# SOFTWARE DEVELOPMENT WITH MODULA-2

# INTERNATIONAL COMPUTER SCIENCE SERIES

*Consulting editors*  **A D McGettrick**  University of Strathclyde
                      **J van Leeuwen**   University of Utrecht

## SELECTED TITLES IN THE SERIES

The UNIX System   *S R Bourne*

Software Specification Techniques   *N Gehani and A D McGettrick (Eds)*

Introduction to Expert Systems   *P Jackson*

Modula-2: Discipline & Design   *A H J Sale*

The Craft of Software Engineering   *A Macro and J Buxton*

Prolog Programming for Artificial Intelligence   *I Bratko*

Pop-11 Programming for Artificial Intelligence   *A M Burton and N R Shadbolt*

Cost Estimation for Software Development   *B Londeix*

Parallel Programming   *R H Perrott*

The Specification of Computer Programs   *W M Turski and T S E Maibaum*

Software Development with Ada   *I Sommerville and R Morrison*

An Introduction to Programming with Modula-2   *P D Terry*

Functional Programming   *A J Field and P G Harrison*

Comparative Programming Languages   *L B Wilson and R G Clark*

Distributed Systems: Concepts and Design   *G Coulouris and J Dollimore*

Software Prototyping, Formal Methods and VDM   *S Hekmatpour and D Ince*

C Programming in a UNIX Environment   *J Kay and R Kummerfeld*

Software Engineering (3rd Edn)   *I Sommerville*

High-Level Languages and their Compilers   *D Watson*

Elements of Functional Programming   *C Reade*

Program Derivation   *R G Dromey*

Programming in Ada (3rd Edn)   *J G P Barnes*

# SOFTWARE DEVELOPMENT WITH MODULA-2

## David Budgen

University of Stirling

ADDISON-WESLEY
PUBLISHING
COMPANY

Wokingham, England · Reading, Massachusetts · Menlo Park, California
New York · Don Mills, Ontario · Amsterdam · Bonn
Sydney · Singapore · Tokyo · Madrid · San Juan

© 1989 Addison-Wesley Publishers Ltd.
© 1989 Addison-Wesley Publishing Company, Inc.

All rights reserved. No part of this publication may be reproduced, stored in a retrieval system, or transmitted in any form or by any means, electronic, mechanical, photocopying, recording or otherwise, without prior written permission of the publisher.

The programs in this book have been included for their instructional value. They have been tested with care but are not guaranteed for any particular purpose. The publisher does not offer any warranties or representations, nor does it accept any liabilities with respect to the programs.

Many of the designations used by manufacturers and sellers to distinguish their products are claimed as trademarks. Addison-Wesley has made every attempt to supply trademark information about manufacturers and their products mentioned in this book. A list of the trademark designations and their owners appears on p. xiv.

Cover designed by Crayon Design of Henley-on-Thames
and printed by The Riverside Printing Co. (Reading) Ltd.
Typeset by CRB Typesetting Services, Ely, Cambs.
Printed and bound in Great Britain by Mackays of Chatham PLC, Kent.

First printed 1989.

**British Library Cataloguing in Publication Data**
Budgen, D.
  Software development with Modula-2 –
  (International computer science series).
  1. Computer systems. Programming languages:
  Modula-2 language
  I. Title  II. Series
  005.13'3

  ISBN 0-201-18482-6

**Library of Congress Cataloging in Publication Data**
Budgen, D. (David)
  Software development with Modula-2.

  (International Computer Science series)
  Bibliography: p.
  Includes index.
  1. Modula-2 (Computer program language)
2. Computer software–Development.  I. Title.
II. Series.
QA76.73.M63B83  1989  005.13'3    88-8040
ISBN 0-201-18482-6

# Preface

One of the things that has most impressed me about the Modula-2 programming language is the enthusiasm that it engenders among its users. When I first began to use it for programming, I too soon found myself enthusing about Modula-2, and have seen the same response from many of my students when they have first been introduced to the language. So while this text tries to avoid an excess of proselytizing zeal, it *has* been written from the viewpoint of an enthusiastic *user* (and not from the viewpoint of an enthusiastic compiler-writer, a very different thing!). It is a sort of zeal that is similar in some ways to that commonly found among the users of the UNIX operating system – inspired by an affinity for a software tool that is elegant and simple, and yet can be used in so many powerful combinations. (Mercifully though, Modula-2 is largely free of the UNIX system's associated problem of encouraging a programming style that can be so imaginatively obscure on occasion!)

One question that needs to be considered at the outset is why we need Modula-2, when there are so many similarities to Ada. Both are 'modern' imperative programming languages that provide such features as information-hiding, concurrency and modular construction, and they both have a strongly 'Pascal-influenced' style. In particular, both contain the features that are needed for building large and complex software-based systems.

In practice there are a number of good reasons for having two languages, and most are on the basis of 'horses for courses'. Modula-2 is a much smaller language than Ada, and hence easier to learn; and it requires much lower overheads of compilation. For that reason alone it is likely to retain a strong hold for use in teaching as well as for general-purpose programming. For the programmer who has been trained using Pascal, it provides the next (large) natural step, and its relative ease of use is undoubtedly a strong asset. It is not the purpose of this book to draw comparisons between the two languages, nor to push the case for one against the other.

This text has one simple objective, which is to show how Modula-2 can be used to *engineer* programs that are elegant, clear and efficient. As such in addressing itself to the details of the language it tries to place its various features into a broader context, so as to guide the user towards a style of programming that is well organized and well disciplined. Modula-2 offers some powerful aids to the production of programs that are well structured and robust but, as with all such tools, it still requires designers and programmers to make craftsmanlike use of these features. No more than any other programming language can it offer remedies against the ills of inadequate specification, poor design and careless documentation. The emphasis on an *engineering* approach to programming is reinforced further by the structure of the book, in which the details of the language are deferred until the underlying principles have been explained.

Inevitably what is offered here are the experiences and views of one person, albeit modified (or moderated) by the comments and advice of colleagues and the comments of those ultimate victims of zeal – the students. The contribution from six generations of student classes should be acknowledged here, for their collective experiences of learning and use provide much of the foundation for the core material of this book.

## Uses for this book

This is not intended as an introductory text on programming. Rather, it is intended to be used by those who have mastered at least the rudiments of 'programming in the small', and who are, or are likely to be, concerned with the problems that arise when 'programming in the large'. For students, this latter emphasis is an important one, since many of the important concepts that distinguish Modula-2 from other programming languages are concerned with this theme. Indeed, one role that this book can perform is to provide a natural way of introducing the issues that are involved in programming in the large at a relatively early stage in a student's career (the second year of programming may well be an appropriate time), by building upon the experiences and skills gained in an initial programming course.

This book is by no means structured for use by students alone, and it is to be hoped that its organization will also be helpful to the professional programmer. The 'separation of concerns' underlying its structure should assist professional readers rapidly to extract knowledge about the key issues that concern them, and in particular, to gain an appreciation of how the features of Modula-2 can be used to good effect.

One vital point arises here. Those learning a language such as Modula-2 are likely to have widely varying backgrounds and experience, particularly as this has so far tended to be the second (or umpteenth) programming language that a programmer learns rather than the first one.

While every attempt has been made to rely upon no more than a general familiarity with the form and style of high-level programming languages on the part of the reader, it may well be that at times some dependence upon a knowledge of the (earlier) programming language, Pascal, has crept in. For this I apologize, and hope that any such peccadilloes will not be a barrier to making an acquaintance with this very useful and practical programming language.

## Structure of the book

The theme is developed in three parts. Part I provides some basic background to the ideas and concepts that are developed in the rest of the book by describing the origins of Modula-2 and how it fits into a software engineering context. In doing this it examines the general structure of a software module as implemented in Modula-2 and *why* this takes the particular form that it has. In the later chapters of this part, the language is described in much greater detail, supported by a variety of examples. The examples have been kept as brief as the topic will allow to avoid an excess of detail at this stage. It is these chapters that provide the programmer's guide to the main structures of Modula-2.

Part II builds upon this and describes how large systems may be designed, developed and tested using Modula-2. It is here that the theme of 'program development' is fully brought out and discussed within the context of programming in the large.

Finally, in Part III some of the more specialist features of Modula-2 are described, including its quasi-concurrency and machine-dependent aspects, as well as an appraisal of the ways in which these features can be exploited using software engineering methods.

The need to keep the book to manageable proportions has required that the later chapters can provide only an overview of a few issues within the very large field of software engineering. There is much more to these methods than it has been possible to present here, and the reader is directed to the ample range of texts on this subject for further details on any of the more general issues described.

## Acknowledgements

In writing this book I have drawn help from many sources, including my own students, fellow staff, the anonymous reviewers, and the members of the British Standards Institution working group on Modula-2 standardization. All of these have striven hard to correct my misconceptions and to help me to clarify my thoughts. I am duly grateful to them for all their efforts – any errors that remain are my responsibility alone. Last but not least, I would like to express my thanks to my long-suffering wife and family, who at times were beginning to believe that this was really becoming rather too much of an exercise in 'book-writing in the large'!

*David Budgen*
June 1988

# Contents

Preface ........................................................................... v

**Part I  MODULA-2 AS A PROGRAMMING LANGUAGE** ........... 1

**Chapter 1  The Modula-2 Programming Language** .................. 3

    1.1  Introduction ............................................................ 3
    1.2  Some history behind Modula-2 .................................. 6
    1.3  Program development ............................................... 9
    1.4  Some assumptions ................................................... 10

**Chapter 2  Modularity and Separate Compilation in Modula-2** ... 11

    2.1  Modularity in programs ............................................ 11
    2.2  Independent compilation .......................................... 14
    2.3  An introduction to separate compilation ..................... 16
    2.4  Some practicalities of separate compilation ................. 20

**Chapter 3  The Organization of a Modula-2 Program** .............. 23

    3.1  More about MODULEs ............................................ 23
    3.2  Controlling visibility: IMPORT and EXPORT .............. 26
    3.3  The Modula-2 program module ................................. 28
    3.4  Library modules ...................................................... 29
    3.5  Character handling in Modula-2 ................................. 30
    3.6  The MODULE InOut .............................................. 31
         Exercises ............................................................... 32

**Chapter 4  The Syntax and Conventions of Modula-2** .............. 35

    4.1  Introduction ............................................................ 35
    4.2  The character set ..................................................... 35
    4.3  Conventions for identifiers ....................................... 37

|     |     |       |                                                          |     |
|-----|-----|-------|----------------------------------------------------------|-----|
|     | 4.4 | Statements                                                       | 38  |
|     |     | 4.4.1 | Separators within a statement                            | 38  |
|     |     | 4.4.2 | The assignment statement                                 | 39  |
|     |     | 4.4.3 | Sequencing of operations                                 | 40  |
|     |     | 4.4.4 | Statement separators and the null statement              | 40  |
|     |     | 4.4.5 | The statement sequence                                   | 43  |
|     | 4.5 | Operators                                                        | 43  |
|     | 4.6 | Delimiters                                                       | 46  |
|     |     | Exercises                                                        | 48  |

## Chapter 5  Simple Data Structures in Modula-2 — 49

|     |     |       |                                                          |     |
|-----|-----|-------|----------------------------------------------------------|-----|
|     | 5.1 | Simple data types                                                | 49  |
|     | 5.2 | Standard data types in Modula-2                                  | 50  |
|     |     | 5.2.1 | The integer types INTEGER and CARDINAL                   | 50  |
|     |     | 5.2.2 | Characters                                               | 58  |
|     |     | 5.2.3 | The type BOOLEAN                                         | 62  |
|     |     | 5.2.4 | The fractional number type REAL                          | 65  |
|     | 5.3 | The set type BITSET                                              | 66  |
|     |     | Exercises                                                        | 71  |

## Chapter 6  User-defined Data Types — 73

|     |                                                                        |     |
|-----|------------------------------------------------------------------------|-----|
| 6.1 | Introduction                                                           | 73  |
| 6.2 | Enumeration types                                                      | 74  |
| 6.3 | Sub-range types                                                        | 75  |
| 6.4 | Set types                                                              | 77  |
| 6.5 | Transferring details of user-defined types via EXPORT and IMPORT       | 80  |
|     | Exercises                                                              | 81  |

## Chapter 7  Control Structures in Modula-2: Selection — 83

|     |     |       |                                         |     |
|-----|-----|-------|-----------------------------------------|-----|
|     | 7.1 | Structuring control flow                        | 83  |
|     | 7.2 | Two-way selection: the IF statement             | 84  |
|     |     | 7.2.1 | Conditional expressions                 | 85  |
|     |     | 7.2.2 | The ELSE clause                         | 89  |
|     |     | 7.2.3 | ELSIF clauses                           | 91  |
|     | 7.3 | The CASE statement                              | 95  |
|     |     | Exercises                                       | 98  |

## Chapter 8  Control Structures in Modula-2: Iteration — 101

|     |                                                      |     |
|-----|------------------------------------------------------|-----|
| 8.1 | The role of the iteration forms                      | 101 |
| 8.2 | Counting and the FOR statement                       | 102 |
| 8.3 | Conditional loops: the WHILE statement               | 107 |
| 8.4 | Conditional loops: the REPEAT UNTIL statement        | 109 |
| 8.5 | The LOOP statement                                   | 111 |
|     | Exercises                                            | 114 |

## Chapter 9  Subprograms in Modula-2  115

- 9.1 The procedure as a structural element — 115
- 9.2 Transferring information: parameters — 118
- 9.3 Transferring information: function procedures — 123
- 9.4 Standard procedures — 125
- 9.5 Recursive operations with procedures — 130
- 9.6 Procedure types — 134
- Exercises — 136

## Chapter 10  The Role of the MODULE  137

- 10.1 MODULEs reviewed — 137
- 10.2 The MODULE main body — 139
- 10.3 Information-hiding in MODULEs — 143
- 10.4 MODULEs within MODULEs — 146
- 10.5 Partitioning the declarations within a MODULE — 152
  - 10.5.1 The definition part — 152
  - 10.5.2 The implementation part — 152
  - 10.5.3 Local modules — 154
- Exercises — 155

## Chapter 11  Structured Data Types  157

- 11.1 The use of structure — 157
- 11.2 The ARRAY — 159
  - 11.2.1 Strings — 161
  - 11.2.2 Open arrays — 163
- 11.3 The RECORD — 165
  - 11.3.1 The WITH statement — 167
  - 11.3.2 Variant sections — 168
- 11.4 Pointer types and dynamic storage allocation — 169
  - 11.4.1 Creating and deleting dynamic variables — 177
- Exercises — 178

## Part II  DEVELOPING PROGRAMS IN MODULA-2  179

## Chapter 12  The Software Development Process  181

- 12.1 Programming in the large, and the software life cycle — 181
  - 12.1.1 The software life cycle — 183
- 12.2 Software design — 186
  - 12.2.1 Modula-2 objects — 189
  - 12.2.2 Top-down decomposition — 189
  - 12.2.3 Decomposition by data flow — 194
  - 12.2.4 Designing around the data structure — 196
  - 12.2.5 Information-hiding — 200
  - 12.2.6 Object-Oriented Design — 201

|      | 12.3   | Design representation and implementation | 203 |
|------|--------|------------------------------------------|-----|
|      |        | 12.3.1 Data flow diagrams                | 205 |
|      |        | 12.3.2 Structure charts                  | 205 |
|      |        | 12.3.3 Block diagrams                    | 209 |
|      |        | 12.3.4 Detailed design                   | 210 |
|      | 12.4   | Assessing design structure               | 213 |
|      |        | 12.4.1 Cohesion                          | 215 |
|      |        | 12.4.2 Coupling                          | 217 |
|      |        | 12.4.3 The cyclomatic complexity metric  | 220 |
|      | 12.5   | Re-using designs                         | 220 |
|      |        | Exercises                                | 224 |

## Chapter 13  Constructing a Modula-2 Program  227

| 13.1 | Selecting an example problem | 227 |
|------|------------------------------|-----|
| 13.2 | A solution based on Structured Analysis and Structured Design | 230 |
| 13.3 | A solution based on Object-Oriented Design (OOD) | 242 |
|      | 13.3.1 Develop an informal strategy | 245 |
|      | 13.3.2 Formalize the strategy | 246 |
| 13.4 | Completing the Object-Oriented Design | 254 |
|      | Exercises | 257 |

## Chapter 14  Program Development, Testing and Documentation  259

| 14.1 | A model of the software development process | 259 |
| 14.2 | Testing strategies | 261 |
| 14.3 | Module testing | 265 |
| 14.4 | Integration testing | 267 |
| 14.5 | Documentation | 268 |
|      | Exercises | 272 |

## Part III  SYSTEM PROGRAMMING IN MODULA-2  275

## Chapter 15  Breaking the Rules!  277

| 15.1 | Why Modula-2 includes rule-breaking mechanisms | 277 |
| 15.2 | The module SYSTEM | 278 |
| 15.3 | The type WORD | 279 |
| 15.4 | The type ADDRESS | 283 |
| 15.5 | Some other non-standard facilities | 285 |
|      | 15.5.1 Code inserts | 285 |
|      | 15.5.2 Absolute addressing | 286 |
|      | Exercises | 287 |

## Chapter 16  Forms for Use with Concurrent Programming  289

| 16.1 | Principles of concurrent programming | 289 |
| 16.2 | The co-routine concept | 293 |

|      |                                               |     |
|------|-----------------------------------------------|-----|
| 16.3 | Co-routines in Modula-2                       | 296 |
| 16.4 | Some examples of co-routines                  | 298 |
| 16.5 | Co-routines as concurrent processes           | 314 |
|      | Exercises                                     | 321 |

## Chapter 17  Low-Level Input and Output            323

|      |                                                    |     |
|------|----------------------------------------------------|-----|
| 17.1 | Background issues and device input and output      | 323 |
| 17.2 | Memory mapped input/output                         | 326 |
| 17.3 | Controlling input and output by device polling     | 329 |
| 17.4 | Interrupts and concurrency                         | 334 |
| 17.5 | Handling multiple interrupts                       | 343 |
|      | Exercises                                          | 344 |
|      | Postscript                                         | 344 |

## References                                        345

## Selected Solutions to the Exercises               349

## Index                                             355

**Trademark notice**
PDP-11™, VAX™, VAX-11™ and VMS™ are trademarks of Digital Equipment Corporation.
Motorola™ and MC68000™ are trademarks of Motorola Corporation.
UNIX™ is a trademark of AT&T.

# Part I
# MODULA-2 AS A PROGRAMMING LANGUAGE

Chapter 1  **The Modula-2 Programming Language**
Chapter 2  **Modularity and Separate Compilation in Modula-2**
Chapter 3  **The Organization of a Modula-2 Program**
Chapter 4  **The Syntax and Conventions of Modula-2**
Chapter 5  **Simple Data Structures in Modula-2**
Chapter 6  **User-defined Data Types**
Chapter 7  **Control Structures in Modula-2: Selection**
Chapter 8  **Control Structures in Modula-2: Iteration**
Chapter 9  **Subprograms in Modula-2**
Chapter 10 **The Role of the** MODULE
Chapter 11 **Structured Data Types**

# Chapter 1
# The Modula-2 Programming Language

1.1 Introduction
1.2 Some history behind Modula-2
1.3 Program development
1.4 Some assumptions

## 1.1 Introduction

The principal aim of this book is to describe some of the ways in which it is possible to use Modula-2 to create and maintain large well-engineered programs. Its features and facilities will be described and illustrated from the viewpoint of their suitability for this purpose, and so while the examples have been kept relatively small, they have generally been selected to exemplify the larger-scale issues.

In particular, the emphasis is not placed solely upon the programming issues. We will examine the structures of Modula-2 to see how these can be used with a number of design methods, and will also consider such issues as the testing strategies that might be best suited to these features. In the final three chapters we will extend the large-scale viewpoint still further and examine the use of Modula-2 as a systems programming tool.

However, when learning to use a programming language such as Modula-2, it is always useful to begin by finding out a little about its background. This then provides a context within which it is easier to see the reasons why some of its features have been included. From that, we can acquire a better understanding of how they can be used in order to construct effective and elegant solutions to a range of problems.

Modula-2 is what we usually term an *imperative* or *procedural* programming language. This form is generally less attractive to theorists and mathematicians than the functional form of programming language such as LISP, because it offers significant difficulties for rigorous analysis.

However, it is a form that has proved popular with programmers in general.

In the late 1950s, when programmers increasingly needed some means of creating programs in a more abstract and less machine-oriented form than was possible by using assembler code alone, a number of 'high-level' languages were developed. The three that came to dominate the programming field in the sixties (and beyond) were FORTRAN, COBOL and ALGOL. (All of these names are written with upper case characters, as they are acronyms.) FORTRAN (FORmula TRANslation) contained features designed for use in numerical work, and was therefore well suited to use by scientists and engineers; COBOL (COmmon Business-Oriented Language) was designed to meet the needs of the business community; while ALGOL (ALGOrithmic Language) was a vehicle for the purists, created by the computer scientists themselves (and mostly used by them alone).

Although FORTRAN and COBOL have been used much more widely than ALGOL and its many derivatives, they have also proved barren: while their form has evolved to some degree (but not necessarily improved, as an inspection of the thinking behind FORTRAN 77 soon reveals), they have not provided the initial models for the development of any later programming languages. ALGOL, on the other hand, has spawned a whole host of programming languages, which in turn have developed a number of further ideas ('block' structuring, flexible statement organization with clear syntax, and data declaration requirements, to mention just some of these). Figure 1.1 shows a 'family tree' for these programming languages, in a fairly general way (detailed analysis would obviously show many more branches). Modula-2 (Wirth, 1980, 1985) is one of the descendants of ALGOL, its immediate precursors being Pascal and Modula (Jensen, 1974; Wirth, 1977).

Pascal and Ada are the languages most often compared with Modula-2. Pascal is often cited because it is here that Modula-2 has its roots, and because in Pascal the ALGOL-like forms have been extended to include what we normally term 'strong typing'. Through this latter feature it has been possible to increase the extent to which the compiler can perform consistency checking on a source program. Ada is also compared with Modula-2, because the design of both was influenced by Pascal, and because Ada incorporates many of the facilities and concepts to be found in Modula-2, although Ada is a much larger language.

We should take some care in making comparisons with Pascal and Ada. Pascal was designed with different objectives in mind, being intended as a teaching language. In a sense, Modula-2 encapsulates the same basic thinking in a more flexible and powerful framework, constructed to be used in a much wider variety of programming tasks. Similarly, Ada was designed with much larger objectives in mind, and with a willingness to accept larger consequent overheads during program construction. Much of the success of Modula-2 lies in its ability to provide many important new

INTRODUCTION 5

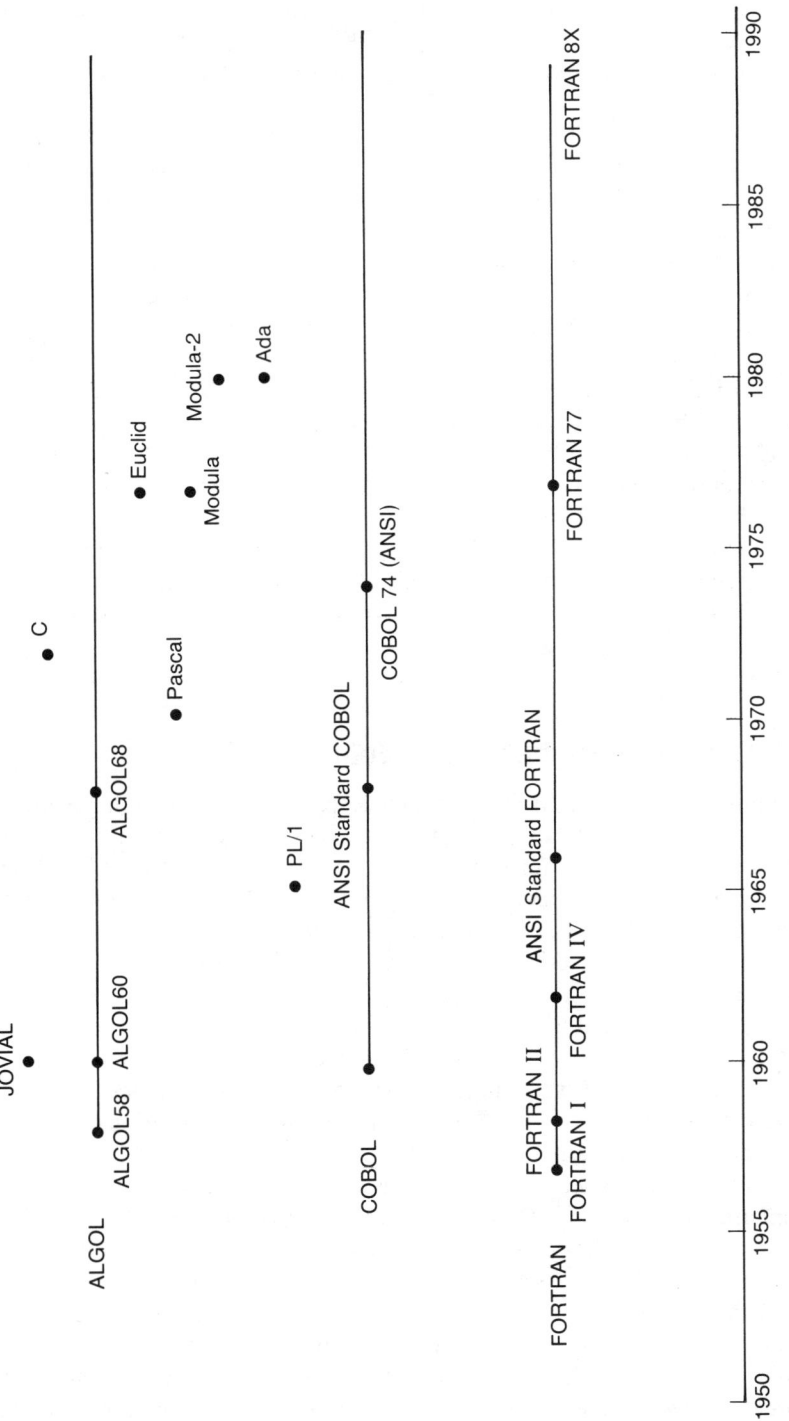

**Figure 1.1** Outline of the chronological development of some major imperative programming languages.

features with fairly low overheads in terms of compilation time and execution time. This makes it especially attractive for use in teaching, since it provides a practical step onwards from Pascal and provides access to important new programming ideas in a largely familiar format.

Like Pascal and Modula, Modula-2 was the product of one man. Professor Niklaus Wirth's name is firmly associated with all of them. This is one factor that has helped to constrain the design of Modula-2 to manageable proportions.

Not every feature of Modula-2 can be regarded as perfect. There are some awkward limitations and some areas of ambiguity that could certainly have been bettered. (Quite a few of these have been handled more sympathetically in the design of Ada.) Some of these points have been revised and clarified by the work of the group from the British Standards Institution (BSI) that has been striving to produce a standard definition for Modula-2 (Cornelius, 1988); while others have been left unaltered, since a working language does deserve a degree of respect, even from committees. Throughout this book, any limitations or ambiguities that might arise within implementations of Modula-2 have been drawn to the attention of the reader when necessary. It is the task of a book of this nature to describe the form of Modula-2 as it is – and not as the author would like it to be!

## 1.2 Some history behind Modula-2

A prominent feature of ALGOL and its descendants has been the need for the programmer to **declare** any symbolic objects (usually variables, constants or procedures) before they can be used. A declaration of such an object must specify its **identifier** (name) and its **data type**. This feature makes it possible for the compiler to check what use is being made of a variable or constant within the program, and to identify such inconsistent operations as copying a floating-point (real) value into a variable that has been assigned to contain integer data (which will differ markedly from floating-point data in the way that it is stored). In particular, the ability to declare new types as sub-ranges of values from other types makes it possible to ensure consistency in the results of any operations that are performed by a program.

This is in contrast to a language such as FORTRAN, in which compilers treat such declarations as optional. In FORTRAN, any reference to a new identifier anywhere in a program will be treated by the compiler as equivalent to a declaration of a variable with that identifier. The data type of such a variable is assigned according to a convention which is based upon the value of the first character of its identifier. In a similar manner, the FORTRAN compiler is not expected to check that subprograms are called with the correct number of parameters and the correct type of value for each parameter. Not surprisingly, FORTRAN programs may take less time to key in than ALGOL programs, but this needs to be offset against the very considerable amount of time that can be spent chasing errors that arise from mis-spelling identifiers (so creating new variables unintentionally). This type of error can result in data of the wrong type being copied into a variable.

For Pascal, Professor Wirth set out to extend the amount of checking that could be performed by the compiler. This was partly achieved by requiring that the compiler should be able to check all references made to data objects in a program, in order to ensure that the correct types were used; this particularly concerned such items as the parameters of subprograms. He extended this checking still further by also allowing programmers to *create* their own data types – and requiring the same degree of checking to be applied. Even though the properties of such user-defined types are rather limited, this facility greatly assists in producing a clear programming style.

A compiler for Pascal can consequently check thoroughly all use that is made of identifiers within a program to ensure that it is consistent, and can check the values that are assigned to variables to ensure that these are within the correct range. As a consequence of the latter, however, there are some additional overheads involved during program execution. Since it is not possible to perform all the necessary checking during compilation, particularly where the results of calculations are concerned, the compiler needs to insert additional code that will perform such checks dynamically during execution. For example, suppose we declare a new type such as

**type**
    *days* = [1..31];

This specifies that a variable of type *days* can take a value in the range 1 to 31 only, and so a statement such as

    *newmoon* := *lastmoon* + *lunarcycle*;

where *newmoon* and *lastmoon* are variables of type *days*, will need a run-time check to ensure that the value generated and assigned to *newmoon* does not exceed the upper bound for a variable of this type.

A more significant restriction is that the complete program needs to be compiled as a unit, so that the compiler can be provided with all the information necessary to perform this degree of checking.

To some extent the overheads that result from this requirement to compile the complete program after every change are offset by the presence of a few further restrictions upon the ordering of declarations. These enable a Pascal compiler to perform its task using only a single pass through the source file, which in turn permits a fast and efficient compilation stage.

In practice, Pascal has proved to be a very successful language for use in teaching computer programming, and since student programs are rarely very large and are rarely executed more often than necessary to demonstrate that they work, the overheads are not usually a problem. (Many students would probably regard one successful run of a program as sufficient to demonstrate success anyway!)

However, as the benefits of the strong typing features of Pascal have been recognized more widely, and as a generation of Pascal-trained students has moved out into commerce and industry, there has been a growth in the use of Pascal for programming larger and more complex systems. An example is Donald Knuth's T$_e$X program (Knuth, 1986). In many cases, various extensions have been incorporated into the language to enable the programmer to utilize machine-related features, and to avoid the overheads of compiling a complete program each time it is modified. Unfortunately such extensions are far from 'standard', and of course their use is apt to weaken some of the main benefits available from the use of Pascal.

It was partly to meet the needs of those creating larger and more complex systems that Modula-2 was produced. This has been designed with the aim of providing a more general-purpose programming language, suitable for use with larger systems, while still providing the features that programmers and designers have come to expect from their experience with Pascal. To further extend its usefulness, it also provides a rather limited form of concurrency, as well as a number of features that allow access to the 'low-level' facilities of a computer system. The syntax of the language has also been very much rationalized, and is generally more consistent in form than that of Pascal.

Having got this far, it may help to illustrate these points a little more by looking at a very simple example of Modula-2. The short list below is a classical 'hello world' program of the sort that programmers often write to test their ability to handle the basics of program construction in a new programming language or operating system:

```
MODULE Hello;
FROM InOut IMPORT WriteString, WriteLn;
BEGIN
  WriteString('Hello World');
  WriteLn
END Hello.
```

As an example this is hardly enough to demonstrate very much, but it does show something of the general style, and anyone who is familiar with ALGOL-style programming languages should at least feel re-assured!

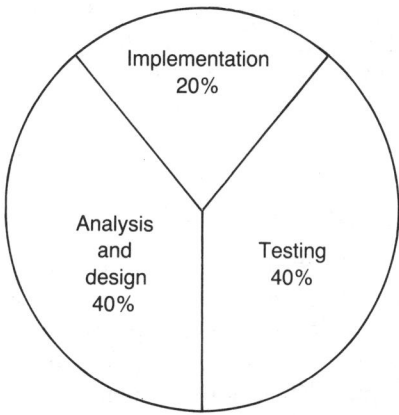

**Figure 1.2** Typical distribution of effort for the development of large systems.

## 1.3 Program development

Modula-2 enables the programmer to divide a program both *logically* and *physically* into separate parts or sections. It also exploits the ideas of **information hiding** through the use of local data structures that have a permanent nature and through concealment of physical representations. So the programmer needs to be aware of the criteria that might be used for dividing a program into separate physical parts, and how this division can reflect the *logical* structuring of the program.

The concept of 'software engineering' has made slow but consistent progress since the term was first coined (Naur and Randell, 1968) – although the idea of using 'engineering' techniques for programming is still apt to remain rather more of an aspiration than a reality. But the subject of software design is still by no means a widely understood area of software engineering, although a number of models and principles have gradually emerged over the last 15 years.

Figure 1.2 shows a typical breakdown of the effort that is involved in developing a large software-based system (Fairley, 1985). As we can see, the specification and design stages are major components of this (the implementation in the form of the actual programming requires proportionally less effort overall), and this book has tried to recognize this balance in its treatment of the subject matter. So we not only examine programming practices but also look at the design task and how this relates to the specific needs of Modula-2. The role of the specification and design phases will be examined more fully in Part II.

The aim throughout this book has been to try to make maximum use of such principles and methods of software engineering as may be appropriate for each aspect of Modula-2, and so to introduce the language within this context, rather than concentrating upon details of syntax. Wherever possible, we not only describe a feature of the language, but also try to show how it fits into the type of programming practice that is needed for a language like Modula-2.

## 1.4 Some assumptions

As this book originated in the experience of teaching Modula-2 to classes of students who already had a grounding in Pascal, it is somewhat oriented towards the assumption that the reader already has a working knowledge of at least one of the programming languages in the ALGOL family, such as Pascal. However, since the author will openly admit to having begun his programming experiences with FORTRAN, the programmer who has a background in FORTRAN may also hope to find salvation here!

Each feature of Modula-2 is therefore described on the assumption that the reader already knows something about programming in an imperative language. Where comparisons are drawn with other programming languages, these will usually be either Pascal or FORTRAN. (The BASIC programmer can be regarded as more or less equivalent to a FORTRAN programmer for such purposes.) So this is not really a book on introductory programming for anyone wishing to make Modula-2 his or her first programming language.

The examples given have been kept as short as possible, and usually only a section of code is given, rather than a complete program. This is in keeping with the assumption that the reader can already program in an imperative language to some degree, and it allows the reader's attention to be focused upon a particular feature.

The first part of this book is largely concerned with aspects of what can be termed 'statement syntax'. The second part then examines ways of designing large programs so that the strengths of Modula-2 can be exploited. Finally, the third part examines the issues of concurrency and low-level programming and some ways in which these can be used. A major objective throughout is to show not only how the language is structured but also how this structure can be used in an effective form – particularly for what is sometimes termed 'programming in the large'. Modula-2 programs need to be written with a 'Modula-2 style' rather than a 'Pascal style' or a 'FORTRAN style' to make the most of the language. Learning Modula-2 requires more than just learning a new syntax, and the next section elaborates a little more on this point.

# Chapter 2
# Modularity and Separate Compilation in Modula-2

| | | | | |
|---|---|---|---|---|
| 2.1 | Modularity in programs | 2.3 | An introduction to separate compilation |
| 2.2 | Independent compilation | 2.4 | Some practicalities of separate compilation |

## 2.1 Modularity in programs

Since the very early days of computers, programmers have found it convenient to divide a large program into both *logical* sub-units (or subprograms), which relate to the structure of a problem, and *physical* sub-units, which are used for convenience of editing and compilation. So programming languages have usually incorporated, in some fashion or other, the features that are needed to support these. Typically the physical subdivision of a program has involved partitioning its code into separate units, each containing a group of one or more of the subprograms that usually form the means of logical subdivision in a particular language. FORTRAN is one example of a programming language with such features, and FORTRAN SUBROUTINEs and FUNCTIONs may usually be compiled independently of a main program, either individually or in groups.

The use of logical subdivision via subprograms also dovetails conveniently into the top-down approach to the design of programs – sometimes known as 'step-wise refinement' or 'divide and conquer' (Wirth, 1971). When using this method, we design the structure of our program by first producing a description of the tasks that are to be performed by the complete program, and then successively refining each of these down into a set of specifications for the individual subprograms. This process of refinement should stop only when each subprogram is considered to be performing a single simple subtask of the overall problem. Figure 2.1 shows the

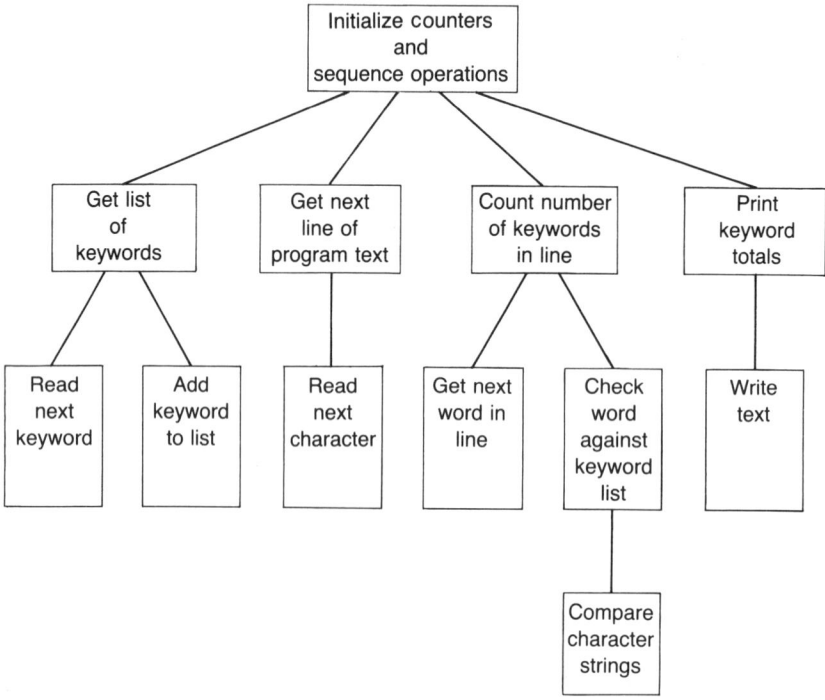

**Figure 2.1** Example of program structure produced through the use of step-wise refinement.

sort of tree structure that can be produced by using this method, and is based upon a design for a program that is required to read through a disk file containing the source code of a Pascal program and count the number of times it detects certain keywords.

All practical imperative programming languages provide some form of subprogram facility, allowing the lowest-level tasks that are identified in the design process, such as getNextSymbol, to be programmed as separate logical units of code. For practical purposes, the subprograms must also be able to accept and return information through the mechanism of **parameters**. This is the means by which the calling unit can specify a set of values that are to be made 'visible' to the subprogram, usually as a set of 'local' variables, and that can also be used to transfer information back to the calling unit from the subprogram. The allocation of the initial 'actual' values to the parameters is organized by the calling part of the program, before it passes control to the subprogram itself. Less structured languages such as FORTRAN are apt to be rather casual about the way that this is done. In such languages, the compiler is not required to perform checks to ensure that the number of parameters *provided* by the caller, and their data types (integer, floating-point, character etc.), are consistent with those that are *expected* by the subprogram.

As an example of this point, it is possible to write a FORTRAN subroutine which begins with the declarations

```
SUBROUTINE MODULO(IX,IY)
INTEGER IX,IY
...
```

which declares that the subprogram MODULO expects to receive the values for two parameters, both of which are of integer (whole number) type. These *formal* parameters are designated IX and IY within the code of the subprogram. In the main body of the program, or in another subroutine, a programmer can then include a call to this subroutine, and needs to provide specific *(actual)* values for these parameters. One example of such a call would be

```
CALL MODULO( LIMIT , 5 )
```

where the variable LIMIT is of type INTEGER. The subroutine MODULO will then have these values passed to it in a correct form and order (the value of LIMIT will be assigned to IX, and IY will take the value 5), since the actual parameters are consistent with the formal parameters. However, a programmer could equally well write a calling statement such as

```
CALL MODULO( LIMIT , 2.5 , 2 )
```

which uses three parameters instead of two, and in which the second parameter is of REAL (fractional) type, instead of INTEGER. The internal forms used within a computer to represent numbers of these types are quite incompatible and so, quite apart from the presence of an additional unwanted parameter, the effects of the call are likely to be rather different from those intended. Yet the FORTRAN compiler may accept both the subprogram declaration and the calling statement without indicating that anything is inconsistent. Indeed, if the part of the program that calls MODULO and the code of MODULO itself are stored in separate files, and possibly compiled at different times, then there is no way that a FORTRAN compiler *could* make any checks for consistency. So in a language such as FORTRAN, it is the responsibility of the programmer alone to ensure that the program is consistent in its use of actual parameters.

Pascal, which was designed much later than FORTRAN, is very much tighter about such things. The form of a procedure or function call (the Pascal forms of subprogram) must correspond *exactly* with that which is used in the declaration of the subprogram itself, and the compiler will check to ensure that this is so. In Pascal, our previous example would need to be declared as

>    **procedure** *modulo* (**var** *ix*, *iy* : **integer**);

with the type and number of the parameters being specified in the declaration, as well as the way that these can be used for information flow. In exchange for this there is a price to pay, for in order to provide the compiler with all the information that is necessary in order to make such checks, the compiler must normally have access to the source code of the complete program. (At least, this is the case for 'standard' Pascal, although there are extensions that circumvent this requirement.)

## 2.2 Independent compilation

An additional benefit of the subprogram facility is that programmers are able to re-use existing subprograms. In this way, programmers can build up their own libraries of useful program segments.

To make this re-use of subprograms even more convenient, and to avoid the programmer having to copy the source code of the subprogram(s) into each new program, a scheme of **independent compilation** is provided in FORTRAN, and in a number of similar imperative programming languages (including C). This makes it possible for the various sub-units of a program to be held in separate files, compiled without reference to one another, and finally joined up to form the complete program by means of another system utility program. This latter program is known by various names in different operating systems, usually some variation on 'link-editor', 'link-loader', 'linker' and so on.

Independent compilation has been a feature of FORTRAN and similar languages from the earliest days, and is the main reason why the compilers for such languages perform little or no checking of references to subprograms to ensure consistency. If the source code for the subprogram(s) being compiled at any particular time is alone available to the compiler, then there is no means by which the compiler may verify that any calls to other subprograms are using consistent and correct types, or even the correct number, of parameters.

That said, the benefits of independent compilation should not be under-rated. One such benefit, namely that of being able to re-use proven and tested code, has already been mentioned. By making use of this feature, the details of the structures and algorithms of subprograms can be kept concealed from the programmers who re-use them, by providing them with only the binary output form produced by the compiler. In this way, as there is no need to supply each user with the source code, they cannot modify it or misuse it in any way, and hence a degree of standardization can be achieved.

A further benefit that arises from such physical partitioning of a program is that a single-functioned item of code may be much more rigorously tested in isolation than is possible when a whole program is being tested at once, since the task of selecting a set of suitable test cases to exercise its functionality becomes much more straightforward. An independently compiled subprogram can be tested as a 'black box', simply by creating a 'test harness' made up from a temporary main program that makes calls to the subprogram using a set of test data, and then prints out an analysis of the results. The tester can be supplied with the binary form of the routine alone, so that the testing exercise cannot be influenced by the tester reading any of the source code.

On a rather different basis, independent compilation also makes it practical for a team of programmers to work together to create a large program, with each programmer being made responsible for producing particular sub-units. However, it is here that the lack of consistency checking by the compiler can become particularly significant. If a group of programmers are to work together to produce a program, each of them needs to be kept fully informed about the exact form of the parameters used by each subprogram, together with the details of any 'global' data that may be used (and changed) by the subprogram. And each programmer needs to be kept informed of any changes that are made to any of this information. While the problem may not sound unduly complex, the evidence suggests that this is a major practical problem in creating large programs, as well as forming a sizable overhead in terms of the amount of programmer time that needs to be spent on keeping up to date with the effects of changes. The problems of program development are as likely to arise from inadequate control of changes to the code, or not communicating the knowledge of such changes to others, as from any technical difficulties or complexities.

(In some programming languages, such as C and CORAL 66, an attempt has been made to restrict this latitude by requiring that the programmer must declare at the head of each program unit the details of any items that are used but not declared within that unit. Such declarations typically use keywords such as DEFINE, EXTERNAL or LIBRARY, and specify the details of the procedural interfaces and parameter types used by such items. While this does make it possible for the compiler to perform additional consistency checking, there is still the problem of ensuring that the declarations are themselves consistent and up to date. Furthermore, this form cannot easily be extended to support the use of user-defined types in general, and as parameters in such a procedure declaration in particular.)

When Wirth designed Pascal as a teaching language that should encourage good programming practices, independent compilation was discarded for the reasons just described. A 'standard' Pascal compiler requires access to the complete source of a program in order to check it for consistency: there is no provision for compiling any of the sub-units of a program separately from the whole. This is sometimes referred to as 'monolithic' compilation.

Unfortunately, while 'monolithic' compilation provides major benefits, it has resulted in Pascal in its pure form being largely confined to the role of a teaching language, and used mainly for writing programs of moderate size. It is difficult for a team of programmers to construct a large Pascal program between them, except by using the various 'extensions' that allow a program to be partitioned and compiled as a set of separate units. Given that the benefits of Pascal and the ideas it contains are now so widely accepted, it is hardly surprising that such extensions have been developed.

Modula-2 has been provided with the necessary features to allow a program to be constructed in separate units, while still providing the high degree of consistency checking that is possible with standard Pascal. The form of this is explained in the next section. In addition, the way that these features have been constructed means that both the *physical* and the *logical* structuring of a system are made clear to the reader of a program. The physical partitioning has been designed into the language, rather than 'bolted on' through such mechanisms as macros or 'include' files. This in turn makes a program easier to read and understand, and hence to maintain and modify.

A question that obviously arises at this point is whether the 'link-editor' program, which is used to join the compiled program units to form the complete executable program image, can be used to perform any checking for consistency. Unfortunately link-editors are usually rather general-purpose programs, which are primarily concerned with machine-related matters and do not have access to the necessary forms of information. A link-editor can rarely do more than ensure that symbol values are consistent, and it usually cannot make any checks concerning their *use*. One reason for this is that some programming languages require that the machine-level organization of subprogram calls should use specific forms, and these are not necessarily consistent from language to language! So the most effective point at which to perform consistency checking is clearly during the process of compilation.

## 2.3 An introduction to separate compilation

From the description of independent compilation in Section 2.2, we can see that a major deficiency with such a scheme is that the *compiler* cannot then be required to check that any references made in the code of one unit of the program to external items are consistent with the actual form of those items as declared within another unit. The link-editor in turn is also unable to provide any significant degree of checking, other than ensuring that the names of any referenced items are correct, since it is working at a much lower level than that of the original source language.

The solution to this problem adopted in Pascal is to require that the entire program be compiled each time: while the solution adopted for Modula-2 (and, in a rather different form, for Ada too) is to separate the information about a re-usable program unit or 'module' into two parts. The purposes of these two parts are quite distinct: one contains the instruction and data statements, while the second acts as a 'window' on the first part, and defines how much of it can be accessed by the rest of a program.

This latter part of such a module is termed the **definition part**, and it contains the specifications of all those components of the module that may be used by other modules. These specifications usually take the form of declarations of data types, constants, variables and the external forms of procedures. Ada uses the term **visibility** for this feature: anything that is declared in the definition part can be made *visible* to other parts of the program.

The other part of such a module is termed the **implementation part**. This contains the declarations for those data types, constants, variables and procedures that are to be *local* to the module – that is, not to be seen or used by other parts of the program – together with the bodies of any procedures that were declared in the definition part.

In Modula-2 these two parts are normally stored in separate files, and on the UNIX, VAX/VMS and many other operating systems the names of the files will by convention have the following extensions

.def   for the definition part;
.mod   for the implementation part.

(The main part of each filename will usually correspond to the module name itself.)

At this point, a simple example may help to make the concept a little clearer. For this we construct a module that contains two procedures to assist with handling strings of characters. The first is a function procedure that checks a character passed to it to see if it is a digit (in the range 0–9). The second checks whether or not a character whose value is passed to it as a parameter is a lower case letter. As the code for each of these tasks is very simple, the example can be kept fairly short. It nevertheless contains a number of features whose significance may not be immediately obvious, but these should not obscure the basic format, and will be explained more fully later on.

If we name the two procedures as

Isdigit

and

>   Islowercase

then the definition part will look like:

>   DEFINITION MODULE Charchecks;
>
>   EXPORT QUALIFIED Isdigit, Islowercase;
>
>   PROCEDURE Isdigit( ch : CHAR ) : BOOLEAN;
>   PROCEDURE Islowercase( ch : CHAR ) : BOOLEAN;
>   END Charchecks.

and this will be stored in a file named Charchecks.def. The corresponding implementation part, which is stored in the file Charchecks.mod, will in turn have the form:

>   IMPLEMENTATION MODULE Charchecks;
>   PROCEDURE Isdigit( ch : CHAR ) : BOOLEAN;
>   BEGIN
>     IF ( ch >= '0' ) AND ( ch <= '9' ) THEN
>       RETURN TRUE
>     ELSE RETURN FALSE
>     END;
>   END Isdigit;
>
>   PROCEDURE Islowercase( ch : CHAR ) : BOOLEAN;
>   BEGIN
>     IF ( ch >= 'a' ) AND ( ch <= 'z' ) THEN
>       RETURN TRUE
>     ELSE RETURN FALSE
>     END;
>   END Islowercase;
>   END Charchecks.

In order to be able to make use of this module, the contents of Charchecks.def need to be compiled first. While it may seem unnecessary to compile a definition part, there are good practical reasons for doing so. For the moment, the only point that concerns us is that it allows the compiler to check the declarations for consistency of form – that is, that they are correctly structured and that the parameters make use of data types known to the compiler. The output from the compilation process is then placed in a file that will normally have an extension of .sym. The contents of this file consist of the original information provided in the .def file, stored in a compressed form for later use by the compiler, together with some additional information that is not of immediate concern. So in our example the output resulting from successfully compiling the contents of Charchecks.def will be placed in the file Charchecks.sym.

Once this has been done, we are able to compile the implementation part held in Charchecks.mod. This must be compiled *after* the definition part, as the compiler will need to make reference to the .sym file during compilation of the contents of the corresponding .mod file. This is to ensure that the procedures have been declared with consistent forms and that all those declared in the definition part are actually present in the implementation part, and to obtain the details of any data types, variables or constants that may be declared in the definition part. (These latter declarations are 'visible' to the implementation part without any redeclaration.) For simplicity, our example contains only procedures in the definition part. Assuming all to be well with the implementation part, the compiler will generate a file that contains the intermediate object code and is usually tagged with an extension such as .obj or .lnk. Optionally it may also generate some form of compiler listing.

So for our module we will now have the following files:

Charchecks.def   Charchecks.mod   Charchecks.sym   Charchecks.obj

and these together form a complete definition of the MODULE Charchecks, which is now ready for use in a program or another module.

To make use of these procedures, the programmer must include a directive to the compiler of the form

FROM Charchecks IMPORT Isdigit, Islowercase;

at the beginning of the MODULE that makes use of these two routines. If only one of the procedures is needed, then only that one need be named after the reserved word IMPORT. Once this has been done, these two procedures can be used in the program in just the same way as any items declared locally: for example, in such a statement as:

IF Isdigit(bufferchar) THEN ...

When the Modula-2 compiler compiles a program that contains an IMPORT directive such as the one in the example above, it will consult the contents of the file Charchecks.sym to obtain the details of the procedures listed in the directive. This information can then be used to check any statements that make reference to these procedures, such as the IF statement above. In this way the compiler can ensure that any calls to external procedures make use of the correct number and type of parameters. Of course, this mechanism is not restricted to procedures only: it can also be used to pass the details of constants, variables and user-defined types between modules too.

By partitioning a program into a set of separate modules of this form, one can have the convenience of being able to handle and test smaller units of code, while still being able to declare and use one's own data types, and one can also have the same degree of consistency checking as in a language such as Pascal. Through this mechanism Modula-2 can also provide some further features that are of assistance in constructing large systems, and these will emerge as we continue to examine the language in increasing detail.

## 2.4 Some practicalities of separate compilation

One item that may need to be clarified is the method that the compiler uses to find the appropriate .sym files. When it encounters a line such as

    FROM Charchecks IMPORT Isdigit;

the compiler needs to find the appropriate .sym file and read its contents, in order to know the details of Isdigit. To do so, it needs to know the name of this file, and where it is located.

This feature is handled differently according to the particular form of compiler and the particular operating system being used. In one widely used form, the compiler uses the name of the module as the base for the name of the file that it wants, and then appends the extension .sym to this. So the choice of the filenames Charchecks.mod and Charchecks.def to hold the two parts was not purely one of convenience. Having determined the name of the .sym file to be Charchecks.sym, the compiler seeks this file in the directory that contains the file currently being compiled. If it fails to find it there, it will seek it in other system directories, with the number of these and their names depending upon the conventions used in a particular operating system. (Most compilers allow the user to override this naming convention, but for administrative reasons alone there needs to be a very good reason for giving a file a name that is not derived from the name of the module.)

At the risk of pre-empting later topics, there is one point that should perhaps be introduced at this stage. Modula-2 is a **case-sensitive** language – that is, it does *not* regard upper and lower case letters as being synonymous, and hence interchangeable. However, the underlying operating system may well not be case-sensitive (VAX/VMS is not case-sensitive, but UNIX is) and this will of course affect the construction of the filename. If we had called our module charChecks, beginning with a lower case letter, then on UNIX we would have needed to use the filenames charChecks.def and charChecks.mod in order to maintain consistent use of the character cases, whereas on VAX/VMS, where all names are mapped to upper case, this would be unnecessary. We will be returning to this important feature in later chapters.

To complete this introductory discussion of the use of separate compilation in Modula-2, some additional points need to be made about the linking of the intermediate code files that are generated by the compiler from the implementation parts of modules.

The link-editor that is used to bind the intermediate code files together will need to perform some additional consistency checking. The reason for a feature that received an indirect mention earlier will become more apparent as this is explained.

The procedures contained within a program component such as Charchecks may well be used in several other MODULES making up a particular program. In each of these we will need to incorporate a directive of the form

```
FROM Charchecks IMPORT ...
```

and the compiler will then consult the contents of Charchecks.sym when it compiles any of these other modules. Because the contents of the file Charchecks.sym fully describe the external form of the MODULE Charchecks, the implementation part can be extensively modified and recompiled without it being necessary to recompile any other parts of a program, provided that the changes do not affect the *external* form of the MODULE. To show this, we could reconstruct the contents of Charchecks.mod with a much more elegant and efficient form by rewriting it to make better use of BOOLEAN expressions. In its new form it now looks like:

```
IMPLEMENTATION MODULE Charchecks;
PROCEDURE Isdigit( ch : CHAR ) : BOOLEAN;
BEGIN
   RETURN ( ch >= '0' ) AND ( ch <= '9' )
END Isdigit;

PROCEDURE Islowercase( ch : CHAR ) : BOOLEAN;
BEGIN
   RETURN ( ch >= 'a' ) AND ( ch <= 'z' )
END Islowercase;
END Charchecks.
```

Because the *external* appearance of the MODULE is unchanged (the procedures still have the same names and parameters), this new version could completely replace the previous one without the need to recompile anything other than Charchecks.mod itself.

However, if at some point we were to decide to modify the *external* interface of our module Charchecks in some way, perhaps by adding an extra component such as the additional routine Isuppercase, it then becomes necessary to change *both* parts of the module, and to recompile them in the correct order (the definition part first, followed by the implementation part).

Having done this, it is then necessary to recompile *all* those parts of the program that make use of the module Charchecks, so that these now make use of the new definition. To help ensure that this has been done correctly and consistently, the compiler inserts a 'key' into a .sym file, using a different value of the key for each version of the .sym file that it generates. In addition, whenever it compiles another module that makes use of that .sym file, it copies the value of the appropriate key into the intermediate code file produced. It then becomes a task for the link-editor to ensure that all the intermediate code files contain consistent values of the appropriate keys – that is, that they have all been compiled using the same version of a .sym file. This feature provides a valuable consistency check and ensures the consistency of the final program.

In the example above, the suggested change to Charchecks would not be particularly crucial, although of course the consistency check would still be performed by the link-editor. If instead we had changed the form of the parameters used with one of the routines, then this additional checking would become extremely important.

On some operating systems, a separate link-editor may be required to support this feature. On others it may be possible to utilize key-checking features that are already available within the standard link-editor program.

We are now in a position to consider the form of a Modula-2 program more fully, and this will form the basic subject matter of the next two chapters.

# Chapter 3
# The Organization of a Modula-2 Program

3.1 More about MODULEs
3.2 Controlling visibility: IMPORT and EXPORT
3.3 The Modula-2 program module
3.4 Library modules
3.5 Character handling in Modula-2
3.6 The MODULE InOut
Exercises

## 3.1 More about MODULEs

The discussion of Chapter 2 has involved some of the more detailed aspects of program construction, because an understanding of the influence of these issues is rather important as a background for understanding how Modula-2 can be used. Such an understanding also helps with appreciating the reasons for the existence and forms of some of the features and structures of Modula-2. The example of the MODULE Charchecks given at the end of Chapter 2 has provided a brief introduction to the organization and form of the Modula-2 language, and in this chapter we begin to examine the use of the MODULE concept in rather more detail, noting some more general points in the process.

It has already been explained that Modula-2 is case-sensitive, and that a compiler will distinguish between upper and lower case characters. So the three identifiers (names) Charcheck, CharCheck and CHARCHECK will be regarded as representing three distinct and separate components of a program.

For the moment, it is important to note that a Modula-2 compiler will require that any of the words that have a special meaning in the language (the 'reserved' words and the standard identifiers) should always be entered in *upper* case. As an example of this, the compiler will recognize the character string WHILE as being the particular reserved word that comes at the start of a particular form of looping structure, whereas the identifier while will be regarded as belonging to some object created by the user. (If this occurs because we have mistakenly typed it in place of WHILE, the compiler may well inform us that the identifier while has not been declared.)

In Modula-2 a program unit always begins with the reserved word MODULE. Given that we often use the word 'module' to refer to units of source code in an abstract sense (for example, to refer to a subprogram, or perhaps a set of subprograms), this choice of name is perhaps a little unfortunate. The term **package** which is used in Ada to describe a fairly similar entity, avoids this clash with existing terminology more effectively. In this book, the word MODULE in upper case, and in a sans-serif typeface, will only be used in the specific context of the programming language, while the word 'module', in lower case and an ordinary typeface, will continue to be used to refer to some (rather loosely defined) logical or physical unit of code – usually either a MODULE or a PROCEDURE, but not necessarily so.

Modula-2 supports three forms of MODULE. (Strictly speaking, the 'internal' MODULE is a fourth form, but we will leave discussion of this form until Chapter 10.) Two of these were encountered in the previous chapter, namely the DEFINITION MODULE (DEFINITION is a reserved word too) and the IMPLEMENTATION MODULE. (It may be obvious by this point that the Modula-2 language requires an ability to spell, together with a degree of dexterity from the typist!) These two forms are always paired together, and of course are really two parts of one MODULE.

The third form can be considered as a special form of the IMPLEMENTATION module, and is referred to as a 'program module'. A program module begins with the reserved word MODULE alone ('program' is *not* a reserved word in Modula-2). A MODULE is not a hierarchical unit in the same way that a procedure is, since a MODULE is not an executable subprogram unit but rather a packaging of such units. However, the code of a program module's main body will always form the 'main body' of a program when it begins execution, and so it essentially acts as the 'top level' of a program. Because of this, while the code within a program module may access data and subprograms that are contained in other modules, a program module may not provide anything for use by other parts of the whole program, and hence it requires no DEFINITION part. (We should perhaps consider that there are three *physical* forms of MODULE, but only two *logical* forms, with the program module being a degenerate form of the more general module.) So any Modula-2 program must contain one program module, and only one.

In its simplest form, a Modula-2 program consists of a program module alone. It then closely resembles a Pascal program, in that all the information that is needed by the compiler to compile the complete program is contained in the one compilation unit. This will be stored in a single file (and on most systems this file will have the extension .mod). In practice, though, this is rarely the exact form, since any practical program will need to perform input and output, which in turn requires the use of a set of procedures provided from another module.

All three forms of MODULE require that the reserved word MODULE must be followed by an identifier that will act as the name of the module, and which is then followed by a semi-colon to show that this is the end of that particular declaration. The identifier used in the DEFINITION and IMPLE-MENTATION parts of a single module must, of course, be identical.

To see an example of this, we can return to our earlier example of the module Charchecks, where the two parts contained the lines

    DEFINITION MODULE Charchecks;

and

    IMPLEMENTATION MODULE Charchecks;

The code of any of these three forms of MODULE is terminated by the reserved word END, followed by the identifier of the module, and then by a period character, as in

    END Textanalyser.

or

    END Charchecks.

Note that, except in program modules, there does not need to be a BEGIN to partner this particular END, a point about Modula-2 syntax that we will be returning to later.

A Modula-2 MODULE is rather like a block that has some form of 'socket' on its outer surface. The size and shape of the socket determines how much of the inner structure of the block can be accessed, and can be considered as being specified by the contents of the DEFINITION module. To form a complete program we need to connect, or 'plug', several such blocks together. These will then act as a whole program by exchanging control and data via the plugs and sockets in their 'surfaces'.

If Charchecks were to be included as a component of some program that was to perform (say) a textual analysis on some stored data, then the program might have some 'top level' module, in the form of a program or IMPLEMENTATION module to perform the required analysis, and this would

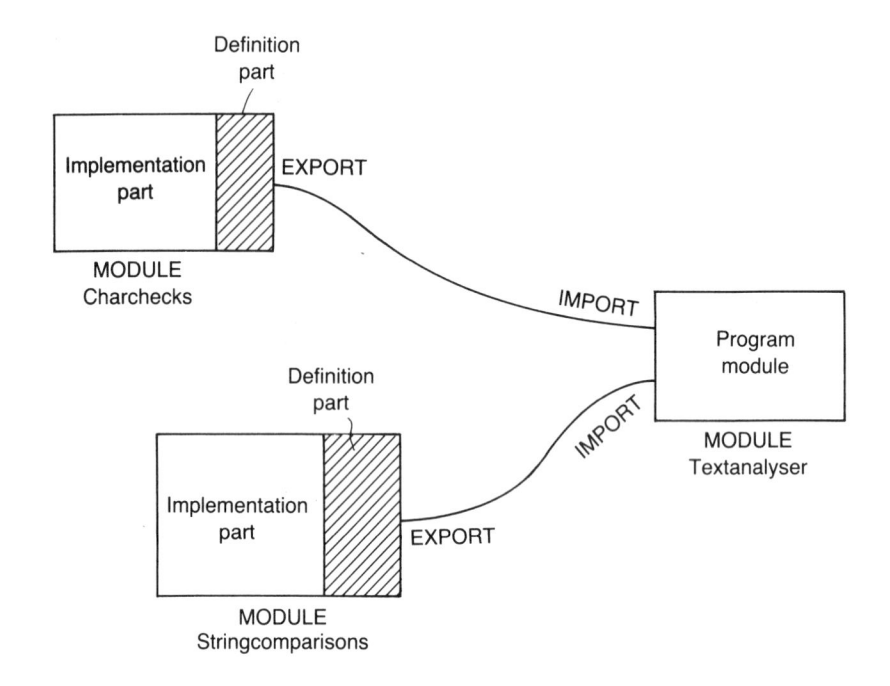

**Figure 3.1** Schematic view of module interfaces.

make use of the routines contained in Charchecks. The code at the beginning of such a program module might look something like

```
MODULE Textanalyser;
FROM Charchecks IMPORT Isdigit, Islowercase;
  ...
```

and this describes the type of 'plug' to be used. This mechanism is explained more fully in Section 3.2. Figure 3.1 shows the concept of module interfaces in a schematic manner.

## 3.2 Controlling visibility – IMPORT and EXPORT

The IMPORT and EXPORT directives provide the programmer with the means of controlling the interchange of information about the component parts of a module. The IMPORT directive may be used within all three forms of MODULE, and usually has the form

```
FROM ⟨modulename⟩ IMPORT ⟨list⟩;
```

where the identifier modulename directs the compiler to the particular .sym file that it needs to consult in order to obtain information about the items in the list, and the list consists of a sequence of names (identifiers) of items to be used from the chosen module.

Returning to our earlier example the following are all valid IMPORT directives that might be contained in a MODULE that needs to use items from the module Charchecks:

FROM Charchecks IMPORT Isdigit;
FROM Charchecks IMPORT Isdigit, Islowercase;
FROM Charchecks IMPORT Islowercase;

Note that the order of the required items within the list is not significant.

As a matter of practicality and style, it is better to avoid using IMPORT directives within DEFINITION modules whenever possible. However, it is not always practical to avoid them, as in the case where a user-defined type exported from one module is in turn required for use in specifying the parameters of procedures provided from another module.

(Note that an IMPLEMENTATION module will automatically IMPORT anything declared within its DEFINITION part. It does not need a specific IMPORT directive for this.)

The EXPORT directive can be considered as defining a 'window' on the contents of a module, by providing a list of the items in that module that are to be made visible to another. As a matter of good style, the list should contain only those items that are essential, since the amount of information EXPORTed from a module largely determines the amount of coupling (Page-Jones, 1983) that will exist between it and its client modules. The less information that client modules have about a lower-level module, the less tightly they can be coupled to it, and hence the more likely it will be that the lower-level modules can be modified without the necessity of changes to the client modules as well.

Since the compiler will already possess information about the identity of the particular module that it is compiling at any given time, the EXPORT directive needs only to specify a list of those items that are to be made visible to other modules. The usual form for this is

EXPORT QUALIFIED ⟨list⟩;

(the reserved word QUALIFIED will be explained later).

This form is used only within DEFINITION modules (at least, for the purposes of the present explanation it is), and the EXPORT directive will be positioned following any IMPORT directives that might be required. The list itself will normally contain the identifiers (names) of all the items declared within the DEFINITION module itself. As an example of this, in module Charchecks we used the directive

EXPORT QUALIFIED Isdigit, Islowercase;

in order to specify that the procedures Isdigit and Islowercase were to be made 'visible' outside the module. (A change in the third edition of *Programming in Modula-2* (Wirth, 1985), reflected in some Modula-2 compilers, is that all items in a DEFINITION module are automatically EXPORTed. Where this is the case, no specific EXPORT statement is required. However, this modification has not been adopted universally, and has specifically not been adopted by the BSI standards group.)

There is quite a lot more that can, and will, be said about IMPORT and EXPORT directives, but for the moment the summary provided in this section should suffice. For the next few chapters, we will concentrate upon the use of IMPORT, and will return to the issues of MODULE structure in Chapter 10.

## 3.3 The Modula-2 program module

The following (rather contrived) program provides a simple example of a program module. When compiled and executed, it will print four copies of the message 'Hello user' on the user's terminal.

```
MODULE Message;
FROM InOut IMPORT WriteString, WriteLn;
  CONST
    NumberOfMessages = 4;
  VAR
    MessageNumber : INTEGER;
  PROCEDURE Printout;
  BEGIN
    WriteString('Hello user');
    WriteLn;
  END Printout;
BEGIN
  FOR MessageNumber := 1 TO NumberOfMessages DO Printout END;
END Message.
```

(This program *may* work with your system, but the detailed form of the library module InOut and the exact form of the parameters used with the procedure WriteString could be different.)

This example makes use of the standard 'library' procedures that are provided in the MODULE InOut, although only two of those available from InOut are used on this occasion. (The issue of 'library' modules is described in the next section.) That apart, the program module looks very much like a Pascal program.

Compared with Pascal, though, there are some other differences. For example, the name of a MODULE or PROCEDURE is now coupled with the reserved word END. But this is hardly fundamental, and the Pascal programmer should find little difficulty in creating a program module.

Since Chapters 4 to 9 are concerned with the data forms and syntax of Modula-2, the examples in those chapters will be based largely upon the use of program modules, IMPORTing items from standard library modules as required, but otherwise ignoring the issues of separate compilation.

## 3.4 Library modules

Strictly speaking, there is no such thing as a 'library' MODULE in Modula-2, and so there is no reserved word LIBRARY. However, this term is commonly used when referring to a MODULE provided as part of the support package for a Modula-2 compiler or written locally to form part of a package used to support some particular facility (say a graphics system). A MODULE of this type will usually contain fairly low-level procedures, and be intended for use by many programs.

As Modula-2 was designed to be a general-purpose programming language, and contains features intended to assist with systems programming, those features that might need to be specific to a particular operating system have been kept out of the language. As a result, the procedures used to perform input and output are not in any sense a part of the language (as is the case for Pascal and FORTRAN), and are provided through a 'library' module. We usually expect to have a set of such modules providing a series of 'layers' to give different levels of file access and device handling, with the procedures in these modules becoming more system-dependent as we descend towards the device-handling level.

Some 'standard' library modules are used quite widely, and help to make Modula-2 programs more portable. They provide a fairly basic and machine-independent level of terminal input/output and file handling, but even these may not (currently) be standard on any given operating system.

A library module is made up from DEFINITION and IMPLEMENTATION parts in just the same way as any other module that is designed to provide a service. Library modules are usually stored within one or more system directories, which will be consulted by the compiler and link-editor. (To support separate compilation, the compiler needs access to a series of .sym files, corresponding to each of the intermediate code files used by the link-editor. This is unlike most other programming languages, which only require the link-editor to consult the intermediate code files in a central library directory.) The compiler and link-editor will then search these directories automatically when encountering any reference to a module that is not present in the user's directory.

The most important library module, for initial programming purposes at least, and the one that we will be using in most of our examples, is the module InOut. This provides a set of facilities for basic file handling and a number of routines to handle input and output of characters at a user's terminal. (Note the somewhat idiosyncratic convention that is used to form the identifier for this module. Using an initial upper case letter for each of the words making up a compound name is widely practised by Modula-2 programmers. However, it can be over-done and can complicate the task of keying in a Modula-2 program.)

The module InOut has been designed so that it is sufficiently abstract to be independent of the detailed form of the underlying file system. It is then serviced by procedures in other modules that operate at a lower level, in order to maintain a desirable degree of logical abstraction for performing input and output within the user's program. The next two sections describe the procedures that this provides for the handling of simple input and output.

## 3.5 Character handling in Modula-2

Many programs need to perform at least some input and/or output of characters, usually from and to the user's terminal, so character handling is probably the most basic form of input/output to consider. It is also a fairly simple form, being concerned only with sequences of characters. (The standard module InOut provides a set of procedures that will default to the user's terminal, but which can also be redirected to use a text file instead.)

The first significant point that the Pascal programmer will notice about the form of character input is that lines of characters are terminated by a special character, which is read in by the program using the same Read(ch) procedure as the other characters. It is not necessary to know what value this character has in any system, since that is provided from InOut as the constant identifier EOL, but the use of a character rather than a BOOLEAN function (EOLN) does influence the form of testing for the end of a line of input. One advantage of this form, however, is a greater consistency of program style, since the operation of reading characters is now solely concerned with handling character data.

For the output of characters, the procedure WriteLn (note the use of mixed upper and lower case characters again) is equivalent to a call of Write(EOL).

In the original Modula-2 report (Wirth, 1980) the module InOut is described as providing a BOOLEAN variable Done. If this variable is imported from InOut, it can be tested after a call to any of the procedures in the module, in order to determine whether the operation involved succeeded or failed. This is quite an attractive mechanism, although it easily becomes overloaded (as occurs with Done itself). Such a 'status return' can be particularly useful when using those procedures that perform such tasks as opening files or seeking for a file in some way. As a BOOLEAN variable, it can conveniently be used in expressions such as IF Done THEN ... .

When using the procedure Read, a return value of FALSE in Done is used to indicate the 'end of file' for that particular input device. When output is redirected in order to write characters to a file, a separate procedure CloseOutput is provided in order to write an 'end of file' to that device or file.

Section 3.6 provides a summary of those components of the module InOut that will be used in the examples of the next few chapters, as a reference that will help the reader to understand these a little more easily.

## 3.6 The MODULE InOut

The module InOut provides a set of procedures that are primarily concerned with simple character input and output. The form given below is something of an extract, since the detailed form of this module varies between systems. Here it has been reduced to a number of fairly general procedures that will be useful in examples: on most systems other procedures will be included in InOut. The description below is in the form of a DEFINITION MODULE.

```
(* Definition Module for InOut.            *
 * A simplified version for use with       *
 * our examples. Based upon a UNIX         *
 * implementation of InOut.                *)

DEFINITION MODULE InOut;
IMPORT FileSystem;                         (* use a lower-level module for
                                              file-handling *)
EXPORT QUALIFIED EOL,Done,Read,ReadLn,ReadInt,ReadCard,ReadReal,Write,
           WriteLn,WriteString,WriteInt,WriteCard,WriteReal;
CONST
  EOL = FileSystem.EOL;                    (* defined for us by the lower
                                              module *)
VAR
  Done : BOOLEAN;                          (* used as a status return
                                              indicator *)

PROCEDURE Read( VAR ch : CHAR );           (* Done := NOT end of file on
                                              input *)

PROCEDURE ReadLn;                          (* skips to start of next input
                                              line *)

PROCEDURE ReadInt( VAR i : INTEGER );      (* read string and convert to
                                              INTEGER, leading blanks
                                              ignored *)

PROCEDURE ReadCard( VAR c : CARDINAL );    (* read string and convert to
                                              CARDINAL, leading blanks
                                              ignored *)

PROCEDURE ReadReal( VAR r : REAL );        (* read string and convert to
                                              REAL, leading blanks ignored *)

PROCEDURE Write( ch : CHAR );
PROCEDURE WriteLn;
PROCEDURE WriteString( s : ARRAY OF CHAR );
```

```
            PROCEDURE WriteInt( i : INTEGER ; n : CARDINAL );           (* writes out i in a field of at
                                                                          least n characters, padding
                                                                          with leading blanks if fewer
                                                                          than n characters needed *)
            PROCEDURE WriteCard( c : CARDINAL ; n : CARDINAL );
            PROCEDURE WriteReal( r : REAL ; n : CARDINAL );
            END InOut.
```

## EXERCISES

To perform the following exercises, it would be useful if you were first to enter and compile the example module Charchecks that is used in this chapter.

**3.1** Enter the following program (into the file 'Chartest.mod')

```
MODULE CharTest;
FROM InOut IMPORT WriteString, WriteLn;
FROM Charchecks IMPORT Isdigit, Islowercase;

BEGIN
  IF Isdigit('9') THEN WriteString('9 is a digit');
  WriteLn; END;

  IF Isdigit('u') THEN WriteString('u is a digit!');
  WriteLn; END;

  IF Islowercase('t') THEN WriteString('t is lower case');
  WriteLn; END;

  IF Islowercase('T') THEN WriteString('T is lower case!');
  WriteLn; END;
END CharTest.
```

Compile and run this program, observe the results. Are they as you expect them to be?

**3.2** Using the program produced in Exercise 3.1, try modifying the parameters of Isdigit and Islowercase so that their form is invalid (for example Isdigit(9)) and observe the results of this

(a) for compilation,

(b) for execution.

**3.3** Design a new procedure, Isparenthesis (which returns TRUE only if its input parameter is a right or a left parenthesis character), and add this to the module Charchecks. Modify the program Chartest to make use of this new procedure. Think carefully about the order of compilation when making this change.

**3.4** In Charchecks.mod add the following lines before the procedure declarations

    CONST
      period = '.';

and then recompile Charchecks and Chartest. Because the value of period is not exported, it cannot be used in Chartest (try making a reference to it there).

# Chapter 4
# The Syntax and Conventions of Modula-2

4.1 Introduction
4.2 The character set
4.3 Conventions for identifiers
4.4 Statements
4.5 Operators
4.6 Delimiters
Exercises

## 4.1 Introduction

For a programmer who is already acquainted with Pascal, or indeed with any of the ALGOL family of programming languages, there is much about Modula-2 that will be familiar. However, there *are* some differences – and the general similarity with the form of Pascal can be quite deceptive on occasion.

This chapter is more concerned with introducing the general style of the language than with the details of the algorithmic forms that are used to specify the intended actions of a program. It provides some of the groundwork needed for the following chapters, which look at such issues as operations and data structures. Having so far been mainly concerned with considering the aspects of Modula-2 that are concerned with supporting 'programming in the large', we now need to fill in some aspects that are more concerned with 'programming in the small'. The emphasis will therefore be on the structuring of a Modula-2 program, and how we can use the language in an algorithmic sense.

## 4.2 The character set

In Modula-2, the **identifiers** (that is, the 'names' that we assign to the variables, constants, types and procedures used within a program) are constructed from the set of upper and lower case alphabetical characters

35

and the decimal digits, 0–9. As already mentioned, Modula-2 is a case-sensitive language, in that the upper and lower case forms of a letter are not treated as being equivalent when used in an identifier. In practice, this feature can be used to enhance the readability of a program, and should not cause any problems as long as we avoid selecting identifiers that might strain our typing skills!

An identifier *must* begin with an alphabetical character, so that

>    alpha    Alpha    twosquared    Nextchar2    pi2    The12th

are all examples of valid identifiers, while

>    2totheN    20times

are invalid. Many compilers will also impose some sort of limit upon the number of leading characters within an identifier that must be unique. (On compilers that run under an operating system that is not case-sensitive, such as VAX/VMS, this constraint may be even tighter, in that the leading sequence of characters in a name may need to be unique independently of their case. This constraint arises because the link-editor used on such systems is unlikely to be able to handle case-sensitive forms, and so any identifiers that need to be passed to the link-editor will be converted into a single case by the compiler. Thus this constraint represents an influence of the underlying operating system.)

The rest of the Modula-2 character set, which is used for the delimiters and operators, comprises the fairly standard characters found on most keyboards. Their individual uses will be introduced as we encounter them. The non-alphanumeric symbols that are used are the set

>    ;  :  ,  .  '  "  <  >  *  /  +  -  =  &  ~  (  )  [  ]  {  }  ↑  |  #

with only the latter three being likely to vary. The ↑ character (up-arrow) is sometimes replaced by a circumflex character ^. The vertical bar character | is sometimes shown with a break in the middle and on some terminals, the # character may be replaced by a £ (sterling symbol). Only the latter variation has any significant effect upon the readability of a program – and this will be explained later.

Unfortunately, unlike Ada, the Modula-2 character set does not include the underscore character '_', which can be a useful aid to forming composite names in a readable form, as in

>    Is_digit    Is_lower_case    Line_Count

and so on. Some Modula-2 compilers do accept this character as valid, in an extension to the language, but, since other compilers do not, its use could cause problems in transporting a program between different systems.

## 4.3 Conventions for identifiers

From the description of the library module InOut given in Section 3.6, it could be seen that the forms for the identifiers already made use of a convention based on a mix of upper and lower case letters. Indeed, this form has been used for most of the library modules proposed in the language definition (Wirth, 1983). The form makes use of upper case letters at the beginning of each part of a composite name – that is, an identifier that has been constructed from (possibly abbreviated) item names. Examples of such identifiers are

> WriteString    WriteLn    ReadCard

Although, perhaps, this convention causes more difficulties when typing, it does make a program easier to *read*, which is, of course, vital in terms of maintenance and support.

A useful convention that makes use of a mix of cases, but which avoids excessive mixing of cases, is: use identifiers that begin with lower case letters for *variables* and *constants* while still using upper case characters in the middle of such identifiers; and begin *module*, *type* and *procedure* identifiers with an upper case character, but not using upper case characters to begin further syllables. Also, procedure identifiers should be 'verbs', while constants and the like should be 'nouns'. One attraction of this convention is that it helps to distinguish visually between invocations of 'executable' items, such as procedures, and references to data items. As a further extension to this convention, user-defined types should be given a plural form for their name.

Using this convention, identifiers such as

> total    width    processBlock    maxCount

will be used for the identifiers of variables and constants, while

> Getscale    Openparser    Thirdpass    Classrecords

will be used for procedure, module or type identifiers. (Classrecords is clearly a type, since it has a plural form.)

The rest of this book largely makes use of these conventions, both to aid readability and to provide consistency of style. However, since we cannot influence the naming of standard library procedures and modules, these will of course remain in their normal form.

At this point we should also mention the use of reserved words in Modula-2. A **reserved word** is a character string (or identifier) to which a particular meaning or value has been allocated as a part of the language definition. As such, it cannot be re-used or re-assigned in any way by the programmer. (This is in contrast to a language such as FORTRAN, where

**Table 4.1** The reserved words used in Modula-2.

| | | | |
|---|---|---|---|
| AND | ELSIF | LOOP | REPEAT |
| ARRAY | END | MOD | RETURN |
| BEGIN | EXIT | MODULE | SET |
| BY | EXPORT | NOT | THEN |
| CASE | FOR | OF | TO |
| CONST | FROM | OR | TYPE |
| DEFINITION | IF | POINTER | UNTIL |
| DIV | IMPLEMENTATION | PROCEDURE | VAR |
| DO | IMPORT | QUALIFIED | WHILE |
| ELSE | IN | RECORD | WITH |

the meaning of a symbol will depend upon its context, so that a programmer *could* declare variable names IF, DO, END etc!) Table 4.1 shows the full set of 40 reserved words used in the Modula-2 language.

## 4.4 Statements

A Modula-2 program normally contains a mix of **declarations**, **statements** and **comments**. The statements are used by the programmer to tell the compiler how the program should act when it is executed (through the use of **expressions**), while the declarations are used to specify information about the forms of data to be used, and about the operations which are to be performed upon these. An executable statement usually contains some combination of **identifiers** (to specify the data elements), and of **operators** (to specify the actions), and these may need to be identified to the compiler by placing **separators** between them.

### 4.4.1 Separators within a statement

Concentrating upon these for a moment, since we will consider operators individually in later chapters, the separators used are the 'space' and the 'newline' characters, as well as comments. By virtue of its role, the space character of course cannot be used within an identifier. In particular, the number of spaces (above one) used between any of the operators and operands of a statement is quite immaterial, and so extra spaces can be used to produce a suitable layout for our code. This is very unlike a language like FORTRAN, where each statement has a number of 'fields' that are distinguished from one another by their position along a line. Indeed, in Modula-2, the 'end of line' is itself merely a separator and does not act as the terminator of a statement, as it does in FORTRAN.

When combining identifiers with operators in order to create expressions, declarations and statements, it is not normally necessary to provide separators between the identifiers and the operators. So the statement

```
x:=x+1
```

is a valid Modula-2 statement. Because the operators := and + are made up using unique characters that cannot appear within an identifier, there is no need to include any spaces or tabs between them and the identifiers. However, as a matter of style and layout, there is little doubt that the form

```
x := x + 1
```

is much more readable. For more complex statements this becomes even more true. (As an added point, we of course cannot put any spaces between the characters which make up a reserved word or a symbol such as the operator :=.)

A statement is one of the basic elements of a program. Each statement in a program specifies either an action or a set of actions that is to be performed when the program is executed. Declarations are also used in programs, and these specify a set of conditions that the compiler is to apply when constructing the program. A statement may also have a structure, in that it might have further subordinate statements within it.

### 4.4.2 The assignment statement

The simplest executable statement in an imperative programming language is the **assignment statement**, which is used to copy a new value into a program variable. The assignment operator is a composite of two characters, and takes the form

```
:=
```

(which can usefully be read as 'takes the value of'). This particular choice will be familiar to Pascal programmers. The two characters must be in strict sequence, and may not be separated by any tab or space characters. We have already seen an example of an assignment statement in the previous section, as in

```
x := x + 1
```

This statement copies a new value into the variable x, and specifies that the new value is to be obtained by adding 1 to the previous contents of the variable x. In Modula-2, as in most similar languages, the assignment destination is a variable on the left of the assignment operator.

In this example of an assignment statement, the clause x + 1 on the right of the assignment operator is an example of an **expression**, that is, a component of a statement that specifies how a new value is to be constructed. The simplest form of expression simply involves a constant as the source, as in the statement

```
x := 10
```

In the examples to be found in this book there will be many examples of both simple and complex forms of expression.

### 4.4.3 Sequencing of operations

An executable statement specifies a complete operation that the computer is to perform when the program is executed. The executable statements within a program are executed in strict sequence, and so the execution of the statement following the one currently being executed will not begin until the current one has completed execution. So in writing the following sequence of statements

```
xUnit := xUnit + 1;
length := xUnit*6 + 10;
```

the programmer will expect that, when these statements are executed, the value of xUnit which is used in the second statement will be that which was generated from the previous statement. So if xUnit has an initial value of 4 (say), a new value of 5 will be copied to it by the first statement, and then this value will in turn be used to compute a value of 40, which is then assigned to the variable length.

### 4.4.4 Statement separators and the null statement

As with most ALGOL-like programming languages, a Modula-2 programmer is not confined to writing only one statement per line, or equally to using one line for a statement. While this freedom may allow a more pleasing and supportive layout to be used in programs, a compiler needs to be able to distinguish the different statements which make up a program. To assist with this, we use a **statement separator**, which is the ';' (semicolon) character. This allows the layout of a program to be organized so as to reflect the structures of a particular algorithm, or to emphasize the logical structuring of the program.

As a part of this flexibility of layout, there is no specific position at which the semi-colon must appear in the region between two statements.

The following are all equally valid forms for describing a particular sequence of two statements:

```
xUnit := xUnit + 1 ; yUnit := xUnit*2 + 1
```

is equivalent to

```
xUnit := xUnit + 1;
yUnit := xUnit*2 + 1
```

and also to

```
xUnit := xUnit + 1
; yUnit := xUnit*2 + 1
```

However, we would normally adopt the first two forms rather than the last, since these make the position of the end of a statement more evident to the reader.

This use of the semi-colon as a separator is one of the issues that can sometimes bother a programmer who has not previously used a language of this form. Making use of it with sequences of statements is simple enough, but confusion may arise when there are subordinate statements nested within an outer statement. However, this is one area where the structures of Modula-2 are much better than those of Pascal and similar languages, as we will see in the examples of the next few chapters.

One aspect of the use of the statement separator that should be mentioned here is the concept of the **null statement**. The need for this arises precisely from the role of the ';' character as a separator rather than as a terminator.

Strictly speaking, within a sequence of statements, be it the main routine of a program, the centre of a looping construct, or the body of a subprogram, no semi-colon is required after the last statement. This is because the compiler recognizes the reserved word (usually END) that is used to terminate the structure as completing the particular sequence of statements. An example of this was the procedure Printout that was used in Chapter 3. The body of this procedure can be written as

```
PROCEDURE Printout;
BEGIN
  WriteString('Hello User'); WriteLn
END Printout;
```

with no need for a ';' following the call to WriteLn, because the END that follows this terminates the procedure. So there is no statement following the call to WriteLn, and so no separator is required.

However, a Modula-2 compiler *will* accept a semi-colon after the last statement of such a sequence as being a valid form, so that writing the procedure as

```
PROCEDURE Printout;
BEGIN
   WriteString('Hello User'); WriteLn;
END Printout;
```

is quite acceptable, and is equivalent to the previous form. This is made possible through the use of the concept of a null statement, which is an 'empty' statement lying between the superfluous ';' and the reserved word END. When a compiler encounters something of this form, it assumes that a null statement is present, and as such a statement does not represent any form of action, no code need be generated for it.

Including a null statement at the end of a sequence of statements is sometimes convenient, and particularly so if it is likely that we will need to add further statements to the sequence at some future time (a realistic assumption – if not an ideal one). This is because we can add extra statements on the lines following the last statement of such a sequence, without also needing to remember to add a semi-colon after that statement. (This is an easy error to make when editing a file of text!) It is not a major point since, if we add extra lines and forget to provide it, a compiler should indicate an error to us, but adopting this practice does avoid the need to re-edit on such occasions.

To clarify this last point by using the previous example, if we wanted to add an extra call of the form

```
WriteString('This is a Modula-2 program')
```

at the end of the procedure Printout, then the first form would require us to modify the existing line by adding a semi-colon after the WriteLn. We could then add the new statement so that Printout now becomes (the new code is underscored for emphasis):

```
PROCEDURE Printout;
BEGIN
   WriteString('Hello User'); WriteLn;
   WriteString('This is a Modula-2 program')
END Printout;
```

Using this form, we really need to modify one line as well as adding a line, whereas by using the second form we would only need to add one line. For this reason, any examples in this book that only use single statements will frequently show them terminated by a semi-colon, for example

```
x := x + 1;
```

However, it should be realized that the semi-colon may not always be necessary, and that this will depend upon the context in which the statement is placed.

### 4.4.5 The statement sequence

Throughout this chapter, associated with the idea of the statement as a component of a sequentially executed program unit, there has been the underlying concept of a **statement sequence**.

While the most elementary form of program will consist purely of an ordered set of statements, intended to be executed one after another, most real algorithms require the programmer to specify a number of optional paths for the flow of control. The choice of path will be determined by evaluating some condition during the execution of the program. Each such optional path will in turn consist of an ordered set of statements, and of course may involve further selection between options too. So we can think of our algorithm (expressed as the executable statements of the program) as being made up of a set of statement sequences. Any one statement sequence will be executed as an ordered sequence of operations. The idea of the statement sequence will prove very useful when we come to examine the ways in which a programmer may specify how control is to flow during execution of the program. Figure 4.1 shows the idea in symbolic form.

## 4.5 Operators

A computer program can be viewed as an ordered set of statements that together specify how and in what order the computer should modify the values of a set of variables. To perform the task of modifying a variable, the computer needs to **operate** upon it in some manner. The operations performed on the variables are themselves relatively simple ones, though they can of course be combined to form very complex structures.

The available operators are denoted in two different ways in Modula-2. One form is to use particular characters, or combinations of characters. Examples of this are the ':=' used to denote assignment, and the '+' used to denote the addition of two values. Assignment of course is an operation, and consists of evaluating an expression and then copying its value into the destination.

Table 4.2 shows the characters and character combinations that are used to denote operations in Modula-2. Most of them will be familiar enough to anyone who has used Pascal or a related language, and the discussion that follows is largely concerned with those that are additional to this base set.

```
                S1;
                IF condition1
                   THEN S2
                   ELSE
                      S3;
                      IF condition2
                         THEN S4
                      END (* if *)
                END (* if *)
                S5;
```

S denotes a statement sequence.

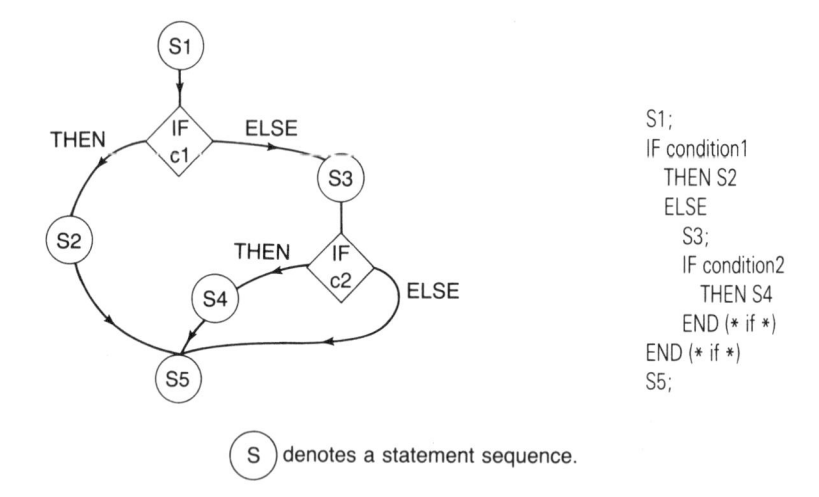

**Figure 4.1** Graphical illustration of the control flow representing the accompanying program segment.

**Table 4.2** Symbolic operators in Modula-2.

| Operator symbol | Operation |
| --- | --- |
| + | addition; set union |
| − | subtraction; unary negation; set difference |
| * | multiplication; set intersection |
| / | real division; symmetric set difference |
| := | assignment |
| & | logical AND |
| ~ | NOT |
| ↑ | pointer dereferencing |
| = | definition (types and constants) |
| # | not equal to |
| <> | not equal to |
| < | less than |
| > | greater than |
| <= | less than or equal to; subset |
| >= | greater than or equal to; superset |
| : | declaration (variables) |

**Table 4.3** Reserved words used as operators in Modula-2.

| Reserved word | Operation |
|---|---|
| AND | logical AND |
| DIV | integer division |
| IN | set membership |
| MOD | modulus |
| NOT | logical negation |
| OR | logical OR |

The second form for operators is to use a reserved word. Table 4.3 shows those used in Modula-2, together with their meanings. In keeping with the Modula-2 convention, these must always be in upper case.

This chapter is concerned only with the general form of a Modula-2 program, and so a more complete description of the operators and their effects will be given in the following chapters, as the structure of the language is described in more detail. In the rest of this section and in the following one, the main differences between the operators used in Modula-2 and those used in Pascal are outlined, and some of the possible hazards that lie in wait for the Pascal programmer migrating to Modula-2 are indicated.

The Modula-2 character set contains three characters additional to the set of characters used in Pascal that should be particularly noted.

The first is the ampersand '&', used as a synonym for the reserved word AND, denoting the 'logical AND' operator. It conveniently shortens long expressions but has no other advantages or disadvantages.

A second new character, the tilde '~', is a synonym for the reserved word NOT, used as the negation operator.

The third additional character is the hash character '#', which is used as a synonym for the opposed character pair '<>', signifying 'not equal to' in a relational expression. While at first this might appear to be a very convenient synonym, it is less convenient for those users of Modula-2 who have terminal devices that use the British form of the ASCII (American Standard Code for Information Interchange) character set (UKASCII) rather than the American form (USASCII). This character happens to be one of the very few that differ in the two sets, and in the British form it is printed as a sterling currency character, '£'. When encountered in the context of a relational expression, the purpose of this latter symbol is far less clear. For example, the statement

    IF x#y THEN ...

makes the relational expression fairly evident, while

    IF x £ y THEN ...

46  THE SYNTAX AND CONVENTIONS OF MODULA-2

**Table 4.4**  Characters and symbols used as separators and delimiters.

| Symbol | Purpose |
|---|---|
| . | field separator (RECORD) |
| , | list element separator |
| ; | statement separator |
| { | set element list |
| } | set element list (closing) |
| [ | array index |
| ] | array index (closing) |
| (* | comment |
| *) | comment (closing) |
| ( | parameter list (PROCEDURE) |
| ) | parameter list (closing) |
| : | label separator (CASE) |
| \| | statement sequence separator (CASE) |

**Table 4.5**  Reserved word used as delimiters.

| Reserved word | Purpose |
|---|---|
| BEGIN | begins MODULE/PROCEDURE body |
| END | terminates construct or structure (IF, CASE, LOOP, WHILE, FOR, PROCEDURE, MODULE, WITH, RECORD) |
| MODULE | begins MODULE structure |
| PROCEDURE | begins PROCEDURE structure |

is rather harder to interpret! So, tempting though the extension is, its use is not advised where there may be devices that use the UKASCII form, or where portability might be regarded as important.

## 4.6 Delimiters

The delimiters are the group of characters and reserved words that are used to form the boundaries around the different components of a program (that is, to delimit the **scope** of an item). Again, most of those used will be familiar to the Pascal programmer, though there are some differences too. Table 4.4 lists the characters that are used for delimiters, and Table 4.5 lists the reserved words that are also used for this purpose.

Some, like the semi-colon and the words MODULE and END, we have encountered already, and the use of the others will be developed further in the following chapters. For this introductory chapter, there are only two significant points to be noted.

The first of these particularly affects the Pascal programmer, and involves the delimiters normally used to enclose a comment. In Pascal the programmer has a choice of delimiters: the pair of braces { }, or the form that we are about to describe. Modula-2, however, provides only one form: in Modula-2, a comment begins with the pair of characters '(*' and ends with the pair '*)'. The comment itself may run over any number of lines, and may be placed within a statement anywhere where a space character could be used. However as such forms as

   IF xUnit < (* test for upper bound *) 100 THEN ...

are not particularly readable, programmers are advised to position comments between statements.

Each pair of characters must be treated as an 'atom', and may not be separated by spaces, tabs, newlines or any other characters. So if we type something such as

   (* test for lower bound * )

in which the final '*' and ')' accidentally get separated by a space, the compiler will regard any following statements as being a part of the comment. The compiler is therefore expected to count the opening and closing comment delimiters and inform us if these two counts do not tally. Comments can be 'nested' within one another, and this way it is possible to detect errors arising from improperly formed comment delimiters.

It is obviously possible that an error could lead the compiler to inform us that a structure is incomplete or incorrect. An example of this is the sequence

   (* now test for a letter q * )
   IF (nextChar = 'q') THEN Callexit
   (* and if not found, call the parser *)
   ELSE Parse(nextChar,code) END;

where the incorrect ending of the first comment will cause the compiler to treat the line beginning with IF as a part of the comment. The second comment is correctly terminated, so the compiler regards this as simply being nested within the first comment, and will continue to regard the following statements as being a part of the comment. Such errors are usually signalled to the user by compiler error messages that report that the end of the module has been encountered unexpectedly.

The second point to be noted is also connected with the Pascal comment forms. In Pascal the braces { } form an option for comment delimiters. In Modula-2 these are no longer available for this purpose.

Instead they have quite a different role, and are used to delimit the elements of a set constant.

We are now in a position to describe the form of Modula-2 in more detail. The points raised here will mostly reappear in the next few chapters and will be elaborated more fully there, as well as being set more fully into context.

## EXERCISES

**4.1** Which of the following are valid Modula-2 identifiers?

        PiSquared    sevenUp    6by10    linecount    page_length    $size

**4.2** Since the sequence

    ; END

is regarded as valid (because of the concept of the null statement), how would you expect a compiler to treat the sequences

    ; ;

and

    ; ; END

and why? (Try these on your own compiler.)

**4.3** Is the following statement sequence a valid or an invalid one, and why?

```
x := x + 3(*
    and
      now
        for a
          comment
*) ; y := y + 6;
```

What does this suggest about the forms of commenting that are possible with Modula-2?

# Chapter 5
# Simple Data Structures in Modula-2

5.1  Simple data types
5.2  Standard data types in
     Modula-2

5.3  The set type BITSET
     Exercises

## 5.1 Simple data types

Modula-2 is what we term a 'strongly typed' programming language. For any statement that specifies a transfer of data, whether by assignment or as a parameter of a procedure (say), the compiler will check whether the actual data item is assignment-compatible with the type that has been specified for the item used as the destination. Before proceeding to examine the standard data types provided with Modula-2, it may be useful to enlarge upon this point.

In Modula-2, each variable or symbolic constant used in a program unit must be declared before it may be used in any way. The **declaration statements** are placed at the beginning of the program unit, headed by the reserved words VAR and CONST. (A 'program unit' in this case may be a module or a procedure.) The declaration of a variable must specify both its identifier and also its **type**, which specifies the form of data that it will hold when used.

In any subsequent reference to that variable made in the executable statements of the program, only data values of an appropriate type may be assigned to that variable, or used in combination with it in expressions. During compilation, a compiler will check each statement of the program to ensure that only appropriate combinations of data types are used, and will mark any transgressions as errors. (Note that while variables do have an associated type in a language such as FORTRAN too, the rules concerning their use are much less rigid.)

49

Rather usefully, we are also able to define data types of our own, and to make use of them in our programs. When we do so, the type-checking rules are then applied to these in just the same way as they are applied to the standard types that are provided within the language.

The following sections give an introduction to the standard data types available in Modula-2, and describe the operations that can be performed upon objects of those types. Chapter 6 will look at the ways in which we can define our own data types, and at the rules which govern their use within modules.

## 5.2 Standard data types in Modula-2

### 5.2.1 The integer types INTEGER and CARDINAL

The type INTEGER is one that can be found in most programming languages. An integer object is one that may be used only to represent whole numbers, with no fractional parts being permitted. The actual range of values that can be represented is dependent upon the particular implementation of a language.

INTEGER objects are 'signed', and so can represent values that are either positive or negative. The range of values available is usually more or less symmetrical about zero. (For computers that use twos-complement arithmetic, the range is not *exactly* symmetrical, since the total number of possible values is even, being a power of two. Since zero is neither odd nor even, there must be one odd or even value that has no equivalent of opposite sign, and usually this is the most negative value.)

For example, with a 16-bit-memory word as used in computers such as the PDP-11, the range of values that can naturally be stored in a single word is −32 768 to 32 767. By contrast, for a 32-bit-memory word as used in larger machines such as the VAX, the range becomes −2 147 483 648 to 2 147 483 647. (In each case, the total range of values is determined by the number of different bit patterns that can be held in a single word.)

INTEGER variables can therefore be used to handle normal, everyday signed arithmetic involving the use of whole numbers, provided that the values do not go outside the appropriate range. Before going on to examine the operations that can be performed with this data type, though, it is necessary to introduce the closely associated CARDINAL type.

A variable of CARDINAL type is also used to hold representations of whole numbers, with the difference that it can represent a range of positive numbers only. (Essentially it represents an unsigned interpretation of the range of bit patterns held in a memory word.) For INTEGER data the stored bit patterns are interpreted using a convention that allows for a sign to be included, while for CARDINAL data, the contents of a word are treated as being a straight binary number.

This dual form for interpreting the contents of a memory word is very closely related to the manner in which the computer's central processor operates. When performing arithmetic operations upon integer data, it will normally treat this as a signed number, and apply the appropriate rules. However, when interpreting the contents of a memory as the address of data held in the main memory, this is normally regarded as being an unsigned value. Any intermediate calculations required in constructing an address will assume that the final value is to be unsigned.

The CARDINAL type is mainly of benefit when it is used with the smaller range of values that is supported on a 16-bit machine, since it allows a larger limit upon the representation of magnitude. Using CARDINAL, the 65 536 possible patterns are now interpreted as representing the range of values 0 to 65 535. However, the underlying hardware of the processor must be able to support this interpretation efficiently, and this may not always be so. The full range of values provided for the type CARDINAL may therefore be less than that possible for the word size, and this point will depend upon the particular compiler used.

The availability of the CARDINAL type makes it possible for the compiler and its support system to perform extra checking for the validity of results in situations where only positive integer values should be used and generated. However, since the same effect can be achieved by using subranges (see Chapter 6), this benefit alone would hardly merit the provision of a separate fundamental type.

As the type CARDINAL is used extensively in some of the standard library modules, it will appear in many of the examples of this book. Undoubtedly though, the presence (and use) of two such similar types as INTEGER and CARDINAL does sometimes cause additional problems when formulating algorithms.

Although the types INTEGER and CARDINAL are distinct, and may not be mixed within a statement, the same set of operations may be performed on variables of both types, and constants of both types are expressed using the same form. The rest of this subsection therefore applies equally to both INTEGER and CARDINAL types, and these will be referred to collectively as 'integer' (using lower case) types.

Variables of all types are normally declared in a segment headed by the reserved word VAR and containing a set of declarations of the form

⟨identifier_list⟩ : ⟨type⟩

Examples of declarations for the INTEGER and CARDINAL types are

```
VAR
  charCount : CARDINAL;
  offset : INTEGER;
  width, length, depth : CARDINAL;
```

Note that each of these declarations is terminated by a semi-colon.

In order to be able to assign particular values to the variables used in a program, we also require a means of specifying **constants** of a given type. An **INTEGER constant** is a signed string of digits, such as

```
100  +50  -10400
```

(note that a positive value does not necessarily require the use of a '+' character), while a **CARDINAL constant** is a positive string of digits – for example

```
100  +4010
```

Some examples of assignment statements that make use of constants are:

```
charCount := 0;
offset := -24;
width := length - 10;
```

We may also use symbolic constants in Modula-2, and the reserved word **CONST** is used to declare the start of a group of definitions, which should be placed at the head of a module or procedure body. Symbolic constants are an important feature in programming, especially where a program may be concerned with handling some particular ranges of data values. If the values of the limits for these are encoded as symbolic constants, and the symbolic form rather than the numeric value of the constant is used in the statements of the program, it becomes much easier to modify the program to accommodate new limits or ranges, since only the definitions of the symbolic constants need to be changed.

As an example of the use of constants, the constant declarations in a program unit might take the following form:

```
CONST
   maxLength = 23;
   wordLimit = 15;
```

(note that the character '=' is used to assign values in the declaration, rather than the operator ':=' which is used for assigning values to *variables*). These constants can then be used in later declarations such as

```
TYPE
   bits = [0..wordLimit];
```

as well as in executable statements such as

```
offset := wordLimit;
```

and

```
IF count > maxLength THEN ...
```

Besides being able to assign values to simple constants in the form shown above, we can also use a **constant expression** in a statement. Such an expression includes constants only, and since their values will be known to the compiler it can be evaluated by the compiler during compilation, with no need to generate any executable code. Some examples of constant expressions are:

```
CONST
    mostSigBit = wordLimit −1;
    overFlow = maxLength + 10;
    maxVolume = (maxLength + 10)*wordLimit ;
```

So far, all numeric constants used have been regarded as being decimal (base ten) values, in the form in which we handle numbers in everyday life. Since it may sometimes be convenient to express numbers within a program in a form related to the binary representation, Modula-2 provides forms for expressing the value of an integer constant to either base 8 (octal) or base 16 (hexadecimal).

An **octal constant** consists of an ordered sequence of digits in the range 0..7, followed by the upper case character B (there must be no space characters between the last digit and the B). Examples of this form are the constant declaration

```
mask = 177400B; (* decimal equivalent is ... *)
```

and the assignment statement

```
size := size + 1000B; (* size + 512 *)
```

A **hexadecimal constant** is formed from an ordered sequence of digits in the range 0..9 together with upper case letters in the range A..F (representing the decimal values 10..15), followed by the character H. An additional constraint is that such a constant must begin with a digit, and so any constant that has one of the letters 'A' to 'F' as its leading character must be prefixed with a zero character. Using the same binary values as before, the two previous examples now become

```
mask = 0FF00H; (* decimal equivalent is ... *)
```

and

```
size := size + 200H; (* size + 512 *)
```

Examples of the use of these forms will occur in some of the later chapters, especially when considering some of the machine-dependent aspects.

The *operations* that can be performed upon INTEGER and CARDINAL variables are mostly arithmetic in form. Each of these is described below.

*Addition*: The addition operator consists of the '+' character, and it is placed between any pair of integer operands (which of course must both be either of INTEGER or of CARDINAL type). Some examples are:

```
i := i + 3;
```

and

```
length := width + margin + 10;
```

*Subtraction*: This operator is the '−' character, which can be used in the same way as the '+' character in order to produce such expressions as:

```
result := base − offset;
```

It may also be used as a unary operator, where it operates upon a single integer operand in order to reverse its sign. An example of this is the expression:

```
offset := −difference;
```

which is the equivalent of the expression:

```
offset := (−1) * difference;
```

*Multiplication*: The multiplication operator is the asterisk character '*', as used in many other programming languages. Examples of its use are:

```
area := width * length;
newUnits := scale * oldUnits;
```

(The use of the '*' is essential: we *cannot* write a statement such as

```
area := width length;
```

with the multiplication operator being implicit as occurs in algebraic notation.) As in the case of the addition operator, the order in which the two operands appear is not significant, since the operation is commutative, that is, x * y is always equivalent to y * x. Note that the spaces around each of these operator characters are purely cosmetic, and used solely as a help to the reader. Because these three characters are not part of the character set that is used to construct legal identifiers or constants, they need no delimiters around them. The use of the spaces as in the examples is, however, easier on the eye, and is recommended as a practice worth adopting.

*Division*: The form used for this is rather different from that used for the previous three operations, though it will be familiar to the Pascal programmer: we use the reserved word DIV, rather than a single character. Examples of its use are:

```
oldUnits := newUnits DIV scale;
width := count DIV 5;
```

This operator nearly always requires spaces around the reserved word, so that a compiler can distinguish it from any identifier names or constants. If one or both of the spaces were missed out, to create a statement such as

```
width := countDIV5;
```

then a compiler would attempt to create the necessary code to copy the contents of a variable whose identifier was countDIV5 into the variable width, and would of course then issue an error message to inform us that countDIV5 had not been previously declared.

An integer division that does not produce an integer result will cause the fractional part of the result to be truncated, so that the result will still have the appropriate integer form (either CARDINAL or INTEGER). For example, the expression

```
7 DIV 4
```

will produce a result of 1. Integer division always *truncates* the result, rather than rounding it to the nearest whole value.

*Modulus*: This is a useful operator, denoted by reserved word MOD. Its operation returns the value of the 'remainder' that is generated by an integer division. So using the values of the last example, the expression

```
7 MOD 4
```

will produce a result of 3; similarly

```
9 MOD 3
```

will produce a result of 0 and so on. The MOD operation is defined only for positive operands, so that the expression

```
-27 MOD count
```

will produce an unspecified result.

For certain arithmetic expressions, it may be necessary for the programmer to know in which order the individual operations will be performed. As an example, the value that will result from executing the expression

   2 + 3 * 4

will be 20 if the addition operation is performed first, and 14 if the multiplication operation is performed first. To enforce a particular precedence of operations it may be necessary to enclose parts of expressions in parentheses, as in

   (2 + 3) * 4

which will ensure that the addition operation will precede the multiplication. Parentheses can be nested to any necessary depth.

In Modula-2 the *precedence* of these operators (i.e. the order in which they are performed if no parentheses are present) is defined as: first the NOT operator, followed by the multiplying operators, then the adding operators, and finally the relational operators. That is, multiplication and division will be performed before addition, so that in the above example, the result of evaluating

   2 + 3 * 4

should be 14. Where operators are of equal precedence, a left–right order of precedence will be applied. However, the use of parentheses should always be regarded as highly desirable, as it makes the intended form of evaluation clear, without the need to remember the precedence rules.

One problem that can arise from the existence of two whole-number arithmetic types is that there will be occasions when we require to form an expression using variables of both types. As the strict type-checking rules of Modula-2 regard these as being incompatible, the compiler will not accept such an expression, however sensible it may be in an arithmetical sense. To enable us to use such expressions when necessary, two **type transfer** functions are provided, which will effectively 'switch off' this form of type checking for a particular operation. The type transfer functions are: INTEGER(c), which causes the compiler to treat the CARDINAL value c as an INTEGER value; and CARDINAL(i), which causes the compiler to treat the INTEGER value i as a CARDINAL value. These functions make it possible to construct such expressions as

   location := base + CARDINAL(offset);

where location and base are of type CARDINAL, and offset is of type INTEGER.

A further group of operations is the comparison operations performed by the **relational** operators. These are introduced here, but are relevant to almost all the types described in this chapter. All the relational operators use two operands, which must be type-compatible, and compare these in order to produce a BOOLEAN result of TRUE or FALSE.

*Equality*: The operator used in testing for equality is the character '=', as in the example

    IF ( charCount = lineLimit ) THEN ...

This will return a value of TRUE if and only if the two operands (charCount and lineLimit) have identical values.

*Inequality*: This operator has already been mentioned in connection with the operator synonyms discussed in Chapter 4. We can choose between using the character pair '<>' and the single character '#' for this operator. So the expression

    IF ( charCount <> lineLimit ) THEN ...

will return a value of TRUE if and only if the two operands have different values and is equivalent to the expression

    IF ( charCount # lineLimit ) THEN ...

*Greater than*: This is denoted by the character '>'. In the expression

    IF ( charCount > lineLimit ) THEN ...

the result will be TRUE only if the value of charCount is larger than that of lineLimit.

An additional form, which also allows equal values of the operands to produce a result of TRUE ('greater than or equal to') is denoted by the character pair '>='. Using this in the previous example we get

    IF ( charCount >= lineLength ) THEN ...

which will now return a value of TRUE if and only if charCount has a value larger than or equal to that of lineLimit.

*Less than*: The operator for this is '<', and there is also the form '<=', which denotes 'less than or equal to'. They complement the forms just described, so that the expression

    IF ( charCount < lineLimit ) THEN ...

will return TRUE if and only if the value of charCount is less than the value of lineLimit.

The relational operators are very widely used, and will appear in many examples throughout this book.

### 5.2.2 Characters

The type CHAR enables a program to store and operate upon data in the form of characters. The standard data type CHAR is essentially the same as that provided in Pascal, though some aspects concerning its use are a little different.

In the memory of the computer each character is stored as a bit pattern, with numerical interpretation usually in the range 0..127 (decimal). Unfortunately the mapping between character symbols and their numerical values is not universal, and care is needed when writing programs that may need to make reference to the numerical representations of characters (termed the *ordinal* values) in any way. The ASCII character set is very widely used, but unfortunately even that is subject to some necessary variation in European hands. The earlier example of the '#' symbol and its UK alternative demonstrates the point. However, when we work directly with the type CHAR the level of data handling involved is so abstract that there is no need to concern ourselves with how the characters are represented in memory.

Variables of type CHAR are declared in the normal manner; for example:

```
VAR
   ch, testChar, sentinel : CHAR;
```

Character constants can be represented using two different forms. For the printing characters we can most conveniently enclose the character in either single or double quote marks, as in:

```
'a'    "a"    'T'    't'    "e"
```

(Note that either form of quote mark can be used in Modula-2, unlike Pascal, in which only single quote marks can be used.) An additional, more general, form is to use the ordinal value of the character, expressed as an octal value. When used with a variable of type CHAR, such a constant must be terminated by the character C, rather than a B, and of course the range of possible values will be limited by storage considerations (usually the range is 0..127). An example of a conditional test written using this form might be

```
IF ( ch = 15C ) THEN ...
```

This form is especially convenient when it is used with the non-printing characters, but of course its use may very well make a program non-portable. Some examples of declarations that make use of the two forms are:

```
CONST
    EOL = 15C;
    Alpha = 'A';
    Beta = 102C;
```

The operations that can be performed upon a variable of type CHAR include those of assignment and comparison, as in:

```
ch := 'f';
sentinel := Alpha;
```

and

```
IF ( ch = EOL ) THEN ...
```

The relational operations can be applied to the ordinal values of the CHAR operands, as in:

```
IF ( ch > 'a' ) AND ( ch < 'z' ) THEN ...
```

There are also two standard functions that are provided in the language in order to allow the programmer to make reference to the numerical representation of characters when required.

The CARDINAL function ORD returns the ordinal value (position) of the character that is supplied as its parameter. For example, using the ASCII character set, the assignment statement

```
testPattern := ORD('A');
```

will result in the CARDINAL variable testPattern being assigned a value of 65 when the statement is executed.

The complementary operation is performed by the function CHR, which takes as its parameter the CARDINAL value of a character's ordinal position and returns a value of type CHAR. So the effect of the previous example could be reversed by a statement of the form

```
ch := CHR(testPattern);
```

or

```
ch := CHR(65);
```

Unlike the type transfer functions, which simply override the type-checking rules of a compiler, these type conversion routines may involve a modification to the form of data storage. They can be useful when we need to handle the 'non-printing' characters that are used for control purposes, such as the 'line feed' or 'newline' character (12C), and the 'carriage return' character (15C).

Two examples of using CHR with such non-printing values are

    Bell := CHR(7);

which assigns the 'bell' character to the CHAR variable Bell (the 'bell' character causes a terminal to produce a bleep); and

    IF (ch = CHR(15B)) THEN ...

which tests the variable ch of type CHAR to see if its value is equal to that of the 'carriage return' character. Obviously for these particular examples, which use constants as source values, the C form is generally clearer, but these functions are of course essential when using variables of type CHAR.

Since the two functions are complementary, they completely reverse each other's actions, so that we have the equivalences

    ch = CHR( ORD( ch ) )

and

    n = ORD( CHR(n) )

The short program module in Figure 5.1 uses some of the features discussed in this and the preceding sections. It may be a useful exercise to enter this program into your own system and, after running it, to try rewriting it to use alternative forms wherever possible.

**Figure 5.1** A simple program using CHAR and CARDINAL.

```
(* Textcount reads a file of characters from the terminal input, until it encounters the
   end-of-file character. It counts the following features:
    * the number of words
    * the number of lines
    * the number of sentences
   present in the text read in. Words are terminated by
    * spaces
    * commas
    * semi-colons
    * periods (full-stop)
    * end of line
   Sentences are terminated by a period. *)
```

MODULE Textcount;

FROM InOut IMPORT Read, Write, WriteLn, WriteString, WriteCard, EOL, Done;

CONST
  period = '.';                      (* character constants *)
  comma = ',';
  semicolon = ';';
  space = 40C;                  (* example of ordinal form *)
  null = 0C;

VAR
  previousChar : CHAR;      (* buffer for previous character read *)
  currentChar : CHAR;       (* buffer for current character read in *)
  wordCount : CARDINAL;     (* counter for words in text *)
  sentenceCount : CARDINAL; (* counter for sentences in text *)
  lineCount : CARDINAL;      (* counter for lines of text *)

BEGIN
  currentChar := null;       (* initialize buffers and counters *)
  wordCount := 0;
  sentenceCount := 0;
  lineCount := 0;

  LOOP
    previousChar := currentChar;
    Read(currentChar);
    IF NOT Done THEN EXIT END;   (* exit on end-of-file *)

  (* convert all characters to lower case to help with counting *)

    IF (currentChar >= 'A') AND (currentChar <= 'Z')
    THEN
      currentChar := CHR( ORD(currentChar) – ORD('A') + ORD('a'));
    END; (* if *)

  (* check for end of a simple word *)

    IF (currentChar = space) OR (currentChar = comma) OR
      (currentChar = semicolon)
    THEN
      IF (previousChar >= 'a') AND (previousChar <= 'z')
      THEN
        INC(wordCount);
      END; (* if *)
    ELSE
      IF (currentChar = period)     (* check for end of sentence *)

```
          THEN
            IF (previousChar >= 'a') AND (previousChar <= 'z')
            THEN
              INC(wordCount);
              INC(sentenceCount);
            END; (* if *)
            IF (previousChar = space)
            THEN
              INC(sentenceCount);       (* have already incremented wordCount *)
            END; (* if *)
          ELSE
            IF (currentChar = EOL)
            THEN
              INC(lineCount);
              IF (previousChar >= 'a') AND (previousChar <= 'z')
              THEN
                INC(wordCount)
              END; (* if *)
            END (* if *)
          END (* if *)
        END (* if *)
      END; (* loop *)
      WriteLn;
      WriteCard(wordCount,4); WriteString(' words'); WriteLn;
      WriteCard(lineCount,3); WriteString(' lines'); WriteLn;
      WriteCard(sentenceCount,3); WriteString(' sentences'); WriteLn;
    END Textcount.
```

**Figure 5.1** *cont.*

### 5.2.3 The type BOOLEAN

Although the type BOOLEAN plays a very important role in programming, it is often used in an indirect way, as when we evaluate BOOLEAN expressions for use with conditional statement forms (IF, WHILE, REPEAT UNTIL). This is often combined with the use of a BOOLEAN status return value from a function subprogram, which can be used to indicate the success or failure of the specific operations performed within the subprogram.

There are only two BOOLEAN constant values, TRUE and FALSE. BOOLEAN variables are declared in the normal manner, as in:

```
    VAR
      Done : BOOLEAN;         (* indicates effect of operation *)
      fileStatus : BOOLEAN;   (* set true when file is opened *)
      Active : BOOLEAN;       (* indicates if device is responding *)
```

and assignment is performed in the usual way, as in

> fileStatus := TRUE;

BOOLEAN expressions may also be formed by using objects of other types, combined with relational operators. Besides being used in conditional statements, such BOOLEAN expressions may be used in assignment statements too, with a destination variable of type BOOLEAN being designated to receive the result of the operation. An example of this form is the statement:

> fileStatus := fileCount > 0;

Another example with a slightly more confusing appearance might be:

> ioBalance := readerCount = writerCount;

In the first of these examples, a value of TRUE will be assigned to the variable fileStatus if the value of the variable fileCount (which will be of type CARDINAL or INTEGER) is greater than zero; otherwise it will be assigned a value of FALSE. In the second example, a value of TRUE will be assigned to the variable ioBalance only if the value of the variable readerCount is equal to that of the variable writerCount (of course, these two variables must be of the same type). Otherwise ioBalance will be assigned a value of FALSE.

In Modula-2 BOOLEAN variables can sometimes provide a convenient means of communicating status information between modules. An example of this is where we have a module containing a number of procedures concerned with handling some particular data item. The success or failure of the requested operations can be signalled back to the calling routines via such a variable. The BOOLEAN variable Done that can be found in the standard library module InOut is used in exactly this way. It indicates the result of performing the various possible file input/output operations (for example, to inform the caller whether a call to the 'file open' routine was successful, or whether the operating system was unable to locate the required file).

There are three operations that can be performed upon BOOLEAN operands, and hence three operators: logical AND, logical OR and negation. Their effects are as follows.

AND (also denoted by the '&' symbol): This operates upon two operands and the BOOLEAN result produced is determined according to the truth table shown in Table 5.1 (denoting the two operands as a and b).

To determine the result of the operation a AND b we select the row and column according to the actual values of a and b, and the result is shown at their intersection in the matrix. That is, the result of the operation will be TRUE only if both a and b are TRUE, otherwise it will be FALSE.

**Table 5.1** Truth table for AND.

|  | operand a |  |
|---|---|---|
|  | TRUE | FALSE |
| operand b TRUE | TRUE | FALSE |
| operand b FALSE | FALSE | FALSE |

OR: The corresponding truth table for this operation is shown in Table 5.2.

In this case, the result of the operation is TRUE if either a or b is TRUE, and hence it produces a result of FALSE only if both operands have a value of FALSE.

**Table 5.2** Truth table for OR.

|  | operand a |  |
|---|---|---|
|  | TRUE | FALSE |
| operand b TRUE | TRUE | TRUE |
| operand b FALSE | TRUE | FALSE |

Examples of the use of these operations would be the statements

IF ( count > 0 ) AND fileStatus THEN ...

and

WHILE ( Done OR Active ) ...

NOT (also denoted by the '~' symbol): This operator has only one operand, and it produces a result that is the reverse of the value of the operand; for example:

NOT Done

will return a value of TRUE if Done has a value of FALSE, and will return a value of FALSE if Done has a value of TRUE.

The type BOOLEAN will feature in quite a lot of the discussions of the next two chapters when we come to examine the IF, WHILE and REPEAT UNTIL statements.

### 5.2.4 The fractional number type REAL

The type REAL is used to store fractional numbers, in what is sometimes referred to as a 'floating-point' form. Constants of this type can be expressed in either standard decimal form, as in

    12.3    2091.032

or by using a **scale factor** (the letter E followed by a number) to denote the power of 10 by which we must multiply the stated value in order to obtain its actual value. Some examples of numbers expressed in this form are:

    2.34E3    1.1E−1    9.6E3    0.2301E2

each of which corresponds to the following values expressed in normal decimal form:

    2340.0    0.11    9600.0    23.01

Note that the value of the exponent (the number following E) must be an INTEGER constant (as the value is signed). Also a REAL constant must *always* have a digit before the decimal point.

The operations that can be performed on REAL objects are similar to those used with the integer types. All except division use the same forms as are used for INTEGER and CARDINAL variables, for example:

    diameter := 2.0*radius;

and

    perimeter := 2.0*( length + width );

However, the division operator for REAL values is the symbol '/', rather than the reserved word DIV. An example of its use is:

    radius := circumference/(2.0*pi);

(Note the use of parentheses to establish the required order of evaluation.)

As types cannot be mixed in expressions, a pair of type conversion functions is provided to handle expressions that mix REAL values with INTEGER or CARDINAL values. These are: FLOAT(c), which returns the REAL equivalent of the value contained in the CARDINAL operand c; and TRUNC(x), which returns the integer part of the REAL operand x as a CARDINAL value. Note that, as indicated by the identifier, it *truncates* the value of x, rather than rounding it.

These functions handle only CARDINAL operands, and so to use them with INTEGER operands a further type transfer operation will be needed.

As with the INTEGER and CARDINAL types, the range of values that can be represented in a variable of type REAL is dependent upon the particular implementation of REAL itself. In particular, the degree of precision available is highly machine-dependent, and the programmer always needs to be aware of this when using REAL values.

## 5.3 The set type BITSET

Modula-2 provides some support for the use of sets, although a particular implementation may involve constraints upon the size of sets, which may reduce their usefulness. The standard type of this form is known as BITSET, and one of its roles is to enable the programmer to treat the contents of the computer's memory as a series of binary patterns rather than as numerical values. Using BITSET, a programmer is able to express operations that set and clear individual bits within a word in a clear and explicit form. This feature becomes an especially useful facility on computers that support the type of internal architecture sometimes known as 'external page', which provides for the control of attached physical devices through the use of registers that can be accessed in the same manner as memory locations. (The PDP-11, VAX-11 and Motorola MC68000 families all support this type of architecture.)

A BITSET variable or constant is a **set** of ordered elements, whose identities consist of the integer values between 0 and $N-1$, where $N$ is normally the number of bits in the computer's memory word. Some typical values for $N$ are 16, 24 and 32.

BITSET constants are expressed as a sequence of values enclosed in braces, and these values correspond to the set elements that are present. Examples of BITSET constants are

    {1}   {2,3}   {7,13..15}   {0..7,14,15}

For a 16-bit word ($N=16$), these will correspond to the bit patterns

```
0000000000000010
0000000000001100
1110000010000000
1100000011111111
```

(where bit 15 is on the left and bit 0 on the right of these patterns). The null (or empty) set is denoted by { } and comprises a word containing all zeros. Note that the specification of a set constant is concerned only with the presence or absence of elements, and so does not require that we specify the elements in a particular order. This means that the constant {2,3} is equivalent to {3,2}.

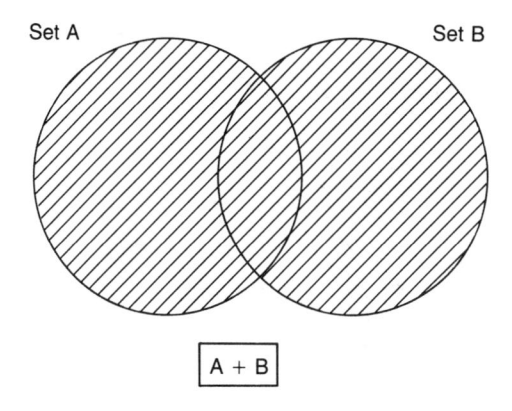

**Figure 5.2** Union of two sets.

BITSET variables are declared in the usual manner, as in

```
VAR
    printerStatus, printerControl : BITSET;    (* device registers *)
```

There are four logical operations that can be applied to variables and constants of this type. These are:

*Set union*: This is denoted by the operator '+'. The **union** of two sets is a set that consists of all those elements which are in either of the two sets, or both. So if we have two BITSET variables p and q, and assign to them the values

```
p := {1,6,7,15};
q := {0..3,14,15};
```

then the expression

```
r := p + q;
```

will assign the value

{0..3,6,7,14,15}

to the BITSET variable r.

The order of p and q is immaterial, so that if we had written

```
r := q + p;
```

then the result would have been the same (the operation is commutative). Figure 5.2 shows the effect in diagrammatic form.

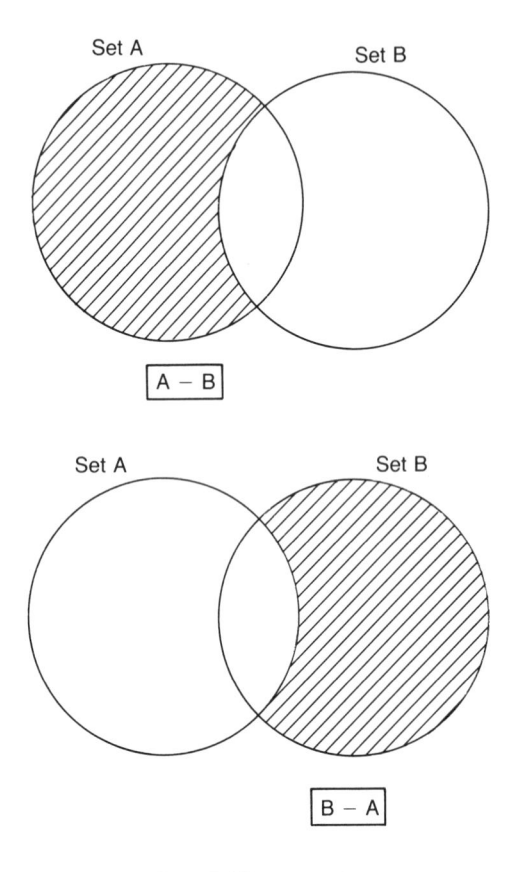

**Figure 5.3** Difference of two sets.

*Set difference*: This is denoted by the operator '−'. The **difference** of two sets is a set comprising those elements that are present in the first set but not in the second. Using the same values for p and q that were used in the previous example, the expression

```
r := p - q;
```

will assign a value of

{6,7}

to the variable r, because the elements 6 and 7 are in p, but not in q, whereas the elements 1 and 15 are in both sets and therefore do not qualify to be included in r.

This operation is *not* commutative for, given the same initial values, the expression

```
r := q - p;
```

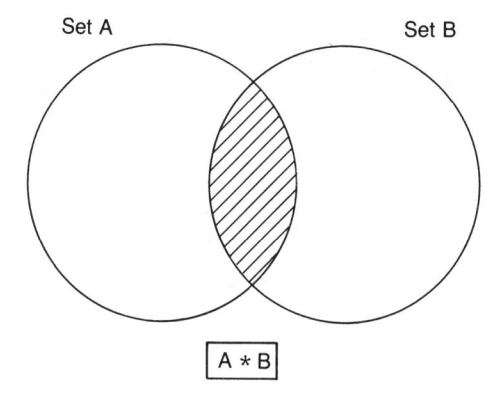

**Figure 5.4** Intersection of two sets.

will assign a value of

{0,2,3,14}

to the variable r. (The analogy with the arithmetic operation of subtraction is fairly strong, in that this is not commutative either, whereas addition is.) Figure 5.3 shows the effect of the two operations.

*Set intersection*: This is denoted by the operator '*'. The **intersection** of two sets is the set of elements that are present in both of the original sets, as shown in Figure 5.4. Using the previous values of p and q, the expression

r := p * q;

will assign a value of

{1,15}

to the variable r. This operation is commutative, and so the operation

r := q * p;

will produce the same result. (Again, this is rather like the arithmetical operation of multiplication.)

*Symmetric set difference*: This is denoted by the symbol '/', and the result of applying it to two sets is a new set whose elements are in one set or the other, but not in both. This operation is the complement of intersection. Using the previous values of p and q again, the expression

r := p / q;

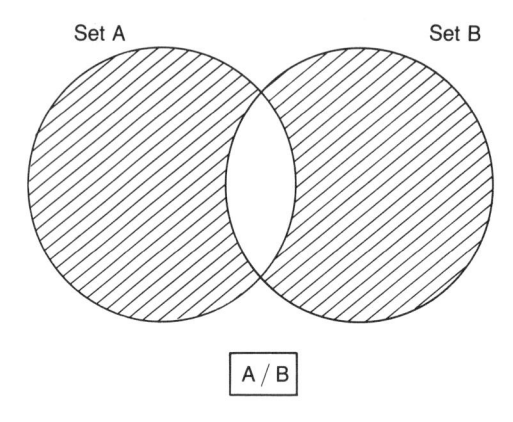

**Figure 5.5** Symmetric difference of two sets.

will assign a value of

{0,2,3,6,7,14}

to the variable r. Unlike the use of this operator in arithmetic operations, this operation is commutative, and so the expression

r := q / p;

will give the same result, as is shown in Figure 5.5.

A particularly convenient place in which to make use of set types is in conditional expressions (IF, WHILE, REPEAT UNTIL) since, instead of using a simple relational expression to produce a BOOLEAN result, we can use the **set membership** operator, denoted by the reserved word IN. This provides a means to test for the presence of a given element within a set value, and its use will be examined in the examples of Chapters 7 and 8.

The type BITSET enables the programmer to make optimum use of packed information. Apart from the device-handling purpose mentioned earlier (and developed more fully in Part 3) it can be used to manipulate word-sized fields of data for various purposes.

One example of the use of such a structure is in encoding the 'file access permissions' that many operating systems use. On an operating system such as UNIX, each file possesses an associated set of access permissions. The forms of access controlled by these are *read from*, *write to*, or *execute* a given file (denoted by r, w, and x respectively). For each file, the states of these permissions (either granted or not granted) are recorded for each of three classes of user: the 'owner' of the file (denoted by o), the members of the same 'group' as the owner (g), and the 'world' – all other users – (denoted by w). Since each permission has only two possible states, we can represent the complete access status by a set of nine binary digits. Where a particular access form is granted for a class of user, then the associated bit will be set to 1 (say) if the permission is granted, and 0 if not.

## EXERCISES

**5.1** For your particular computer system and Modula-2 implementation, check:

(a) the range of permissible INTEGER values;
(b) the range of permissible CARDINAL values.

If MaxInt is the largest positive INTEGER value allowed, what will be output by the call

   WriteCard ( CARDINAL(MaxInt +1), 12);

and by

   WriteInt( MaxInt + 1, 12);

**5.2** Write a program that reads in the value of a CARDINAL number from the keyboard, and then prints out the equivalent value to base eight, using only ReadCard and Write.
   [Hint: use DIV 8 and MOD 8, and convert the results to ASCII characters by using a sequence such as

   asciiChar := CHR( ORD('0') + octalDigit); ]

**5.3** Use the symbolic constants

   NewLine  = 12C;
   Bell     = 7C;
   Formfeed = 14C;

in a small program module that outputs the values of these characters to your terminal. What results do you observe on the screen, and how do they match your expectations?

**5.4** Write a small program that uses BITSET variables in such a way as to demonstrate that both set intersection and symmetric set difference operations are commutative.

**5.5** Enter and run the program that is listed in Figure 5.1. Try making each of the following changes in turn:

(a) change the definition of the constant space to have the same form as period, comma and semicolon;

(b) add the exclamation mark '!' and the question mark '?' to the list of word terminators and to the sentence terminators (remember to modify the initial comment block too);

(c) replace all of the CARDINAL variables with INTEGER variables.

# Chapter 6
# User-defined Data Types

6.1 Introduction
6.2 Enumeration types
6.3 Sub-range types
6.4 Set types

6.5 Transferring details of user-defined types via EXPORT and IMPORT
Exercises

## 6.1 Introduction

Modula-2 provides programmers with the facilities to define a data type and to declare variables of that type in expressions and statements. The compiler will check for consistent use of such a type, using the same type-checking rules that it applies to statements specifying operations on the standard types defined in the language. The main restriction upon the use of a user-defined type is that only a limited number of operations can be performed upon the elements of the type.

User-defined types can be used for various purposes, but a major use is to assist in demonstrating how a program is related to the problem that it is intended to solve. Being able to declare new types can sometimes help with this, because the 'objects' of such a type can be identified as representing corresponding 'objects' in the problem.

The types that users can define fall into a number of distinct categories: enumeration, sub-range, set, procedure, pointer, array and record. Only the first three forms will be described in this chapter, the other forms will be described in later chapters. Type definitions are placed at the beginning of a module or procedure, and are preceded by the reserved word TYPE.

## 6.2 Enumeration types

An enumeration type is essentially unstructured (that is, it is a **scalar** type), and it is defined by naming (enumerating) the sequence of constant elements that form it. An enumerated type is declared using the form

⟨typename⟩ = ( ⟨elementlist⟩ );

(Note that this declaration uses the '=' character in the same way as the constant declarations. This is because both 'type' and 'constant' declarations provide information that is required at compilation time, unlike the assignment statement, which specifies an operation that is to take place during program execution.) Some examples of the declaration and definition of enumerated types are:

```
TYPE
    Days = (Monday,Tuesday,Wednesday,Thursday,Friday,Saturday,
            Sunday);
    Languages = (FORTRAN,Pascal,BASIC,PROLOG,LISP,Modula2,
                Ada,CORAL,ALGOL,COBOL);
    Suits = (Spades,Hearts,Diamonds,Clubs);
```

Once a type has been defined in this way, the compiler will recognize any declarations for variables of the type as being valid. So using the three types declared above, some associated variable declarations might look like:

```
VAR
    today, payDay : Days;
    source : Languages;
    cut, trumps : Suits;
```

and so on. It is not always necessary to declare an enumerated type in this way, though. The following declaration is also a valid form, if more restricted in its potential application:

```
VAR
    primaryColour : (Red,Blue,Yellow);
```

Using this form of declaration limits the ability to declare further variables of the type elsewhere in a module, since the further declaration

```
VAR
    newColour : (Red,Blue,Yellow);
```

would not be compatible with the declaration of primaryColour, since the compiler would not be able to recognize that the elements making up the type were logically the same for the two declarations.

The only operations that can be performed upon a variable of an enumerated type are those of assignment, comparison, and passing as parameters of procedures. Examples of assignment are

```
today := Monday;
source := Pascal;
trumps := cut;
```

The value assigned must of course correspond to one of the constants of the enumerated type. Any other operations required must be provided through the use of user-defined procedures, and this is where the structure of the MODULE can prove convenient, in that such a 'library' of procedures can be provided as a MODULE.

The constant elements that appear in the definition are identified internally by their position in the list (their ordinal value), with the first element having an ordinal value of 0. In the above examples:

Sunday will have the highest ordinal value of type Days (6)
Monday will have the lowest ordinal value of type Days (0)
Diamonds will have an ordinal value of 2

Because the elements of an enumerated type are ordered, we can use the relational operators with them, as in the statements:

IF today < Saturday THEN ...

and

IF cut = Diamonds THEN ...

The built-in function ORD, as used with variables of type CHAR, can be used to return the ordinal value of any element of an enumerated type. In addition, given a particular element, we can obtain the ordinal value of its predecessor in the definition list using the built-in procedure DEC, and of its successor by the built-in procedure INC. These two functions will be described more fully in Chapter 9.

It might seem that the lack of operations that can be applied directly to variables of such a type will limit its use to little more than occasionally providing stronger type checking. In practice this is not so, and the examples of the next sections and chapters should make the usefulness of enumerated types rather clearer.

## 6.3 Sub-range types

A sub-range type is defined as a new type which is formed by taking a contiguous group of elements from the range of values for another type, termed the 'base type'. The base type might be a standard type, such as CHAR, INTEGER or CARDINAL, or it might be user-defined, either enumerated or, of course, another sub-range type. The most significant restriction upon the definition of such a type is that it must consist of a group of *contiguous* elements within the original type.

In defining a sub-range type, the declaration statement must specify the range of values from the base type. To do this, the limit values are enclosed in square brackets, and the '..' symbol can be used to indicate 'elements between'. Some examples of sub-range declarations are:

```
TYPE
   Lowercase = ['a'..'z'];
   Weekdays = [Monday..Friday];
   Dicevalues = [1..6];
```

In these examples, the base types are respectively CHAR, the user-defined type Days encountered in Section 6.2, and the type CARDINAL.

The base type does not need to be specified in the declaration, and is normally evident from the values cited. For integer sub-ranges, the base type will be determined by the actual values specified in the range. If the lower limit is negative, then the base type will be taken as INTEGER, otherwise it will be assumed to be of type CARDINAL. Hence the statement that Dicevalues will be a sub-range of CARDINAL.

Note that, because the sub-range is required to consist of contiguous elements of the base type, declarations such as:

```
TYPE
   Odddays = [Monday,Wednesday,Friday];
   Realids = ['A'..'H','O'..'Z'];
```

are not permitted.

There are some other limitations on the use of this form. A particular case to note is that of the type REAL. We cannot define sub-ranges of this type, as it is not represented consistently on different machines.

A sub-range type is compatible with the original base type, and so the two may be combined in expressions, so long as any values that are assigned to the variables of the sub-range type remain within the specified range. As an example of this, using the earlier definition of the type Days, together with that used for Weekdays above, and the following variable declarations:

```
VAR
   today : Days;
   workingDay : Weekdays;
```

then the assignment statement

```
   workingDay := today;
```

will be valid as long as the variable today does not contain a value of Saturday or Sunday. (Obviously this cannot be checked by the compiler, and so must be checked by the run-time support software.)

Sub-range types provide a means by which run-time and compile-time checking on the values taken by variables can be tightened, in exchange for slightly larger overheads of run-time checking. Where the possible values of particular variables are constrained in some way by the nature of a problem, then such checking can provide a useful verification feature, and in general the use of sub-ranges is a practice to be encouraged.

The operators that can be used with the elements of a sub-range type are the same as those that are available for use with the elements of the base type.

## 6.4 Set types

Modula-2 provides quite strong support for the use of set types. When used in appropriate situations, such types can indeed provide for elegant and well structured programs, although the limitations imposed upon set size by implementational constraints are apt to restrict the usefulness of sets, especially for portable programs. (Unfortunately, because Modula-2 supports sets in a different way from Pascal, the rather convenient Pascal form for creating small sets, as in:

**if** *ch* **in** ['y','Y'] **then**

is not available in Modula-2.)

A set type is defined in the same manner as other user-defined types: by declaring the members of the set, together with the reserved words SET OF. The general form of declaration is

```
TYPE
   setidentifier = SET OF ⟨basetype⟩;
```

For example, we can use the elements of type Suits defined earlier to form the elements of the set type Cards, using the declaration

```
TYPE
   Cards = SET OF Suits;
```

Where the set members can be directly expressed as a sub-range of the base type, the element list is enclosed in square brackets. As an example, by using the elements of the type Days which was defined earlier, we can define a set type Workdays as

```
TYPE
   Workdays = SET OF [Monday..Friday];
```

The main restriction that applies to this process is that the base type must be either an enumerated type or a sub-range type. There is also a restriction upon the maximum number of elements in the set, which usually cannot be greater than the number of bits in the computer's word. As a further extension of this, those elements of the base type used to make up the set must not possess ordinal values of the base type that are greater than $N-1$, where $N$ is often defined as being the number of bits in the computer's word. So the following declaration will be invalid:

```
TYPE
    Wholenumbers = SET OF CARDINAL;
```

because the base type is too large, whilst in the declarations

```
TYPE
    Lowercase = SET OF ['a'..'z'];
    Integervars = SET OF ['I'..'N'];
```

the ordinal values of the elements will probably be too large for most values of $N$, assuming that we are using the ASCII character set.

One way in which to overcome the restriction upon the size of a base type is to use a sub-range of values where appropriate. This can be done by first enumerating a suitable sub-range, as in the declarations

```
TYPE
    Values = [1..6];
    Dicefaces = SET OF Values;
```

or more directly, as

```
Dicefaces = SET OF [1..6];
```

(The base type will be determined using the same rules as for sub-range types.) The four set operations that can be applied to BITSET, and the membership operator IN, can also be applied to operands of compatible user-defined set types.

Set variables are declared in the usual manner – for example:

```
VAR
    workingWeek : Workdays;
    redDice,blueDice : Dicefaces;
```

Set constants are described by enclosing the list of elements in braces, in the same way as for BITSET, with the addition that a set constant of a user-defined type must also include the set type identifier before the braces. This allows the compiler to perform type checking on both the set constant and the set elements. Using the set types declared earlier, some examples of the use of set constants are:

```
workingWeek := Workdays{Monday,Thursday,Friday};
redDice := Dicefaces{6};
workingWeek := Workdays{};
```

(In the last example, the constant is the null set.)

Not surprisingly, Modula-2 requires that a set constant must be specified using only constant values for the elements of the set – that is, the elements cannot be variables of the base type. So we cannot have a variable today of type Days, and use this when defining a constant of type Workdays, as in

```
daysOff := Workdays{Monday,today};
```

since we would then have a set constant that was not actually constant!

In order to use variables of the base type to construct the value of a set variable, we need to make use of two special procedures within Modula-2, which allow for an element to be added to or removed from a set variable. The element itself may be specified using either a constant or a variable of the base type, and so these procedures provide the means of getting around this particular problem. The two procedures are INCL(s,x), which includes element x in the set variable s, and EXCL(s,x), which removes element x from the set variable s.

As an example of this mechanism, if the set variable staffHoliday has been assigned a value, as in:

```
staffHoliday := Workdays{Monday,Tuesday};
```

then the operation of the procedure call

```
INCL(staffHoliday,Wednesday);
```

will change the value of staffHoliday to

```
Workdays{Monday..Wednesday};
```

and then the further operation

```
EXCL(staffHoliday,Tuesday);
```

will change the value of the variable staffHoliday to

```
Workdays{Monday,Wednesday};
```

and so on.

80   USER-DEFINED DATA TYPES

Because the set element used as the parameter of INCL and EXCL can be a variable of type Days (the base type of the set), this form also allows us to use a variable such as today, which is of type Days, and then the procedure call

   INCL(staffHoliday,today);

will include an element corresponding to the value of today in the set variable staffHoliday. This overcomes the problem of having two levels of constant and variable declaration and assignment, which is the basic issue that leads to this problem in handling set types.

As a last point about set types: if the element specified in a call to INCL is already present in the set variable, nothing will be changed, as each element can only be present in or absent from a set – there is no sense in which it can be present twice! Similarly with EXCL, if the element being removed is not present in the set variable, no changes will occur. Such null operations are not necessarily errors, of course.

## 6.5 Transferring details of user-defined types via EXPORT and IMPORT

Having looked at the general subject of user-defined types in this chapter, it is appropriate to mention briefly how the information about these can be shared between separately compiled modules.

When we considered the IMPORT and EXPORT directives in Chapter 3, it was emphasized that the list of elements associated with each of these could include the identifiers used in both type definitions and variable declarations, as well as the procedure headings. One reason for needing to be able to exchange definitions of types is that it may be necessary to make use of user-defined types as parameters of certain procedures, or to access them in some other way in different parts of a program. For example, in one module we might have a definition of the type Days in the following form:

   TYPE
      Days = (Monday,Tuesday,Wednesday,Thursday,Friday,Saturday,Sunday);

If another module needs to IMPORT some procedures which have parameters of type Days from this first module, and if it does not also IMPORT the type Days, then of course the compiler will not permit any variables of type Days to be declared for use as parameters for the procedure calls either. (An important observation is that IMPORTing the type Days has the effect of IMPORTing all of the constants Monday..Sunday without the need to list these explicitly.)

If the type Days is redefined (in identical form) in the second module, this will not be accepted either, as the compiler is concerned only with physical equivalence in terms of the source, rather than logical equivalence in terms of identifier or role. So if the MODULE is to EXPORT procedures with parameters of the type Days, then it will need to EXPORT the type Days as well. Similarly, the modules which make use of these procedures will need to IMPORT the type Days, rather than redeclare it.

As a slightly more subtle variant, where programmers writing the second module want to use only a sub-range of the enumerated type, they might define a new type

Days = (Monday,Tuesday,Wednesday,Thursday,Friday);

and attempt to use this with the procedures imported from the first module. Again, this will be rejected by the compiler for the same reasons as before.

One solution to the latter problem is to IMPORT the type Days from the first module, and then define a sub-range type such as

Mydays = [Monday..Friday];

which might then be used with the procedures that have parameters of type Days. (Unfortunately this will not always be possible, as *variable* parameters of a procedure need to be of identical type, and so variables such as a sub-range type can be used only as *value* parameters of procedures.) The only other limitation on using such a form is that the sub-range must contain contiguous values from the first type. For enumerated types this should be no problem, since of course the ordering of the elements of the base type is under the programmer's control.

Having now considered the simple types of Modula-2 in some detail, we go on in the next two chapters to use variables of these types with the control statements of the language.

## EXERCISES

**6.1** For the example definitions given for the types Days, Languages and Suits in Section 6.2, what are the ordinal values of:

Wednesday    Saturday    Modula2    COBOL    Hearts

82    USER-DEFINED DATA TYPES

**6.2** One reason for using enumerated types is to make 'visible' the representation of certain 'objects' that are modelled in a program, and that are used to represent some external situation or status. Try to think of situations where you could have made use of such a type in a program that you have written recently. If you had done this would the program have been any easier to understand?

**6.3** Enter and run the following simple program module, and observe what happens.

```
MODULE BoundTest;
TYPE
  Days = (Monday,Tuesday,Wednesday,Thursday,Friday,
          Saturday,Sunday);
  Weekdays = [Monday..Friday];
VAR
  Holiday : Weekdays;
  today : Days;
BEGIN
  today := Saturday;
  Holiday := Saturday;    (* should create a compiler error *)
  Holiday := today;       (* should cause a run-time error *)
END BoundTest.
```

(To compile this program you may need to comment out the second statement, but see what happens first!)

**6.4** What sub-ranges of standard base types might be useful for representing:

(a)   the days in a month;

(b)   numeral characters;

(c)   the range of temperatures outside your home throughout the year (in degrees Celsius)?

**6.5** Think of reasons for EXPORTing the following from a MODULE:

(a)   an enumeration type;

(b)   a sub-range type;

and provide an example for each case.

# Chapter 7
# Control Structures in Modula-2: Selection

7.1  Structuring control flow
7.2  Two-way selection: the IF statement
7.3  The CASE statement
Exercises

## 7.1 Structuring control flow

In a structured programming language such as Modula-2, a programmer is provided with three basic forms of structure that can be used to specify the algorithm of a program. Each of these forms describes a particular form of control flow, and so determines how the computer will select the next statement to be executed. These three forms are **sequence**, **selection** and **iteration**.

A *sequence* of statements consists of an ordered list of statements, positioned in the order in which they will be executed by the computer. So each statement is executed after the computer has completed the operations of the previous statement. In Modula-2, this is described as a **statement sequence**.

While much of the code in our programs may take this form, at least over short samples, in order to implement any practical algorithm we will need to make use of the other two forms as well. The concept of a statement sequence is fairly straightforward, and has already been covered in previous chapters. This chapter is concerned with describing the two forms of selection control that are provided in Modula-2; Chapter 8 will then cover the four forms of iteration control.

The process of *selection* requires the computer to determine which path of execution is to be used, selected from a number of optional statement sequences. This choice is in turn dependent upon some condition which is to be evaluated as a part of the selection operation. Two forms of selection are provided in Modula-2 and they will both be familiar to the Pascal programmer.

The first form, which is usually described as the IF statement, provides the means for a programmer to specify a choice between two possible paths of execution. This is the most fundamental form of choice that can be made and, indeed, we can then construct complex multiple choice forms by combining a sufficient number of such basic two-way decisions. The second form is the CASE statement, which provides a means of specifying a selection between any number of possible execution paths, with the choice being determined by the value of some 'selector'. (FORTRAN programmers should be familiar with the first form; in FORTRAN the nearest to the second form is probably the computed GOTO statement.)

Although the general forms of both these statements will be familiar to a Pascal programmer, it should be emphasized that the details of form and syntax for both statements have been extended from those used in Pascal.

## 7.2 Two-way selection: the IF statement

In its most basic form, an IF statement contains the specification of a BOOLEAN condition that must be evaluated by the computer, together with a statement sequence that is to be executed if the condition is met (that is, if the result is TRUE). We can describe this basic form by the following regular expression:

IF ⟨booleanexpression⟩ THEN ⟨statementsequence⟩ END

(As usual, the reserved words IF, THEN, END are in upper case.) At this point, the *statement sequence* that was introduced in Chapter 5 can be seen as forming an element of a larger construct and, of course, any one of the statements in such a sequence can in turn be a further IF statement. In many cases the BOOLEAN expression will be a conditional expression, but it can also be a BOOLEAN variable or function call, or any other operation that produces a single BOOLEAN value.

When an IF statement is used in Pascal, the reserved word THEN is followed by either a single or a compound statement (this is usually referred to as the THEN clause). If it is the latter form, then its component statements must be bracketed by BEGIN and END. This can be an irritating feature when a single statement used in such a construct later needs to be replaced by two or more statements, since the programmer must also remember to insert the necessary BEGINs and ENDs to create the compound form.

In Modula-2 this problem does not arise. The compiler *always* expects that the reserved word THEN will be followed by a statement sequence, which of course can be a single statement, and that this sequence will be terminated by the reserved word END. So when using the Modula-2 form, expanding the clause from a single statement to many statements does not require any other changes to the basic form of the clause.

### 7.2.1 Conditional expressions

A conditional expression yields a BOOLEAN result, and is normally formed using one of the relational operators. These operate on a pair of operands, which can be of any type appropriate to the relation but must of course be of the same type. The operation will then produce a result which is of type BOOLEAN. As a reminder, the relational operators are

|      |                          |
| ---- | ------------------------ |
| =    | equal to                 |
| #, <> | not equal to            |
| <    | less than                |
| >    | greater than             |
| <=   | less than or equal to    |
| >=   | greater than or equal to |

These relational operators may be used with any standard type, including BOOLEAN. For the set type BITSET the operators '<=' and '>=' are used to denote 'subset' and 'superset', but the operators '>' and '<' have no meaning.

Some examples of this simple form of IF statement are

```
IF x <> y THEN i := i + 6; total := total + x END;
```

and

```
IF (pitchLength > 20)
   THEN pitchWidth := pitchWidth +4
END;
```

In the first case, the contents of the variables x and y are compared and tested for equality, and the statement sequence consisting of two simple statements that make up the THEN clause will be executed only if x contains a value different from that of y. If x does have the same value as y, then the whole statement will be skipped. In the second example, the contents (value) of the variable pitchLength are compared with the constant value of 20, and the single statement making up the THEN clause will be executed

86  CONTROL STRUCTURES IN MODULA-2: SELECTION

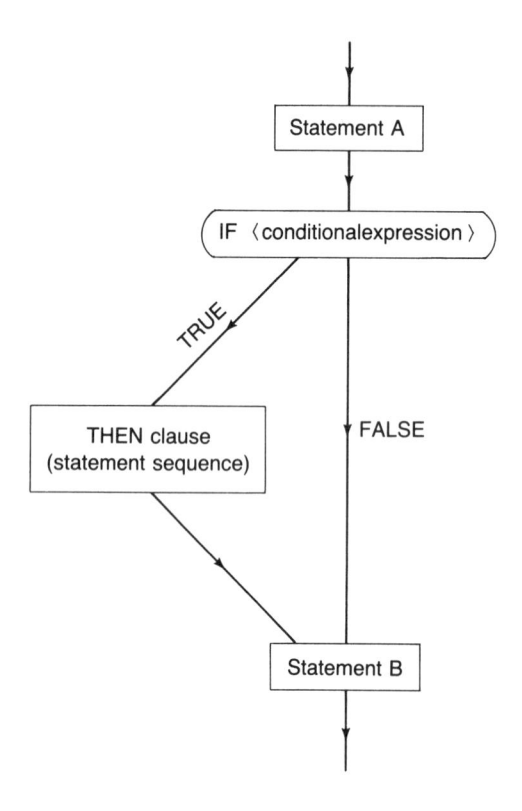

**Figure 7.1**  Flow of control for a simple IF statement.

only if the value of pitchLength is larger than 20. The parentheses in this case are unnecessary, but help to make the code more readable. Because these comparisons make use of the value of one or more variables, they must obviously be evaluated during program execution, rather than during compilation.

Figure 7.1 demonstrates the flow of control in graphical form, where statement A precedes the IF statement, and statement B follows it. If the condition within the IF is evaluated to be TRUE, then the execution path specified by the arc between A and B is traversed (that is, the group of statements concerned will be executed), otherwise it will be ignored and statement B will be executed directly after statement A.

The conditional expression used in an IF statement can also be compound in form, since the logical operators AND and OR can be used to combine a series of BOOLEAN values and provide the necessary BOOLEAN result. An example of such a compound condition is

```
IF (pitchLength > 20) AND (pitchWidth < 15 )
  THEN
    rate := 20.5
END;
```

For this particular conditional expression, it will be necessary for both of the individual relational expressions to be satisfied before the THEN clause can be executed. When the IF statement is executed, the first condition will be evaluated and, if this results in a value of TRUE, the second condition will be evaluated to determine which execution path is to be selected. (In Modula-2 the operation p AND q is defined as IF p THEN q ELSE FALSE, which also defines the order of evaluation. Similarly the operation p OR q, is defined as IF p THEN TRUE ELSE q.)

The BOOLEAN unary operator NOT can be used with conditional expressions, and an example of an IF statement which uses this might be:

```
IF NOT (pitchWidth = 20) THEN ...
```

which is an alternative to the form

```
IF (pitchWidth <> 20) THEN ...
```

and which may sometimes be clearer (and vice versa!).

When using several BOOLEAN operators in a compound condition, the individual expressions should be separated out by using parentheses, in order to make the intentions of the programmer clear. (As with most programming languages, we can add paired parentheses both for clarity, and more particularly to enforce the intended order of evaluation.) An expression such as

```
IF (i=10) AND ( (j=14) OR (k=20) ) THEN ...
```

needs to make use of parentheses in this way, because the AND operation is of a higher precedence than the OR perator. In this particular example, there are two conditions that can cause the THEN clause to be executed, namely:

(1)   i has a value of 10, and j has a value of 14;
(2)   i has a value of 10, and k has a value of 20.

If the parentheses were not placed around the second pair of relations, the THEN clause would be executed if either:

(1)   i has a value of 10, and j has a value of 14;

(2)   k has a value of 20.

The set membership operator IN is also counted as being a relational operator. This makes it possible to use set types within a conditional expression, as in such statements as:

IF 7 IN deviceStatus THEN ...

and

IF gameScore IN {4,5,15} THEN ...

In the first example, the variable deviceStatus must be of the type BITSET, or of some user-defined set type which has a CARDINAL base type, and the condition will be satisfied (the result will be TRUE) if the current elements of deviceStatus include the element 7. In the second example, the variable gameScore must be of a CARDINAL type, and preferably be of a subtype which has the same upper limit as BITSET.

This form of conditional expression may be especially useful when a programmer needs to make use of enumerated types in forming a conditional expression. The following example shows how this might be done, using the following definition of an enumerated type, Languages:

TYPE
   Languages = (FORTRAN,Pascal,BASIC,PROLOG,LISP,Modula2,
               Ada,CORAL,ALGOL,COBOL);

and using this as the base type, we can define an associated set type as

Vocabulary = SET OF Languages;

which defines the type Vocabulary as a set type whose members are the elements of the base type Languages.

To show how this can be used in a condition expression, at the head of a MODULE or procedure we can now use a declaration such as

VAR
   programSource : Languages;

and then, within the executable code of the module, it is possible to make use of such statements as:

IF programSource IN Vocabulary{BASIC,PROLOG,LISP} THEN
   Interpret(source) END;

or similarly:

```
IF programSource IN Vocabulary{Pascal,Modula2..ALGOL} THEN
    structured := TRUE;
    expectBlocks := TRUE
END;
```

(Remember that the set constants for a user-defined type require the set type to be stated before the braces. This can only be omitted when using the standard type BITSET.) What these provide is a quite elegant way of avoiding the equivalent sequences of BOOLEAN expressions, which would be:

```
IF (source = BASIC) OR (source=PROLOG) OR (source=LISP) THEN ...
```

and

```
IF (source = Pascal) OR (source=Modula2) OR (source=Ada) OR
   (source = CORAL) OR (source=ALGOL) THEN ...
```

Not only is the set notation much more concise but, on such occasions, it is eminently more readable too. (As a proviso, though, the second example uses the .. notation to indicate a range of values: for an enumerated type such as this one, where the ordering is not obvious, it might be better to state the list explicitly.)

This form of expression can be used with any set type, regardless of the base type of its elements. When used with BITSET it rather resembles the form available for use with sets of integers in Pascal. (A standard Pascal implementation may also have a restriction on the size of the range of permissible integer values within the elements of a set.)

Unfortunately, one convenient feature of Pascal that is not always included in Modula-2 implementations is the facility to use sets of type CHAR with the membership operator IN. A Pascal program may contain a statement such as

**if** *ch* **in** ['*a*','*i*'..'*n*'] **then** ...

but it is not always possible to express this condition so easily and neatly in Modula-2, depending on the extent to which the compiler restricts the size of sets. (This feature is probably the principal example of a significant feature of Pascal lost on the way to Modula-2!)

### 7.2.2 The ELSE clause

So far, discussion has been concentrated largely on the forms of conditional expression that can be used with an IF statement. The examples given have all assumed that the reserved word IF is followed only by a THEN clause,

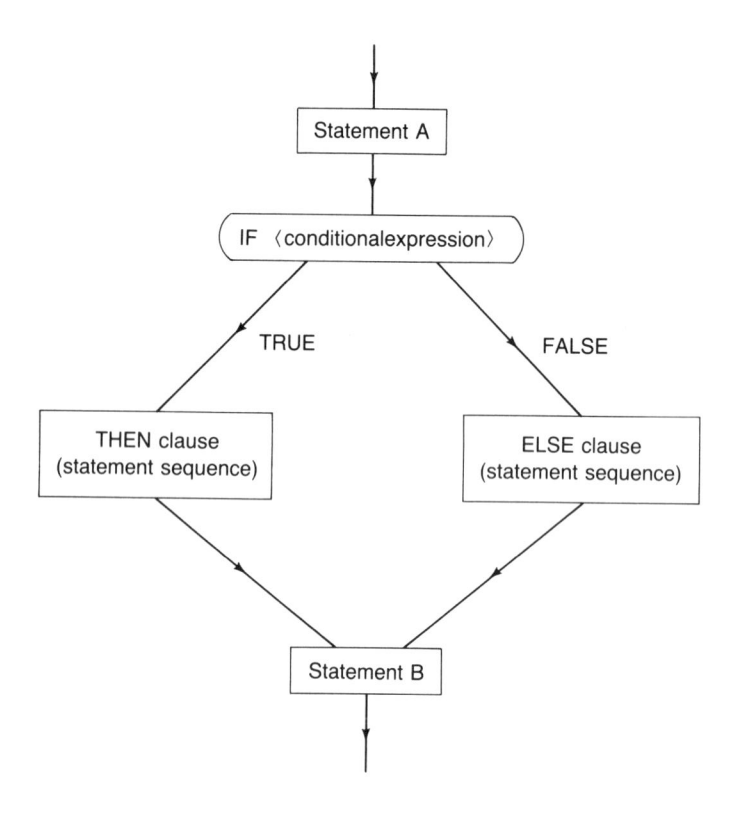

Figure 7.2 Flow of control for an IF statement with THEN and ELSE clauses.

which consists of a statement sequence to be executed if evaluation of the conditional expression gives a result of TRUE when the IF statement is executed.

Every IF statement *must* have a THEN clause, but the programmer can choose to specify an alternative path of control, consisting of a statement sequence that is to be executed if evaluation of the conditional expression gives a result of FALSE. This path is declared using the reserved word ELSE, and is usually termed the 'ELSE clause'. So the IF statement can now be described as having the form

```
IF ⟨conditionalexpression⟩ THEN ⟨statementsequence⟩
[ ELSE ⟨statementsequence⟩ ]
END
```

Note that the first statement sequence comprising the THEN clause will be terminated by the reserved word ELSE if the optional clause is present, and that the reserved word END is always used to terminate the complete structure of the IF statement. It is important to remember that statement sequences have no BEGIN or END, so that the only occurrence of the reserved word END is the one that is used to terminate the complete IF statement. Figure 7.2 shows the resulting flow of control in diagrammatic form.

The ELSE clause enables the programmer to specify a choice between two distinct execution paths, as in the following example:

```
IF (pitchLength > 20)
  THEN
    pitchWidth := pitchWidth + 4
  ELSE
    pitchWidth := pitchWidth + 2;
    goalHeight := goalHeight - 1
END
```

If the condition is satisfied when this statement is executed (that is, the value of pitchLength is greater than 20), then the single statement in the statement sequence between the reserved words THEN and ELSE (the THEN clause) will be executed. If the condition is not satisfied, then the statement sequence between the reserved words ELSE and END (the ELSE clause) will be executed instead.

Although the use of an ELSE clause is optional, we frequently refer to the IF statement as having an IF...THEN...ELSE form.

### 7.2.3   ELSIF **clauses**

While an IF statement must have only one THEN clause, and may (optionally) have one ELSE clause, it may also have any number of ELSIF clauses. The ELSIF clause can be regarded as a form of ELSE clause that contains a further subcondition, and which has the form

```
ELSIF <subconditionalexpression> THEN <statementsequence>
```

The conditional expression that follows the ELSIF will be evaluated only if the evaluation of the conditional expression of the original IF statement returned a value of FALSE (so that the THEN clause was not selected), and also only if the conditional expressions of any preceding ELSIF clauses have also returned values of FALSE. This is because there can be only one path of execution through an IF statement, and if a preceding clause is selected as a result of evaluating a conditional expression, then any following conditions will not be evaluated. Figure 7.3 shows the structure that results from this.

An ELSIF clause will be terminated by one of the reserved words ELSIF, ELSE or END. (Of course, any ELSIFs used must precede the ELSE clause – if this is present – if they are to be evaluated at all.)

So the complete form for an IF statement now looks like:

```
IF ⟨conditionalexpression⟩ THEN ⟨statementsequence⟩
{ ELSIF ⟨subconditionalexpression⟩ THEN ⟨statementsequence⟩ }
[ ELSE ⟨statementsequence⟩ ]
END
```

## 92 CONTROL STRUCTURES IN MODULA-2: SELECTION

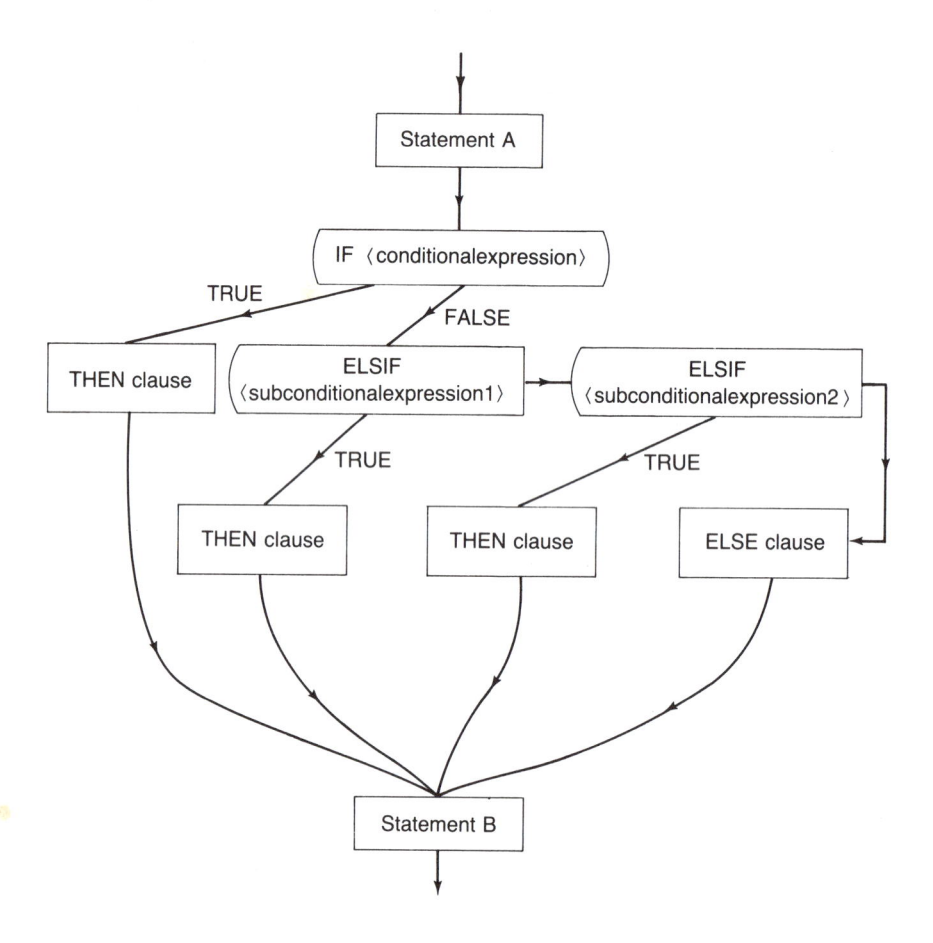

**Figure 7.3** Flow of control for an IF statement with two ELSIF clauses and an ELSE clause.

Note particularly that an ELSIF clause has no ELSE part within it. It is an extension of the original IF statement, inasmuch as it involves a subcondition, and it is relevant only when the main condition is FALSE and the subcondition is TRUE. As such the ELSIF is *not* a synonym for the two reserved words ELSE IF, which are used where the statement sequence within the ELSE clause contains another IF statement. While the structures produced by the two forms will be *logically* equivalent, the syntax will differ slightly.

So it is possible to express the structure of Figure 7.3 using just the IF...THEN...ELSE form (Figure 7.4 shows this), but using this form results in the use of multiple ENDs, and so emerges as rather less readable. To see the difference between them, we should consider the following example of a

TWO-WAY SELECTION: THE IF STATEMENT    93

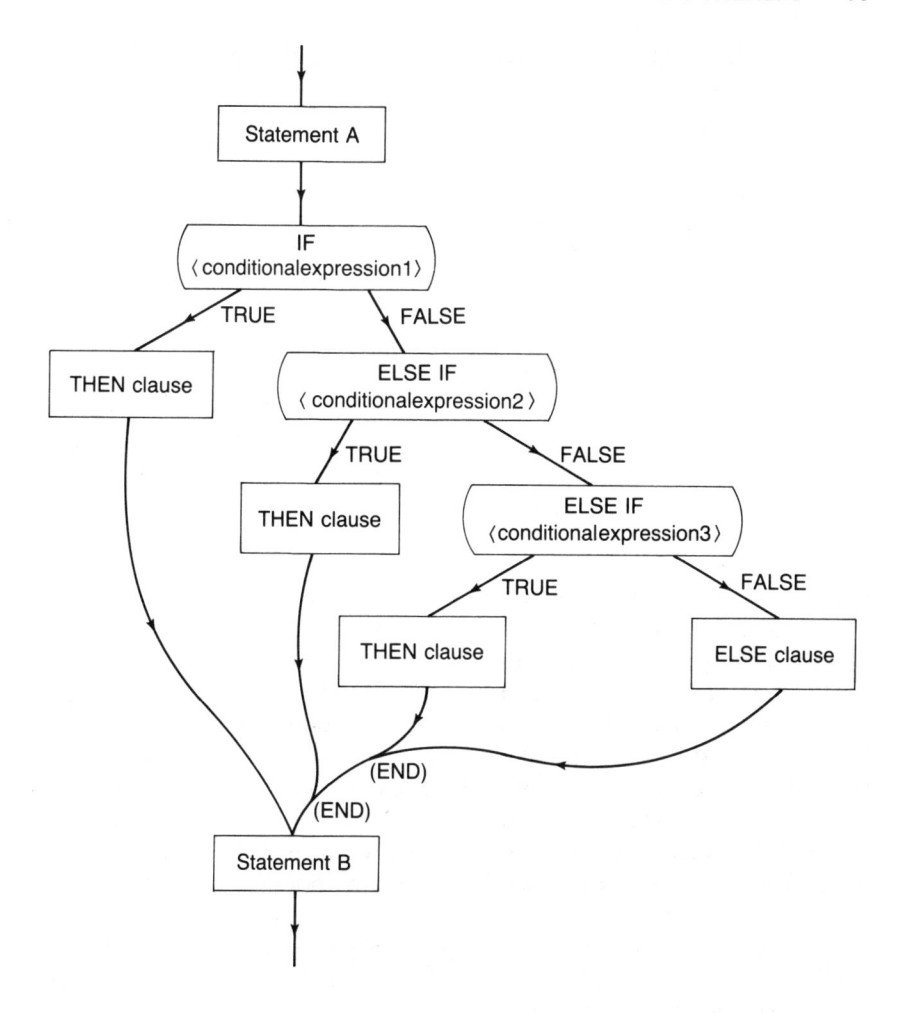

**Figure 7.4**  Flow of control using multiple IF...THEN...ELSE constructs.

complete IF statement, which has been constructed using ELSIF clauses:

```
IF ( ch >= 'a' ) AND ( ch <= 'z' )
   THEN ...
   ELSIF ( ch >= '0' ) AND ( ch <= '9' )
     THEN ...
   ELSIF ( ch = ' ' )
     THEN Skipnext
   ELSIF ( ch = FormFeed )
     THEN Skipnext ; Newpage
   ELSE ...
END
```

The equivalent expression constructed using only the basic IF...THEN...ELSE form is as follows:

```
IF ( ch >= 'a' ) AND ( ch <= 'z' )
  THEN ...
  ELSE IF ( ch >= '0' ) AND ( ch <= '9' )
    THEN ...
    ELSE IF (ch = ' ')
      THEN Skipnext
      ELSE IF (ch = FormFeed)
        THEN Skipnext ; Newpage
        ELSE ...
      END
    END
  END
END
```

(Each IF statement used will require a corresponding END.)

Since the ELSIF and ELSE clauses are optional, they can be included or omitted as required. The only constraint upon their use is in the ordering of the clauses: the THEN clause must precede all others, and any ELSIF clauses need to precede an ELSE clause. It is generally good practice to include an ELSE clause, and this is especially so when using a number of ELSIF clauses, since the ELSE clause can function as a 'catch-all' sequence to allow the program to deal with any conditions that have not been previously specified in the sequence of subconditions. The need for such a role may occur when there is a need to include error-handling operations, since the ELSE can be used to 'catch' any invalid conditions.

The ELSIF clause is useful, but its use should not be pursued to exhaustion! The CASE statement, described in the next section, offers an alternative, and sometimes rather clearer, form that can be used for handling those situations needing multiple branches in the flow of control based upon a single selector. It may be rather more readable, since it expresses the multiple branching form directly, rather than by using a sequence of binary divisions.

However, the use of the ELSIF clause *is* necessary where the subconditions involved are quite different from the original condition of the IF statement. A structure such as:

```
IF today <> Saturday AND today <> Sunday
  THEN ...
  ELSIF programSource IN Vocabulary{Prolog}
    THEN ...
  ELSIF userIdentifier < 700
    THEN ...
```

can hardly be expressed in any other way, and certainly not through a CASE statement. (Whether we would want to create such a structure in the first place is another matter, but there are definitely situations where such structures are almost unavoidable.)

## 7.3 The CASE statement

An IF statement is particularly suitable for use in the situation where an algorithm requires a binary choice to be made between two sets of actions, and where the choice can be expressed as some form of conditional expression. (Of course, one of the choices could be 'do nothing' – which is represented by the use of a THEN clause alone.) While the IF statement can be extended further through the use of ELSIF clauses, the form is still essentially a binary one, in that each sub-choice is made between two possible options, and so a choice between multiple options requires the programmer to describe a hierarchy of choices.

Such forms of choice occur very widely in programming problems, perhaps partly because we try to structure some of our solutions in that form. But there are also algorithms that require the selection of a single course of action from more than two possible routes, in a non-hierarchical manner. In such situations the CASE statement provides a selection mechanism that does not need to use subconditions. (For example, where a program needs to handle a 'menu', through which the user is presented with a choice of actions.) Of course, as in the case of the IF statement, only one path of action will be selected on any particular invocation.

The CASE statement has the general form

```
CASE ⟨expression⟩ OF
{ ⟨label⟩ : ⟨statementsequence⟩ | }
  ⟨label⟩ : ⟨statementsequence⟩
  [ ELSE ⟨statementsequence⟩ ]
END
```

The initial expression used in a CASE statement acts as the 'path selector', and it can have a value from any of the scalar types except REAL. (This is excluded because the form of representation used for floating-point arithmetic in a computer renders exact comparison difficult.)

The **labels** that are used in the CASE statement must be constants of the same type as that of the selector, and their values represent the set of selector values that are to be associated with each statement sequence. A label can represent a single value of the selector or a group of values, but it must consist of one or more constants, and it cannot be modified during the execution of the program. No constant value can appear more than once within the list of labels. Each label is separated from its associated statement sequence by a colon.

The CASE statement as used in Modula-2 differs significantly in two ways from that used in Pascal. The first of these is the form of **separator** that is used to distinguish between the statement sequences representing the different paths, while the second is the inclusion of an optional ELSE clause.

A separator between the paths is necessitated by the use of statement sequences in Modula-2. In Pascal, each option in a CASE statement is either a simple statement or a compound statement, and in the latter case it is terminated by an END. In either case, the extent of the optional path is well defined. In Modula-2, which uses statement sequences, we need to indicate where a statement sequence terminates and the next label begins. The vertical bar character '|' rather than a reserved word is used for this purpose. It acts as a separator of statement sequences in the same way that the semi-colon acts as a separator of statements. Of course, the last statement sequence must be terminated by the reserved word END and, where an ELSE clause is used, the reserved word ELSE will similarly act as a separator.

The following example shows the use of a CASE statement where the selector expression is a variable of type CHAR:

```
CASE ch OF
  'a'..'z' : Readstring; symbol := charString |
  FormFeed,Space : Readoperand(newOperand);
     symbol := operand |
  '.' : symbol := endstate
END
```

The label 'a'..'z' is an example of a range, and specifies the course of action to be followed if the character variable ch contains any values within this range (any lower case letter). The labels FormFeed and Space are character constants – in this case the values of the space and form feed (newpage) characters.

Note particularly that the last statement of the statement sequence following a label does not require a following semi-colon before the vertical bar (since the semi-colon is a statement *separator*), but if one is used, then the compiler will simply assume that a null statement is present (this was described in Chapter 4). Similarly the last option, labelled by EOL, needs no vertical bar at the end of the associated statement sequence, as it is terminated by the reserved word END.

A CASE statement may also possess an ELSE clause, which can be used to provide a 'catch-all' label through which the programmer can specify a course of action to be followed if the selector value matches none of the label values of the statement. The ELSE clause can thus be used in 'defensive programming' techniques, to cover those situations in which, if the program behaves as intended, it should never be executed. This option must be positioned at the end of the CASE statement, and *after* all the valid labels.

To show the use of this option, the last example can be extended to:

```
CASE ch OF
    'a'..'z' : Readstring ; symbol := charString |
    FormFeed,Space : Readoperand(newOperand);
        symbol := operand |
    '.' : symbol := endstate
    ELSE symbol := unknown; error := TRUE;
        INC(errorCount)
END
```

As this example expects that the selector variable ch should always contain a legal value when the correct form of input is used, the ELSE statement is used to detect an error in the form of the input. (Note that the vertical bar and the reserved words ELSE and END are all valid separators for the component statement sequences.)

The next example of the CASE statement uses a CARDINAL selector expression rather than a single selector variable:

```
CASE systemStatus DIV 512 OF
    1 : Teststatus |
    0 : Initializetransfer |
    2..5,8..14 : |
    6 : Setinterrupt ; interruptFlag := TRUE |
    7 : deviceReady := TRUE; Servicebuffer(bufferAddress)
    ELSE Returnerror
END
```

This example is loosely based on the functions performed by the individually numbered bits of a register used to control an external device, as with a PDP-11 computer. Note that the label values need not be ordered, in that the value 1 can precede 0 (although from the viewpoint of readability, this practice is rather questionable). Note too that the values used for the third label are not all contiguous, with non-contiguous values being separated by commas: 2..5,8..15. This particular label has a null statement sequence associated with it, to make the distinction between a value of position that is valid but nonetheless requires no action to be taken, and an invalid value that is outside the range 0..15, and which will be handled by the ELSE clause.

Our third and final example of the CASE statement shows its use with one of the enumerated types that was introduced in an earlier example:

```
CASE programSource OF
   Prolog : form := logic ; action := Interpret |
   Lisp : form := functional ; action := Interpret |
   BASIC : form := imperative ; action := Interpret |
   FORTRAN : form := imperative ; action := Translate |
   Pascal,Modula2..Algol : form := blockImperative ;
                           action := Translate
   ELSE form := unknown ; WriteString('unknown source');
      WriteLn
END
```

The CASE statement is a useful general purpose form that is suitable for use when there is a multiple choice of execution paths that lack any implicit hierarchy. The provision of the ELSE clause makes it possible to include additional defences against run-time errors, and programmers should seek to make use of this wherever possible.

## EXERCISES

**7.1** (a) Re-construct the program listed in Figure 5.1 using ELSIF clauses. Does this make the structure of the program any clearer than the previous form?

(b) Why is there little scope to use a CASE statement within the body of this program?

**7.2** Given the following type definitions:

```
TYPE
   Months = (Jan,Feb,Mar,Apr,May,June,July,Aug,Sept,Oct,
             Nov,Dec);
   Days = [1..31];
```

and the variables

```
VAR
   thisMonth : Months;
   yesterday, today : Days;
```

(a) write a set of nested CASE statements that will calculate the value of today from the current value of yesterday;

(b) explain how the form of the solution might be improved (neatened) through the definition of further sub-range types or set types.

**7.3** While British telephone numbers are somewhat variable in length and format, telephone numbers in the USA all have the form

> *xxx yyy zzzz*

where

> *xxx* is a three-digit area code
> *yyy* is a three-digit code for an exchange in an area
> *zzzz* is a four-digit code for a number on a given exchange.

Sketch out the form of nested CASE structure that could be used to determine the origin of a given phone number. What types would you use for this?

# Chapter 8
# Control Structures in Modula-2: Iteration

8.1 The role of the iteration forms
8.2 Counting and the FOR statement
8.3 Conditional loops: the WHILE statement
8.4 Conditional loops: the REPEAT UNTIL statement
8.5 The LOOP statement
Exercises

## 8.1 The role of the iteration forms

The previous chapter described the two forms of selection control that can be used to specify a choice between different execution paths within a program. This chapter concentrates upon the other major class of structured flow control: iteration. It describes the forms that are provided in Modula-2 for organizing the repetition of actions within a program, often referred to as **looping**. In Modula-2 iterations involve the repeated execution of a statement sequence, and this is usually termed the **loop body**.

There are two principal ways of organizing the control of iteration, although one of them has a number of variants. The first is concerned with the situation in which the number of iterations required is known at the start of the iterations, making it possible to count them using a built-in counter mechanism. In the second, the entry to each iteration cycle is conditional upon the evaluation of an expression, so that the number of iterations needed cannot be determined when the iterations start. Strictly speaking, the first form can always be replaced by the second, simply by selecting some particular value of the counter as the termination condition. However, a separate control structure is provided for the counting form, not least because it helps to improve the clarity and readability of a program to have the form of condition involved made explicit.

The second and more general form can be organized in a number of ways, and the Modula-2 language provides three different control structures of this type. Again, it is possible to contort almost any algorithm so that it could be expressed using just one of these: but an appropriate choice of form makes a programmer's intentions much clearer to anyone who needs to read the program code.

The material of this chapter is as central as that of the previous one to using Modula-2 well, since iteration is a powerful facility that is essential to solving many of the problems that can be tackled well with a computer. Programmers often make extensive use of iteration for handling some of the more common forms of compound data structures, such as arrays and linked lists. Indeed, one of the particular strengths of the digital computer is its capacity for performing work of a repetitive nature.

This chapter begins by describing the 'counting' form for controlling iteration, not least because similar constructs occur in so many other programming languages and so are likely to be familiar to almost all programmers.

## 8.2 Counting and the FOR statement

The FOR statement in Modula-2 is similar to that found in most ALGOL-like programming languages. Syntactically it differs more from the Pascal form than the other looping constructs that are common to both languages.

Since the FOR statement is concerned with counting the number of iterations, it needs to make use of some (suitably pre-declared) **control variable** to act as its counter, or **index**. INTEGER, CARDINAL (as well as subrange types derived from these) and CHAR are convenient types to use, but a variable from any enumerated type can also be used as the counter. A variable of type REAL cannot be used for this task, though, owing to the problems of precision that occur when handling fractional numbers, nor can we use a variable of a structured type. As a further restriction, the control variable cannot be one of the components of a structured type (such as an element of an array or record), even where the type of the component is itself valid.

The control variable must be declared within the MODULE in which it is used. Additionally, where a loop occurs within a procedure, it may not use one of the parameters of the procedure as the control variable.

While this last point may seem rather restrictive, in practice we are very unlikely to encounter situations in which it is necessary to do other than use a locally declared control variable. When using a FOR loop within a procedure, many experienced programmers will declare the control variable within the body of the procedure (this is a requirement in Pascal), and this is a good practice to adopt.

In order to perform its counting task, the FOR statement must specify an **initial value** to be assigned to the control variable, as well as a final value, or **limit**. Since loops can count downwards as well as upwards, the limit may be lower than the initial value, and may of course be negative. The program will exit from the loop when the value of the control variable becomes equal to the limit or passes it. Both the initial and the limit values can be specified using either expressions (so allowing the bounds to be selected during execution) or constants (including constant expressions). Of course, these must also be consistent with the type of the control variable.

So the structure of the FOR statement includes an assignment (to specify the initial value), and a limit value, which is prefixed by the reserved word TO. Its normal form is as follows:

```
FOR 〈controlvariable〉 := 〈initialvalueexpression〉 TO 〈finalvalueexpression〉
  DO 〈statementsequence〉 END
```

An example of this form is:

```
FOR footSize := 1 TO 18 DO shoeStock[footSize] := 0 END;
```

In this example, the variable footSize, which is used as the control variable, will probably be of the type CARDINAL or a sub-range of CARDINAL (although it could of course be INTEGER), and it is used to access each element of the array shoeStock in turn. (More about arrays later: for the moment we should just note that the FOR loop is particularly useful when handling arrays.) In this case the value of each element of the array is set to zero, as an example of the sort of initialization step that is frequently needed at the beginning of a module. Note that the statement sequence is bracketed by the reserved words DO and END, unlike Pascal, where the END would be omitted for a statement sequence that consisted of only a single statement.

In this example, the initial value and the limit value were expressed using numeric constants. In the next example, the limit value is specified by means of a variable (which must of course be initialized with a value prior to use). In the example an array of type CHAR, containing a line of characters typed in from a terminal, is being processed to remove any 'tab' characters and to replace them by single-space characters. The upper limit (that is, the number of characters read in) is held in the variable lineLength, and will have been determined when the line of characters was read into the buffer.

```
FOR position := 1 TO lineLength DO
  IF (character[position] = TAB ) THEN
    character[position] := SPACE
  END
END;
```

(In this case the statement sequence consists of a single statement, which is an IF statement.)

It is also possible to specify the size of the **increment** that is to be used during the iteration – that is, the amount by which the control variable is to be changed at the end of each pass through the body of the loop. If no value is specified for this, then the default is +1. The increment *must* be a constant expression of type INTEGER or CARDINAL, regardless of the type of the control variable. Note too that, since it can be of type INTEGER, it is permissible to use negative values for the increment, in order to count downwards. In such a case the initial value would, of course, normally be larger than the limit. When the size of the increment is specified, it is preceded by the reserved word BY. So the more general form of the FOR statement is

```
FOR ⟨controlvariable⟩ := ⟨initialvalueexpression⟩ TO ⟨finalvalueexpression⟩
  [ BY ⟨incrementvalue⟩ ]
  DO ⟨statementsequence⟩ END
```

A very simple example of using an increment within a FOR loop is

```
total := 0;
FOR i := 1 TO 1000 BY 2 DO
  total := total + i;
  WriteInt(i,4); WriteInt(total,8);
  WriteLn
END;
```

This time, while the control variable is again an integer type, we are also using BY, so that the loop is repeated only for the sequence of values 1,3,5,7,...,997,999. This also shows that when the BY form is used the control variable does not necessarily ever contain the actual value of the upper limit. On the last test for the end of the loop, adding the increment can, as in this case, raise the value of the control variable above the limit.

This last example simply works out the arithmetic sum of the odd numbers between 1 and $i$ (the current value of the counter) and prints out a table of these values for a range of values of $i$. While fairly trivial in itself, it forms a simple example of the sort of task that can usefully be performed using this type of looping structure.

Note that the control variable $i$ can be used both in the assignment statement

```
total := total + i;
```

and as a parameter of the procedure WriteInt, since in neither case will the actual *value* of $i$ be modified in any way. However, it is illegal to use any statement within the loop that modifies the control variable in any way, as in:

```
i := i + 4;
```

Such a statement should be rejected by the compiler.

Modula-2 does not specify the value that should be left in the control variable when the loop has terminated, so in the above example the value of *i* at the end of the loop might be 999, 1001 or anything else. This is a good example of a situation in which the programmer should take care to avoid building in any dependence upon the behaviour of a particular compiler. The control variable should never be re-used after the loop without first having a specific value assigned to it.

This leads on to another point, and one that should be familiar to a Pascal programmer, although possibly not to others. During the execution of a FOR loop, the current value of the control variable is compared with the value of the limit at the *beginning* of each iteration. So if, for example, the limit value were less than the initial value and a positive increment were specified, then the statement sequence making up the body of the loop would never be executed at all, since the loop would terminate on the first test. In some other languages of this style, and in early versions of FORTRAN, this is not necessarily the case, and the body of a loop of this form will be executed at least once, regardless of the initial values of the control variable and limit.

This behaviour is an important factor in the design of a program, since both the initial value and the limit can take the form of an expression whose value cannot be determined at compilation time. By organizing the execution of the loop in this way, the Modula-2 language ensures that a FOR loop will always execute in a consistent and sensible manner.

The next two examples show FOR loops that use control variables of other scalar types. The first uses the standard type CHAR for the control variable, while the second uses an enumerated type, Months.

The first example consists of a trivial exercise – to print out the lower case letters of the alphabet in order along a line:

```
FOR ch := 'a' TO 'z' DO Write(ch) END; WriteLn;
```

When using a control variable of an enumerated type, the value of the optional increment usually has no sensible meaning, and any attempts to use it may produce peculiar results. However, we *can* use a value of −1 for the increment in order to invert the sequence, so to print the alphabet in reverse order the FOR statement would be written as:

```
FOR ch := 'z' TO 'a' BY −1 DO Write(ch) END; WriteLn;
```

The second example involves both the enumerated type Months and a set type based upon it. These are defined as follows:

```
TYPE
  Months = (Jan,Feb,Mar,Apr,May,June,July,Aug,Sept,Oct,Nov,Dec);
  Term = SET OF Months;
```

For this example, we also need to declare the following variables:

```
VAR
  thisMonth : Months;
  autumn, winter, spring : Term;
  workMonths : CARDINAL;
```

The example consists of a section of code that first sets up an information base, describing each school term by its component calendar months, and then counts the number of months of the year when a school will be in use by using a FOR loop.

```
(* define the three terms *)
autumn := Term{Sept..Dec};
winter := Term{Feb..Apr};
spring := Term{May,June};
workMonths := 0; (* initialize the count *)
(* now the loop used to perform the count *)
FOR thisMonth := Jan TO Dec DO
  IF ( thisMonth IN autumn+winter+spring ) THEN
    workMonths := workMonths + 1
  END
END;
(* print out the result *)
WriteString("The school will be open during ");
WriteCard(workMonths,2);
WriteString(" months of the year"); WriteLn;
```

(It may be a useful exercise to try putting all this together into a small program module.) Note particularly the use of the set union operator '+'; this makes it possible to cope with terms that overlap a little. If the winter term ends in early April, and the spring term begins in late April, then modifying the third assignment statement to read

```
spring := Term{Apr..June};
```

will still produce the correct result.

The examples have shown a number of occasions that require a counting structure, and, although all have been rather contrived, their extensions can be very wide and varied. As far as possible the examples have made only minimal use of arrays, although it is in handling these that the FOR loop becomes particularly useful. When we come to examine the use of arrays in Chapter 10, there will be more opportunity to see how FOR loops may be used.

## 8.3 Conditional loops: the WHILE statement

This style of loop control is an example of a conditional form of looping structure. In a way it resembles a repetitive form of the IF statement. At the beginning of each pass through the loop a conditional expression is evaluated, and if this produces a result of TRUE then the statement sequence making up the loop body is executed (rather like the THEN clause of the IF statement). When the result is FALSE, the loop terminates and control is transferred to the statement following the loop. As a structure it is one that we are all familiar with in everyday life, as in the advice: 'While it is raining, keep your umbrella up.'

However, as we will see in the later discussion, this form of conditional loop may well require some initialization steps to be completed beforehand (in the above example this might be the act of raising the umbrella in the first place). This assumption of some possible initial condition may be an important factor in selecting this form within a part of a program.

The selection of an initial status or condition is not always necessary, of course, as the instruction 'While the coffee is not sweet enough, add more sugar,' illustrates. Returning to Modula-2, the general form of a WHILE loop is.

    WHILE ⟨conditionalexpression⟩ DO ⟨statementsequence⟩ END

Since the conditional expression is always evaluated *before* the code of the loop body is executed, it is always possible that this statement sequence might not be executed at all, since the first evaluation of the conditional expression might produce a value of FALSE. (In the last example, some of us drink coffee with no sugar at all!) For this reason, the WHILE loop is often useful in situations such as searching a data structure for a particular entry, since it is able to cope with the special case of an empty data structure. This point will become clearer when examining the use of linked list structures. In the example below, a WHILE loop is used to search along an array of characters containing a variable-length line of text, and to count the number of space characters that are present in the line.

```
spaceCount := 0;
characterIndex := 0;
WHILE characterBuffer[characterIndex] <> EOL DO
  IF ( characterBuffer[characterIndex] = '' )
    THEN INC(spaceCount)
  END;
  INC(characterIndex)
END;
```

When the WHILE loop terminates, the variable spaceCount will contain the number of space characters found. This segment of code will be able to cope quite adequately with an empty line, where the first character examined will be the end-of-line character: in this case the IF statement within the WHILE loop will never be executed.

This particular example also brings out a couple of other points about this form of loop.

Firstly, the programmer needs to specify explicitly any changes that are to be made to the value of any variable that may be used as a counter or for control (in this example, the variable characterIndex). This is unlike the case of the FOR loop, where such changes are made only as a part of the looping construct and would be illegal within the loop body.

Secondly, it is often necessary to set up initial values for some of the variables that are to be used within the conditional expression, before entering the loop (in this case, assigning a value of 0 to the variable characterIndex). This is to avoid an error when the conditional expression is first evaluated. Such initialization can sometimes be rather inelegant, as in the next segment of code, which can be used to read a line of characters into an array, taking them from a user's keyboard.

```
characterCount := 0;
Read(ch);
WHILE (ch <> EOL) DO
  textBuffer[characterCount] := ch;
  INC(characterCount);
  Read(ch)
END;
textBuffer[characterCount] := EOL;
```

In this example it is necessary to perform a preliminary call to the procedure Read before entering the loop, so that the character variable ch will be assigned a value before it is first used in the conditional expression. Ensuring that this occurs often requires some care when using the WHILE form, although, in exchange, it provides a powerful means for handling a variety of tasks in a clear and concise manner. The section of code just given is also an example of the type of loop that needs to be performed 'one and a half' times. In practice, the other forms of conditional loop are generally better suited to handling this type of requirement.

The final example shows the type of situation in which a WHILE loop may be very effective and yet very simple. It is used when scanning a line of text (characters) that has been read into an array. The objects of interest are the 'tokens' (strings of characters) and the routine is used to skip over any intervening space characters to find the start of the next token. Since there may be any number of space characters between the tokens on a line, a loop such as

```
WHILE textBuffer[characterIndex] = " DO
   INC(characterIndex)
END;
```

will perform this task quite elegantly. On exit from the loop, the variable characterIndex will contain the position of the first character of the next token, or of the end-of-line character. A WHILE loop can cope with such situations as that in which the first token on a line has no preceding spaces, or the last token on a line has no spaces following it.

## 8.4 Conditional loops: the REPEAT UNTIL statement

This is a further form of conditional loop control that will be instantly familiar to the Pascal programmer. It is very similar to the WHILE form in that it does not automatically perform any counting, leaving this to be organized by the programmer if required. It is particularly suitable for those situations in which there will be at least one iteration cycle, which is to be terminated by the occurrence of some event or by the detection of some condition being true. Again, this is a form of iteration that is quite 'natural', as it expresses such everyday operations as starting a car by obeying the instruction 'Repeat turning the key until the engine fires.' Since the engine won't fire until we have turned the key at least once, this describes the situation quite well even if the final condition might need some refinement! Unlike the FOR and WHILE statements, the condition used for termination of this type of loop is not evaluated until the end of the statement sequence that forms the body of the loop. So the statement sequence within the loop will always be executed at least once.

The form of the REPEAT UNTIL is

REPEAT ⟨statementsequence⟩ UNTIL ⟨conditionalexpression⟩

with the loop body being delimited by the two reserved words REPEAT and UNTIL. It is usually unnecessary for the programmer to initialize any variables used in the conditional expression in order to avoid a premature exit from the loop. Of course, where any counting is involved, the variables used as counters will need to be initialised before the loop is entered. So the REPEAT UNTIL form of loop is very useful when it is necessary to perform the operations of the statement sequence in the loop at least once. In the example below, it is used to check input values entered from a terminal to see if they are valid, before they are passed on to the next part of the program.

```
REPEAT
  WriteLn;
  WriteString("Enter size of unit to be used: ");
  ReadCard(value)
UNTIL ( (value >= minSize) AND (value <= maxSize) );
```

Note that as the reserved word UNTIL terminates the statement sequence that makes up the loop body, the last statement does not require a following semi-colon as a separator. (One reason why novice Pascal programmers often seem to prefer this statement to the WHILE form might well be that it avoids the issue of simple and compound statements by using its own reserved words to bracket the loop body.)

Using the WHILE form for a loop requires that the programmer has to perform more initialization than is usually necessary with the REPEAT UNTIL form, but the exit condition may require a little more thought in the case of the latter.

An important role for the REPEAT UNTIL form is to provide a 'conditional delay' through which the program can effectively 'idle' and wait for some event to occur. The following example demonstrates this in outline form:

```
Starttransfer(buffer,size);
REPEAT
UNTIL transferDone;
```

After calling the procedure Starttransfer, the program will 'idle' until the value of transferDone is TRUE. (Since this construct effectively has no loop body, it is perhaps a moot point as to whether the test occurs at the beginning or the end of the loop! However, the form is one that expresses the intentions of the programmer very effectively.) This type of operation is particularly important for programs that interact with external devices. When we come to examine the use of Modula-2 for low-level programming tasks in Part III, we shall encounter examples that show how REPEAT UNTIL can clearly express the need to delay action until some event occurs.

## 8.5 The LOOP statement

In solving problems through the use of iteration, it is not unusual to find that we require some way of specifying the need for '*n* and a bit' iterations. The three forms of iteration control that have been described so far are all very much concerned with performing *n* complete iterations. In each of them the terminating condition is evaluated at either the beginning (FOR, WHILE), or the end (REPEAT UNTIL) of each iteration. So the complete statement sequence making up the loop body will be executed on each iteration.

Obviously these forms can easily be manipulated to provide '*n* and a bit' iterations, largely by using a suitably placed IF statement within the loop body, but this does not always lead to easily readable forms of program structure.

A further need, which is more apt to arise in 'embedded' systems used in process control, is for some means of specifying an 'infinite' loop, which is to continue to run 'for ever'. A common way of constructing this is

```
WHILE TRUE ...
```

which will of course continue to perform loops indefinitely, as the condition is always satisfied. However, this is not really a clear way of expressing the situation.

To help with such problems, Modula-2 includes a more general form of loop control: the LOOP statement, which is intended to provide a more elegant and readable structure. This has the very simple form:

```
LOOP (statementsequence) END;
```

The LOOP statement has no built-in provisions whatsoever for determining when the cycle of iteration should end, and so terminating it requires an additional control statement, the EXIT statement. An EXIT statement provides a very restricted form of unconditional branch, by transferring control to the first statement immediately after the end of the loop. (Note, incidentally, that Modula-2 has no GOTO statement.) The EXIT statement is normally used within a conditional statement form, such as an IF statement.

If no EXIT statement is included within the body of a LOOP, the program will continue to loop forever. As indicated above, in some process control type applications this is actually a desirable feature, since the main body of the program may be required to repeat some task continually, and the use of a LOOP fits well into programs of this type. This sort of use for the LOOP will reappear when we come to look further at the features of Modula-2 that can be used for handling low-level programming tasks.

A rather abstract example of the use of a LOOP is given by the following section of program:

```
LOOP
    Initializeinputtransfer(buffer);    (* get more data if available *)
    IF NOT Done THEN EXIT END;   (* no data available at present *)
    Checkdata(buffer);
    Addtoqueue(buffer)
END; (* loop *)
```

This is an example of the '$n$ and a bit' requirement, roughly modelled on a form of input/output handling that might be used within an operating system. When receiving data, we may not always know whether it will be available at a particular time, and so the 'bit' part of the loop performs the task of initiating a transfer, while the rest of the loop is concerned with the actions required if data is available. Control is transferred out of the LOOP when an attempt to initiate a transfer finds that there is no data available.

While the LOOP statement can always be used in place of any of the other three forms, it is generally better to reserve it for those occasions when the other forms cannot conveniently describe the form of iteration required. One problem with using LOOP is that any terminating condition may well become hidden away in the middle of the code, so reducing the clarity of the code – especially if the loop body is fairly long. What is worse still, though, from the point of view of understanding the code, is that there might be more than one exit point, since it is permissible to use more than one EXIT statement within a LOOP. For these reasons, the LOOP statement has been introduced only at the end of this chapter, and it should be reserved for use on those occasions when generality of form is a genuine need.

As an example of this, we can extend the last example to include a guard condition that will pick up any error occurring during a data transfer:

```
LOOP
    Initializeinputtransfer(buffer);    (* get more data if available *)
    IF NOT Done THEN EXIT END;   (* no data available at present *)
    IF Checkdata(buffer) THEN
        Addtoqueue(buffer);             (* data has no errors *)
    ELSE EXIT END                       (* exit on error in data *)
END; (* loop *)
```

Since each form of iteration construct contains statement sequences, which can contain further iteration forms, we can of course 'nest' loops where required. For the LOOP statement, the effect of an EXIT in such a case is to terminate only the innermost level of iteration. It is also possible to use EXIT statements within the other forms of loop construct, although it is usually hard to justify doing so! Again, when used in these forms, the effect is to terminate the innermost level of iteration. Figure 8.1 shows the effect of

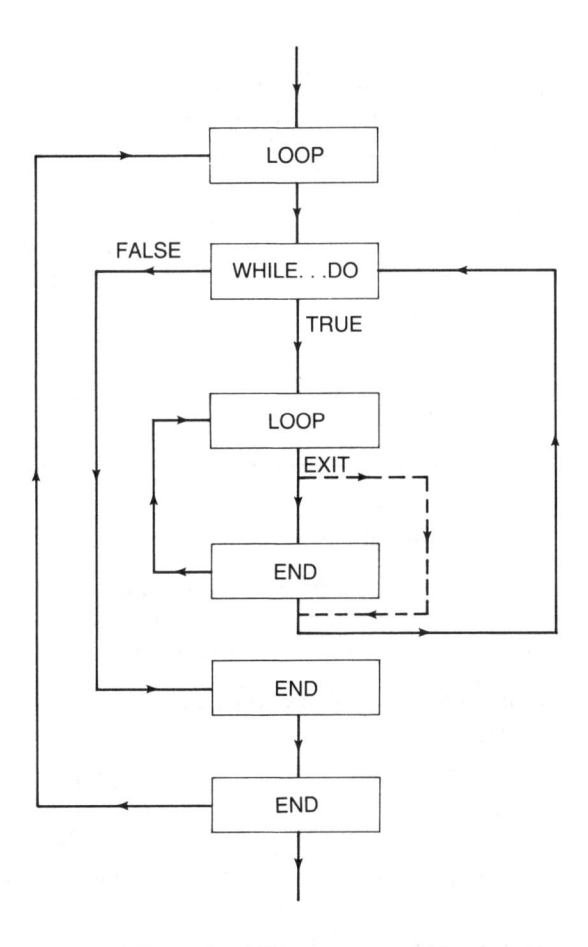

**Figure 8.1** Effect of an EXIT statement within nested loops.

the EXIT statement when used within a number of different nested constructs.

One final point about the LOOP statement is that, like the WHILE and REPEAT UNTIL forms, it often requires the initialization prior to entering the loop of any variables that are to be used within its body. Only the FOR statement contains a built-in initialization step, although the effect of this is limited to the control variable.

The Pascal programmer will already be familiar with the previous three forms, and will have some experience of the issues involved in choosing between them on any occasion. For a programmer who is more familiar with a language such as BASIC or FORTRAN, where the looping forms are more restrictive, the choice of form provided in Modula-2 may seem almost excessively generous. However, this choice is necessary if our code is to be structured so that another programmer (and we ourselves) is to be able to understand it. The correct choice of form can help to make a program clearer by avoiding the need for convoluted code. This is important since, regardless of intentions, a program usually ends up receiving some type of maintenance, whether to fix bugs (*corrective maintenance*), to make improvements or extensions (*perfective maintenance*), or to modify it to run under another operating system, or a new version of an operating system (*adaptive maintenance*). With these needs in mind, there is every reason for striving to produce code that is clear and readable and avoids the use of convoluted constructs.

## EXERCISES

**8.1** Which form of looping construct do you consider to be the most suitable for use in the following tasks?

(a) performing a delay of 30 seconds (assume that a library procedure is available that will return the current time of day as a CARDINAL value in units of one tenth of a second);

(b) setting all the even elements of an array of CARDINALs to some pre-selected value;

(c) counting the number of characters in a line of text read in from a file.

**8.2** Re-write the simple example of counting the months in a year when a school will be in use (Section 8.2) to make use of the LOOP construct rather than a FOR loop.

# Chapter 9
# Subprograms in Modula-2

9.1 The procedure as a structural element
9.2 Transferring information: parameters
9.3 Transferring information: function procedures
9.4 Standard procedures
9.5 Recursive operations with procedures
9.6 Procedure types
Exercises

## 9.1 The procedure as a structural element

The advantages that can be obtained from subdividing a program into smaller units have long been evident to programmers and to language designers. Originally this practice arose in assembler-level programming, where the advantages of being able to call a subprogram rather than repeat whole sections of code are very obvious, not least because this reduces the likelihood of coding errors creeping in. This way of using subprograms to package repeated sequences of operations is encouraged by the fact that assembler-level programmers often find it necessary to re-use sequences of operations at different points.

With the transition to high-level languages, the motivation for using subprograms has become rather different. Indeed, as Constantine and his co-workers have pointed out (Stevens, 1974; Yourdon, 1979), the decision to create a subprogram on the basis that certain sequences of actions are repeated within a program is likely to be unsound, and certainly does not provide a well structured basis for subdividing a program. As a result of such thinking, the subprogram unit is now seen more as an element that is associated with the *logical* structure of a program and that arises from the functional partitioning of the *task* that the program is to perform. Because of the manner in which procedures are invoked, procedures are also *hierarchical* in nature, and this again is concerned with the logical structuring of the solution to a problem. Viewed in this way, the repetition of actions is no longer a dominant issue, and it then becomes quite acceptable practice to create a subprogram that is called only once during the execution of a program, if by doing so the programmer is able to group together all those operations that are related to performing a particular function.

Although this chapter is primarily concerned with the *physical* structures of a procedure, its role in the *logical* structure of a program is extremely important, and we will return to this theme when examining some ways of choosing subprograms in Chapters 12 and 13.

The subprogram unit provided in Modula-2 is termed a 'procedure'. A procedure may be called at any point within a statement sequence, essentially just by using its identifier together with a list of any necessary parameters. (There is no specific 'CALL' statement in Modula-2.) Whenever a procedure is called, it begins execution at the first executable statement (the *entry point*). At the end of the procedure, control will be returned to the calling point and the program will resume execution at the next statement following the one that invoked the procedure.

The general structure of a procedure is very similar to that of a MODULE. The procedure body may contain declarations of types, constants and variables that are local to the procedure, and it may also contain inner procedures. A procedure also has a body that consists of executable code, rather like the main body of a module.

A procedure declaration is introduced by the reserved word PROCEDURE, and this is followed by the name of the procedure (its identifier), and then a list enclosed in parentheses, which gives the details of any parameters that are required. If a procedure has no parameters, then only its identifier is given, and no parentheses are required (unless it is a function procedure). An example of a declaration for a very simple procedure that has no parameters is:

```
PROCEDURE Endline;
CONST
    cr = 15C;    (* carriage return character *)
    lf = 12C;    (* line feed character *)
BEGIN
    Write(cr);
    Write(lf);
END Endline;
```

This is a procedure that will perform a similar task to that of the 'standard' WriteLn procedure contained in InOut, but in a rather device-specific manner. (Of course, WriteLn has no parameters either!)

We can describe the structure of a procedure more formally as:

```
PROCEDURE ⟨procedurename⟩ [ (⟨parameterlist⟩) ];
[ CONST {⟨constantdeclarations⟩} ]
[ TYPE {⟨typedeclarations⟩} ]
[ VAR {⟨variabledeclarations⟩} ]
{⟨proceduredeclarations⟩}
BEGIN
⟨statementsequence⟩
END ⟨procedurename⟩;
```

For the Pascal programmer, the only significant difference to note is the requirement that the reserved word END at the end of the procedure body must now be followed by the name of the procedure (as is the case with a MODULE too). Otherwise the structure of a procedure is much the same as that which is used in Pascal.

Within a MODULE, declarations of procedures will usually follow the declarations of any types, constants and variables used in it, and will precede the main body of the MODULE. Unlike Pascal, there are no constraints upon the order in which procedures may be declared within a MODULE, although to aid anyone needing to read a program, it is essential to ensure that a consistent practice is adopted. The Pascal practice is for a procedure to be declared *before* any procedures that make use of it, but many programmers find this convention less natural than the converse one of declaring a procedure *after* it is first referenced. Whichever practice is preferred, it is certainly necessary for it to be followed in a consistent manner.

The description so far has emphasized the similarities between the structures of procedures and modules, but at this point we should also consider the ways in which they differ. These mainly revolve around the larger issues of data permanency and the 'scope' of data items. To some extent this is complicated by the ability to nest PROCEDUREs within other PROCEDUREs and within MODULEs, and to nest local MODULEs (more about these later) within PROCEDUREs.

To begin with the issue of permanency: any variables declared within the main part of a MODULE that is not itself local to a procedure will be *permanent* – that is, the compiler will allocate storage space for them as a part of the memory image of the program. As such, they will be resident in the computer's memory throughout the execution of the program. So once some value has been assigned to such a variable, it will retain it thereafter until a new value is assigned.

For a PROCEDURE, the situation is rather different. Any variable that is declared within a procedure is purely *temporary*, and so storage space will be provided for it in memory only while the procedure is actually executing (that is, space for the variables will be allocated only when the procedure is called). The space that is allocated for the variables will also be reclaimed when control is returned to the caller. (For most procedures, control will be returned after the computer has executed the last statement within the procedure body.) So any value assigned to such a variable will not be preserved between successive invocations of the procedure. We sometimes refer to such variables as being *transient* in nature.

This manner of handling storage space for variables within procedures is common to very many programming languages, and it is necessary for the support of recursion. Programmers tend to exploit this feature by ensuring that any 'scratch-pad' variables used to hold intermediate calculations or data are declared within procedures, in order to avoid locking up memory storage unnecessarily.

The issue of scope is closely allied to the issue of permanency, since it concerns the extent to which other 'objects' are visible and accessible at any point during the execution of a program. The code of a procedure is able to access any constants, variables or types that are declared within that procedure, and also any that are declared within any outer procedure that might be active when it is called (that is, where the procedure is called from other procedures). Since the highest level is the outermost MODULE, any items that are declared within this will also be 'visible' to all the procedures contained within it. Where identical identifiers are used for items declared at different levels, the item that is most local to the called routine will be selected.

However, this 'visibility' does not apply in reverse, in that the statements in the outer layers cannot make references to data objects that are declared in the called routines. This of course is because no storage space will exist for these items when the code of a higher-level routine is being executed.

The use of procedures as a means of subdividing the structure of a program is a very important technique, and it is one that every programmer needs to master. This aspect will be covered in more detail in Part II. The rest of this chapter will examine how information can be exchanged when using a procedure and give a summary of the 'standard' procedures of the language, before concluding with some more general aspects, including the use of recursion.

## 9.2 Transferring information: parameters

Although, from a structural viewpoint, the number of times that a procedure will be called is not significant, a fairly obvious need is to be able to make use of parameters in a procedure call. By transferring information through the use of parameters, the calling component can select the data values to be used by the procedure during a particular invocation, thus making the procedure into a much more flexible item. This greatly extends the range of tasks that procedures can perform, since information can be conveyed *to* the procedure from the caller in order to direct its actions, and then *back* to the caller from the procedure to indicate the results of those actions.

In assembler programming this can often be achieved by using some of the general purpose registers of the computer to hold the parameters of a call. However, doing so requires some convention to be adopted by which the calling routine will place the items of data into specific registers; and the subprogram will then perform its task using the contents of those particular registers. Using the same scheme, it can return any results from the same registers or from other ones.

A major weakness with such a method lies in the fact that it is only a convention, and there are no checks that can be made when a program is assembled to ensure that it is adhered to. It is entirely up to the programmer to maintain consistency. (As an added point, the number of general purpose registers available to the programmer is usually quite small too.)

With a high-level language such as Modula-2, the physical method by which the data of the parameters is transferred to and from the procedure is transparent to the programmer. However, because Modula-2 supports the use of strong typing, the details of any parameters that are to be used with a procedure must be listed as part of the procedure declaration. For each call of that procedure, the compiler will then check that the correct number and types of parameters are supplied. An example of a procedure with just one parameter is as follows:

```
PROCEDURE Converttouppercase( VAR ch : CHAR );
BEGIN
  IF ( ch >= 'a' ) AND ( ch <= 'z' ) THEN
    ch := CHR( ORD('A') + ORD(ch) - ORD('a') )
  END (* IF *)
END Converttouppercase;
```

Any call to this procedure must provide a single parameter of the type CHAR, as in the call

Converttouppercase(nextch);

or

Converttouppercase( charBuffer[characterIndex] );

where the variable nextch and the element of the array charBuffer must both be of type CHAR.

In this example, the identifier ch is referred to as the **formal** parameter, because it is the one that is used in the declaration of the procedure. The variables nextch and charBuffer[characterIndex] are described as the **actual** parameters that are used for the respective calls to Converttouppercase. A formal parameter is used within the algorithm of the procedure to specify the actions that are to be performed, and the actual parameter of the call will be substituted for the formal parameter when the procedure is executed.

A procedure may have any number of parameters, and a parameter may be of any type that is known within the enclosing MODULE – whether declared there, or IMPORTed from another MODULE, or declared within an outer PROCEDURE. An example of a PROCEDURE heading is:

    PROCEDURE Holidaycheck( initialMonth, lastMonth : Months ;
      VAR leaveGranted : BOOLEAN );

The parameter list that follows the procedure identifier is enclosed by parentheses, and within it any sequence of parameters of the one type can simply be named as a list, separated by commas, while parameters of different types are separated by semi-colons. In each case, the formal identifiers of the parameters must be followed by the identifier of their associated type.

In this last example Holidaycheck has three formal parameters. The first two are both of the enumerated type Months (which we have used previously), while the third is a BOOLEAN variable, which may be used to indicate whether or not the action that was requested was accepted or rejected.

The parameters of a procedure can be used to convey information in both directions. In one direction, they can provide information *to* the procedure (as in the parameters initialMonth and lastMonth in the above example), while in the other they can be used to convey information *from* the procedure to the caller (as in the variable leaveGranted). Like Pascal, Modula-2 differentiates between two forms of parameter, *value* parameters and *variable* parameters. (Ada uses a rather different form, which includes the use of the reserved words *in* and *out*, to indicate the purpose of a parameter. This is actually more powerful since, as we will see, it permits a distinction that is lacking in the form adopted in Modula-2 and Pascal.)

A **value** parameter is one that can only be used to provide input to the procedure, and so this cannot make use of it to return information to the caller in any way. This in turn means that the actual parameter in the calling routine can be any form of expression, since its value is simply copied to the procedure. Unless the programmer specifies otherwise, a parameter is assumed to be a value parameter by default. Examples of this type are the first two parameters of Holidaycheck, so that in

    Holidaycheck(monthOne,monthTwo,holidayGranted);

the values of the variables monthOne and monthTwo are copied to Holidaycheck as the actual parameters, and in:

    Holidaycheck(Jan,lastMonth,holidayGranted);

the first parameter is specified by using the constant element Jan from the enumerated type Months instead of a variable.

Within the procedure itself, a value parameter can be used as though it were a locally declared variable, and values may be assigned to it during the execution of the procedure. If it is used in this way, such an assignment will overwrite the value passed to it by the caller, but it will not affect the value of any object used as the actual parameter within the caller.

A **variable** parameter is one that can be used to transfer information both into and out of the procedure. It may be given a value by the caller when calling the procedure, or may just be provided by the caller for the purpose of receiving returned information. A parameter is declared to be variable by preceding its identifier in the parameter list with the reserved word VAR, as in the example of the parameter leaveGranted that was used in the definition of Holidaycheck. (The BOOLEAN variable holidayGranted is also an example of an actual parameter that is provided by the caller to receive a value.) Where there is a list of several parameters of the same type, separated by commas, these will all be of the form selected for the first parameter, the effect of the reserved word VAR being terminated by the next semi-colon or bracket. So if we have two parameters of the same type, and wish one to be a value parameter and the other a variable parameter, these will require separate declarations in the list, as in

```
PROCEDURE Bitwiseand(maskValue : INTEGER ; VAR statusValue : INTEGER);
```

where both parameters are of type INTEGER, but maskValue is a value parameter and statusValue is a variable parameter.

If any value is assigned to a variable parameter within the body of a procedure, the actual parameter as used in the caller will be modified too. (The first example of Converttouppercase shows this. If the parameter ch is found to be a lower case character, it is changed, and this operation will alter the value of the actual parameter used in the call to the procedure.) So a constant cannot be used as the actual parameter, where a parameter is a variable parameter, since it is illegal to assign a new value to a constant! Neither can we use an expression as the actual value of a variable parameter, of course.

FORTRAN programmers are provided with parameters of only one form, which is something akin to the variable parameter form. Ada is more subtle, since it distinguishes the case where a parameter is used only to return information to the caller, as in the variable leaveGranted used in Holidaycheck, and allows this to be declared as an *out* parameter alone. (A variable parameter in the Modula-2 sense would be one that had both the *in* and the *out* attributes.) In many ways the Ada form is the better one, as it makes the intentions of the programmer much clearer, although the form of a procedure declaration does become a little longer and slightly more complex.

As a general rule, we should try to limit the number of parameters that are used in a procedure. Having too many parameters in the declaration suggests that the procedure might be performing too many operations and should be subdivided. It is also quite difficult to use procedures that have many parameters, since the programmer must remember the order and types of the parameters when coding each call. Certainly a parameter list that contains more than (say) six parameters should be viewed with concern.

As a further point of good practice, we should also take care that a procedure does not receive any information not directly necessary to its task. One of the basic tenets of 'information hiding' (discussed further in Chapter 12 ) is that each component of a program should receive only data that is absolutely necessary for it to perform its task. There is then no opportunity for the programmer to include any extra coding that might add undocumented (and unwanted) side-effects, however good the intentions. Yourdon and Constantine (1979) give a good example of this in 'Charlie's telephone number checking routine'.

One aspect of handling parameters in which Modula-2 differs from Pascal is in the transfer of information that is stored in an array, and this will be covered more fully in Chapter 11. For the moment it is sufficient to note that we no longer need to declare the size of an array which is to be used as a parameter: it is necessary to declare only that it is an array and the details of its element type. (The size can be declared, but this is optional.) An example of a procedure heading that contains such an **open array** is

```
PROCEDURE Countspaces( buffer : ARRAY OF CHAR ;
  VAR spacecount : CARDINAL );
```

(This example also reminds us that a declaration can be spread over any number of lines, and that it is only terminated by the semi-colon that separates it from the following statement.) Chapter 11 will cover the use of open arrays more fully, as well as describing the facilities provided to support their use.

So far we have concentrated on describing how to pass information in and out of a procedure via its parameters. However, a different mechanism is available to us where only a single value needs to be returned from a procedure, and it is one that can sometimes help with a clearer style of programming – namely, the use of function procedures. These are described in the next section, and it is worth observing that this is a language feature in which Modula-2 uses a form quite different from that used in Pascal.

## 9.3 Transferring information: function procedures

Most high-level programming languages support the use of a form of procedure, termed a 'function', that generates a single return value and is constructed so that it can be used as a component within an expression, rather than as a stand-alone statement. FORTRAN has its FUNCTION subprograms, likewise **function** is a reserved word in Pascal, and all procedures in C are constructed as functions by default.

We have already come across examples of the use of function procedures in some of the earlier program examples, through the use of standard functions such as ORD and CHR. When we declare our own function procedures, Modula-2 does not use a separate reserved word to denote a procedure that returns a value in this way. Instead, this is made implicit by including a type for the procedure itself within the procedure declaration. This in turn will determine the type of value that will be returned from a call to that procedure. So the procedure heading for a function procedure looks like

   PROCEDURE ⟨procedurename⟩ ( [ ⟨parameterlist⟩ ] ) : ⟨proceduretype⟩

As an example of this form, the heading for the procedure Countspaces that was used in the last section could now be redesigned to make use of this form, and would then be:

   PROCEDURE Countspaces( charBuffer : ARRAY OF CHAR ) : CARDINAL;

Countspaces could then be used directly within an expression such as the assignment statement

   whiteSpace := Countspaces( thisLine );

or in a conditional expression such as:

   IF ( Countspaces(thisLine) = 0 ) THEN ...

The same can be done with the procedure Holidaycheck introduced in the last section, transforming this into a BOOLEAN function procedure with the heading

   PROCEDURE Holidaycheck(initialMonth, lastMonth : Months) : BOOLEAN;

so that it can be used in an expression such as:

   WHILE Holidaycheck(Jan,request[staffNumber]) DO ...

Holidaycheck is an example of the situation where a parameter is required only for the transfer of information out of the procedure (thus this facility meets the lack of the more rigorous Ada *out* – in a limited way though, since of course we can have only one parameter of this form). A function procedure may also return further information to the caller through the use of variable parameters – but as a matter of style it is better to avoid doing so, since it introduces a source of potential side-effects.

The nature of a function procedure requires that there should be some mechanism within the procedure for assigning the value that is to be returned to the caller. In Modula-2 a RETURN statement can be used both to return control and to transfer a value to the caller. When used in a function procedure, the reserved word RETURN must be followed by an expression that specifies the value that is to be returned to the caller as the value of the function call. More than one RETURN statement is permitted within a function procedure, since there may be multiple control paths within the procedure. As the RETURN statement also terminates execution of the procedure, this means that it is possible to have multiple exit points within a procedure. In many ways the RETURN statement performs a very similar role to that of the EXIT used in the LOOP statement, by providing a structured way of breaking out from a segment of the program. Its use requires a similar degree of discipline to that needed for the use of EXIT. If used badly, it can render the structure of a procedure indistinct or obscure, but if used with care it can avoid the need to use a convoluted flow of control within the procedure. (A RETURN statement may also be used in a normal procedure, where of course it does not need any following expression. However, the use of the RETURN statement other than within function procedures should generally be avoided.)

For a more complete example of a function procedure, we reconstruct our very first example of a procedure, which was Converttouppercase. We rename it as Uppercase and give it the form

```
(* function procedure Uppercase
    if argument is in the range a–z, then return upper case character
    else return original argument *)
PROCEDURE Uppercase( ch : CHAR ) : CHAR;
BEGIN
  IF ( ch >= 'a' ) AND ( ch <= 'z' ) THEN
    RETURN CHR( ORD('A') + ORD(ch) – ORD('a') )
  ELSE RETURN ch
  END (* IF *)
END Uppercase;
```

This can then be used in the following statement:

```
FOR i := 0 TO lineLength DO
  newBuffer[i] := Uppercase( buffer[i] )
END;
```

which copies one array of characters into another, and converts all the lower case characters that it finds into their upper case form. This form of routine might be useful in scanning through a block of text, where the interest lies in the sequencing of characters, regardless of their case.

Since the parameter of this routine is now a value parameter, it will be unchanged by the procedure, so that in the statement

```
IF ( Uppercase( ch ) <> 'Y' ) THEN ...
```

the actual value of the variable ch itself will be unchanged by the call. Obviously this is a much more secure feature than would be provided by the use of a variable parameter.

One obvious role in which function procedures are useful is for converting between two forms of data: either type conversion and type transfer, such as ORD, CHR, INTEGER, CARDINAL, or format conversion, such as Uppercase above. Function procedures are particularly suitable for such single-valued operations, where a single input parameter will generate a single output value.

Used with care, function procedures can form a powerful addition to the programmer's set of structuring facilities. Within Modula-2 they also take a form that in many ways is much more consistent than that which is used in most other languages of this style, by simply extending the procedure declaration to specify a type for the procedure itself. This concept will be taken a step further when we come to look at procedure types at the end of this chapter. First though, the next section gives an overview of the standard procedures provided in Modula-2 (which are mostly function procedures too).

## 9.4 Standard procedures

The standard procedures of Modula-2 are largely concerned with such tasks as obtaining execution-time 'status' information or performing type transfers and type conversions. So most of them are structured as function procedures, the form most appropriate for these roles. We have already encountered many of them in the examples of the previous chapters, although there are some concerned with tasks that have not yet been delineated. There is also a group of standard procedures concerned with simplifying some frequently repeated tasks.

Following the convention that is also used for the reserved words and predefined types in Modula-2, the standard procedures have identifiers that are made up from upper case characters. With the exception of HALT, they can all be identified as procedures by their use of parameters.

The group of procedures that are concerned with type conversion and form conversion, most of which should be familiar to some degree, are as follows:

ABS(s)   A function procedure that returns the absolute value (or unsigned magnitude) of its parameter. It is a rather special form of function procedure in that the parameter can be of more than one type (INTEGER or REAL), and it returns a value of the appropriate type in each instance. As an example, if the variable basicStep is of type INTEGER, and contains the value −20, then the statement

   nearestRadius := ABS(basicStep);

will copy the value 20 into the INTEGER variable nearestRadius.

CAP(ch)   This is another function procedure, which performs a task essentially identical to that performed by Uppercase in the previous section. It takes a parameter of type CHAR and, if this is a lower case alphabetical character, returns the corresponding upper case character, otherwise it returns the character unchanged. For example

   IF ( CAP( ch ) = 'Y' ) THEN ...

CHR(n)   A function procedure that should be familiar to the Pascal programmer. Given a value of $n$ for its parameter, CHR will return the character of type CHAR that corresponds to the ordinal position $n$ within the character set. As an example,

   nextChar := CHR(65);

will place a value of 'A' in the CHAR variable nextChar.

FLOAT(c)   A function procedure that takes an argument c of type CARDINAL, and returns the REAL value which corresponds to this. As an example of its use, the statement

   pathLength := FLOAT(20);

will set a value of 20.0 into the REAL variable pathLength. (Note that because the argument is of CARDINAL type, this can only be used with positive numbers!)

CARDINAL(i)   This is really a function procedure that is concerned with *type transfer* rather than *type conversion* (as is the next procedure), but it has the same form as the previous procedures. It takes a parameter $i$ of type INTEGER, and returns the corresponding value with type CARDINAL (obviously negative values of $i$ are invalid).

INTEGER(c)   Performs the complement of the action of the preceding function. It takes a CARDINAL parameter $c$, and returns its INTEGER value. (These two type transfer procedures are used to overcome some of the problems that arise when using two integer types in a strongly typed language. They are considered as being 'unsafe' conversions, since an operation such as

 CARDINAL(-1)

can yield a value of 65 535 on a 16-bit twos-complement machine.)

 ORD(x)  A function procedure that returns the CARDINAL value corresponding to the position of the input parameter within the appropriate enumerated type (that is, its *ordinal* value). It is not simply a complementary function to CHR since, besides the obvious use with type CHAR, it may also be used with *any* enumerated type. As an example:

 charPosition := ORD('A')

sets the value of 65 into the CARDINAL variable charPosition, while

 monthOrdinal := ORD(Feb)

will set the ordinal value of Feb (which is 1) into the CARDINAL variable monthOrdinal. (Note that ordinal values start from 0.)

 TRUNC(r)  A function procedure that returns a CARDINAL value comprising the integer part of a real number. (There are obviously potential problems when using negative real numbers, so we may need to use ABS too.) In the statement

 basicLength := TRUNC( fullLength )

if the REAL variable fullLength has the value of 21.784, then basicLength will be assigned a value of 21.

 VAL(T,n)  This procedure is an extension of the idea of CHR (note that its complement ORD is already extended to types other than CHAR alone). Instead of operating on just one type, VAL can be used with any enumerated type T (as well as CHAR too, of course). It takes an ordinal value *n* as its parameter and returns the corresponding element from the enumerated type T. Rather like ABS, it is a special form of function procedure since the type of the value returned is determined by one of its parameters (T). As examples of its use:

 VAL(CHAR,n)

is equivalent to

 CHR(n)

and

> VAL(Months,3)

will generate a return value of Apr when used with the enumerated type Months.

The following three procedures are concerned with providing *information* about data types, rather than with conversion tasks. (They were all added to Modula-2 by Wirth in the 1983 revision.)

> MAX(T)   Returns the maximum value of an element of type T, which may be a standard type or a user-defined type. (Clearly T must also be an ordered type, and so it cannot be an array type or a record type.)

> MIN(T)   Similar to MAX, but it will return the smallest value that an element of type T can possess.

> SIZE(T)   Can be used either with a type identifer as its parameter, or with the identifier of a variable. In either case it will return a CARDINAL value that corresponds to the number of storage units that will be required by its argument. Examples of this are:

> numberOfBytes := SIZE(Headerblocks);

when used with the type Headerblocks, and

> numberOfBytes := SIZE(newRecord);

where newRecord is a variable of some (presumably structured) type.

A (truly) odd function procedure is

> ODD(x)   A BOOLEAN function procedure that performs a test for the condition

> (x MOD 2) <> 0

where $x$ is a variable of either of the integer types. ODD will return a value of TRUE if the value of $x$ is odd, and of FALSE if it is even.

Programmers make frequent use of counters when programming in imperative languages such as Modula-2, and they normally use integer variables for this purpose, incrementing and decrementing these at various points in the code. So statements such as:

> count := count + 1;

and

> index := index − 1;

are frequently encountered in programs. To help make such code more readable, Modula-2 provides the following two procedures

    INC(x)    Performs the operation $x := x + 1$;

and

    DEC(x)    Performs the operation $x := x - 1$;

These two procedures also help to reduce the risk of a particular form of programming error. Entering the line

    $x := x + 1$;

when we had intended to type

    $x := x - 1$;

will generate no compiler errors, since it is purely a logical error and can be very hard to detect. However, we are far less likely to type INC in place of DEC! Besides being used with the integer types INTEGER and CARDINAL for handling counters, these two procedures can also be used with the type CHAR and with enumerated types, where they perform the operation of replacing the given parameter element with its successor or predecessor. (In Pascal, these operations are performed by the **succ** and **pred** functions.)

    There are also more general forms of these two procedures, which permit the size of the increment to be specified as a second parameter. These are:

    INC(x,n)    Performs the operation $x := x + n$;

and

    DEC(x,n)    Performs the operation $x := x - n$;

Since in most applications we step only one point at a time, these are likely to be far less widely used.

Some further standard procedures that can be used for manipulating data types are the following pair, which have already been described in Chapter 6.

    EXCL(s,e)    Removes the element $e$ from the set variable $s$.
    INCL(s,e)    Adds the element $e$ to the set variable $s$.

The final two standard procedures cannot really be fitted into any of the above categories, nor do they even go together. These are:

    HALT    A procedure that terminates program execution when called, and which can be used for exception (error) handling.

    HIGH(a)    A function that returns the value of the upper limit of an array used as a parameter of a procedure. Its use with open arrays will be described in Chapter 11.

## 9.5 Recursive operations with procedures

The concept of recursion may already be familiar to the reader, and especially to anyone who has programmed in Pascal. While recursion provides a powerful facility that can help in producing elegant solutions to a large class of programming problems, a comprehensive description of its use is beyond the scope of this book. For a more complete treatment of the use of recursion, the reader is advised to consult a suitable text on programming methods. However, since recursion is a feature of Modula-2, a brief introduction to its use is included in this section; those readers who are already familiar with the topic may well choose to omit this section.

Since a procedure body consists of a statement sequence, it can of course contain calls to further procedures. In a programming language that supports the use of recursion, the calling procedure itself is one of those that may be called in this way. This self-referencing can be continued until some suitable terminating condition occurs, whereupon control is returned to the original calling level, step by step.

Whenever a procedure is executed, new instances of its local variables will be created (since these occupy temporary storage), and this will also occur when a procedure is called recursively. So recursive calling of a procedure will create a nested series of instances of local variables, with the only instance that is 'visible' to any particular activation being that which is declared within it: hence this will be the only one that is 'visible' during its execution. Figure 9.1 shows the effects of recursive calling for a very simple procedure.

Recursive methods can provide very elegant solutions for certain classes of problem and may be preferable to a looping construct such as WHILE, LOOP or REPEAT UNTIL on such occasions, especially for data structures such as trees, which are not sequential in form. However, if a procedure is to be used in this way it needs to contain a conditional expression that will ensure that the sequence of recursive calls is correctly terminated.

In Modula-2 all procedures may be used recursively, although of course they need to be suitably organised and structured for the purpose. So, just as in Pascal, there are no reserved words needed to indicate recursion. (The concept of recursion is missing from FORTRAN.)

As with all language features, recursion should be reserved for use on suitable occasions – not least because the repeated calling of a procedure represents an overhead at the time of execution, and it would be pointless to incur this without a genuine need for the flexibility of structure. Quite a number of mathematical operations lend themselves to elegant representation through the use of recursive forms and, together with such tasks as accessing tree-like data structures, provide scope for using the power of recursion.

As an example of the use of recursive techniques, the following procedure performs the task of calculating $n$ factorial ($n!$). The factorial of

# RECURSIVE OPERATIONS WITH PROCEDURES

```
PROCEDURE Decrement ( value : CARDINAL );
BEGIN
  IF value > 0 THEN
    WriteCard(value,2);
    WriteLn;
    Decrement(value−1);
  END; (* if *)
  RETURN;
END Decrement;
```

A call of Decrement (3) would generate the sequence:

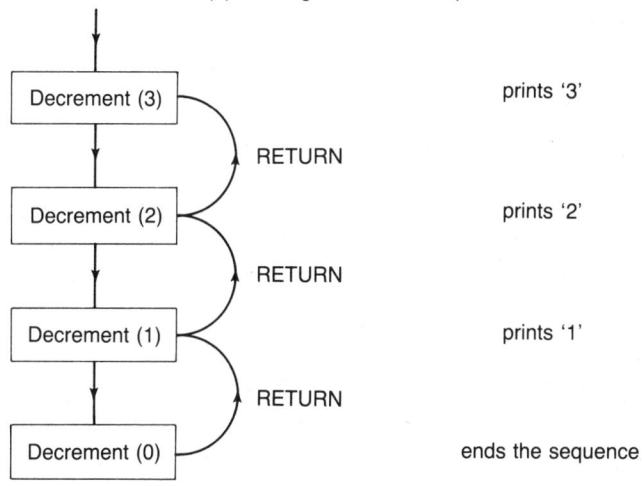

```
Decrement (3)               prints '3'
       RETURN
Decrement (2)               prints '2'
       RETURN
Decrement (1)               prints '1'
       RETURN
Decrement (0)               ends the sequence
```

**Figure 9.1**  Effect of recursive calling.


a positive integer *n* is the product

$$n * (n - 1) * (n - 2) * \ldots * 3 * 2 * 1$$

For example, 4! is 4 * 3 * 2 * 1. The method used in the example simply evaluates this series directly using the relationship

$$n! = n * (n - 1)!$$

(While this is not the most efficient way of calculating factorials, it does show the use of recursion quite concisely.)

132    SUBPROGRAMS IN MODULA-2

```
MODULE Printfactorial;

FROM InOut IMPORT WriteString, WriteCard, WriteLn, ReadCard;
CONST
  maxvalue = 7;          (* largest value permitted *)
VAR
  userEntry : CARDINAL;  (* value entered by user *)

PROCEDURE Factorial( n : CARDINAL) : CARDINAL;
BEGIN
  IF (n > 1)
  THEN
    RETURN n*Factorial(n−1)
  ELSE
    RETURN 1             (* factorial 1 *)
  END (* if *)
END Factorial;

BEGIN
  LOOP
    WriteLn; WriteString("Please enter a number between 1 and 7 : ");
    ReadCard(userEntry) ; WriteLn;
    IF (userEntry = 0) OR (userEntry > maxvalue)
    THEN
      EXIT
    ELSE
      WriteString("Factorial "); WriteCard(userEntry,2);
      WriteString(" is "); WriteCard(Factorial(userEntry),5);
      WriteLn;
    END; (* if *)
  END; (* loop *)
END Printfactorial
```

**Figure 9.2**  A simple program using a recursive procedure.

```
PROCEDURE Factorial( n : CARDINAL ) : CARDINAL;
BEGIN
  IF (n > 1) THEN RETURN n*Factorial(n−1)
  ELSE RETURN 1    (* factorial 1 *)
  END              (* if *)
END Factorial;
```

The program module in Figure 9.2 makes use of this, together with some standard procedures from the InOut library, and will calculate the factorial of any positive integer that is entered from the user's keyboard. (To avoid overflow when this is run on a 16-bit machine, a limit has been placed upon the size of number that can be entered.)

RECURSIVE OPERATIONS WITH PROCEDURES    133

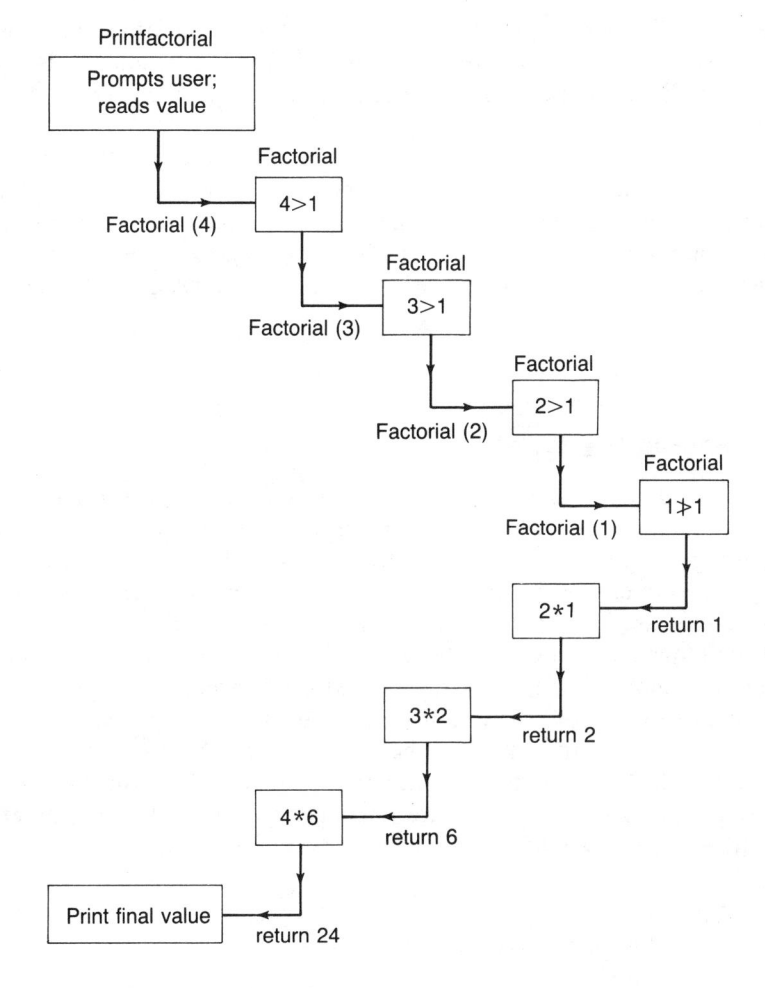

[Diagram showing recursive call sequence for Printfactorial with input 4:
Printfactorial (Prompts user; reads value) → Factorial(4) → [4>1] → Factorial(3) → [3>1] → Factorial(2) → [2>1] → Factorial(1) → [1≯1] → return 1 → [2*1] → return 2 → [3*2] → return 6 → [4*6] → return 24 → Print final value]

**Figure 9.3** Sequence of transfers of control when entering 4 into Printfactorial.

For those who may be unfamiliar with recursion and its use, Figure 9.3 shows the sequence of actions that will occur when the user enters the number 4 into this program.

This example exhibits one structural feature that is to be found in all recursive procedures, in that, in order to ensure the correct termination of the sequence of calls, the recursive procedure call needs to be placed inside some form of selection operation, such as an IF statement.

(It is worth emphasizing that the recursive procedure could be much more complex, and could call other procedures – nothing constrains us to this rather limited size and form of procedure, nor need it be a function procedure. However, in practice most recursive routines are apt to be quite short, as their power lies in the repetition of a task, rather than in complexity of coding. In addition, a recursive routine that is very long is also very difficult to understand, and so is better divided into recursive and non-recursive procedures.)

Combinatorics exercises can make very good use of the power of recursion and, as already mentioned, recursive routines can be useful in making searches up and down complex data structures such as trees. This sort of data structure is described in Chapter 11, and we will be encountering some examples of recursive procedures as we progress through the rest of the book.

## 9.6 Procedure types

So far in our discussion the idea of associating a type with a program element, giving the compiler an opportunity to perform consistency checking during compilation, has been restricted to the idea of data types, which can be used to create the 'passive' elements of a program via declarations of variables and constants of the type. In Modula-2 this idea has been extended further to include the idea of **procedure types**. However, it should be emphasized that in this context the concept of a type is essentially confined to those aspects of procedures that could be considered as essentially passive, and which can hence be checked by the compiler.

A definition for a procedure type consists of a **template**, which describes the form of a procedure heading – particularly the number of parameters that it will have, and their types. For example:

```
TYPE
   Integerfunction = PROCEDURE ( INTEGER ) : INTEGER;
```

Here the type Integerfunction is declared as representing a function procedure that has a single value parameter of type INTEGER, and which returns a value of type INTEGER too. If we declare a variable of this type within our program, the only 'value' that can then be assigned to it must take the form of a procedure identifier, which in turn must be for a procedure of the corresponding form. Since such a type may itself be used for a parameter of a procedure, this mechanism provides the means for passing a procedure as one of the parameters of another procedure (curiously enough, a similar feature is provided in FORTRAN).

There are some restrictions that limit which specific procedures can be assigned and used in such a way. Neither the standard procedures nor procedures with declarations that are nested within another procedure may be used in this way. (The standard procedures are ruled out because in practice they may be implemented as in-line code, and so may not exist as callable procedure bodies.) So if nextFunction is declared as a variable of type Integerfunction, we cannot use the assignment

    nextFunction := ORD;

but if our MODULE contains a procedure that is declared as

    PROCEDURE Cubeof( x : INTEGER ) : INTEGER;
    BEGIN
        RETURN x*x*x
    END Cubeof;

then we can use the assignment

    nextFunction := Cubeof;

in order to assign the identifier Cubeof to nextFunction. (Note that only the *identifier* of the procedure is used in this assignment: no parentheses are required.) When we have done so, the further assignment of

    result := nextFunction(length);

will be executed as if it had been written as the statement

    result := Cubeof(length);

This feature provides a means of selecting between procedures at time of execution. However, to keep our code clear and understandable we would not use this facility in this manner as part of our normal programming. Rather, it is provided so that we can select a procedure as a parameter of another procedure, and when we come to examine the co-routine facility of Modula-2 we will see one of the situations where it can be useful. It also provides a way of selecting a particular option at execution time rather than at compilation time. This might be convenient when selecting the form of terminal handling required, or to make use of a particular 'error handler'. Apart from such cases, procedure types should be treated with care, to avoid creating obscure structures in programs.

Modula-2 includes one standard procedure type in addition to the standard predefined data types described in Chapter 5. This is the procedure type PROC, which is used to denote a parameterless procedure. Its definition is therefore of the form

    TYPE
        PROC = PROCEDURE;

This type will be encountered again when we come to examine the use of co-routines in Modula-2.

Procedures are an important tool for creating structure within programs, and the choices of procedures and their interfaces have important implications for the way in which a program can be constructed, as well as the ease with which it can be modified or maintained. We will be returning to this theme in the second part of this book.

## EXERCISES

**9.1** Re-write the program listed in Figure 5.1 to make use of procedures and function procedures wherever possible.

**9.2** (a) Create a program that contains an ordered type such as Days, and then apply the standard procedures MAX and MIN to this type, printing out the ordinal positions corresponding to the values that these return.

(b) Repeat the above exercise for a sub-range type.

**9.3** What do you expect will happen when we use the value of the highest element of an enumerated type as the argument of the standard procedure INC (such as INC(today), where today has the value Sunday)? Likewise, what will happen if we use the value of the lowest element as the argument of DEC (such as DEC(today), where today has a value of Monday)? Write a small program to experiment with these operations.

**9.4** Repeat Exercise 5.3, but this time use a recursive form for the procedure that prints the base eight number.

# Chapter 10
# The Role of the MODULE

10.1 MODULEs reviewed
10.2 The MODULE main body
10.3 Information-hiding in MODULEs
10.4 MODULEs within MODULEs
10.5 Partitioning the declarations within a MODULE
Exercises

## 10.1 MODULEs reviewed

The MODULE construct is a feature that distinguishes Modula-2 from almost all other imperative programming languages. However, since the brief review of the forms of MODULE back in Chapter 3, most of the subsequent examples have involved only program modules, which have in turn IMPORTed items from other modules as needed. Having now covered the main structures of the language and their syntax, it is an appropriate time to examine the roles performed by MODULEs rather more fully. This material is important to obtaining a proper understanding of the material in Parts II and III, where we examine how the Modula-2 language can be used to best effect.

It is important to reiterate that the MODULE is basically a packaging feature and is not concerned directly with the logical structure of a program, unlike the procedure. Because the role of the program module implies a degree of hierarchy, it is sometimes tempting to regard MODULEs as being more like 'super-procedures', and this view needs to be resisted. In Part II of this book we will be much more concerned with the issues of choice that arise in grouping objects within a module, but for the moment we will mainly concentrate upon the MODULE mechanism itself.

The idea that a program module contains the 'top level' of a program (and that a program can therefore contain only one such module) should now be familiar enough. A program module is identified to the compiler (and to the reader) by the single keyword MODULE at the beginning, and, organizationally, its structure does not differ very much from that of a Pascal program. When the program formed from a program module is executed, the main body of this module provides the top-level algorithm of the program – and when this algorithm terminates, it ends the execution of the program.

Each separately compiled 'subordinate' module is divided into two parts, a definition part and an implementation part, respectively identified by the pairs of reserved words DEFINITION MODULE and IMPLEMENTATION MODULE. It should be emphasized that these distinguish two parts of *one* module, and so must always be followed by the same module identifier.

The definition part defines a 'window' for the facilities provided by the module. The details of any constants, types, variables and procedures that are to be made available to other modules need to be declared in this part. It is stored in a separate file (typically distinguished by the extension .def), and on compilation this is processed into a compressed form, which in turn is stored in another file (typically having the extension .sym). As a matter of good practice we try to avoid including anything that is not essential in the definition part – a point that will be expanded upon later.

The implementation part of a module contains all the *executable* code of the module, and also the declarations for the local structures of the module, including further declarations of constants, types, variables and procedures. On many operating systems it is stored in a file with the extension .mod. When this part is compiled, the compiler generates a file of intermediate object code, which can then be integrated with other such modules by the link-editor, in order to create the executable program file.

Like the program module, the code of an implementation module can in turn make use of the facilities that are provided from other modules – and, indeed, it is essentially identical in form to a program module. However, when compiling an implementation part, the compiler will automatically read the associated .sym file, so that anything declared in the definition part concerning the module will be known to it while compiling the implementation part. This has two consequences. One is that the code of the implementation part can use any constants, types and variables that are declared in the definition part, without needing to redeclare them or to IMPORT them specifically; the second is that the compiler is able to check that the forms declared for any 'visible' procedures are actually consistent with the procedural interfaces that are specified in the definition part.

As a practical point, this means that, in order to be able to read and understand the code of an implementation part, it is also necessary to have access to the code of the definition part, since any data items declared there can be freely used in the implementation part. This feature can be rather confusing in practice, since it means that the implementation part may refer to items that are neither declared within that part, nor explicitly imported from another module! This is not a major issue, however, as one of the points about this form of separate compilation is that we only need to read the definition part of a module in order to be able to make use of it. Hence the need to read implementation parts is largely confined to maintenance programming and the task of marking student exercises!

So the source code of a Modula-2 program will consist of a single program module, together with any number of other modules, each of which will be divided into two parts. (The criteria that might be used in dividing the contents of the module between them will be discussed in a later section.) When the program is executed, the main body of the program module forms the 'top level' of the program.

The use of definition parts is the key to the scheme of separate compilation as used in Modula-2, since it allows the compiler to check for consistency of the interfaces between the different parts of a program that might have been constructed by different members of a programming team at different times.

## 10.2 The MODULE main body

In the preceding section, it was observed that the structure of the implementation part of a module is very similar to that of a program module. Since the main body of a program module functions as the top level of the program, this leads to the question of what role the main body of an implementation module can perform.

Whereas any practical program module must *always* have a main body, which is declared after any declarations of data items and procedures, and is preceded by the reserved word BEGIN, this is an optional feature for an implementation module. However, where an implementation module does have a main body, this will be treated as though it were an 'anonymous' and parameterless procedure, and it will automatically be called during program initialization — that is, *before* the body of the program module is executed.

In a sense, we can regard the main body of an implementation module as though it were a parameterless procedure possessing the same identifier as the module. Since it is called and executed as a part of the complete program, it might be sensible to include it in any structure diagram used to describe the hierarchical form of a program.

This means that the main body of a module can contain code that will initialize the values of any of the data structures declared in the module. This makes it possible for such variables to be assigned an initial value before any of the component procedures of the MODULE are called. This quite important feature will be examined more fully in the next section, where we consider how this can be most effectively used in the design and construction of a program.

(* Provides a definition part for a simple integer stack module in which the stack is completely concealed and may only be accessed via the procedures
  * PushInteger
  * PopInteger
which respectively add one integer to the top of the stack and remove an integer from the top of the stack. Both procedures provide BOOLEAN parameters to indicate overflow or underflow *)

DEFINITION MODULE IntStack;

EXPORT QUALIFIED PushInteger, PopInteger;

PROCEDURE PushInteger(newValue; INTEGER; VAR overFlow : BOOLEAN);

PROCEDURE PopInteger(VAR topValue: INTEGER; VAR underFlow : BOOLEAN);

END IntStack.

**Figure 10.1** A simple module definition part.

**Figure 10.2** A simple module implementation part.

(* Provides an integer stack facility. See comments in the definition part for further details. *)

IMPLEMENTATION MODULE IntStack;

CONST
  stacklimit = 20;

VAR
  stack : ARRAY [0..stacklimit−1] OF INTEGER;     (* actual stack space *)
  stackpointer : [0..stacklimit];

PROCEDURE PushInteger(newValue: INTEGER; VAR overFlow : BOOLEAN);
BEGIN
  IF stackpointer < stacklimit THEN
    stack[stackpointer] := newValue;
    INC(stackpointer);
    overFlow := FALSE;
  ELSE
    overFlow := TRUE
  END; (* if *)
END PushInteger;

```
PROCEDURE PopInteger(VAR topValue: INTEGER; VAR underFlow: BOOLEAN);
BEGIN
  IF stackpointer > 0 THEN
    DEC(stackpointer);
    topValue := stack[stackpointer];
    underFlow := FALSE;
  ELSE
      underFlow := TRUE;
  END; (* if *)
END PopInteger;

BEGIN (* main body *)
  stackpointer := 0;     (* initialize stack *)
END IntStack.
```

**Figure 10.2** *cont.*

For the moment, an example may help to clarify the point, and for this we will consider a module that implements a stack. Before the stack can be used, the stack pointer needs to be set to a value that corresponds to the top of the stack. We can place the statements assigning an initial value to the stack pointer in the main body of the implementation part, so that when the procedures used by the rest of the program for accessing the stack are first called, the stack will have been set up correctly. Figures 10.1 and 10.2 show the definition and implementation parts for just such a stack module.

In Chapter 3 it was observed that modules are primarily a packaging feature, and that they are used to group data items and executable items (procedures). If we draw a hierarchical diagram (structure diagram) to represent a complete program, then we may well find that the procedures contained within a particular module can be all at one level of the hierarchy or that they may be spread around several levels. So the module itself has no hierarchical role in terms of its contents.

Figure 10.3 shows an example of a structure diagram (Stevens *et al.*, 1974; Yourdon and Constantine, 1979) that describes a fairly simple program (we will discuss this form of program representation more fully in Part II). Figure 10.4 shows how these same procedures might be grouped within a set of MODULEs. This emphasizes the need for any descriptions of a Modula-2 program to include forms that represent both *hierarchy* and also *packaging*. In a sense, the two representations of Figures 10.3 and 10.4 are 'orthogonal', in that they embody quite different views of the structure of a program.

This orthogonality arises because a structure diagram is primarily concerned with showing the hierarchy that exists among procedures in

142   THE ROLE OF THE MODULE

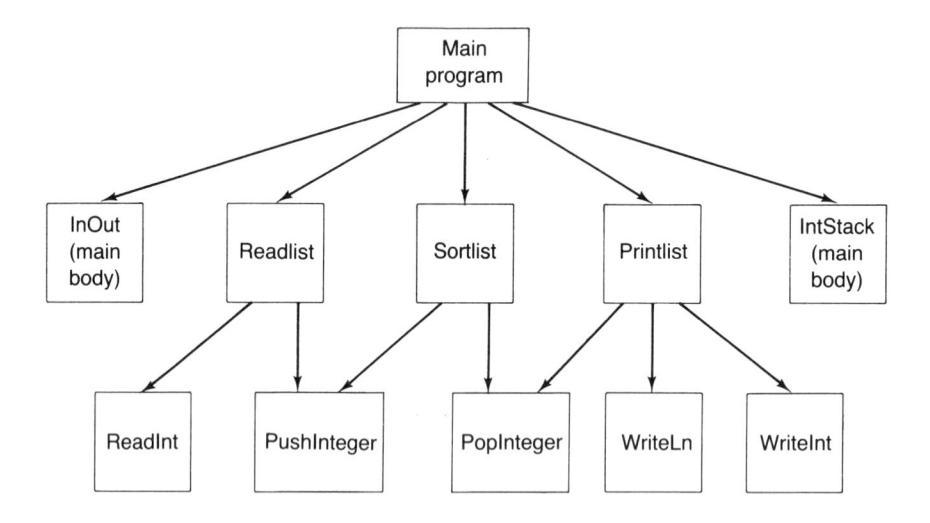

**Figure 10.3** A simple structure diagram for a program (for clarity, details of parameters have been omitted). This diagram shows the run-time call hierarchy.

terms of the flow of control (which procedures call which other procedures) and the flow of data that occurs as a part of that flow of control (the parameters of a procedure call). It does not show any information about the data structures that may be common to a group of procedures and that can therefore be accessed directly by them. Since this latter feature is one of the most significant factors in determining which elements are combined into a module, it is not surprising that the hierarchical forms of representation are not able to show module structure in any form. Hence the need for more than one form of representation.

However this lack of involvement in the logical structure of a program does not strictly apply to the main body of a module. Since a module may well IMPORT items from other modules, there is a degree of hierarchy among such modules: the main body of a 'lower' module needs to be executed first, so that any data items that are used by its procedures can be initialized correctly.

According to our normal view of dependencies, this is the inverse of what we might expect, since the main body of the 'lowest' module is the one that needs to be executed first. In fact this is not a true hierarchy at all, since several 'higher' modules might depend upon a single 'lower' one – yet its main body should be executed only once. What we are really observing is the need for a definite *sequence* to be established for the initialization of the modules, so that the anonymous procedures are executed in the correct order. In this way, any relevant data items will be initialized correctly before they are used.

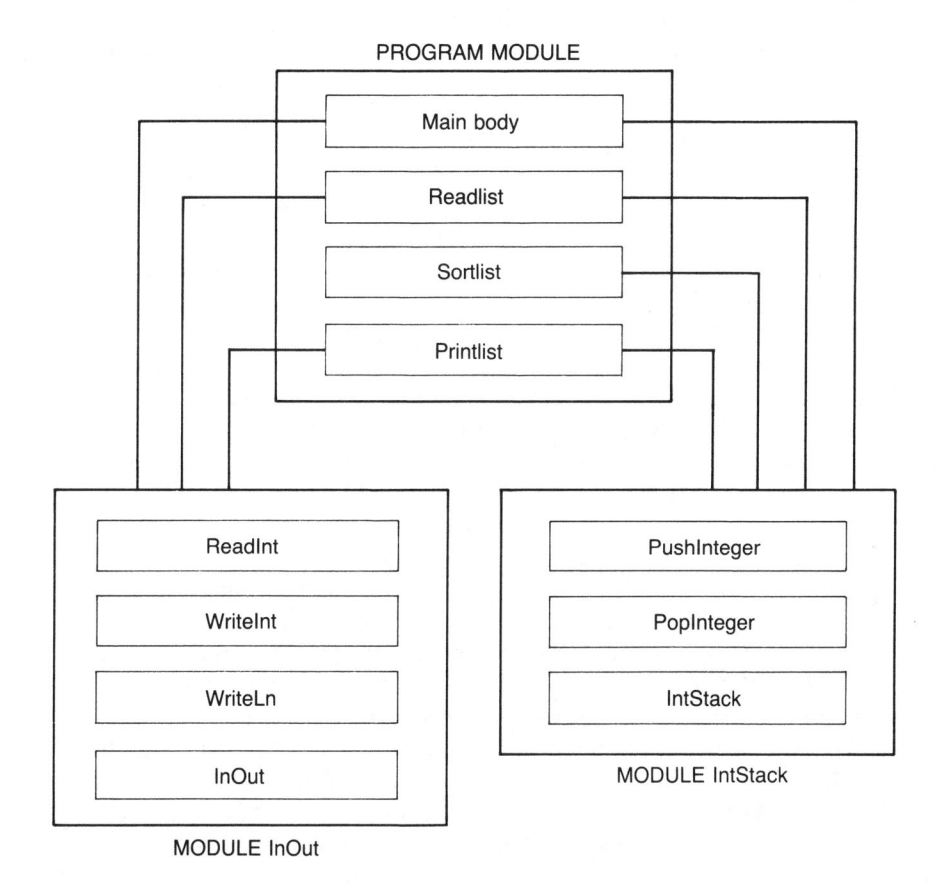

**Figure 10.4** Packaging of the elements of the program in Figure 10.3. This diagram shows compile-time dependency.

## 10.3 Information-hiding in MODULEs

Although the concept of information-hiding will be discussed more fully in Chapter 12, this is a useful point at which to consider the influence that it has had upon the design of the Modula-2 programming language.

The idea of information-hiding was first introduced in two very influential papers by David Parnas (1972a, 1972b). In these he emphasized that an important criterion for successful modularization was that details about the nature and form of data and control structures should be kept concealed from the rest of the program wherever possible. Such items should be accessed and manipulated only via a well defined set of associated 'access procedures', the interfaces of which should ensure that the details of how data is stored should not be visible to the calling module.

We need not go into the details of this concept more fully at this point but, in order to see its influence on the language structures, it may help to consider two simple examples of how the idea might be used.

The first, more general, example is not specifically related to Modula-2. Most programmers are familiar with the use of information-hiding in the design of operating systems, particularly in terms of the abstract idea of a 'file'. While the actual physical disks are 'block structured' devices, and a file needs to be mapped onto a set of physical blocks, chained together in some way, none of this information is normally visible to the user at all. The program interface to a file of (say) text is usually concerned only with providing the means of reading lines of characters. The way in which these characters are actually stored in the files is normally concealed from the user. In turn, a file is accessed only by its name, or identifier, which reveals nothing about the way in which it is held in the physical blocks of the disk. All accessing of files by a program is then performed via a set of library routines that are a part of the operating system and provide the necessary buffering and decoding. The parameters of such procedures use only such abstract links as the name (identifier). Because of this, provided that we design programs so that they use only 'standard' file-handling routines (Pascal provides these, as does FORTRAN), it should be a fairly simple task to recompile these to run on a different operating system, even if this has a set of very different underlying file structures. So the organization of a file system can usually be considered as an example of 'information-hiding' put into practice.

This last point about a change of operating system is quite important, for one of the reasons why Parnas argues that we should seek to adopt such a scheme is that it makes code much more portable and easy to change. This is on the basis that a change of environment (such as the operating system) should affect only one part of our program, namely the part that interfaces with the area that has changed.

The second example is more program-oriented: an integer stack. As already observed, a stack needs to be initialized by giving the stack pointer an initial value. In a Pascal program, any need for the stack to occupy permanent data storage means that it must be declared in the outer block, which renders it impossible to enforce concealment from the rest of the program, since the code of any procedure can bypass the 'push' and 'pop' routines provided and manipulate the stack directly.

In Modula-2, it becomes possible to conceal the structure of the stack. By placing the stack structure within a module, together with its push and pop procedures, and then EXPORTing only these procedures, it is possible to keep the form of implementation used for the stack completely concealed from the user. This is because the code of push and pop can directly access the local data structure used for the stack, so that it need not be passed as a parameter, and, since the structure is local, it is invisible to the rest of the program outside that module. Furthermore, since the main body of the module can be used to initialize the value of the stack pointer, all the 'house-keeping' aspects are also kept concealed. Indeed, if at some point we decide that the form of implementation used for the stack structure needs to be changed, the change can be kept wholly concealed from the rest of the program and from other programmers since it has no effect on the external form of push and pop. This is because in Modula-2 there is no way in which the other parts of the program can possibly access a local data structure, other than by calling the procedures that are provided for that purpose, and hence any references that are made to the stack *must* make use of the procedures that are provided by the stack module.

The key issue in doing this is that we are able to declare *permanent* data objects in a module, and then conceal their *existence* as well as their form from the rest of the program by not EXPORTing them. In Pascal, by comparison, it is possible to create a permanent data structure only by including its declaration in the main part of the program.

The variables declared in the main part of a Pascal program will be *visible* to all sections of the program, and may be directly accessed from them (this is not good practice where subprograms are concerned). Pascal does not provide us with any means of building local 'scope walls' around our permanent variables, in order to restrict access to them. If variables are to be permanent, then they must also be global and hence their form and very existence cannot be concealed.

The scope rules for a Modula-2 module are similar. Like Pascal, any variables that are declared within a procedure (subprogram) will exist only while the procedure is being executed. Also, any variables that are declared in the outer part of a MODULE will normally be permanent, regardless of the actual type of MODULE involved (with the one exception of local modules that are declared within procedures). Within a MODULE, any variable that is declared in the outer part will be visible to all the components of the MODULE: but unless it is specifically EXPORTed such a variable will not be visible to the components of any other MODULE. (Of course, where a variable *is* EXPORTed, its value can then be altered by 'client' modules.) In particular, any items declared in a DEFINITION module can be regarded as having also been declared in the outer part of the corresponding IMPLEMENTATION module.

For a large program, and especially for one being constructed by a team of programmers, the consequences of all of this are important. Once an agreed interface to a module, as represented by its DEFINITION part, has been determined, it is possible for the implementation part to be written and tested in isolation, provided that this does not IMPORT objects from modules that are being developed in parallel. Apart from any such IMPORTs, the only coupling that exists between the module and the rest of the program is defined by the procedures, types and variables in the definition part: and so it is possible for the local data structures to be chosen (and

```
                    OUTER MODULE A
```

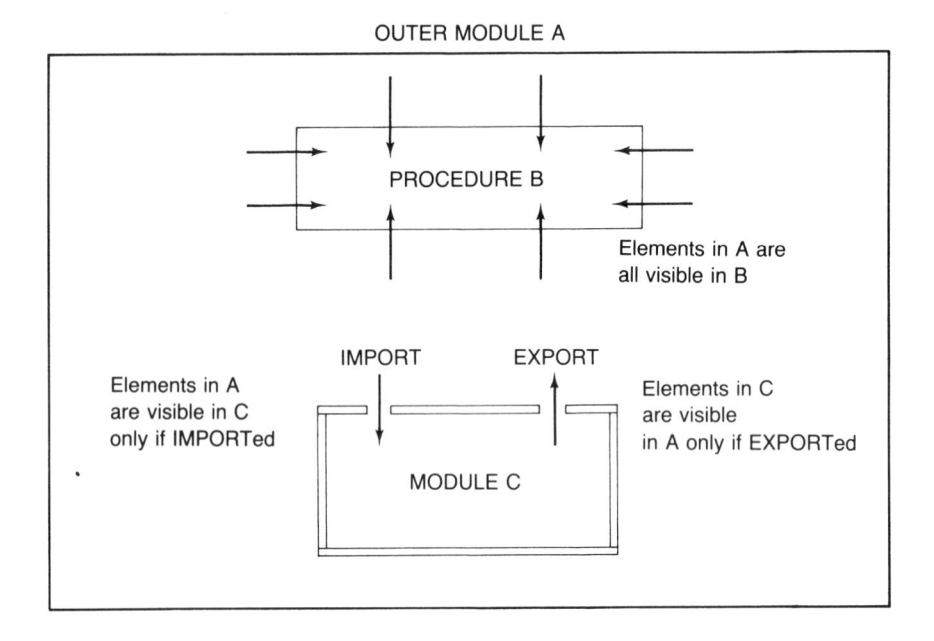

**Figure 10.5** Scope rules for procedures and local modules declared within a module.

changed if necessary) solely to suit the needs of the functions that are provided by the module.

We will be examining the issues involved in this at a later point, but even at this stage it may already be apparent that a Modula-2 program needs to be designed in a rather different way from (say) a Pascal program, if we are to make good use of such features of the language.

## 10.4 MODULEs within MODULEs

So far, all discussion about modules and their component parts has assumed that each part of a MODULE will be stored in a separate file, and that it can be compiled as a physically distinct entity. However, as was emphasized in the last section, the purposes of the MODULE construct are to provide a means of enforcing scope control and to provide a way of packaging 'objects' together with the procedures that operate on them. So it is a logical extension to find that a MODULE structure can be created *within* another MODULE, in order to 'draw a wall' around a section of its workings. Such an internal MODULE can have the full MODULE structure of types, constants, variables and procedures, and may even have further MODULEs nested within it. However, it cannot have definition and implementation

**Table 10.1** Visibility of 'objects' in the procedures and modules of program Wordcount (Figure 10.6).

|  |  | Wordcount | Readfile |  | Display |  |  |
|---|---|---|---|---|---|---|---|
| Declared in |  |  | main body | Getword | main body | Incrementcount | Total |
| Wordcount: |  |  |  |  |  |  |  |
|  | length | √ | x | x | x | x | x |
|  | Read | √ | √ | √ | x | x | x |
|  | WriteLn | √ | x | x | √ | √ | √ |
| Readfile: |  |  |  |  |  |  |  |
|  | endFile | √ | √ | √ | x | x | x |
|  | period | x | √ | √ | x | x | x |
|  | currentChar | x | x | √ | x | x | x |
| Display: |  |  |  |  |  |  |  |
|  | numberofWords | x | x | x | √ | √ | √ |
|  | Total | √ | x | x | √ | √ | √ |

parts, because it is not compiled separately from the containing MODULE. Such a MODULE is referred to as a **local module**, and it can be used to define further scope limits, as well as to provide a further degree of information-hiding when required. The *scope* of a local module is very similar to that of a procedure, in that any objects that are declared within the module will be visible only within that module.

However, unlike the case of the procedure, variables declared in the local module will be permanent, unless the module is declared within a procedure, and a local module can use the EXPORT statement to make 'gaps' in the scope wall, in order to make some of its objects visible to the code of the outer module. Furthermore, again unlike the case of a procedure, for which any permanent data objects declared in the surrounding module are visible, the objects of the outer module are visible to the code of the inner module only if they are included in its IMPORT list. So the scope wall acts as a two-directional constraint upon the flow of information between the nested modules.

Figure 10.5 shows these ideas in a diagrammatic form. It also compares the situation for a procedure declared within a MODULE to that for a MODULE that is declared within a MODULE.

Figure 10.6 shows a small program module that contains two inner local modules (it is a rather artificial division of information, purely for the sake of the exercise). Table 10.1 shows the visibility of objects at any of the key points in the code.

148   THE ROLE OF THE MODULE

**Figure 10.6** Example program using local modules.

(* This program is a modified version of the program Textcount that was used in Chapter 5. Unlike Textcount, it simply counts the number of words in a file. Words are terminated by one of the characters
* space
* comma
* semi-colon
* period (full stop)
* end of line
and for each word found the program prints a period character on the user's screen. *)

(* The program is constructed in the form of an outer module that makes use of two inner modules. One of these handles the word recognition, while the other maintains a count of words and prints the period characters. The division is very artificial, but demonstrates the use of inner modules. *)

MODULE Wordcount;          (* this is the outer module *)
FROM InOut IMPORT Read, Write, WriteLn, WriteString, WriteCard, EOL, Done;

VAR
    length : CARDINAL;     (* used to hold word length from Getcount *)

(* now the first inner module *)

    MODULE Readfile;
    IMPORT Read, EOL, Done;
    EXPORT Getword, endFile;

    CONST
        period = '.';       (* the character constants used as word terminators *)
        comma = ',';
        semicolon = ';';
        space = 40C;
        null = 0C;

    VAR
        endFile : BOOLEANS;  (* used to indicate no more words available *)

    (* Getword returns the number of alpha characters in the next word in the file – this is not used in this version of the program. *)

    PROCEDURE Getword (VAR charCount : CARDINAL);
    VAR
        currentChar : CHAR;   (* holds each character read in *)
    BEGIN
        charCount := 0;
        LOOP
            Read(currentChar);

```
        IF NOT Done       (* check for eof *)
        THEN
          endFile := TRUE;
          EXIT;
        ELSE
          IF (currentChar >= 'A') AND (currentChar <= 'Z')
          THEN
            currentChar := CHR(ORD(currentChar)−ORD('A')+ORD('a'));
          END; (* if *)
          IF (currentChar >= 'a') AND (currentChar <= 'z')
          THEN
            INC(charCount);
          ELSIF (( currentChar = space) OR (currentChar = comma)
            OR (currentChar = semicolon) OR (currentChar = EOL))
            AND (charCount > 0)
          THEN
            RETURN
          END; (* if *)
        END; (* if *)
      END; (* LOOP *)
    END Getword;

BEGIN (* main body of Readfile *)
  endFile := FALSE;
END Readfile;


(* now the second inner module, which handles display of the final count and prints a dot
   for each word read in *)


MODULE Display;

IMPORT WriteString, WriteCard, Write, WriteLn;
EXPORT Incrementcount, Total;

CONST
  maxline = 40;            (* max no of dots per line *)
VAR
  numberofWords : CARDINAL;
  dotCount : CARDINAL;


  (* Incrementcount adds one to internal word count, and prints a dot *)


PROCEDURE Incrementcount;
BEGIN
  INC(numberofWords);
  Write('.');
  INC(dotCount);
```

```
        IF (dotCount > maxline )
        THEN
          WriteLn;
          dotCount := 0;
        END; (* if *)
     END Incrementcount;

     (* Total prints the final word count on the screen *)

     PROCEDURE Total;
     BEGIN
       WriteLn;
       WriteCard(numberofWords,6); WriteString(' words ');
       WriteLn;
     END Total;

     BEGIN (* main body of Display *)
       numberofWords := 0;
       dotCount := 0;
     END Display;

  BEGIN (* main body of outer module *)
    LOOP
      Getword(length);
      IF (length > 0) THEN Incrementcount END;
      IF endFile THEN EXIT END;
    END; (* loop *)
    Total;
  END Wordcount.
```

**Figure 10.6**  *cont.*

Note that in this example the IMPORT directive used with a local module does not require the use of a FROM, and the EXPORT directive does not use a QUALIFIED. One reason for the first point is fairly evident: we do not need a FROM to instruct the compiler to search for any external files. The second needs to be explained a little more fully and also involves expanding a little more on the first point.

When using an EXPORT directive within a definition module, we must use the reserved word QUALIFIED with it. The reserved word QUALIFIED enforces a requirement that any reference made in another module to one of the objects in the QUALIFIED export list should have the identifier of the module preceding that of the object, separated from it by a period character. For example, if we were using the library module InOut, we would expect to refer to the procedures Read and WriteLn by their full identifiers, which are:

>    InOut.Read(ch);

and

>    InOut.WriteLn;

However, the reserved word FROM has the secondary effect of automatically 'de-qualifying' the items in its list, so that we can just use their identifiers without the additional qualifying field.

In a large program, the use of QUALIFIED makes it possible to avoid clashes of identifiers, which can occur if different modules EXPORT objects that have the same name, and hence its use with definition parts is mandatory. To use the mechanism to avoid such clashes, though, it is necessary to avoid de-qualifying the object names using FROM. We do so using a special form of IMPORT directive:

>    IMPORT <modulename>;

Using this form, the only field following the reserved word IMPORT will be the name of the relevant module. When the compiler encounters this, all the items in the EXPORT list of that module will be made accessible automatically, and any references to their identifiers must use the full form, as in

>    〈modulename〉.〈itemname〉

So for the case of the library module InOut, using the statement

>    IMPORT InOut;

in a MODULE will render all the items in InOut visible, and then they must be referenced by using the qualified form, as in:

>    InOut.Read(ch);

and

>    InOut.WriteLn;

Most programmers soon weary of typing identifiers when using this form of IMPORT!

Since local modules can be regarded as a special form of MODULE, and as their compilation involves no reading of separate files, we can usually omit QUALIFIED, and the use of FROM in identifying a .sym file has no meaning. However, since it is still possible (though unlikely) that we can encounter the conflicting use of identifiers, it is possible to use QUALIFIED and FROM with such a module.

## 10.5 Partitioning the declarations within a MODULE

All of the discussion about module structure in this chapter has so far been largely concerned with describing the scope rules that determine the 'visibility' of data, together with examining the requirements that arise from the use of separate compilation. These issues are very much concerned with the *mechanics* of constructing a program in Modula-2. However, to construct our programs in an effective manner, we also need to understand the *logical* basis that should underlie any partitioning of a program into modules, so as to be able to exploit its benefits as fully as possible.

In this section we address the issues of *where* within a module particular declarations might best be positioned, leaving the discussion about the actual criteria that should be used for decomposing a program into modules for consideration in Chapters 12 and 13. For the moment we are concerned with finding answers to the two questions of how to divide the declarations of objects between the definition and implementation parts of a module, and when to make use of a local module.

### 10.5.1 The definition part

As a fairly sound rule of thumb, the definition part should not normally contain any declarations for items that are not also included in the EXPORT list. As a corollary to this, no item should be present in the EXPORT list of a MODULE unless it is really necessary for it to be visible outside that module.

Apart from the matter of good style, there is an important practical point here. Changes that are made to declarations that occur within the implementation part of a MODULE will require only that the implementation part be recompiled, whereas any change to the form of the definition part will require that *all* the modules that IMPORT from it should be recompiled. The latter may be a very large and complex task for some systems.

In particular, it is important to avoid positioning the declaration of any item in the definition part solely on the basis of 'we might want to EXPORT it later'. If such a change does become necessary, then the relevant declaration will have to be placed in the definition part at that time – but only then. Things that we 'might' want to do ought to be confined to those considerations that have a sound basis in our design strategy, and will occur only rarely. Indeed, when we look at the question of design we will see that some methods place great emphasis upon fixing the form of the definition part as early as possible.

### 10.5.2 The implementation part

Every data object that does not need to be declared in the definition part must be declared in this part, so its contents are determined largely by default. The experienced Modula-2 programmer will also make maximum use of the facilities of the main body of the module for initializing variables. Where initialization is concerned, it is important to ensure that there are no items in the EXPORT list that are included solely for the purposes of initialization, and that could therefore be more appropriately placed in the main body of the module. For the programmer who is writing Modula-2 programs for the first time, this feature does require a different approach to program design, but it is one that can be of great help when seeking to use information-hiding within a design, since it enables the local initialization of global structures.

At this point, one other feature that is concerned with declarations made within separately compiled modules should be mentioned, namely **opaque export** of a type.

Where a type is declared within a definition part, the full details of the declaration will be available to any importing modules. For an enumeration type, the export of the type identifier will automatically cause the export of the identifiers of the enumerated constants. Similarly, for a record type (as described in Chapter 11), export of the type identifier automatically causes export of the identifiers and form of the record fields too. In such cases, the export can be considered as *transparent*.

In the case of opaque export, only the type identifier is declared in the definition module, and the full declaration is then provided in the implementation part. For practical purposes, opaque export is limited to use with pointer types (which are also described in Chapter 11). However, because a pointer type is bound to another type, which is usually a record type, the use of opaque export makes it possible to hide the details of this latter type, and hence provides additional support for the ideas about information-hiding that underlie much of this chapter.

As a very simple example of this form, we may have a definition part structured as follows:

```
DEFINITION MODULE Booklist;
(* example of declaring an opaque type *)


EXPORT QUALIFIED bookptr, NextTitle;
TYPE
    bookptr;    (* this is opaque export *)


(* now a procedure which makes use of this type *)
PROCEDURE NextTitle(VAR title: ARRAY OF CHAR; nextbook: bookptr);
END Booklist.
```

where the type bookptr is an opaque export. The first part of the corresponding implementation part may then look something like the following:

```
IMPLEMENTATION MODULE Booklist;
CONST
   titlelength = 49;                          (* max length of title stored *)
   authorlength = 29;                         (* max length of author's name *)
TYPE
   bookptr = POINTER TO bookrecord;           (* now declare this fully *)
   bookrecord = RECORD                        (* details of a book *)
      title : ARRAY [0..titlelength] OF CHAR;
      author: ARRAY [0..authorlength] OF CHAR;
      instock: BOOLEAN;
   END; (* bookrecord *)
VAR
headoflist : bookptr;


(* example of a procedure that uses the type bookptr *)
PROCEDURE NextTitle(VAR thistitle: ARRAY OF CHAR; nextbook: bookptr);
BEGIN
   ...
```

By using opaque export in this way, any programs that make use of this module can access and manipulate records of the type bookrecord indirectly, while the actual form of bookrecord is kept completely concealed.

### 10.5.3 Local modules

Local modules are not really a general purpose programming feature, since a well constructed module will rarely require to have 'inner' scope walls drawn around its information structures. However, the use of a local module may occasionally avoid the need to construct a trivially small separate module, in order to conceal the knowledge of some low-level feature, and that is unlikely to be utilized by any other module than the one that encompasses it.

When we come to examine concurrency and exception handling in Modula-2, we will find that they have a number of roles that can usefully be performed by inner modules. For the moment, the best guideline is to avoid making use of local modules as a general programming device, since their presence generally does not make the code of a MODULE any easier to read or modify.

# EXERCISES

**10.1** Re-write the simple stack module shown in Figure 10.1 to provide a more general facility so that a type Stack is also exported, and so that variables of the type Stack can be declared in other modules. In modifying this module so that it can be used with any such stack, what other items need to be made 'visible', and what other procedures are needed?

**10.2** Modify the program shown in Figure 10.6 so that it uses conflicting identifiers (for example, both Getword and Incrementcount could be renamed Next), and then use the qualified form of EXPORT with these so that the program will work.

**10.3** Write (and test) a separate module (with definition and implementation parts) that provides a simple buffer to hold a single string of characters, together with Putstring and Getstring procedures that can be used to enter and extract a message.

[Hint: select an 'end of string' character which can be used to indicate the end of a transfer.]

# Chapter 11
# Structured Data Types

11.1 The use of structure
11.2 The ARRAY
11.3 The RECORD
11.4 Pointer types and dynamic storage allocation
Exercises

## 11.1 The use of structure

Most of the predefined and user-defined data types that we have encountered so far, such as INTEGER, CHAR etc, can be considered as being unstructured. This means that variables of these types have no internal components, so that a data element of such a type will have only a single *scalar* value associated with it. The main exception to this in the types described so far is the idea of a set type, since a set does have a number of distinct elements, and so a set type should perhaps be considered as a semi-structured type.

There are various reasons for making provision for the use of *structured* types in a programming language, where these are data types that have some internal structure in the form of identifiable elements. One reason is that our programs often need to model the real world in which we work and operate. In the real world we are likely to find that data has some form of structure associated with it: for example, a person's name has a structure (although not necessarily the same structure in all countries), being formed from an ordered sequence of strings of characters, where both the ordering of characters in a string and the ordering of the strings are significant. Likewise, a ship's position has a two-component structure (latitude and longitude), while an aircraft's has a three-component one.

In these examples, the components of an item of data are likely to be of the same form or type, and such a structure is often referred to as a **vector**. (You might not think of your name as a vector, but it conforms to the idea, since it is formed from an ordered sequence of strings of characters.) Note too that a vector implicitly contains the idea of ordering within it, in the sense that some convention must be adopted so that we can correctly identify the individual components. In the domain of computer programming, the fact that this is a *convention* is especially noticeable when we need to express a date as a sequence of integer values. People in the UK normally order the components of a date in the following way:

> day, month, year

so that the 26th August 1987 is:

> 260887

In the USA, however, the date is normally ordered as

> month, day, year

so that the same date is represented as:

> 082687

A further convention sometimes used is

> year, month, day

which gives

> 870826

providing obvious opportunities for confusion!

Within a program, of course, we may find it convenient to store such a form of data as a mix of different data types (for example, an enumerated type Months could be used when storing the date). Often this may be the most practical form to use, since it allows the structures within a program to reflect the real-world structures that are familiar to the people that will use it. For example a program may store some data about a book. The details of the book might include such information as author, number of pages, size, publication date, etc. and obviously this combined information really needs to be stored using a mix of data types, rather than trying to contort the information so that it fits into one data type. (It would be possible to store each item of the data as a character string – but this is not necessarily appropriate or efficient for many required operations.) Usually we try to select the form of storage that is most appropriate for each item on the basis of the forms of operation that we will be performing upon it.

So we find that there are two prime requirements for the structured data forms: one is to store ordered sets of data in which each element will be of the same type; and the other is to store data items that have elements of different types.

The next two sections examine the ways in which each of these two forms is handled in Modula-2. The Pascal programmer will find little that is particularly new about these, although there are some changes of notation that may need to be noted.

## 11.2 The ARRAY

The array is the most straightforward form of structured data type, and is one that is to be found in almost all programming languages. An array consists of an ordered list or vector that is composed entirely of elements of the same data type. The elements of an array will effectively occupy a contiguous set of storage locations in the computer's memory, so that there will be no vacant positions in the array.

The elements of an array can therefore be identified by their position, normally by using an **index value**, and the range of possible index values will need to be specified when the array is declared. So the declaration of an array must specify both the type of element and the array size, this being determined from the boundary values declared for the index. The range of values to be used may be specified either by using two constant expressions for the upper and lower bounds, as in [-2..19] or by using the identifier of the type that is used for the index. (For practical reasons this does not apply to standard types such as CARDINAL or INTEGER.) Where specific boundary values are used, these can have positive or negative values, but the upper bound will normally be greater than or equal to the lower bound.

The elements of an array can be of any type, including scalar types, procedure types, and structured data types. However, the index must be of an ordinal type, since it is necessary to enumerate a value of the index in order to determine the position of an element within the array. Most commonly we use such types as sub-ranges of the standard integer types, CHAR and any user-defined enumeration types for the index. (BOOLEAN is also a permissible index type, but is obviously a bit limited.)

An array type will be declared within the TYPE block. Some examples of such declarations are:

```
TYPE
  Dayrange = [28..31]    (* needed for the third example *)
  Velocity = ARRAY [0..2] OF INTEGER;
  Bitmap   = ARRAY [-99..99] OF BOOLEAN;
  Enddates = ARRAY Months OF Dayrange;
```

An array may also be declared directly within the VAR block, as in the following examples:

```
VAR
    textBuffer  =  ARRAY [0..79] OF CHAR;
    shoeStock   =  ARRAY [0..maxFitting] OF CARDINAL;
```

As the elements of an array can be arrays, too, it is possible to declare arrays with as many dimensions as we wish, although in practice it is quite unusual to use arrays with more than three dimensions. A multi-dimensional array may also be declared more directly by specifying the list of ranges, with the elements of the list being separated by commas. An example of this is the following declaration of the two-dimensional array 'Calendar':

```
Calendar = ARRAY [1..31],Months OF Days;
```

which could also be declared as

```
Calendar = ARRAY [1..31] OF ARRAY Months OF Days;
```

Of course, as always with multi-dimensioned arrays, this could also be organized as:

```
Calendar = ARRAY Months,[1..31] OF Days;
```

The two declarations represent the same logical object, although the organization of the physical storage is transposed between them.

A particular element of an array is designated by its index value, as in the assignment statements:

```
shoeStock[3] := 0;
newBitmap[-12] := TRUE;
```

Where the array is multi-dimensional we need to specify the appropriate set of index values, as in:

```
calendar1988[1,Jan] := Fri;
today := calendar1988[day, thisMonth];
```

An index value can be a constant, a variable or any expression of the appropriate type.

An element of an array can be used almost anywhere that it would be appropriate to use a scalar variable of the same element type, as in the conditional statement

```
IF ( textBuffer[0] = EOL ) THEN ...
```

and in the procedure call

    INC(shoeStock[selection]);

Where we need to manipulate complete sections of an array in some way, then we usually make use of the FOR loop, as in the example below of initializing the values of the elements of an array:

    FOR i := 0 TO maxFitting DO shoeStock[i] := 0 END;

The FOR loop is widely used when manipulating arrays, since it is well suited to handling those operations that involve accessing a sequence of array elements.

Where two arrays are of the same type, the complete contents of one array can be copied to the other with a single assignment statement. There will of course be no need to make any explicit use of the array index: the two arrays are specified simply by using their identifiers. An example of this might make use of the following declarations:

    TYPE
      Buffer = ARRAY [0..maxString] OF CHAR;
    VAR
      inputBuffer,outputBuffer : Buffer;

and then, later in the module, the single assignment statement

    outputBuffer := inputBuffer;

provides a valid way of specifying that the contents of the array inputBuffer should be copied to the corresponding elements of the array outputBuffer.

### 11.2.1 Strings

A common need that arises in programming is to handle strings of characters and, like many other programming languages, Modula-2 provides the useful notion of a **string constant**. This consists of a sequence of characters, which are enclosed within quote marks. (Both double and single quote marks may be used for this, but the opening and closing quote marks of a string must be identical.) Some examples of string constants are:

    "Error – open parenthesis expected"
    "Don't give up the ship"
    'Hello user'

Where we wish to use a quote mark of either type within a string, as in the second example above, we must use the other form as the string delimiter.

String constants are treated as arrays of type CHAR, and where a string contains more than one character (that is, it consists of *n* characters, where *n*>1), it is regarded as having been declared in the form

    ARRAY [0..n−1] OF CHAR;

(A revision to the original standard (Wirth, 1985) regards a single character such as "A" as being of the type

    ARRAY [0..0] OF CHAR

for greater consistency.)

In particular, a string constant with fewer than *n* characters can be assigned to an array of type CHAR with dimensions that are greater than *n*, simply by using a single assignment statement. (This can be considered as a type-specific extension to the idea of array assignment introduced above.) So where we have the declarations

    CONST
      Errorstars = " **** error **** ";
    VAR
      errorBuffer : ARRAY [0..79] OF CHAR;

(the upper limit of the range is given specifically in this case, to make the example clearer, but of course it would be better style to express this by using a symbolic constant), then the following assignment statements are all valid:

    errorBuffer := "Error 20 − semi-colon expected";
    errorBuffer := "missing right parenthesis";
    errorBuffer := Errorstars;

So this is one of the few occasions where it is not necessary to include an index value after the name of the array. A string constant is the only form of constant that can be used with array assignment, since there are no means provided for defining any others.

In each of the examples above, the array errorBuffer has bounds that are larger than those of the string constants assigned to it. In such a case, the characters in the string will be copied into the leading elements of the array (regardless of the range of index values), and then a null character (0C) will be copied into at least the first element of the unused portion of the array. This convention of identifying the unused part of an array through the use of the null character is a feature of the language, and so will be recognized by the standard Modula-2 library routines. So a call to a library procedure, such as

    WriteString(errorBuffer);

will produce the appropriate output for each of our previous examples.

Since the value of the packing character used to fill out the end of the array is standard (at least within an implementation), it is also possible to write our own routines to handle variable-length character strings. To show the general form of algorithm that can be used for such a task, the body of a 'personal' version of the procedure WriteString might look like

```
CONST
  null = 0C;
VAR
  characterIndex : CARDINAL;
BEGIN
  characterIndex := 0;    (* initialize the index *)
    (* the test here may not be enough – how big is a buffer ? *)
  WHILE ( errorBuffer[characterIndex] <> null ) DO
    Write( errorBuffer[characterIndex] );
    INC(characterIndex);
  END; (* while *)
END;
```

(It may be convenient to refer to this as the procedure MyWriteString.)

### 11.2.2 Open arrays

As Pascal programmers will be aware, the specification and use of arrays for parameters of procedures is somewhat inconvenient in many implementations of Pascal, since a procedure declaration may need to specify the dimension of any arrays which are to be used as parameters. This is a very inflexible form, and in Modula-2 it has been replaced with the more practical concept of the open array.

In order to use an array as a parameter of a Modula-2 procedure, it is necessary to declare the formal specification of that parameter as an array of the appropriate type, but no size need be specified for it. An example of this is the declaration:

```
PROCEDURE MyWriteString( textBuffer : ARRAY OF CHAR );
```

On a call to this procedure, the formal parameter textBuffer will be replaced by an actual parameter, which in turn can be any array of type CHAR, of any size. Within the procedure itself, regardless of the range of index values declared for the actual array used, the formal array is regarded as having a lower index value of 0, and its upper bound can be determined by using the standard function HIGH that was described briefly in Chapter 9.

So if the actual parameter used in a call to the procedure MyWriteString is an array that was declared as

```
VAR
  outBuffer : ARRAY [ -9..8 ] OF CHAR;
```

that is, as an array of CHAR having 18 elements, then on the call

```
MyWriteString(outBuffer);
```

within the procedure MyWriteString, the formal array textBuffer will be regarded as having a lower bound of 0 for its index, and an upper bound of 17. This latter value will be obtained by using a call of HIGH(textBuffer) from within MyWriteString.

So it is now possible to complete the example that was begun in the last subsection, and to create our own procedure to print character strings, as follows:

```
PROCEDURE MyWriteString( textBuffer : ARRAY OF CHAR );
CONST
  null = 0C;
VAR
  characterIndex : CARDINAL;
BEGIN
  characterIndex := 0;    (* initialize the index *)
  WHILE ( characterIndex < HIGH(textBuffer) ) AND
        ( textBuffer[characterIndex] <> null ) DO
    Write(textBuffer[characterIndex]);
    INC(characterIndex);
  END; (* while *)
END MyWriteString;
```

Of course, the function HIGH can be used with arrays of any element type, not only those of type CHAR. To show this, we can write a short function procedure that is to compare two arrays of integer values. If the two arrays are of equal size and if the value of each element of the first array is equal to that of the corresponding element of the second, then the procedure will return a value of TRUE, otherwise it will return a value of FALSE. So our procedure might look like the following:

```
PROCEDURE Vectorsequal(firstVector,secondVector : ARRAY OF INTEGER) : BOOLEAN;
VAR
  index : CARDINAL;
```

```
BEGIN
  IF ( HIGH(firstVector) <> HIGH(secondVector) ) THEN RETURN FALSE END;
  FOR index := 0 TO HIGH(firstVector) DO
    IF ( firstVector[index] <> secondVector[index] ) THEN RETURN FALSE END;
  END; (* for *)
  RETURN TRUE; (* only get here if vectors are equal *)
END Vectorsequal;
```

This algorithm first checks that the two arrays have the same dimensions, and then compares them element by element. If one pair of elements is found that fails to meet the required condition, the procedure will terminate at that point. Only if the FOR loop terminates correctly, so that no pairs of values have been found that are not equal, will the procedure return a value of TRUE. (This procedure also demonstrates that Modula-2 is suitable for use in constructing mathematical packages, since it can cope with data structures of varying size, unlike the 'standard' form of Pascal.)

Note that we can legally place a RETURN statement in the middle of a loop in this way, and thus break out of the FOR loop – although, as with the EXIT statement, the effect is limited. The only option that this provides is to terminate execution of the procedure, and to return control to the caller along with a status value.

This should be a sufficient description of the form that arrays take in Modula-2. The array is a fairly universal structure, and is also a very powerful one. In the next section we go on to examine the data structure that contains elements of differing types, namely the RECORD.

## 11.3 The RECORD

While an array comprises elements that are all of the same type, the elements that make up the structure of a RECORD can be a mix of many types including other records and arrays too. We refer to the components of a RECORD as its **fields**. The idea of RECORDs will be familiar to anyone who has used Pascal (and the Modula-2 form is very similar), but there is no real equivalent data structure in many older programming languages, such as FORTRAN.

The TYPE declaration for a RECORD must specify the order of the fields, the type of each field, and an identifier for each field. The field identifiers are important, since they are used as 'tags' when accessing and manipulating the individual fields of the record.

A TYPE declaration for a RECORD begins with the reserved word RECORD, and then the fields are declared as an ordered sequence of variable declarations, with the whole structure being terminated by the reserved word END. As usual, the declarations within a record are separated by semi-colons. Two examples of such TYPE declarations are:

```
TYPE
  Dates = RECORD
    day : [1..31];
    month : Months;
    year : [1950..2100];
  END;

    (* an enumerated type needed in the next record *)
  employmentStatus = (working,sick,retired);

  Employees = RECORD
    name : ARRAY [0..Maxnamesize] OF CHAR;
    payNumber : CARDINAL;
    currentStatus : employmentStatus;
    monthlyPay : CARDINAL;
    incrementDate : Dates;
  END;
```

Having declared the types Dates and Employees, we can then proceed to declare variables of those types, and make use of them in our program. Indeed, we might well find it convenient to declare arrays of the type Employees, as in the declaration

```
VAR
  staff : ARRAY [0..Maxstaff] OF Employees;
  today : Dates;
```

The equivalent form, which is

```
VAR
  staff : ARRAY [0..Maxstaff] OF
          RECORD
            name : ARRAY [0..Maxnamesize] OF CHAR;
            payNumber : CARDINAL;
            currentStatus : employmentStatus;
            monthlyPay : CARDINAL;
            incrementDate : Dates;
          END;
  today : Dates;
```

would be equally valid. However, this style can be considered as less practical, since it is essentially less flexible. (This is a point that will become clearer when we consider dynamic storage allocation in the next section.) It is also constraining an abstract concept (that of the 'staff member') by limiting it to this one data structure.

Obviously, for a record structure to be of any real use, we need to be able to access individual fields within a record variable. An individual field of a record is specified by appending the identifier of the appropriate field to the identifier of the record variable, using a period character as the separator. So to refer to the first field of the variable today, we would use the composite identifier today.day. When using this form, this component of the record is treated as being a simple variable of the field type, and so it can be used anywhere that it is possible to use a variable of such a type. This allows us to write such expressions as the following:

```
today.day := 7;
INC(today.year);
today.month := Apr;
IF (today.month = Dec) AND (today.day = 31) THEN INC(today.year) END;
```

When an array of records is used in a module, the variable identifier is extended to include an index value within the identifier field used for the variable. In this way, we get expressions such as:

```
staff[6].payNumber := 100462;
staff[new].name := "John Smith";
staff[i].monthlyPay := payment[ staff[i].payNumber ];
```

In the last case, we have used one of the fields of a record as the index to the CARDINAL array payment. (It is assumed that this particular array can hardly be an array with elements of type INTEGER, of course!)

Records are a very useful facility when handling composite forms of data but, as these examples show, they can involve some rather unwieldy notation. To help with this, Modula-2 provides a shorter form for specifying the fields of a record, by making use of the WITH statement.

### 11.3.1 The WITH statement

A WITH statement is used to 'qualify' a record within a segment of code. The record that is specified as the argument of the WITH statement will be implicit within the scope of the statement sequence bounded by the WITH clause, and so it need not be used to qualify any references that are made to field identifiers within that segment of code. In keeping with the style of Modula-2, the WITH clause is terminated by the reserved word END. So a WITH statement has the form:

WITH ⟨recorddesignator⟩ DO ⟨statementsequence⟩ END;

Using WITH we could rewrite the last example of an expression as:

```
WITH staff[i] DO
   monthlyPay := payment[payNumber];
END; (* with *)
```

168    STRUCTURED DATA TYPES

While in this example there seem to be few reasons for using a WITH statement, it becomes much more useful if we need to manipulate several fields of a record at one time – perhaps for the purpose of initialization or assignment. (When we come to the use of pointers with transient data storage in the next section, this will be seen to apply particularly to the initialization stage.) Still keeping with the last example, we can see how it might be extended to a larger block of statements as in the sequence:

```
FOR i := 0 TO Maxstaff DO
  WITH staff[i] DO
    monthlyPay := payment[payNumber];
    WriteString(name); WriteString(" ");
    WriteString("this month's pay is ");
    WriteCard(monthlyPay,6); WriteLn;
  END (* with *)
END; (* for *)
```

where it qualifies the fields monthlyPay, payNumber and name.

The WITH statement can be used to produce a form of code that is more easily read and understood, and we will return to this issue in the next section. For the moment it is worth looking at the other significant feature in the use of records: the facility for providing different options for the structure of a particular type of record.

### 11.3.2  Variant sections

While many problems can be solved with only one form of data structure within a record, it is sometimes necessary to be able to accommodate a number of possible variations in the data structure used within a single record type.

The structure used in Modula-2 is similar to the form used in Pascal. Where we wish to declare a field within a record that can take different forms, we use a separate **tag field** within the record, the value of which is used to select the appropriate variation in the form of data structure to be used. In the declaration of the RECORD type, the value of the tag field is used within a CASE selector as a means of declaring the optional forms.

At this point, a simple example seems appropriate. This is constructed by making an extension to the earlier example of an employee record, by modifying it to handle employees who are paid weekly as well as those who are paid monthly:

```
Employees = RECORD
  name : ARRAY [0..Maxnamesize] OF CHAR;
  payNumber : CARDINAL;
  currentStatus : employmentStatus;
  CASE weekly : BOOLEAN OF
```

```
         TRUE : weeklyPay : CARDINAL; |
         FALSE : monthlyPay : CARDINAL;
                  companyPensionScheme : BOOLEAN
      END (* case *);
      incrementDate : Dates;
   END; (* employee record *)
```

So now, if an employee is paid on a weekly basis, then each record will contain a field that records the weekly pay. If the employee is paid on a monthly basis, then the record will contain both the monthly pay and also a field that indicates whether the employee belongs to the company pension scheme. Obviously, if we use tags of types other than BOOLEAN, we can declare more than two optional forms.

Note, too, that the tag field is an additional field that has been introduced into the record, and so it can be referenced in the same way as any other field. One example of its use is in such expressions as

```
   IF staff[i].weekly THEN ...
```

The usefulness of variant records is rather offset by the greater complexity that they introduce. For most programming applications they are not particularly elegant or necessary, and so their use should not be emphasized unduly. In particular, they provide an instance where strong typing cannot be used, since the compiler cannot know in advance where a particular form is to be used.

So far in this chapter we have been concerned with data forms that are essentially *static* – that is, they are declared within the program, so that permanent or temporary storage space can be allocated for them by the compiler. The extent of this allocation cannot then be extended or modified in any way while the program is executing. With arrays this is generally convenient, but when using record types this is less likely to be so, especially as the use of large pre-declared arrays of records can tie up a lot of storage unnecessarily. It may also be rather difficult to determine how much storage to allocate in advance, leading to overly large allocations for precautionary reasons. More significantly, though, it restricts the type of large data structure that we can create to those forms that can be represented using an array, and so may make it difficult to write a program that needs to model more complex forms of relationships, such as trees. The next section is therefore concerned with providing a brief survey of the *dynamic* forms of storage allocation, and their use in Modula-2.

## 11.4 Pointer types and dynamic storage allocation

All the structured variables examined so far have been 'static' ones that were declared at the beginning of a module or procedure, and accessed directly by making reference to their identifiers. In this section we consider the use of variables that are created during the execution of a program and can therefore be considered as 'dynamic' structures. Such variables are important when modelling systems and structures in the real world that may vary in size and even in details of form. Where the exact forms of these are not known sufficiently at compilation time, we generally find it particularly convenient to make use of dynamic data structures that can 'expand' and 'contract' as necessary. However, before getting into the details of the creation and use of such forms, we first need to consider how such variables can be accessed. The mechanism for doing this is provided by 'pointer' variables. A pointer type is used when we require a variable to act as an index (or pointer) to another variable. So its value at any time is only of indirect interest, in that it provides a means of accessing data stored in some other location. Hence the use of the term 'pointer'.

We can create pointers to provide access to variables of any type, although in practice they are primarily useful in association with record types. This is because a record type can contain one or more fields of the same type as the pointer used to address the record, which makes it possible to construct quite complex linked structures. Figure 11.1 shows how this scheme might work for some fairly simple linked structures. So while we can declare a pointer type that is to point to data of a scalar type such as INTEGER, or to an array of type CHAR, the usefulness of such a type is rather limited.

In a strongly typed language such as Modula-2, a pointer variable must have a well-defined type. This is determined through the type of the variable that it makes reference to, and the type checking rules can then be applied to any use that is made of a variable of this pointer type. (A pointer type is said to be **bound** to its associated data type.) Examples of such declarations are:

```
TYPE
    dayIndex = POINTER TO Dates;
    staffReference = POINTER TO Employees;
```

The reserved words POINTER TO are used in Modula-2 in preference to the rather terse notation that is used in Pascal, as this makes the role of such a type very much clearer. Having thus defined the type, we can proceed to declare variables of the type in the normal way, as in:

```
VAR
    newEmployee : staffReference;
    today, holiday : dayIndex;
```

and can then go on to assign values to these variables. Indeed, assignment is almost the only operation that we are permitted to perform upon a pointer variable. (We can also test for equality of pointers in a relational

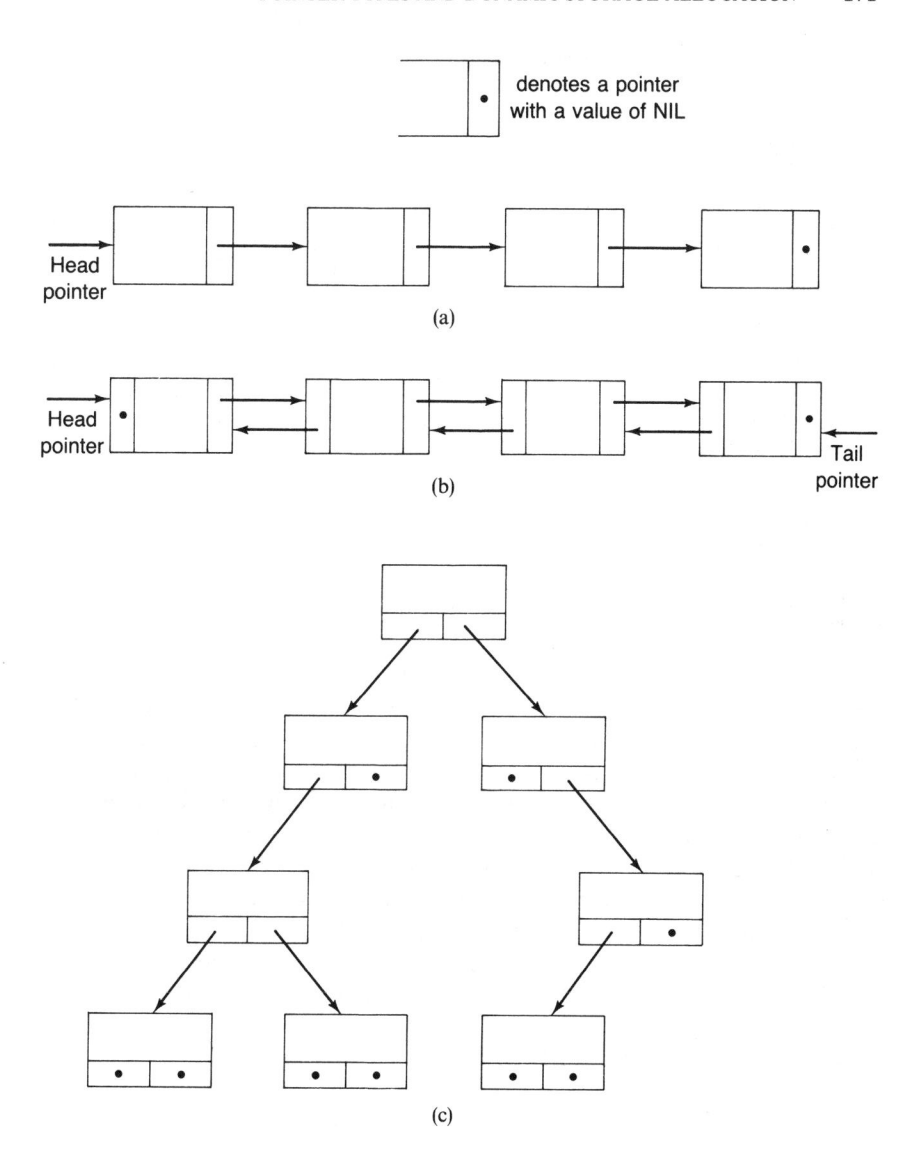

POINTER TYPES AND DYNAMIC STORAGE ALLOCATION    171

**Figure 11.1** Some simple linked data structures: (a) single linked list of records; (b) double linked list; (c) binary tree.


expression. This is something of a potential minefield, since it is the values of the *pointers*, and not the values of the objects that they reference, that is being compared – a point that can easily be overlooked.)

There is only one constant value that can be used with pointers, and this is the constant NIL. It is valid for use with all pointer types, and assigns a value to a pointer that can be considered as effectively 'empty', or pointing to 'nowhere'. So we can write such statements as

    holiday := NIL;

and

    IF ( today <> NIL ) THEN ...

A pointer variable may not be used to refer to any variable that has been declared within a program (and which is therefore 'static'). Such static objects may be referenced only through their identifiers (this permits more thorough checking by the compiler). So a pointer variable can be linked only to a variable that has been declared dynamically during program execution, and which is therefore 'anonymous', in that it does not possess an associated identifier. This means that we need some way of creating such anonymous variables and of removing them when they are no longer needed by the program.

Dynamic variables can be created by using the standard procedure ALLOCATE, and deleted by means of the complementary procedure DEALLOCATE. (Earlier versions of Modula-2 included procedures NEW and DISPOSE, which in turn made use of ALLOCATE and DEALLOCATE, but NEW and DISPOSE themselves have been deallocated in later versions!) Each of these procedures has only two parameters: the first must be a pointer variable, and the second specifies the amount of storage to be reserved for the variable. When the procedure ALLOCATE is executed, it will cause storage space to be allocated for a variable of the associated type for the pointer that is given as the first parameter, and it will place a value within the pointer variable itself that will refer to this storage location. ALLOCATE is usually able to determine the amount of storage required for the variable by using the standard procedure TSIZE, which has as its parameter the type of compound variable being used. (TSIZE is imported from the module SYSTEM, which is described more fully in Part III.) As an example, the call

    ALLOCATE(today,TSIZE(Dates));

will obtain sufficient storage space for a variable of the type Dates, and will copy its location into the pointer variable today. The use of such variables needs care of course, since if we subsequently assign a new value to the variable today, without having first saved its current value in any way, we will have lost the link to the anonymous variable and will be able neither to use it nor to reclaim the memory space that it occupies.

When handling static RECORD variables that have been declared in our program, the individual fields are accessed by using the form

    <identifier>.<fieldidentifier>

But with dynamic data storage, we need a slightly modified form of this mechanism. This requires that the 'identifier' be created by **dereferencing** the value of the pointer variable, through the use of the dereferencing operator. This is an 'up arrow' character, '↑' (on some keyboards this appears as a circumflex character). It is positioned after the identifier of the pointer variable, and has the same effect as a conventional static identifier. (That is, it dereferences a pointer and so gives access to the value in the associated location.) So in our example of the variable today, we can access its fields as

```
today ↑ .day;
today ↑ .month;
today ↑ .year;
```

So far so good, but of course we have not yet created a truly dynamic data structure by these means, since for every dynamic variable used we must declare a static pointer variable that is bound to that particular data type. To construct a data structure that is truly dynamic, and whose size is not constrained in any way by the data structures declared at compilation, we need to modify the form of the record so that it includes a field (or more than one field) that contains a variable of its own associated pointer type. To keep the example simple, we will use a new record type, and one that simply associates two items of data, the name of a town and its population. In addition to these we will include a third field, which will contain a pointer to another record variable of this type and can be used to link the record to another of the same type. The declaration for this looks like:

```
Townptr = POINTER TO Town;
Town = RECORD
   name       : ARRAY [0..Maxnamelength] OF CHAR;
   population : CARDINAL;
   nextTown   : Townptr;
END;
```

These records can now be linked in a 'chain': Figure 11.2 shows an example of such a linked structure, using the type just declared above. (Note that it is common usage to give pointer types an identifier that ends in ptr, in order more easily to distinguish them when in use.) However long the list of such records, we need to use only one 'header' pointer of type Townptr, which has been declared statically in the program and acts as an 'anchor' point by giving access to the 'head' record in the linked list.

The study of dynamic data structures such as single-linked lists, double-linked lists, trees, etc. is a large and important field, and not one that can be adequately covered in this text. So the example in Figure 11.3 contains a short program module that makes use of a simple linked list and shows how it can be manipulated in a simple manner.

174 STRUCTURED DATA TYPES

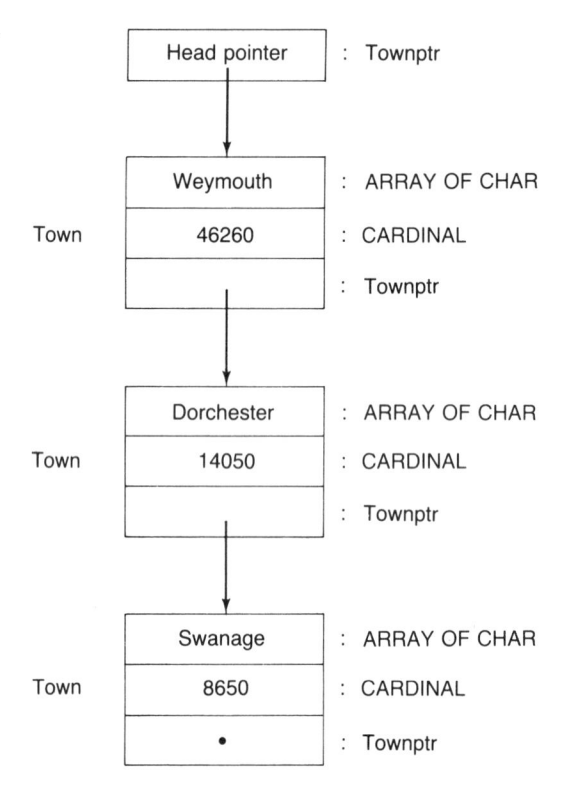

```
                    ┌─────────────────┐
                    │  Head pointer   │  : Townptr
                    └────────┬────────┘
                             │
                             ▼
                    ┌─────────────────┐
                    │   Weymouth      │  : ARRAY OF CHAR
            Town    ├─────────────────┤
                    │     46260       │  : CARDINAL
                    ├─────────────────┤
                    │        │        │  : Townptr
                    └────────┼────────┘
                             │
                             ▼
                    ┌─────────────────┐
                    │   Dorchester    │  : ARRAY OF CHAR
            Town    ├─────────────────┤
                    │     14050       │  : CARDINAL
                    ├─────────────────┤
                    │        │        │  : Townptr
                    └────────┼────────┘
                             │
                             ▼
                    ┌─────────────────┐
                    │    Swanage      │  : ARRAY OF CHAR
            Town    ├─────────────────┤
                    │     8650        │  : CARDINAL
                    ├─────────────────┤
                    │       •         │  : Townptr
                    └─────────────────┘
```

**Figure 11.2** Linked list using types Town and Townptr.


The dereferencing of pointer variables is quite a flexible form. We can chain pointers together too, as in the expression:

next↑.nextTown↑.nextTown↑.population := 0;

which will simply chain the pointers until it reaches the third record. (Note, though, that an expression of this sort is not very secure, since it will be valid only if the list of towns contains at least three entries.) Additionally, we should note that a RECORD is not limited in any way as to the types of pointers that it can contain, and so it is possible to declare quite complex structures, with sub-lists of widely differing types. However, programming with pointers needs practice and an orderly approach, since the consequences of failing to initialize variables correctly, or of losing a link, can be catastrophic!

**Figure 11.3** A simple program that makes use of a linked list.

(* This program maintains a simple linked list of records for the children in a class, ranked by age. The user has the following set of commands that can be used to manipulate the list:
  i – to insert a new entry in the list
  p – to print out the contents of the list, ordered by age
  q – to terminate the program
For simplicity we will assume that age for the children needs only to be measured in months and days, and that all the children have birthdays in the same calendar year. *)

MODULE Classlist;

FROM InOut IMPORT WriteString, Write, WriteLn, WriteCard, ReadString,
    ReadCard,Read;
FROM Storage IMPORT ALLOCATE, DEALLOCATE;
FROM SYSTEM IMPORT TSIZE;

CONST
  maxnamelength = 20;
TYPE
  Months = [1..12];
  Days = [1..31];
  Childptr = POINTER TO Child;
  Child = RECORD
    name : ARRAY [0..(maxnamelength−1)] OF CHAR;
    birthMonth : Months;
    birthDay : Days;
    nextChild : Childptr;
  END;

VAR
  oldestChild : Childptr;          (* points to head of the list *)
  ch : CHAR;                       (* used for command input *)

(* Addchild creates an entry for a new child, and prompts the user for the entries to each field. It then calls Insertrecord to add the record to the list. *)

PROCEDURE Addchild(VAR head : Childptr);
VAR
  newChild : Childptr;             (* temporary pointer for new record *)
BEGIN
  ALLOCATE(newChild,TSIZE(Child));
  WITH newChild ↑ DO
    WriteString("Name of child : ");
    ReadString(name); WriteLn;
    WriteString("Birthday – day : ");
    ReadCard(birthDay); WriteLn;
    WriteString("Birthday – month : ");
    ReadCard(birthMonth); WriteLn;
    nextChild := NIL;

```
        END; (* with *)
        Insertrecord(head,newChild);
      END Addchild;

        (* Insertrecord adds a record to the linked list. It contains clauses to handle the special
          conditions of an empty list and one where the new record becomes the first record. *)

      PROCEDURE Insertrecord(VAR head,newEntry : Childptr);
      VAR
        date : CARDINAL;                    (* compound of month and day for comparisons *)
        temp,last : Childptr;

      BEGIN
        data := newEntry↑.birthMonth*31 + newEntry↑.birthDay;
        IF head = NIL
        THEN
          head := newEntry;                 (* if empty list just add at front *)
        ELSIF (head↑.birthMonth*31 + head↑.birthDay) > date
          THEN
            newEntry↑.nextChild := head;    (* if new head record *)
            head := newEntry;
        ELSE
          temp := head;                     (* scan down the list *)
          WHILE (temp<>NIL) AND ( (temp↑.birthMonth*31 + temp↑.birthDay) < date)
          DO
            last := temp;
            temp := temp↑.nextChild;
          END; (* while *)
          last↑.nextChild := newEntry;      (* now add the record *)
          newEntry↑.nextChild := temp;
        END; (* if *)
      END Insertrecord;

        (* Printentries simply scans down the list and prints the information about each record. *)

      PROCEDURE Printentries(head:Childptr);
      VAR
        temp : Childptr;
      BEGIN
        temp := head;
        WHILE temp <> NIL DO
          WITH temp↑ DO
            WriteLn; WriteString(name);
            WriteString(" was born on "); WriteCard(birthDay,2);
            WriteString(" of month "); WriteCard(birthMonth,2);
            WriteLn;
          END; (* with *)
          temp := temp↑.nextChild;
        END; (* while *)
      END Printentries;
```

```
BEGIN   (* main body of program *)
  oldestChild := NIL;                       (* initialize list *)
  WriteLn;
  WriteString(" i to insert, p to print, q to quit");
  WriteLn;
  LOOP
    WriteString(" Please select option : ");
    Read(ch); Write(ch); WriteLn;
    CASE ch OF
       'i','I' : Addchild(oldestChild); |
       'p','P' : Printentries(oldestChild) ; |
       'q','Q' : EXIT
    ELSE
       WriteString("unknown option"); WriteLn;
    END; (* case *)
  END; (* loop *)
END Classlist.
```

**Figure 11.3**  *cont.*

### 11.4.1 Creating and deleting dynamic variables

In Modula-2, the pair of low-level procedures ALLOCATE and DEALLOCATE are imported from the MODULE Storage rather than being standard procedures. This may seem a little cumbersome (it is), but has a sound logical basis in that the handling of dynamic memory allocation during the execution of a program is not strictly an issue that should be handled by the Modula-2 run-time system, but rather should fall within the province of the underlying operating system. So the MODULE Storage connects the requirements of the program to the facilities of the operating system, and in doing so it reduces the strength of the coupling between the Modula-2 compiler and its operating system. (It is even possible to replace the 'standard' forms of ALLOCATE and DEALLOCATE with your own forms through this mechanism!)

This chapter has dealt with a lot of quite complex material and certainly could not be claimed to have provided more than a rather superficial introduction to dynamic storage and associated algorithms. However, it should be sufficient to indicate how the Modula-2 language provides support for these features, and further examples of their use will appear in some of the later chapters of this book.

This chapter concludes Part I of this book, which has dealt with the basic structures of Modula-2 as a programming language. In Part II we go on to examine some ways of designing programs to make good use of the features of Modula-2, and pay particular attention to the design process involved.

## EXERCISES

**11.1** Create RECORD types which represent:

(a) an INTEGER stack;

(b) the details of a book (as might be used in a library database);

(c) a description of a ship (or a car);

(d) a description of a room in a house.

For each of these, what scope is there for the use of enumerated types, and where might you need to make use of variant records?

**11.2** Using your answer to Exercise 11.1(d), write a short program module that allows you to input and store the details of a house or a flat, and that can output these using a selected ordering of rooms (for example, ground floor rooms first, bedrooms before bathroom etc.).

[Hint: organize the record handling first, using an array of records, and then modify the solution to provide an ordering mechanism through the use of a linked list.]

**11.3** Re-write the example program in Figure 11.3 to use a double linked list (each element should have two pointers, with these being respectively linked to the preceding and the following records).

Part II

# DEVELOPING PROGRAMS IN MODULA-2

Chapter 12  **The Software Development Process**
Chapter 13  **Constructing a Modula-2 Program**
Chapter 14  **Program Development, Testing and Documentation**

# Chapter 12
# The Software Development Process

12.1 Programming in the large, and the software life cycle
12.2 Software design
12.3 Design representation and implementation
12.4 Assessing design structure
12.5 Re-using designs
Exercises

## 12.1 Programming in the large, and the software life cycle

Writing programs in order to practise programming techniques, which is the sort of programming that usually occurs as part of a student course, can provide a rather biased view of the nature of program development. The structure of a small program can often be created using little more than a set of jottings on the back of an envelope. This approach can succeed even when larger programs need to be developed, as long as there is no need to consider the resulting programs as having any use beyond the immediate one of practising technique. Producing programs in such a way will usually involve relatively little effort on design, quite a lot on coding and debugging, and a minimum on testing (after all, the results of effective testing may prove to be too revealing for comfort).

Unfortunately, the sort of programming habits that this creates, where coding is viewed as being the prime task in programming, are all too often then carried on beyond the learning stage. Having come to view programs as relatively small and short-term objects, many programmers find it quite difficult to adopt a longer-term view, and to adapt to the idea that a large program will need the *collective* efforts of a large number of

181

people in its construction. (We will use the terms *program* and *system* interchangeably in Part II, since the solution to a user's needs may well require a number of integrated programs, possibly running concurrently, and usually termed a system.)

That is not to imply that the 'quick and dirty' form of program is never required, although their use may require considerable self-discipline on the part of the programmer. We often use the term 'throw-away' to describe a program written to test out some idea or to perform a simple 'one-off' task, with the intention that it will then be discarded. All too often though, such programs are *not* discarded: if the result has some appearance of success, then the obvious next step is to develop it further – and why start and write another program when we already have one! And so it goes on, typically resulting in a large program that can no longer be modified without a plethora of strange side-effects, and which is probably completely undocumented. When the original programmer leaves the project, all too frequently the only practical option is to begin again – preferably where development should really have begun anyway, namely with the development of a *design* for the program.

So as this is a book about using a programming language, these considerations are very important to us. The material of Part I was concerned with describing the structures of Modula-2 and its *syntax*. This concentration upon the detailed structuring issues and techniques of programming is sometimes termed 'programming in the small'. However, when we come to *use* a programming language as a tool to assist us in producing solutions to real problems, we are far more often concerned with the problems that arise from operating on a larger scale, which is termed **programming in the large**. The questions that go with this are concerned with how our program needs to be organized in terms of much larger and longer-term objectives and requirements. This sort of consideration is at the centre of the material making up this chapter and the following two and it is just as significant to the Modula-2 programmer as the detailed material covered in Part I.

Programming in the large requires a very different approach from programming in the small. We would not expect to be able to build a six-lane motorway bridge over a large river with the same techniques that we might use to build a footbridge over a small stream in a garden. Yet all too often that is what we do try to do in programming. Our program (and its development path) should have a structure appropriate to its size and its role. To use large system engineering techniques on a small program can be just as inappropriate as trying to construct a 20 000-statement real-time process control system in the same way that we might write a 30-statement Pascal program to print out a calendar. The foundations that we provide should be adequate to support the final structure that we erect – and in programming this may well be very much larger than was originally expected!

### 12.1.1  The software life cycle

It is important to appreciate that many of the systems made up from programs that are 'written for real' are used over a relatively long period (10 or 15 years is by no means untypical), and so we need to plan for that fact. The development and use of most programs goes through what we often refer to as a 'life cycle'. This begins when the need for the program is realized, and continues right through until the time when the program is ultimately discarded. During this time, the developers and maintainers of the program will almost certainly find it necessary to repeat tasks. For example, to make a change to the program, either during development or during maintenance, it may well be necessary to repeat some parts of the design task, to re-program sections of the code, and then to re-test large sections of the program. It is this cyclic nature of development and maintenance that has led to the term 'life cycle'. We can also consider a program as having a 'lifetime', which is the time which elapses between the beginning of development and the final withdrawal from use. So when developing a new program, it is helpful if we can keep some model in our minds of the likely life cycle for our program, and to draw up our plans accordingly.

Of course, there isn't really one life cycle that applies to any and every program, and indeed there are techniques for program development (such as prototyping) that do not fit into this model at all (Jackson and McCracken, 1982; Gladden, 1982). In particular, some problems, such as the development of a graphical user interface for a system, will usually require a degree of interaction and iteration that can be met only by such techniques.

All programs are different in detail, but it is at least often possible to recognize a number of distinct phases within the lifetime of any particular program. One version of the generalized life cycle consists of the following phases:

(1) Requirements analysis: trying to determine exactly what is needed by the user of the program.

(2) Specification: expressing the user's requirements in a more formal way, to ensure that these are complete and consistent.

(3) Design: planning the form of a program or set of programs that will meet the user's requirements.

(4) Implementation: coding and constructing the program(s).

(5) Testing: checking to see that each program conforms to the specification – and also that it meets the user's requirements (these are not necessarily the same thing).

(6) Maintenance: adapting the program to meet new requirements, correcting programming errors, etc.

These phases are rarely as well defined and clearly separated as might be suggested by the list above, since most of the tools and techniques

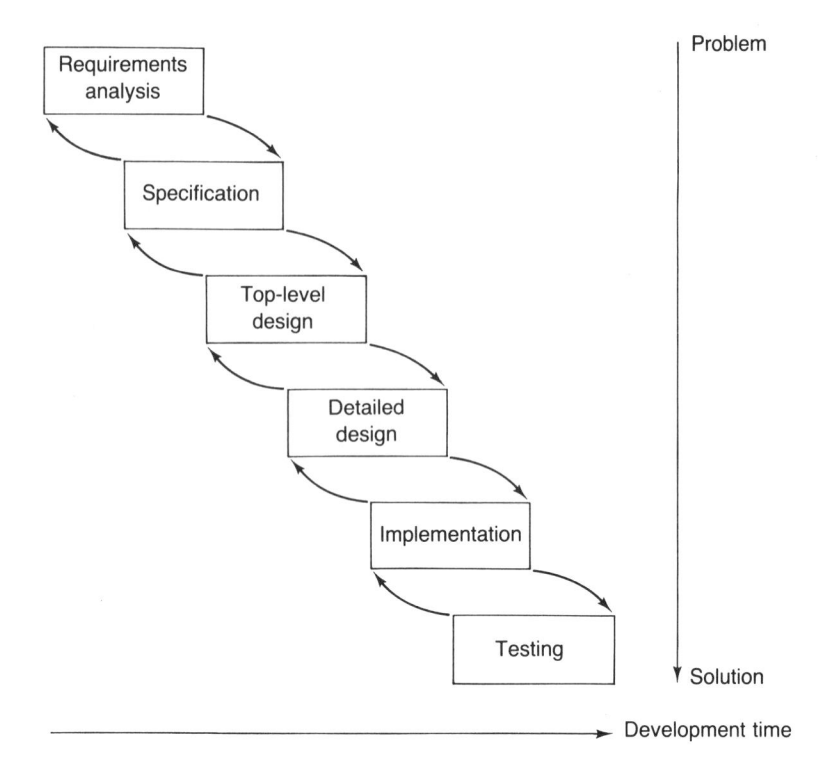

**Figure 12.1** Waterfall model of the software development life cycle.

available to assist with performing the tasks involved in each phase are neither precise nor rigorous. As a result, each phase in turn will reveal errors or omissions in the plans and decisions produced in the preceding phases. For example, the testing phase may reveal not only errors in the detailed coding of a program but also flaws in its very structure. In the extreme, it may well be that the program does not even perform some of the tasks that the original analysis identified as being required.

So there is usually some degree of iteration between these phases, with various sections of the work of earlier phases needing to be revised on each iteration. Figure 12.1 shows a diagrammatic form for the life cycle that reflects this, sometimes referred to as the 'waterfall' model. Like any model, this isn't necessarily an exact description of every program. Nor should the waterfall be regarded as a desirable structure, since it reflects our inability to perform correctly the tasks that comprise the earlier phases of software development. The more successfully we can perform these tasks, the fewer iterations through the early development phases should be needed during program development.

Many of the phases of the life cycle given above can be further subdivided. For example, under 'testing', there are often three distinct subphases. The first subphase is concerned with testing the functions of the individual components of a program (module testing). In the second these are gradually combined (integration testing). Finally the program as a whole is exercised to demonstrate that it meets the original requirement (acceptance testing).

Stages 1 to 5 of this life cycle form can be categorized as 'development'. The development of new programs is usually regarded as a glamorous task for programmers, while 'maintenance' is regarded as dull (though of course worthy), and therefore as really only a task for junior and inexperienced programmers.

If, however, we were to look at some statistics taken from some of the projects that have developed large systems, it would not be unusual to find that the development phase occupied only a very small part of the lifetime of a system. We will also usually find that it accounts for quite a low portion of the total effort expended on the system over its lifetime. Furthermore, maintenance programming can involve a programmer in some very challenging assignments, as well as requiring a lot of basic detective work (Sommerville, 1989).

Over the last 15 years or so, the various problems associated with the different phases of the life cycle have received a lot of attention, and the field of study concerned with the production of large systems on a systematic basis has become known as 'Software engineering'. Under this title a lot of effort has been expended on seeking better ways in which to specify and design systems on a methodical basis, on seeking methods of systematically testing programs, and on finding ways of structuring both design and code so that the task of maintenance is made much easier. Software engineering is a large and developing field: this chapter will simply make use of some of the work undertaken in this area and try to show how the ideas involved can be expressed in using Modula-2.

Part of the motivation for using software engineering methods is simply that we believe that, if we can make a better job of the earlier phases of development, then the final result should be better too. To correct an error that is discovered during testing may involve having to repeat part of the tasks of the specification, design and coding phases. Doing this thoroughly, so that the overall structure of the program is not to be degraded, is inevitably both time-consuming and expensive. So the better the ways that we can find for performing the tasks of analysis, specification and design, the fewer repetitions of these tasks should be necessary, and the greater the possibility of producing the final working system to a higher standard of quality within a shorter time scale.

Despite this, a large proportion of the development and research effort devoted to this field in recent years has concentrated upon improving the implementation tools, largely because this task is better understood and is easier to solve.

Since Modula-2 is a means of *implementation*, the main emphasis in this chapter will be placed upon the phase of the life cycle that precedes the task of implementation, that of *design*, since the two phases are strongly connected. Not only are we concerned with finding the best way to implement possible design concepts in Modula-2 but also we need to identify those methods of program design that can provide the best opportunities to exploit the features of Modula-2. Indeed, one of the points about Modula-2 as a programming language is that it is well provided with features that should assist us with constructing *large* systems.

The rest of this chapter reviews some of the methods that we commonly use for designing programs and considers how well these can be utilized for constructing programs in Modula-2. The following chapter provides a more fully worked example, and considers some issues of implementation a little further. In Chapter 14 we go on to examine how the testing of Modula-2 programs might best be organized, once we have seen how the construction of a program is managed. These are important topics for the engineering of large programs, and are those phases of the life cycle that are influenced most strongly by the choice of implementation language.

Modula-2 provides some very powerful features and, if we design with its facilities in mind, these can aid us in creating large programs that will work and that can be modified without losing their structure. (However, we should take care not to let these features dominate our thinking during the design process. It is important that we should seek to consider *logical* issues during design, and that we should not let ourselves be influenced by the *physical* structures of the eventual programming language.)

## 12.2 Software design

The process of designing a large system is a complex task, and to describe even one method of design with any degree of thoroughness would require a separate book in itself. The objective of this section is to review some of the principles and methods that are in common use for designing large programs (and systems of programs), and in doing so to highlight how we can use the structures of Modula-2 to support the principles involved. As such, this section is intended to set the Modula-2 language into a larger context, and also to identify some of the practices that it is desirable to adopt in our programming to ease the process of transferring into the development of larger programs.

It is also important to appreciate that time invested in the tasks of requirements analysis, specification, and design of systems is invariably time well spent – even if this means that a program development project appears to produce very little 'real output' for a considerable time. (Unfortunately this is not always appreciated by either managers or programmers.) For large systems, these phases may require considerably more

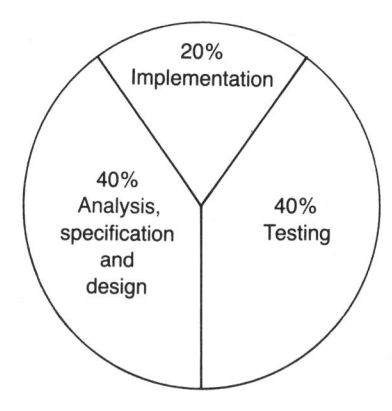

**Figure 12.2** Typical distribution of development effort through the development cycle of a system.

effort than that of coding, and at least as much effort as is expended on testing (Fairley, 1985; Sommerville, 1989). This is the converse of the normal student situation. (In that sense, the proportions of the sections of this book are probably wrong too!) Figure 12.2 is a reminder of the type of effort distribution that might occur in the development of large systems.

The production of a design is important even for small programs, and its importance increases with the size of the problem. Where a team of programmers are working together to produce a system that may consist of many programs needing to interact in some way, a complete and detailed design is essential. Without this, any missing details will be apt to be generated by the programmers on an ad hoc basis, and probably with little or no appreciation of the wider system requirements involved. In particular we should remember that:

- requirements define *what* is needed;
- design defines *how* this should be achieved;
- implementation embodies a description of how this *is* achieved.

The initial phases of the software life cycle are concerned with analysing the objectives for a particular system or program, and with specifying these as rigorously as possible. In practice, designers and programmers often find themselves working on the development of a new system with far from exact specifications. There are various reasons for this: in a pioneering situation it may simply be that no one can determine exactly how a computer system will actually be used, and it may be desirable to produce some prototypes for evaluation. At other times it may prove difficult to obtain a clear statement from the customers as to what exactly is wanted – often because they simply do not really know. Indeed, a particular problem of software development is that we are almost always breaking new ground, and so rarely have the chance to 'build it twice'.

Whatever the reasons, the less precise the statement that emerges from the requirements analysis phase, the more difficult it will be to design the system. The role of the design process is to *transform* the original requirements into a *plan*, or a 'statement' about how these requirements are to be met by a program. The less complete and precise the requirements are, the harder it will be to produce a design. Unfortunately this is a point that is often not appreciated, and all too frequently the process of design becomes entangled in the tasks of the preceding phases.

Even if we have a complete and clearly stated set of requirements, the process of design is far from being a matter of 'handle-cranking'. In any field of work, the task of the designer is usually regarded as having a *creative* component. The tasks of designing bridges, aeroplanes, electronic circuits all require a disciplined approach together with a creative skill, and such a skill is partly something that can be learned and partly personal aptitude. The task of designing programs is like these in many ways, although it is further complicated by the medium that the designer must work with. Whereas the task of design in other fields often involves the designer in handling a medium (steel, plastics, water) that obeys a set of physical laws, and therefore behaves in ways that can be predicted to some degree, the designer of software works in a much less tangible medium. Software design involves producing artifacts with other artifacts, such as editors and compilers, and there are no standard building blocks equivalent to the steel I-beam or the integrated circuit.

However, while the process of software design may be less than rigorous in terms of our ability to determine the likely behaviour of the final system, there are still a number of broad principles that can be used to help the designer to make the choices involved in producing a design. In the rest of this section, some of the more commonly used approaches will be examined, in order to see how well they relate to the structures of Modula-2.

We often recognize two stages to the design process. In the first stage, the designer works with very abstract objects, to model ideas about how the program will be structured on a very large scale. We usually refer to this as 'top level' or 'architectural' design. In the second phase, which is that of 'detailed design', the design is elaborated in order to determine how it will actually be realized in the final programming language. In the first phase of producing the top level design, the designer is concerned with separating out the different tasks that are involved, and with identifying the 'modules' that will make up a system – where a 'module' might be a program, a procedure, a MODULE or even a data structure. When expanding upon this, the designer determines how these will be physically realized and related in a greater degree of detail, and while this latter phase should not involve actually writing any code, it is likely to require the production of what is often termed 'pseudo-code', in order to express the algorithmic forms of the final code itself. The output of the design process should provide a set of 'blueprints' for the programmer(s), usually in the form of structure charts, a 'data dictionary', and pseudo-code.

Before examining some current design practices, a brief diversion may be useful to review the ways in which a high-level programming language such as Modula-2 provides us with the means of implementing the abstract 'objects' that may be manipulated by a designer.

### 12.2.1 Modula-2 objects

In terms of supporting structuring in an abstract sense, Modula-2 possesses three main forms that can be used for containing sub-units of a structure, and that can therefore act as components of the overall structure of a program. The *procedure* provides a means of implementing 'function', in that we usually use procedures to perform the high-level *operations* of a program – and we have already observed that it is generally good style to have each procedure perform only one such task. The *module* forms a 'packaging' structure, which can be used to encapsulate permanent data objects together with the procedures that operate upon them, so hiding the physical form of data structures and providing access to them only on a 'need to know' basis.

Modula-2 also provides the facilities for creating more abstract data types, using complex data forms such as records, as well as creating enumerated types to manipulate data within a program using as abstract a form as possible. So it provides the means by which a program can be organized *logically* (in terms of its operations upon data structures), and *physically*, in terms of information-hiding and data abstraction. This is further supported by the strong typing that is a feature of the language. (Separate compilation assists too, but this feature is really an issue of the construction rather than the logical structuring of a program.)

### 12.2.2 Top-down decomposition

This is often referred to as the 'divide and conquer' approach to determining the structure of a program: the basic principle of the method is that of repeated subdivision of the program's function until a suitably 'atomic' level of functional components is achieved. The whole emphasis in this approach is very much upon analysing the *function* that a program, and its component parts, will perform.

The top-down approach to program design has been in use for a long time, and has even been formalized to some extent (Wirth, 1971). This reflects the historical development of programming languages, in that the form of abstraction most widely provided has been the subprogram facility.

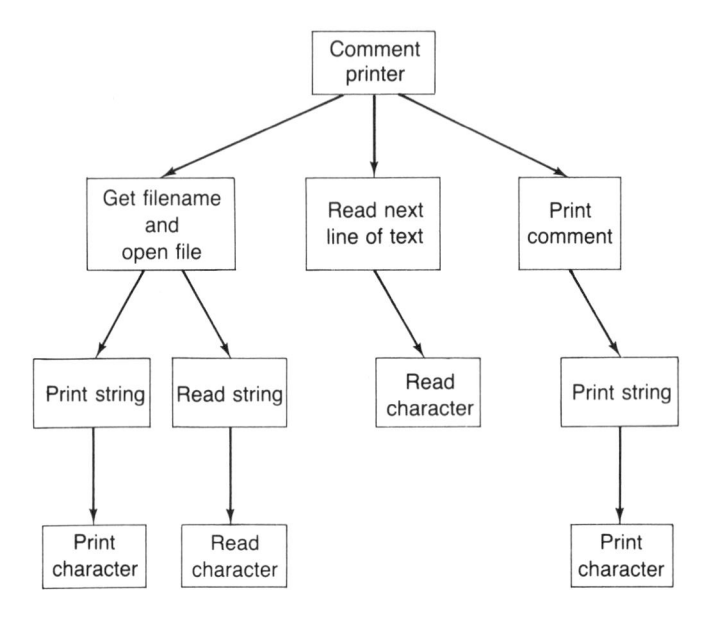

**Figure 12.3** Initial program structure from top-down design.

Sub-programs are basically high-order operations, hence the strong emphasis upon function that permeates this approach.

Despite the long history of the use of the top-down philosophy, there is still a lack of true 'method' in designing programs in this way, simply because there are no clear guidelines as to how the decisions involved in each decomposition step should be made. Different designers are able to produce quite different decompositions from the same starting point, and there are no standard criteria that can be used to choose between them. As an approach to design it is potentially unstable, and the solutions it yields are not necessarily reproducible.

A particular problem is to determine the point at which any further decomposition will produce sub-tasks that are trivially small. To some extent the point that is chosen as the end of the decomposition task will reflect the designer's experience – and possibly the features of the chosen programming language too!

A further problem is that the repeated subdivision of each sub-task leads to a final structure that is apt to have the form of a very wide tree, as in Figure 12.3. As a result, there may well be a very large number of subprograms at the lower levels. When examined, it is likely that many of these will perform very similar tasks, and so the designer will need to review the final decomposition and seek to combine those subprograms that are essentially duplicates of each other. Figure 12.4 shows the type of

SOFTWARE DESIGN    191

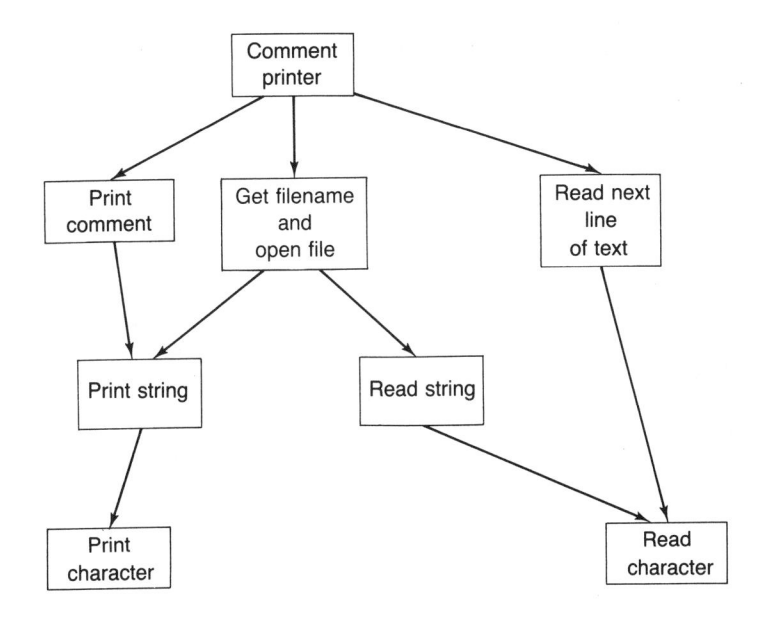

**Figure 12.4**  Program structure after some recombination of operations.

structure that might be achieved by doing this for the program shown in Figure 12.3.

The tree-like representation for showing the hierarchical structure of a program turns out to be very useful, and a very influential paper by Constantine and his co-workers at IBM (Stevens *et al.*, 1974) suggested ways of formalizing this rather more, and including a description of the flow of data that occurs when a subprogram is called from another part of a program. Figure 12.5 shows an example of such a **structure chart**. The notation is a commonly used variation on that used in the original paper. We will make further use of structure charts as descriptions of a program when we come to look at design representations more fully.

As a simple example of top-down design, we can consider its application to the problem of producing a program to extract and print the comments from a Modula-2 module. The output from our program should consist of a copy of the text of the original input source file, but with all those characters that are not part of a comment being replaced by a dash character, '–'.

As an initial decomposition, we can identify the following functions (Figure 12.6):

- open input file;
- read and print comment;
- read and print code (with substitution).

192   THE SOFTWARE DEVELOPMENT PROCESS

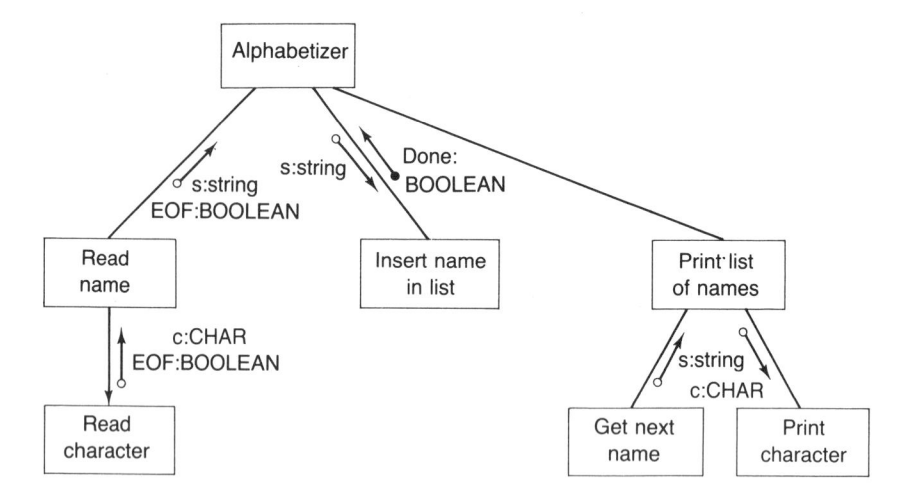

**Figure 12.5**   Example of a structure chart.

If we now examine these more closely, we can see that the task of the subprogram 'open input file' depends on both the way that the input file is identified (this may require a dialogue with the user) and the form of the InOut module. However, it does not involve any other particularly significant tasks and we can therefore consider this to require no further significant decomposition beyond separating the dialogue.

The functions 'read and print comment' and 'read and print code' will obviously use some common low-level procedures to fetch and print characters, and so we can end up with the structure shown in Figure 12.7. Apart from this, the algorithms involved do not really warrant further decomposition of these sub-tasks at this point.

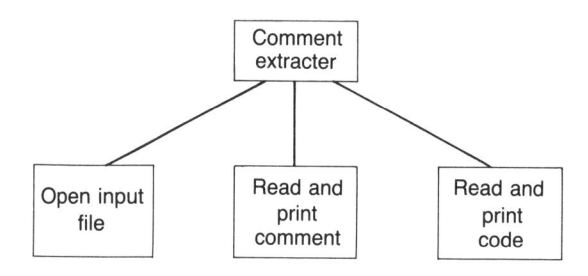

**Figure 12.6**   First stage of top-down decomposition.

SOFTWARE DESIGN 193

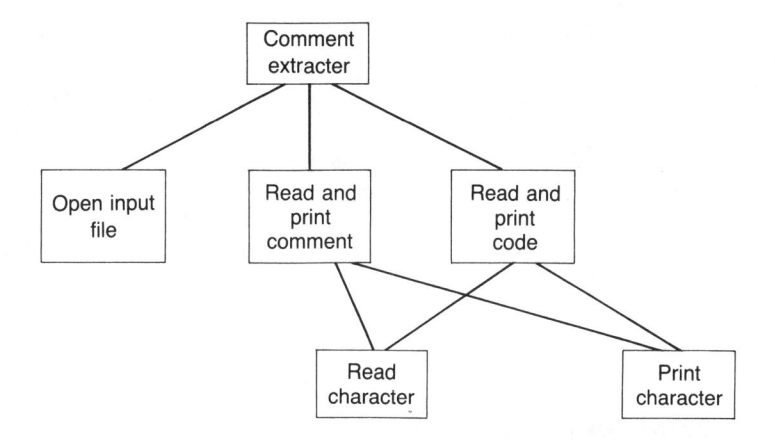

**Figure 12.7** Second stage of top-down decomposition.

We can easily identify a number of potential problems that are likely to arise when expanding this design into a program. The first is that the program needs to begin by performing one of its main operations and has to choose between these in some way. To get around this we need to add an extra task to the 'open input file' routine, or to the main body of the program, which is to read the first few characters so that the program knows whether these are a comment or not. So the task of data input starts to become spread throughout the program, a point that we will return to later.

As a further point about this design, it takes no account of the possible use of nested comments in Modula-2, and already it looks as though it will have to handle these in a less than graceful fashion. Similarly, future modifications that might be required, such as keeping the reserved words and not replacing them with dash characters, will be difficult to incorporate into the structure of this program. (This demonstrates the point that when designing we should always consider likely changes in the requirements. This may in turn influence our design decisions and should encourage us to think of design in a fairly general way.)

It can reasonably be argued that this is a poor decomposition, and that an experienced programmer or designer would not choose such a structure. However, the point is that there are no clearly laid down guidelines to save the inexperienced designer from producing just such a design (or worse).

One frequently used analogy for the form of a computer program is with the structure of an English sentence. Sentences have nouns to describe the objects and use verbs to describe the operations that are applied by or to the objects. As an example, the sentence

The programmer drank another cup of coffee.

contains two objects ('programmer' and 'cup of coffee', and a verb ('drank') that describes how one object modified another object in some way. In a program, the algorithms are concerned with specifying the operations that are to be performed upon the data of the program, in much the same way that the verb(s) of a sentence specifies the operations that affect the objects. When we consider this view, we can quickly see that a significant shortcoming of the top-down approach is that it concentrates wholly upon the operations of the program, and gives no weight to the form of the data structures. In that sense, it is rather like trying to describe something by using only verbs!

### 12.2.3 Decomposition by data flow

This particular approach was developed from the pioneering work of Constantine and his co-workers, and is a way of describing the approach that is often termed **Structured Design**, or **Composite Design**. More correctly, it should really be considered as comprising two distinct techniques, one for analysing the task and the other for producing a design. While the main emphasis of this method is still upon function, it does attempt to use information about the data to provide some form of guidance on *how* the decomposition should be structured.

In the first part of the task, the designer performs a **Structured Analysis** of the problem domain (DeMarco, 1978). This involves tracing the flow of information into and out of the system, and determining how the information is processed between these points. The primary tool used for the analysis is the **Data Flow Diagram**, or DFD. Figures 12.8 and 12.9 show two simple data flow diagrams. The first is a very high-level description of how information is processed in the system, while the second is a more detailed expansion of just one of the 'bubbles' of the first diagram. In these diagrams, the bubbles represent the operations performed by the program, while the connecting lines describe the flow of information between them. As with the top-down approach, the process is repeated until the system has been decomposed to a sufficiently low level, at which point the bubbles can be considered to describe operations that can be implemented as subprograms.

In the second stage, Structured Design, the designer *transforms* the overall non-hierarchical DFD into one or more hierarchical structure charts. (This method is mainly concerned with producing a design for a sequential program, but it is possible to identify concurrency at an early stage, and to 'factor out' the DFD so that it forms the basis for several programs.) During this transformation, the bubbles of the DFD become the boxes on the structure charts, and the flow lines are transformed into the lines that link the elements of the structure chart and show the flow of control and information. This process of transformation is an important

SOFTWARE DESIGN 195

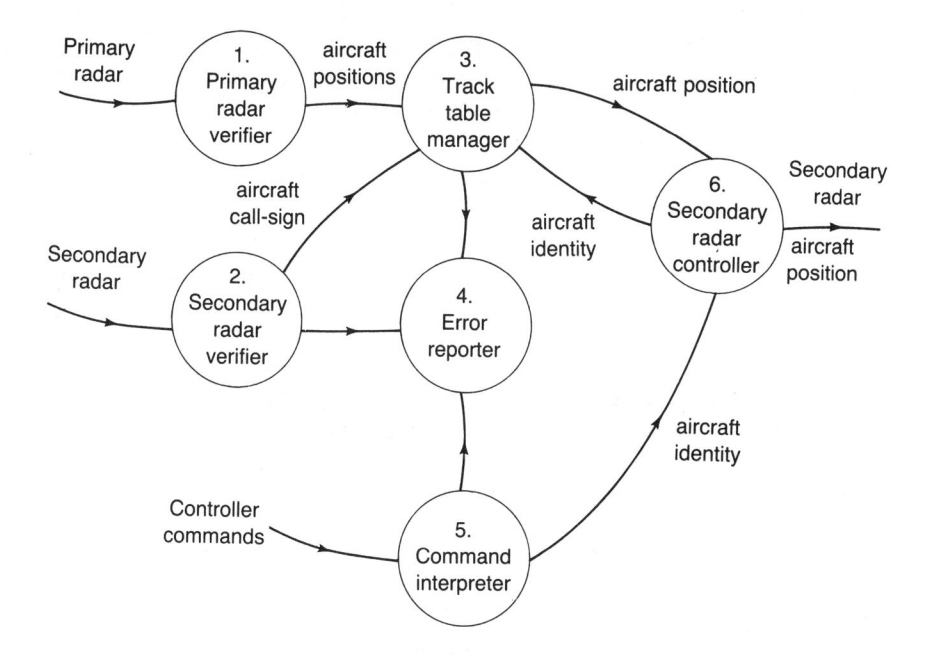

**Figure 12.8** Data flow diagram (for Air Traffic Control System).

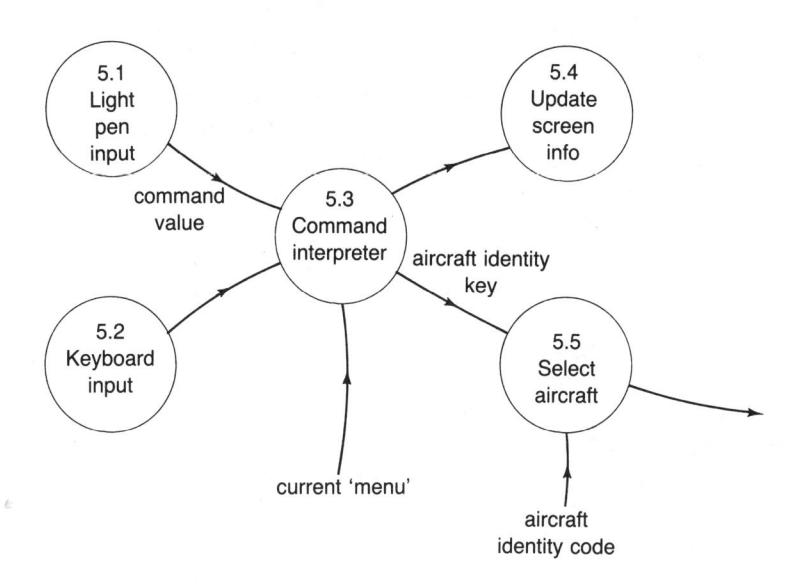

**Figure 12.9** Data flow diagram: expanded version for one activity from Figure 12.8.

step in this method of design, and there are several very good texts that describe how it can be done (Page-Jones, 1980; De Marco, 1978).

This approach can be considered to be more systematic than the top-down approach, and by considering the *flow* of information, as well as the *functions* of the system, it takes a more balanced view in producing a solution. However, the process of transformation between the DFD and the structure chart is fairly complex for all but the simplest systems, and involves the use of a number of 'rules' that are drawn largely from experience and practice.

The method has been widely taught and used in a number of forms since the mid-1970s. The strong emphasis that it places on the role of the data in the system makes it a design approach that is very useful in the data processing field. However, since event-driven systems are also concerned with data flow, this method (or at least the analysis part of it) can usefully be applied in designing quite a wide range of application programs.

### 12.2.4 Designing around the data structure

Determining the structure of a program by modelling it around the *structure* of the data that it processes is the basis of the design methods developed by both Michael Jackson (Jackson, 1975; Cameron, 1983) and J. D. Warnier (1974). (The latter form has been further expanded by K. Orr [1981].) Both of these methods have been extensively used in the field of data processing. The method described here is that due to Michael Jackson – Jackson Structured Programming, usually termed JSP.

This method can most effectively be used for designing programs that handle data streams containing well defined data structures. The basic idea is to construct a tree representation for the data structures used in the input and output, and then to structure the actual program around this tree so that each element of the program describes the operations to be performed upon the data element in the corresponding position. A significant departure from the previous two design methods is that this method can be considered as consisting of a process of *composition*, rather than of decomposition.

As a very simple example of the ideas behind this method, consider a program to read a stream of records generated from the petrol pumps at a self-service filling station and print out a 'log' on the cashier's console giving the details of each transaction. Each time a customer uses a pump, the program will output a record of the type shown in the bottom row of Figure 12.10 to a printer. (Each level in the 'tree' expands the description of the objects above.)

We begin with a tree structure describing the inputs and another describing the outputs, as in Figures 12.10 and 12.11, and then create a tree structure for the program that is a composite of these (Figure 12.12).

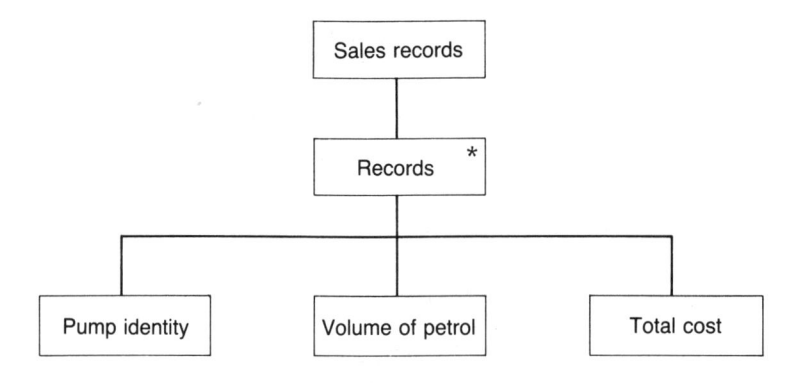

**Figure 12.10** Petrol pump control: structure diagram for the output data stream. (* denotes iteration of structure or action.)

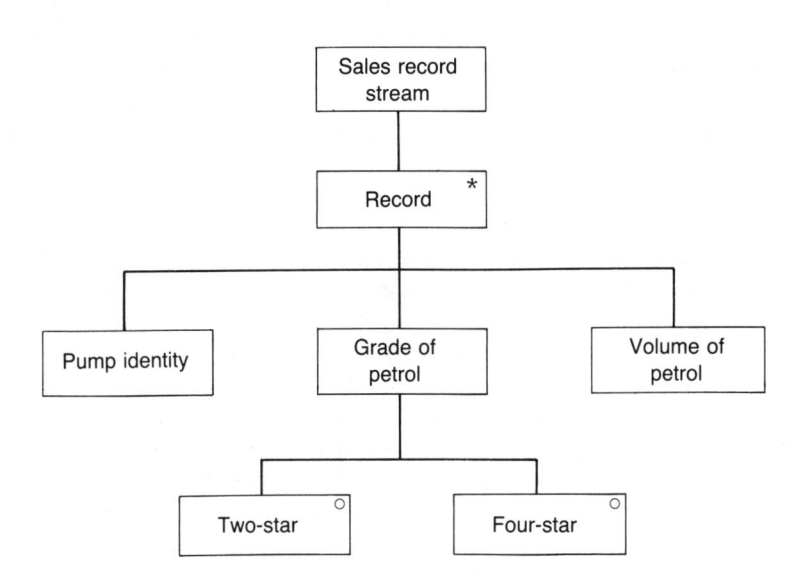

**Figure 12.11** Petrol pump control: structure diagram for the input data system. (○ denotes selection between form or action.)

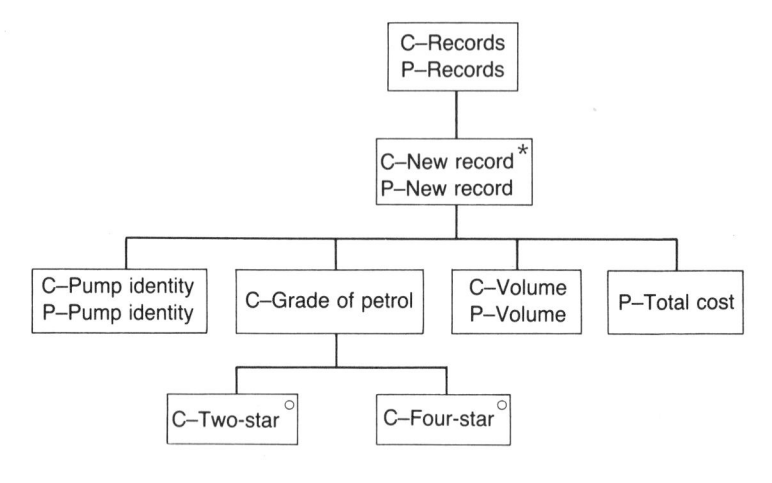

```
              C–Records
              P–Records
                  |
           C–New record *
           P–New record
    _____|_____
    |           |           |           |
C–Pump identity  C–Grade   C–Volume   P–Total cost
P–Pump identity  of petrol P–Volume
                  ___|___
                  |     |
              C–Two-star° C–Four-star°
```

C = *consume* information
P = *produce* information

**Figure 12.12** Petrol pump control: program structure diagram created by merging the descriptions of Figures 12.10 and 12.11.

Operations are then allocated to the elements in the program tree to operate upon the data field in the corresponding position (Figure 12.13). Note that the resulting program tree is not a structure chart of the type that was described earlier, and that Jackson's notation includes information about sequencing, as well as repeated actions/records and selection. (Time ordering is an important aspect of Jackson's method.)

This approach has the attraction that any change in the form of the data can fairly easily be mirrored by making a corresponding change to the structure of the program. This is further eased by the fact that the structure of the program can be understood quite easily from examining a description of the data form. However, there are problems as soon as a program needs to handle multiple types of data record and has to combine the information in some way, since these records or files may not be organized on the same basis. Such problems are not insurmountable, and the method has well developed solutions that can be applied to such problems. (Where information is structured around different 'keys', this is termed a 'structure clash', and before a program can be designed around the relevant data structures, one or more of these must first be modified by a separate program to use a key consistent with those used in the others.) There are also techniques that can be used to extend this approach to produce programs that are interactive with a user or device.

Because the design of a program is systematically derived from the structures of the data, this method is quite prescriptive, and so is more

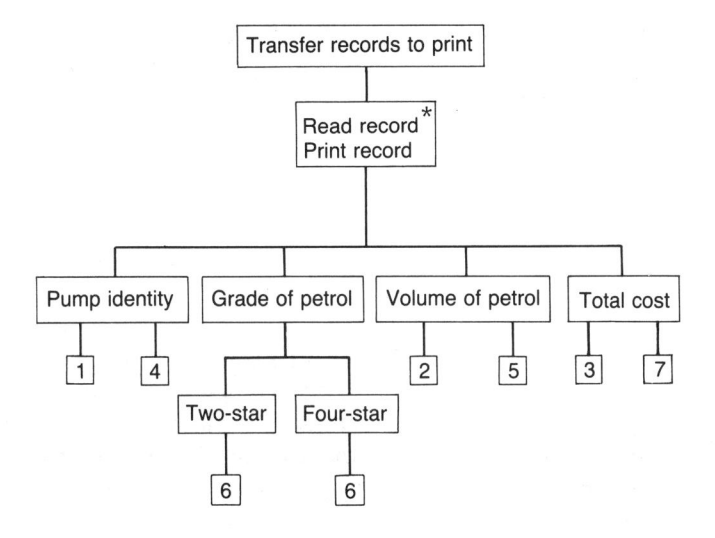

```
                    ┌─────────────────────────┐
                    │ Transfer records to print│
                    └─────────────────────────┘
                                │
                    ┌─────────────────┐
                    │ Read record *   │
                    │ Print record    │
                    └─────────────────┘
                                │
        ┌───────────────┬───────────────┬───────────────┐
┌───────────────┐ ┌───────────────┐ ┌───────────────┐ ┌───────────┐
│ Pump identity │ │ Grade of petrol│ │Volume of petrol│ │ Total cost│
└───────────────┘ └───────────────┘ └───────────────┘ └───────────┘
     │    │            │                  │    │           │    │
    [1]  [4]                             [2]  [5]         [3]  [7]
                  ┌─────────┬─────────┐
              ┌────────┐ ┌────────┐
              │Two-star│ │Four-star│
              └────────┘ └────────┘
                  │          │
                 [6]        [6]
```

Outputs:
(1) write pump identity
(2) write volume of petrol
(3) write cost to customer

Operations to set these up are:
(4) obtain pump identity
(5) obtain volume of petrol
(6) obtain grade of petrol
(7) multiply price for grade by the volume dispensed

**Figure 12.13** Petrol pump control: allocation of operations to elements in the program structure.

likely to produce consistent solutions when used by different designers than the functional or structured design methods (Bergland, 1981). This in turn makes it easier to modify such a design, because the maintenance designer is able to understand the reasoning behind the choices made by the original designer. Forms such as this are also likely to be attractive to large organizations, where staff move frequently between appointments and so may inherit a project already begun. The more prescriptive the design method, the more easily a new designer should be able to take over the responsibility for a system. However, as a design method JSP is somewhat restricted in that it can be directly applied only within a limited problem domain, and tends to be less easily managed for large systems.

A limitation of all three approaches discussed so far is that, when offering guidance as to how the task of a program is to be organized, each tends to put emphasis upon one feature. While each in turn is suited to a particular class of problems, they somewhat lack generality. Furthermore, they provide no particular guidance as to how we can utilize the concept of information-hiding, which we now discuss more fully.

### 12.2.5 Information-hiding

This principle was first described in two very influential papers written by David Parnas (1972a, 1972b). Neither the papers nor the principle of information-hiding are easily digested, nor do they offer a particular approach to producing a design. Rather, the complete concept provides a design philosophy and some criteria that can be used to assist the designer when making a choice between different options during the design process.

The essence of the idea is that the designer should not only consider the actual problem that the program is to address, but also the ways in which the problem itself might be changed in the future. So not only does the designer need to formulate a solution to the immediate problem but this solution should also be structured in such a way that it can be easily adapted when changes occur in the user's needs, or in the environment in which the program runs (for example, the operating system), or in the information that it handles.

In order to achieve this objective, the designer needs to identify those parts of a program that are likely to be affected by the changes arising from (say):

- a new version of an operating system;
- a new format for its input data, which might include new fields in records;
- a change in the dimensions of one of the fields of a record;
- new requirements from the user that will have the effect of extending the original purpose of the program.

The designer having identified these parts, the program should then be structured so that the *details* of the information associated with each such possible change are concealed from the rest of the program as far as possible. For example, the data processing parts of a program should not directly access an input record in order to extract some required field: instead they should access the record via some intermediate procedure, so that the details of the record's structure are concealed inside the code of this 'access procedure'. Then any change that occurs to the form of the input data will require only modifications to the code of the access procedure, rather than changes throughout the code at the points where 'knowledge' about the form of the data is involved. It is then easy for a maintainer to identify where changes should be made, and for such changes to be made without the programmer needing to be concerned about possible side-effects.

So the principle of information-hiding guides the designer to conceal the details of those data structures that are liable to change in the future, so that the effects of a change are confined to a small locality within the program. In some ways this can be seen as a further form of abstraction, and a refinement of the concepts behind the use of symbolic constants and user-defined types.

As already noted in Section 10.3, it is difficult to implement the idea of information-hiding in a language such as standard Pascal, because the scope rules make it difficult to conceal information about the form of any permanent data structure very effectively. However, Modula-2 is very well suited to the idea. The MODULE structure of Modula-2 makes it possible to conceal the internal forms of permanent data objects very easily, since they can be initialized via the main body of the module and access to them can be confined to those procedures that have explicitly been constructed and exported for that purpose. Information-hiding is a particularly important concept, and the examples in this part of the book have largely been constructed around it.

Unfortunately, while the concept of information-hiding has long been widely accepted, and has formed a major influence on the form of such modern imperative languages as Ada and Modula-2, it has proved difficult to incorporate it into a design practice. It can be used as a means of helping the designer make decisions when using a particular method, but there is still no widely accepted method that uses this to guide the designer throughout the design process in any systematic or procedural manner. The remaining part of this section describes a design method that currently seems to offer the best means of utilizing this concept within a procedural development form.

### 12.2.6 Object-Oriented Design (OOD)

Rather than trying to describe the steps in this method for producing a design (Abbott, 1983; Booch, 1986), it may be more useful to summarize the principles that it involves.

Very broadly, OOD is based upon the idea that the task of designing a computer system or program is essentially one of creating a (software and hardware) model of the 'real-world' process that it is to perform. (One can see this as an extension of the ideas of Michael Jackson's data-structured method, where the form of the program is modelled around the form of the data.)

So the task of design requires that the designer first tries to identify the various *objects* or *entities* that make up a real system and then seeks to model these and their interactions with the rest of the 'world' in the form of the program. To do so, the designer not only needs to identify the objects (such as a bank account) but also to determine the *attributes* that these possess (type of account, current balance, overdraft limit) and the *operations* that are performed by or upon them (deposit, withdraw). (The attributes generally determine the *state* of an object, and the operations transform the object to another state.) Within a program, the objects and their attributes can then be represented using abstract data types, and the operations can be represented by the algorithms, which are contained in procedures. Of course, the objects themselves may be composites of further objects, so that design proceeds by a set of refinements.

A good review of the principles used in object-oriented design is provided in Booch (1986), which also explains the relationship of this method to Michael Jackson's JSD design method (Jackson, 1983; Cameron, 1983, 1986). In JSD, Michael Jackson has extended the design philosophy that was described earlier, in order to handle the design of larger and more complex systems. However, JSD is essentially *process-centred*, while OOD is *object-centred*, and so while they use a similar philosophy, the *viewpoints* involved are rather different.

It is fairly easy to see that the OOD approach is more likely to result in a program structure that is well suited to information-hiding, and also suited to being implemented in Modula-2. This is because we can use MODULEs to conceal the data structures, and hence the details of the objects and their attributes, and can export from these the necessary operations in the form of procedures. This is different from the functional decomposition approach, which primarily generates designs that can be implemented using procedures (since these are functional entities), and which provides little guidance as to how these may be packaged with their data by using a facility such as the MODULE. The data flow approach does provide some recognition of data 'objects' through the use of the data dictionary, but the design decisions are still strongly influenced by consideration of function. So even if the object-oriented design method does not explicitly consider information-hiding, the necessary information is available for its effects to be assessed.

The use of object-related methods has attracted considerable interest in the Ada domain, since the Ada **package** provides the programmer with a facility similar to that of the Modula-2 MODULE in terms of its ability to support information-hiding (Booch, 1983). One advantage of such an approach is that it also helps with the task of program maintenance. This is because changes required in a program generally arise because of changes in the external world (new devices, changes in regulations, new facilities), which are changes that occur to the real-world objects or their operations. Provided that the program has been designed to reflect the real-world structures, the task of changing the program is very much simplified. This in turn reflects one of the basic tenets of information-hiding: that by hiding the detail of structures, we are able to confine the required changes to the affected module alone.

Because these methods seek to model the structure of the problem itself, rather than just the data structures or functions involved, their basis is somewhat stronger than those of the methods that were outlined above, although their application is not necessarily a very easy task. However, because the program design is constructed (or 'composed') around the problem structure, different designers are more likely to produce very similar designs, which is not the case for the decomposition methods.

These methods are very important and likely to become increasingly so. While there is not space in this book to elaborate upon them in detail (such a task really requires a specialist text), the would-be designer of large Modula-2 systems is well advised to study some of the references that have been cited in this chapter. In the next chapter, we develop the design for a moderately large program, using both the structured design and object-oriented methods, and then examine how the resultant designs can be expressed using Modula-2.

## 12.3 Design representation and implementation

Of necessity, designers of large programs and systems need to begin by using abstract representations of their ideas, since constructing a large system without some form of plan would be too complex a task. Only when the design has been completed in some fashion can it be realized in the form of a program using a programming language.

While the previous section was concerned with describing some commonly used means of producing a plan (design) for the structure of a system, this section will examine some of the ways that this design can be described. A designer needs to provide the programmer with a 'blueprint' of the designer's intentions, which can then be used as a guide to the task of programming. So it is important to determine exactly what it is that the designer needs to express through any form of representation. The process of design should produce a description of the *logical* structuring of a system, and this must somehow be transformed into the *physical* forms that are provided within the chosen programming language. This consideration alone shows why the top-down and data flow design methods have been popular for so long. These methods place their emphasis upon the operations that are performed within a program, and so the logical design that is produced can then be directly implemented using subprograms to perform the actual operations. Since the subprogram has been the only significant means of providing any form of partitioning in most imperative programming languages (before Ada and Modula-2), these methods are well matched to the facilities usually available to the programmer.

So when translating an abstract design to a form that describes how a system is to be implemented using a programming language such as Modula-2, the designer will need to determine how procedures and data objects should be grouped into modules. The design methods that are primarily concerned with function and hierarchy can provide little guidance on how to package the subprograms into modules, which suggests that object-oriented methods not only provide a more balanced view of the whole design process, but also offer fuller guidance about how to partition the code and data structures physically.

There is an element of the tail wagging the dog here, of course. In an ideal world, we should choose the design method that is best suited to a particular problem and only when the design is complete should the final implementation language be chosen. However, for many programming projects the choice of programming language will precede almost every other step in the software life cycle (perhaps excepting the choice and purchase of the hardware!), and so it is frequently necessary to choose the design method that is best suited both to the problem and to the means of implementation. As a better understanding of the objectives of software engineering practices begins to take hold, we can at least hope that this situation will eventually change for the better.

In the rest of this section we shall consider some ways of expressing a design in such a way that it can be easily transformed into code. There are two levels of description that are generally used for expressing the form of a design, namely:

- the abstract top-level description;
- the detailed design description.

The 'top-level' description is largely concerned with the relationships between the larger components of a program, while the detailed design description is concerned with the algorithms that are used within the program units and the detailed forms of the associated data structures. (We can also consider the former to be mainly concerned with logical design, and the latter as being a part of the process of transformation into a physical design.)

Because these two levels have quite distinct and different needs, it is usually impractical to represent the ideas of both levels by the same form of representation. For representing the abstract ideas of top-level design, the forms that will be considered here are:

- data flow diagrams (DFDs);
- structure charts;
- block diagrams.

while for representing the detailed design, we will simply consider the use of pseudo-code (sometimes termed Structured English).

### 12.3.1 Data flow diagrams

Some examples of these were used in the previous section. Those in Figures 12.8 and 12.9 show how the form of the DFD can be layered, with each subsequent diagram expanding upon the information presented in a previous one. This is an important feature when trying to analyse the form of a large system, since it helps to preserve a clear view of the whole structure. Strictly speaking, the DFD is mainly an *analysis* tool, intended to assist in sketching out the operations that the program will perform upon the data. However, if this information is of use to the designer in creating the final design, then it must also be able to provide valuable information to the maintenance programmer or designer who will later need to modify the design, and so can be duly considered as a design representation.

The form of the data flow diagram is non-hierarchical, in that it represents a network of producer–consumer relationships between the components of the system, describing the activities (nodes) and the information flow between them, but not showing any information about how these will be activated. For systems that make use of concurrently executing components (these will be discussed further in Chapter 16), this is just the type of relationship that does exist between the different parts of a program. In many other systems, the components will be realized as a single sequential task. So the information in the data flow diagram is quite independent of the form of implementation, which might be a single sequential program or a number of concurrent processes.

There are ways of embellishing this form quite considerably, and the use of one such form, the MASCOT representation, in conjunction with Modula-2 is discussed in Budgen (1985). For the moment, though, we will confine our discussion of the DFD to observing that it can be a useful supplement to other forms, but is really too abstract to be used as the sole means of representing the intentions of a designer. In particular, it does not lend itself to providing a sufficiently detailed representation of the final structure of a program.

### 12.3.2 Structure charts

The structure chart was also introduced in the previous section, and Figure 12.5 provides a simple example. There are a number of variants in common use: Figures 12.14 and 12.15 show the same program structure represented using two of the possible forms.

The form used in Figure 12.14 is essentially the one proposed in the original paper by Constantine and his co-workers (Stevens, 1974). The structure chart is drawn using a tree-like form to represent the hierarchical flow of control, together with a separate table to provide a summary of the flow of data at each interface, in terms of the formal parameters of each subprogram and the direction of flow of the information. (The form of the

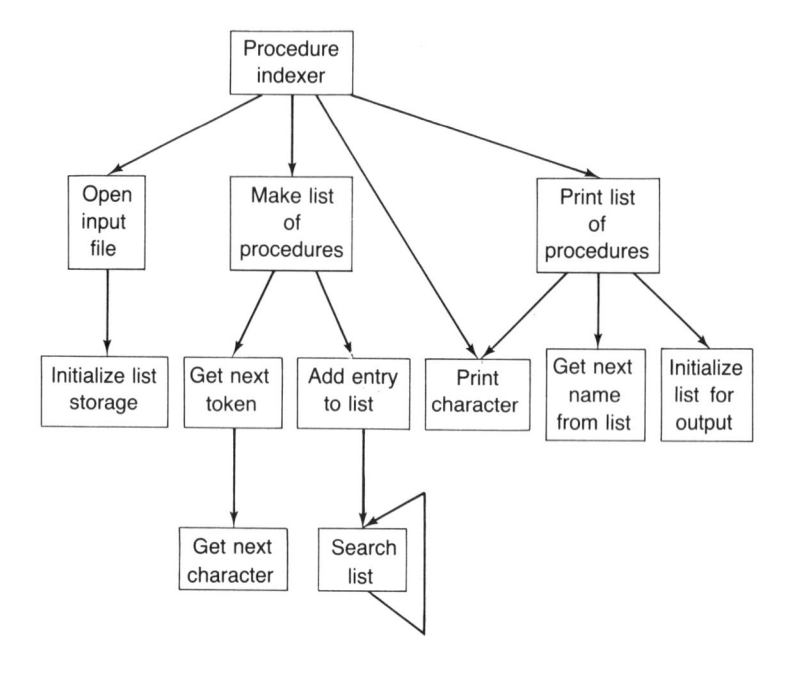

```
                    ┌─────────────┐
                    │  Procedure  │
                    │   indexer   │
                    └─────────────┘
           ┌──────────────┼──────────────────┐
    ┌──────────┐   ┌─────────────┐   ┌─────────────┐
    │  Open    │   │  Make list  │   │ Print list  │
    │  input   │   │     of      │   │     of      │
    │  file    │   │ procedures  │   │ procedures  │
    └──────────┘   └─────────────┘   └─────────────┘
```

| Procedure | In | Out |
|---|---|---|
| GetNextToken | – | s:string |
|  |  | EOF:BOOLEAN |
| GetNextChar | – | ch:CHAR |
| AddEntry | s:string | – |
| InitializeListForOutput | – | Done:BOOLEAN |
| GetNextName | – | s:string |
|  |  | Done:BOOLEAN |
| PrintChar | ch:CHAR | – |
| SearchList | s:string | p:Listpointer |

**Figure 12.14** Structure chart using a separate table of parameters. The program produces an alphabetically ordered list of procedures in a program.

structure chart is not a true tree as the term is generally used in computing science, because a node may have more than one parent node, but the qualification does not reduce its usefulness in any way.)

This form of structure chart provides a clear diagram, and handles complex procedural interfaces well, but the distribution of information

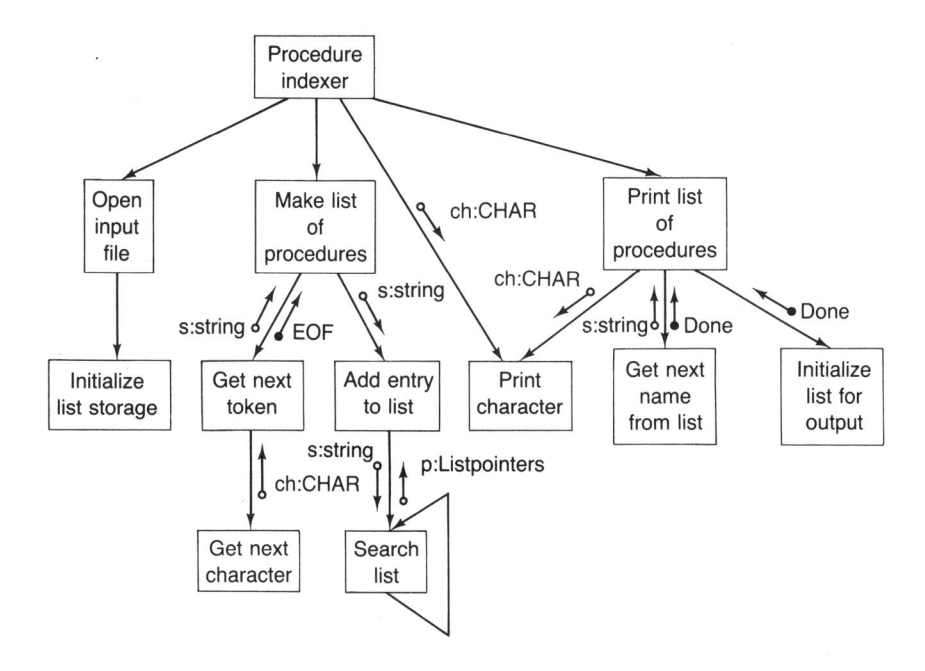

**Figure 12.15** Structure chart using alternative notation to that of Figure 12.14.

between the diagram and the table can make it harder to follow than the form in Figure 12.15, which has emerged as a practical and widely used alternative. It makes use of small flow arrows at the side of the control flow lines in order to show the flow of data across the procedural interfaces. An added convention that is sometimes adopted makes further use of the tails of the arrows by drawing a hollow circle to represent data flow and a filled circle to show the transfer of status information. The diagrams can also show recursion, as represented by the procedure SearchList. However, this form is less well suited for use with those procedural interfaces which may have large numbers of parameters. (Since a large number of parameters usually represents high data coupling, perhaps any difficulty encountered with this form should be considered as indicating that the designer should reconsider the procedural interfaces!)

As with the data flow diagram, it is generally better to use several layers of structure charts to describe a large program, with each lower chart providing an expansion that describes the structure of one of the boxes in a higher chart. The hierarchical nature of the structure chart particularly helps with this.

208    THE SOFTWARE DEVELOPMENT PROCESS

Some practical points that are worth noting about drawing structure charts are:

- *Keep each box at the appropriate logical level.* This is determined by the maximum number of calling routines above it. In Figures 12.14 and 12.15, the routine PrintCharacter is called by procedures at different levels, but it is positioned so that it appears beneath the lowest caller. A structure chart should be strictly *hierarchical*, and should have no horizontal lines of control flow.
- *Keep information concise.* If procedures and variables have been named sensibly, then the use of their identifiers should suffice to label the diagram.
- *Don't try to make the diagram represent too much.* For example, by using coloured lines to indicate how the subprograms are grouped in modules. The role of the structure chart is to describe the run-time call hierarchy of a program, and this does not really allow it to describe this type of information about constructional packaging as well. Trying to contort it in such ways will only reduce its basic clarity and usefulness.
- *The horizontal position of each box should have no significance.* That is, we should not try to indicate such information as the order of calling by the left to right positioning of boxes. Most users seem to observe the convention of keeping inputs to the left and outputs to the right, but trying to stick rigidly to this may produce a mess where lower-level subprograms are called from several different points in the levels above. It is better to try to keep the flow lines as uncluttered as possible.
- *Use only the formal parameters of a subprogram to describe the information flow.* These are then consistent with the actual code, since a given subprogram may be called at several points within the code of a higher subprogram, using different actual parameters. If information about actual parameters is required, then this should be tabulated separately.

When using structure charts to describe Modula-2 programs, one small but useful extension to the basic format is to regard the main body of each module as though it were a procedure (which it effectively is), and to include it on the chart, labelled with the name of the module. The main body of a module is generally used for such tasks as initializing data structures, which is an important part of the program, and hence these operations should be explicitly recognized by including them in the structure chart. Like a normal procedure, it should appear at the appropriate level, which is determined by the depth of the set of modules that make use of it. In Figures 12.14 and 12.15, the procedures InitList and OpenInput are

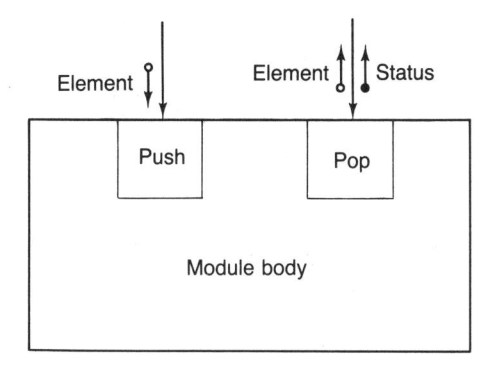

DESIGN REPRESENTATION AND IMPLEMENTATION   209

**Figure 12.16**  Simple structure graph for a stack module.

really the main bodies of the modules ListStorage and Inputs, and ListStorage is drawn at a lower level because it is used both by the main program module via procedure PrintList, and also by module Inputs (if we choose to place MakeList in Inputs).

### 12.3.3 Block diagrams

As already demonstrated, while structure charts can be used to describe the *hierarchical* structuring of a program, they do not provide an adequate description of the grouping of procedures and data into modules. Nor is the data flow diagram suited to describing this type of relationship. So to describe the structuring of modules, a quite distinct form of representation is needed.

In his book *System Design with Ada* R. J. A. Buhr (1984) has suggested the use of a form of block diagram termed a 'structure graph', which shows the interactions between the program components contained within a set of Ada packages. Some of the features of this form seem to be well suited to Modula-2, and so its main features are briefly outlined below.

Using this notation, the MODULE is represented as a block or box, emphasizing the 'black box' role of a module. The procedures that are exported, and hence are visible outside the module, are drawn as smaller boxes on the 'surface' of the module box. Figure 12.16 shows an example of this form for an integer stack module that exports the procedures Push and Pop. (Note that we can denote data flow in much the same manner as with the structure chart.)

This form is quite attractive, since the visible procedures are at the top of the module (on the 'surface'), and the rest of the details are hidden within the box. Following Buhr's ideas a little further, we can also use a

210 THE SOFTWARE DEVELOPMENT PROCESS

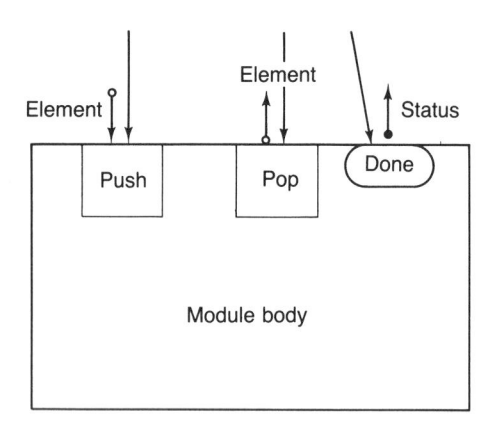

**Figure 12.17** Structure graph for a stack module that exports a status variable.

small rounded box to represent a non-procedural interface (i.e. a variable, constant or type). Figure 12.17 shows the integer stack module again, but now with the BOOLEAN variable Done added. So the 'surface' of the box now represents the contents of the module's EXPORT list. Similarly, the use of local modules can be denoted by creating inner boxes within the main box of the module, as in Figure 12.18.

Finally, in Figure 12.19 we see an example of a complete system design described using this form. This is intended to complement the program description given by the structure charts shown in Figures 12.14 and 12.15, and together the two forms of diagram are able to provide a complete description of the top-level structure of the program – although information about data structures still needs to be handled separately.

This form has been extended considerably for use in describing Ada programs (Buhr, 1984). However, we can adapt this for our own use, and the form shown should be quite sufficient for describing Modula-2 structures.

### 12.3.4 Detailed design

Having now described various means of representing the division of a program into procedures and modules, we need a means for describing the operations of these sub-units. At this level of description, the designer should be providing the programmer with a detailed plan for the structure of the code.

At this level we are concerned with describing algorithms that will perform operations upon data structures. The form of structure diagram devised by Michael Jackson (1975) can help with this (Figure 12.12).

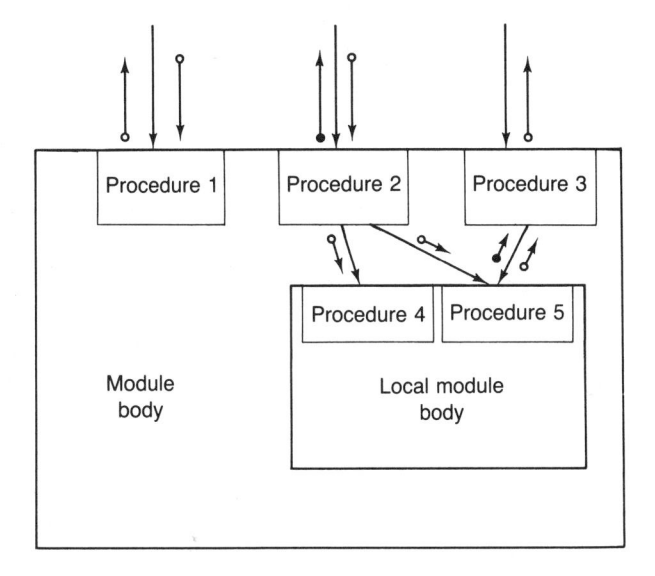

[Figure: structure graph showing Procedure 1, Procedure 2, Procedure 3 in Module body, with Procedure 4 and Procedure 5 inside Local module body]

**Figure 12.18** The structure graph extended to include a local module.

However, while this may show the presence of structures such as iteration and selection, we still need a means of describing their details.

A very widely used way of describing the details of the algorithmic structures of a program is **pseudo-code**. This makes use of the basic structures of sequence, selection and iteration, and includes keywords to indicate where they are used in the real code, but describes the operations of the program using a narrative form. Such a description will contain no specific assignment statements, and actions are described in general terms, rather than in terms of specific identifiers. For example:

```
LOOP until all data has been transferred
   LOOP until the tape controller is ready
      IF this is not the last block of data
         THEN
            transfer this block of data to the tape
         ELSE
            pack out the unused part of the buffer with nulls
            transfer the buffer to the tape
      ENDIF
   ENDLOOP
ENDLOOP
```

Obviously the form of this description can be expanded through a number of stages of increasing detail, still retaining the basic form, until we are

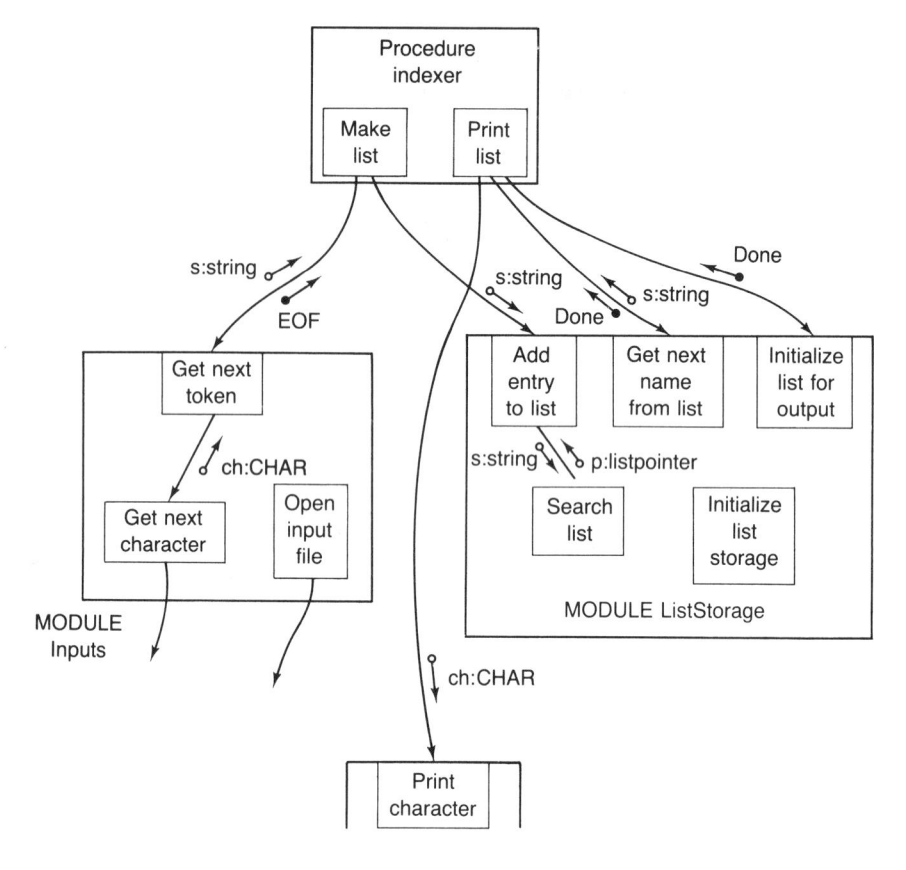

**Figure 12.19** Example of Buhr's structure graph notation using the program shown in Figures 12.11 and 12.12.

ready to write the actual code itself. A few points to note about writing pseudo-code are:

- *Do not try to optimize code or select exact structures too early in the process.* For example, the IF statement in the example above can be considerably improved, but this is a task that should be left until much later, when considering the details of the actual code. For the moment, the narrative form is much more descriptive as it is. Similarly, at this stage it is not necessary to specify the exact form of iteration that is to be used, hence the use of LOOP.

- *Model the form of the pseudo-code upon the structure of the problem.* This is a fundamental step in a method such as JSP, and is one that can be considered as quite general to the design process.

- *Do not introduce variable identifiers and assignment statements into the pseudo-code.* The purpose of pseudo-code is to provide an abstract description of the operations of this piece of a program: any mixing of the level and form of information provided is confusing for the reader.
- *Use indentation to denote blocks.* It is also important to use 'reserved' words such as ENDIF to clarify where these end.

Conventions about the use of upper and lower cases are a matter of preference and local practice. Since upper case letters tend to attract the eye, there is a good argument in favour of keeping the 'keywords' in upper case, while retaining lower case for the narrative descriptions.

Pseudo-code is very much concerned with describing *function*, and the details of local data structures are determined only at a very late stage. While this may be less than ideal, we should remember that decisions about global data structures should already have been made, and only the decisions about local data structures are being deferred to so late a stage.

Pseudo-code is not just a means of sketching out the designer's aims, it is also an important form of documentation, and one that is particularly useful for the maintainer, since it provides a narrative description for the operations of the final program. Even the most 'readable' statements in a program are apt to be heavy going, and the use of pseudo-code enables the programmer to identify quickly which sections of the code need to be read in any detail. For such purposes one is not initially concerned with such questions as 'Which variable is acting as the loop index?', but rather such questions as 'Which operation is performed when...?' While good code should indeed be self-documenting, it is greatly enhanced by the use of narrative forms such as this, which can act as an index to the operations concerned. (As a caveat, this does of course require that the pseudo-code be maintained so that it reflects the structure of the code!)

Figure 12.20 shows the purposes of the different forms of representation that have been discussed in this section, and also suggests what roles they can play in the development of a program. Note that these are mainly concerned with describing the form of the executable statements of the program. Data structures are generally described using words (as in the data dictionary), although it is always good practice to draw diagrams to show the structures of complex forms such as RECORDs, and especially of any linked data structures that might be used.

## 12.4 Assessing design structure

Before the task of transforming a design into program statements (coding) can begin, it is essential for the designer to make some sort of assessment as to how well the design matches the original requirement, and how well

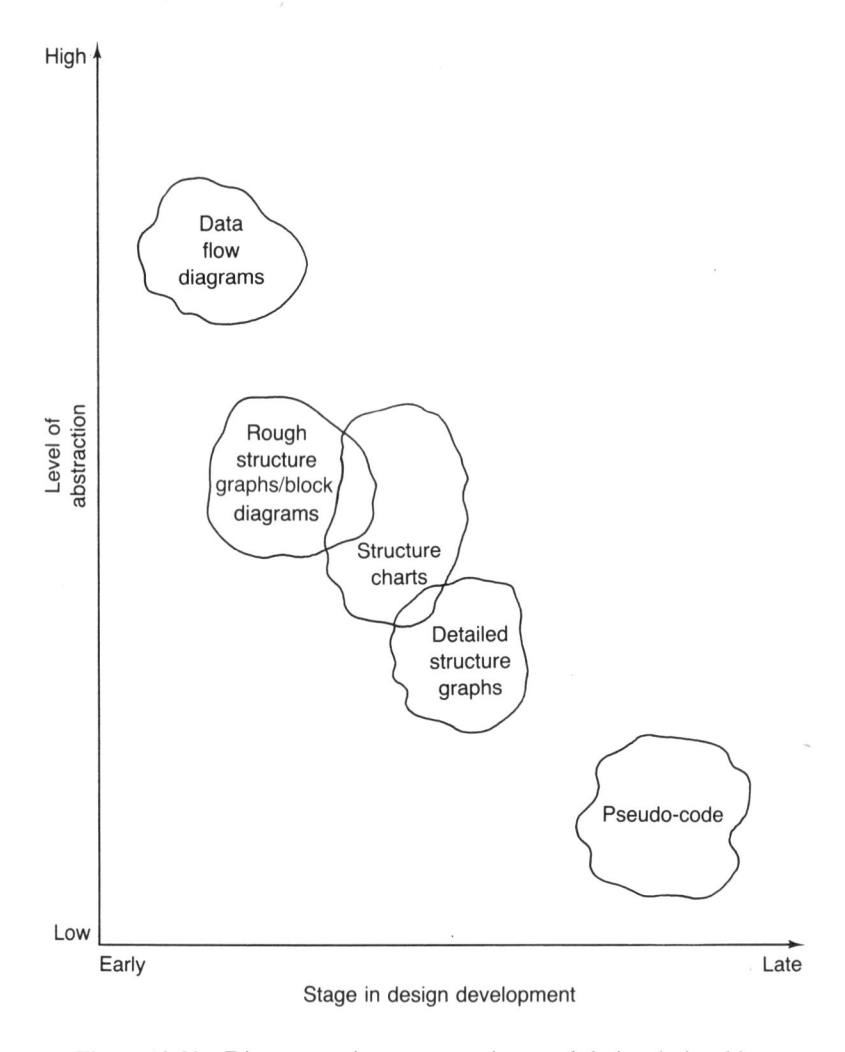

**Figure 12.20** Diagrammatic representations and their relationships.

structured it is. This may also need to be done at various times during the process of design and is largely independent of the design method adopted. The larger the system that is to be produced, the greater is the investment that it represents, and the more it is necessary to review the quality of the design before transforming it to code.

Because of the abstract nature of a design, there are relatively few objective assessment criteria or 'design metrics' available to measure the quality of a design. Indeed, it is hard enough to produce any form of quantitative assessment for something as relatively structured as the code of a program!

However, there are a number of useful guidelines about quality that can be assessed in a largely subjective way, and some of the more effective among these are summarized in this section. In particular, although design is and should be an abstract process, this summary assumes that the final program is to be implemented in Modula-2, and hence emphasizes some of the points that are most relevant to its facilities and structures.

It is now widely recognized that *complexity* is a major factor that makes it difficult to modify or correct the statements of a program (Stevens *et al.*, 1974). There are two measures that are widely used for identifying the forms that contribute to the complexity of a program, **coupling** and **cohesion**. They can provide useful assistance in performing a qualitative assessment of the complexity of a program, although it is difficult to produce any quantitative measure of its extent. In particular, these measures are not dependent upon the design method used.

Both of these measures are concerned with modules in the logical (that is, the abstract) sense of the word. In Modula-2, the term 'module' can be interpreted to include both the PROCEDURE and the MODULE, although, as we shall see, the interpretation that we make might vary somewhat between them. Cohesion describes how well the contents of an individual module are related to one another, while coupling is concerned with the interactions between the components of *different* modules.

### 12.4.1 Cohesion

Yourdon and Constantine (1979) identified some seven different forms of cohesion and ranked them in order of their desirability. A brief summary of these is given in Table 12.1. At the highest level (that is, the most desirable) there is **functional cohesion**, in which each of the components of a module is concerned with performing one and only one task. At the lowest (and hence least desirable) level, there is **coincidental cohesion**, in which the components of a module are included on some rather random basis. (This often arises when a programmer tidies up a program by creating a procedure to perform a set of tasks that are apt to be performed together, but which have no real common purpose other than a chance association.) Not all of the five intermediate forms are necessarily undesirable: for example, **communicational cohesion** occurs when the components of a module are concerned with handling some shared data structure, and this evidently applies to the well structured implementation module. A fuller description of the seven forms can be found in various books on software design (Page-Jones, 1980; Yourdon, 1979).

When implementing a particular design with Modula-2, we need to interpret the meaning of cohesion at two separate levels of abstraction. At the higher level, which is concerned with how procedures and data structures are grouped within a module, we can use cohesion as a measure of

**Table 12.1** Summary of the seven forms of cohesion.

---

*Most desirable*

**Functional** All elements contribute to the execution of a single problem-related task.

**Sequential** The outputs from one element of the module form the inputs to another element.

**Communicational** All elements are concerned with operations that use the same input or output data.

*Less desirable*

**Procedural** The elements of the module are related by the order in which their operations are performed.

**Temporal** The elements are concerned with operations that are related by the time at which they occur, and are usually linked to a particular event such as initialization or 'warm restart'.

*Undesirable*

**Logical** The elements perform logically similar operations that may involve very different actions. (For example, 'read character' is a very different physical task according to whether the data is to be read from a terminal, a magnetic disk or a magnetic tape, yet the logical result is the same in each case.)

**Coincidental** The elements of the module are not linked in any discernible way other than being physically joined within one module.

---

how well the procedures and permanent data structures of a module are integrated. For example, a module that provides an INTEGER stack and solely exports the procedures Push and Pop would exhibit at least communicational cohesion, because it consists of items that make use of a common data structure. Since we could also argue that the module has the single function of providing an INTEGER stack, it could be regarded as having functional cohesion too. So cohesion offers a useful measure for evaluating possible choices of partitioning for the elements of a program. (It can be argued that a design method such as object-oriented design strongly assists in making this type of decision anyway. On the other hand, a method such as top-down design leaves the partitioning of procedures and data structures into modules until late on in the design process, and the lack of guidance on this issue that is implicit in the method emphasizes the need for such a means of assessment.)

At a more detailed level, as when considering the structure of a procedure, we can also make use of the concept of cohesion. Cohesion provides a measure that can be used to determine whether or not the procedure is single-functioned and, if it is not, to what extent its contents could be partitioned differently between a number of procedures. Many textbooks on software design are primarily concerned with just this type of analysis.

Cohesion is a useful concept, although it is not always very easy to identify exactly which of the forms are present in a module. With Module-2, it can serve the double purpose of assessing the structures of both MODULEs and PROCEDUREs.

### 12.4.2 Coupling

There are four major forms of coupling, which will be examined in some detail since they lend themselves to a fuller interpretation with Modula-2 than with some other programming languages. The four forms are:

- data coupling;
- control coupling;
- stamp coupling ('type coupling');
- common-environment coupling.

(There are other forms besides these, but they are not particularly applicable to a language such as Modula-2, and so will not be considered here.)

**Data coupling**

This is, just as the name implies, a measure of the volume and form of information flow between modules. It is generally realized through the parameters of a procedure (at the lower level) and through the variables included in the export and import lists of a module. For procedures, there is also another form of data coupling, which occurs when statements within the procedure make direct references to an external data structure (which might be local to the module, or more global).

While no program could perform very much useful work without the use of some data coupling, we generally regard a high degree of it, as might be revealed by the use of many parameters or by many references to external data structures, as implying that the procedure is likely to exhibit poor cohesion. Similarly, a very long export list, particularly if it includes a large number of variables, can sometimes imply a poor choice of MODULE structure. (The guidelines for MODULEs are less clear than those for procedures.) High data coupling is often associated with low cohesion, for fairly obvious reasons.

One way of keeping the data coupling of a procedure to a minimum is to ensure that only the minimum of data to be used within a procedure should be passed as a parameter. So if a procedure accesses (say) only one field of a record, then that field alone should be passed, rather than the whole record. This ensures that the statements of the procedure are able to use or modify only that field, and cannot contain any undocumented references to the other fields, which could eventually lead to complications for the maintainer. (This also fits in nicely with the concept of information-hiding, since the passing of information is restricted to the relevant data structures.) So any procedure with a large number of parameters, or with structured types in the parameter list, should be viewed with a quizzical eye.

Direct access to external data structures is a form of data coupling that is much harder for the reader of a program to detect without checking each statement in a section of program – and so it is even harder to discover when examining the design for a program. As a general rule, procedures should make direct access only to local data structures (that is, ones that are local to the containing MODULE), and even this form should be used only when it is necessary to preserve information-hiding, and should be clearly documented.

**Control coupling**

The hierarchical run-time nature of a program in a language such as Modula-2 involves transferring control to another segment of the program whenever a procedure is called during program execution. Like some forms of data coupling, this form of control coupling is a necessary and normal feature within a program. However, control coupling can also take other forms, and one of the less desirable of these involves using one of the parameters of the called procedure as a 'switch'. Such a parameter is used within the called procedure to determine how it should perform its task: that is, it conveys information that is used to control the actions of the procedure, rather than information to be used by the calculations of the procedure.

As an example of this, consider the following procedure:

```
PROCEDURE PrintDate(month,day,year : CARDINAL; style : Conventions );
BEGIN
  CASE style OF
    American: WriteCard(month,2); WriteCard(day,2) |
    British: WriteCard(day,2); WriteCard(month,2)
  END; (* case *)
  WriteCard(year);
END PrintDate;
```

Here the parameter style, which is of type Conventions, is used to determine the way that this procedure will perform its actions when it is executed, and hence it acts as a switch. Rather than controlling the operation of PrintDate in this way, it would be better to use two separate procedures whose actions are single-valued, such as PrintAmericanDate and PrintBritishDate. (Note that the use of a switch can also make the exact purpose of a procedure harder to describe through its identifier.)

This form of control coupling is undesirable because it requires that the writer of the calling routine must know something about the form of the called routine in order to determine the appropriate value for the switch parameter. In the above example this means that the calling code must explicitly select the value of the parameter style in order to control the actions of PrintDate. This creates a connection (coupling) between the two routines, and any change that is made to one of them may also require a change to the other. So when designing a program, we need to examine each procedural interface carefully to determine how much of the information being exchanged is necessary (data coupling) and what purpose it will serve.

## Stamp coupling

This form involves two or more modules making use of some common data *type* (although not necessarily by accessing a shared data *structure*, which is really data coupling). Usually some amount of stamp coupling is a necessary feature within a program, although its use should be kept to a minimum. Where complex structured types such as records are used in a program, one of the benefits of Modula-2 is that the details of these can often be concealed within a module, with the knowledge of the structure being confined to the procedures that are provided for accessing its fields. (The use of opaque export can also assist in reducing the amount of stamp coupling present in a program or module.)

It is generally good practice to examine both the EXPORT and the IMPORT lists of modules for the presence of variables and data types, and to question carefully the necessity for including each of these. This is because these forms are major sources of both data coupling and stamp coupling between MODULEs. Ideally, only the absolute minimum of information should be provided in the interfaces to a module.

## Common environment coupling

This feature is rarely present in Modula-2 programs, although it can be present in certain circumstances. Programmers who are familiar with the feature of the FORTRAN language known as a COMMON block will have already encountered the idea of the common environment, in which some shared data area is separately (independently) referenced from different parts of a program. To ensure the integrity of the program, each segment must independently use the same structure to describe the form of the COMMON block, and this creates a coupling between the segments. This is a particularly insidious form of coupling, since a change in a section of a

COMMON block that may be used by only a few routines, such as inserting some new variables used by these routines, will affect *all* of the routines that use that COMMON block, even if they do not use the particular structure that has been changed.

While these particular concepts are not particularly helpful in providing any set of quantitative measures for the complexity of a program, they do assist us in making some qualitative assessments about our design choices. In particular, they can assist us when we wish to determine how well our design ideas conform to the concept of information-hiding, and hence are particularly valuable with a language such as Modula-2. Additionally, by their nature they can be used at a fairly early stage of the development process, and so can reduce the complexity of the eventual coding task.

### 12.4.3 The cyclomatic complexity metric

There are a number of metrics that can be used for analysing the complexity of program code. One of the better known is McCabe's cyclomatic complexity metric (McCabe, 1976; Myers, 1977), which is based upon a fairly simple analysis of the number and type of possible control paths that can arise during the execution of a program. Its validity has been challenged, however (Sheppard, 1988). Like the other metrics that have been described in this section, it is not particularly language-dependent and can form a useful measure for assessing the complexity of individual procedures. However, since its application requires that either the pseudocode or the actual code of a program be available, it can be used only at a fairly late stage of design, where it can be used to identify those modules that need further revision, or are likely to provide problems when it becomes necessary to modify them.

## 12.5 Re-using designs

Regrettably, programming (and hence software design) is currently apt to involve both designers and programmers in repeatedly re-inventing the wheel. Given the cost of developing a new program, it is therefore worth seeking ways to make the most of any previous efforts. One commonly used approach is to construct new programs in such a way that significant portions of them can later be directly re-used in the construction of other programs. Such an approach reduces the amount of effort required for the coding and testing of modules on subsequent occasions. Similarly, we can seek to reduce the (enormous) effort expended on the maintenance of software-based systems by separating out the features that are most likely to need changing at a later date. To some extent these two points are related, since the type of program that is constructed using well tested modules wherever possible is likely to be 'factored out' in such a way that it can be more easily maintained, too.

The idea of re-use is hardly new to the design of programming languages. The *library* facility used to store often used procedures in such well worn languages as FORTRAN has long provided a means of re-using existing code. However, without the use of information-hiding and without the packaging facility that is provided by the MODULE in Modula-2, it is possible to provide support in this way only for the functional components of a program through the re-use of procedures. So the emphasis for re-use is entirely on the separation of such algorithmic tasks as the calculation of mathematical functions or the provision of sorting routines, rather than on reducing the degree of data coupling.

We can further divide the question of re-use into the re-use of *code* in the form of program statements (which is largely provided by the traditional form of library structure), and the re-use of *design*, which involves the description of more abstract concepts. In order to re-use a piece of a design as fully as possible, we need to be able to separate the algorithmic component of the design from the data types that it handles. Ideally this needs the provision of some generic form that can be used for declaring the data types to be used in a re-usable module. Although Modula-2 does not directly provide a facility for generic data types, the concept can still be very useful to us when designing our programs.

The use of **generic data types** with modules parallels the use of formal and actual parameters with procedures. The idea is first to compile the module using a 'place-holder' for the data type that is handled in the module (the generic data type), and then to substitute the 'actual' data type when the module is linked into a program. The difference is that the substitution involved is of data *types* rather than of data *variables*. (There are obviously some limitations as to the type of module that is suited to this idea, since not all algorithms are sufficiently type-independent.)

The idea of generic types may be made clearer by an example. If we wish to construct a generic stack module – that is, one that can be instantiated to provide a stack of INTEGERs or REALs, or CHARs, or any other data type – the module interface, as represented by its definition part, will need to look like:

```
(* a simple stack module defined in generic form *)
DEFINITION MODULE GenericStack;
EXPORT Push, Pop, Done;
    PROCEDURE Push(input : Elementtype);    (* adds element to stack *)
    PROCEDURE Pop(): Elementtype;           (* removes top element from stack *)
    PROCEDURE Done(): BOOLEAN;              (* success/fail indicator *)
END GenericStack.
```

**Table 12.2** Comparison of generic types and procedure parameters.

|  | *Generic types* | *Procedure parameters* |
| --- | --- | --- |
| Formal values act as a template | During compilation | During compilation |
| Formal values are replaced by actual value | When module is bound into the executable program by the link-editor | During program execution |

In this, the formal (generic) type is Elementtype, which is still undefined at this point. Within the implementation part we will also need to construct the stack as a permanent data structure, and the declaration of this might look like:

```
VAR
    stack : ARRAY [0..maxlength] OF Elementtype;
```

or might equally well be based upon the use of a linked list.

The key point is that to be able to make use of true generic types we would need to be able to compile the two parts of the module GenericStack without declaring anything about the actual form of Elementtype. Only when the module is actually linked into the program should Elementtype be replaced by an actual type, such as INTEGER, CHAR or some user-defined type. Table 12.2 shows the steps in constructing a program using generic types in modules, compared with the use of formal and actual parameters of procedures.

The use of generic types in this way has some obvious attractions for the programmer. Provided that the algorithm for such a module can be constructed so that it is sufficiently independent of the actual data type being stored on the stack, then once the module 'template' has been created, an instance of a stack using any appropriate data type can be created from it as necessary. (To be more general, we should also extend the structure of this example module so that it can be used to generate multiple instances of stacks of a given type.) Not only does this reduce the effort needed for designing and programming such modules but, if the module has been tested for an INTEGER stack (say), it should work for a stack of any similar type: only a limited amount of additional testing should be necessary when instantiating it for a similar type.

Unfortunately the provision of a generic typing facility adds considerable complications for the compiler writer, and so Modula-2 does not directly support the use of generic forms as described above. A Modula-2 compiler requires that we should supply the actual type to be substituted for Elementtype when compiling the module described above, instead of deferring this binding until it is used in constructing a program. Ada, a much larger programming language, provides a very powerful facility for using generic types. However, this should not be taken to imply that we cannot make use of the concept in any way. There are a number of opinions on the best way of implementing the use of generic forms in Modula-2 (Wiener and Sincovec, 1985; Beidler and Jackowitz, 1986; Wiener, 1986; Goldsby, 1986), but as our immediate concern in this chapter is the design of systems rather than their construction, we will not attempt to evaluate these here.

Generic data types augment the module facility, in that we can code and test one module and then use this as a template from which to create others that use different data types. Because Modula-2 lacks a true generic type facility, some additional testing of any modules generated from even a well tested template is still necessary. To make effective use of the concept, the designer must ensure that the packaging of a program into modules will seek to identify those modules that are potentially re-usable. These are in turn most likely to be found where we use complex data structures such as trees, stacks or linked lists, for which the algorithms involved are essentially independent of the data type used in the elements.

It should be emphasized that the reduction in programming effort that can result from the re-use of modules is not just saving of time spent on coding – it is also the saving of (some) design time and of some module testing time. Since the testing of large systems at component and integration levels typically requires several times the effort needed to program them, these savings can be significant.

As the example above suggests, a key factor in designing a module for re-use is the choice of its interface form, as specified in the definition part of the module. Ideally the export list should contain:

- no variables (since these create extra data coupling);
- no structured types (which could reveal the details of structures);
- procedures that have only the minimal set of parameters in order to keep data coupling to a minimum.

Within the module, it is also necessary to ensure that any operations using the generic Elementtype are not dependent in any way upon its form – that is, that they are type-independent. Modula-2 provides some useful help here through the standard functions, such as INC, that are suitably type-independent, at least for scalar ordinal types.

Once again it needs to be emphasized that these points only provide a means of *assessing* our decisions about design choices. They prescribe no practices that can be adopted to guarantee that a design will meet our requirements. For the present at least, the available software design methods and practice can offer little better.

224 THE SOFTWARE DEVELOPMENT PROCESS

This chapter has been concerned with some issues taken from a large and complex subject area that still lacks any real theoretical underpinnings. The emphasis has been on fairly abstract issues, yet these are not so abstract that they cannot be related to Modula-2. To make the best use of Modula-2 in writing programs that can be used and maintained or modified over long periods, the issues raised in this chapter need to be considered in detail before any of the code is written. While the process of top-level design largely involves handling abstract ideas, and the detailed forms of the eventual implementation language should not be a major consideration during this phase, expanding a design into declarations and statements is very much influenced by the facilities that are provided in the eventual programming language.

In the next chapter we shall examine two approaches to the design of a modest-sized example program in some detail, using some of the ideas introduced in this chapter. In Chapter 14 we shall consider how the testing of modules can be organized, and the influence that our testing strategy will have on the way that we structure and partition code.

EXERCISES

**12.1** Consider the last few programs that you have written. How closely did their development match the cycle that is shown in Figure 12.1? Which phases of the development part of the life cycle were missing? How well did the distribution of effort match that shown in Figure 12.2?

**12.2** Try sketching some data flow diagrams that represent the following activities:

(a) the way that you create and develop a program on your computer system;

(b) the process of assembling a garden shed;

(c) the process of repairing a puncture in a bicycle tyre.

**12.3** Draw a structure chart for the program listed in Figure 11.3.

**12.4** One of the advantages of a programming language with a form such as that used with Modula-2 is that it is possible to provide support for the concept of *information-hiding* by using separate compilation. This can, in turn, be related to the concept of *objects* within a system. For the following system descriptions, try to identify the objects within the system for which it would be desirable to conceal the detailed form and structure within a module.

EXERCISES     225

(a)   a 'portable compiler' for Modula-2 that is intended to be easily reconfigured to run on a variety of machines and operating systems, and reconfigurable to generate code for different computer instruction sets;

(b)   a screen-based text-editor program that will need to be reconfigured for use with several different types of terminal (assume that there is only one type of terminal used on any particular system);

(c)   a 'mail browser' program that allows users to send, receive and examine electronic mail from their computer terminals.

# Chapter 13
# Constructing a Modula-2 Program

13.1 Selecting an example problem
13.2 A solution based on Structured Analysis and Structured Design
13.3 A solution based on Object-Oriented Design (OOD)
13.4 Completing the Object-Oriented Design
Exercises

## 13.1 Selecting an example problem

The aim of this chapter is to draw together the relatively abstract measures and practices that were described in the previous chapter, and to relate them wherever possible to the issues of implementing designs using Modula-2. It is useful to have a suitable example to assist with this, a problem that is large enough to require a systematic approach to its design, yet not so large that it cannot also be understood fairly quickly and readily.

A further important aspect of our choice of example is the type of programming problem that should be used. We can identify three major domains of computer application, each with its own special characteristics, which commonly provide problems that might effectively exploit the resources of a language such as Modula-2. These are:

- business data processing;
- process control;
- program development tools.

It is possible to use Modula-2 for all three types of problem, but it is designed largely for use with the latter two groups. Since process control problems represent a rather complicated subject area, the best area in which to seek a representative problem that is not too large and complex

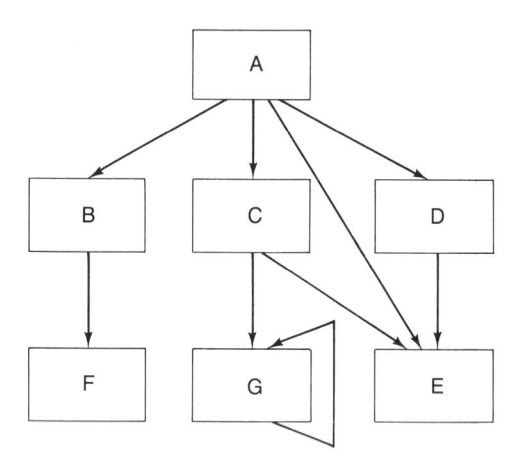

**Figure 13.1** Example structure diagram for a Pascal program. (Procedure G is recursive.)

for our purpose would seem to be that of 'systems' programs, among which we might number such software tools as editors, compilers, directory listing utilities, etc.

The problem chosen for this chapter is fairly straightforward, and results in a useful software tool (always a bonus). If designed carefully, it can also form a source of modules that can in turn be re-used when constructing further tools. We shall design and construct the framework for a program to perform dependency tracing, using as its input the source code of a Pascal program.

Such a tool is useful to anyone who wants to understand, and perhaps modify, an existing program. With the all-too-frequent lack of up-to-date system documentation, a tool that draws a structure chart for a source program (or at least provides the information needed to enable us to draw such a chart for ourselves) can be of great assistance. A structure chart can be considered as forming an index to a program, as well as indicating the general structure adopted by the original designer. Since a Pascal program must all be contained in a single compilation unit, choosing to restrict ourselves to Pascal limits the complexity of the problem. The form of a Pascal program is also reasonably close to that of a Modula-2 program, so we will be discussing structures that will be familiar enough to the reader.

To perform this task, the program will need to read through the source code of a Pascal program and identify the extent and form of the relationships among its procedures. So for each procedure declared in the input source program, our program will need to print out a list of those

|  |  |  |  |  | level | types |
|---|---|---|---|---|---|---|
| Level 1: | A | > | B (list of formal parameters) |  | 2 | p |
|  |  | > | C ( | ) | 2 | f |
|  |  | > | D ( | ) | 2 | p |
|  |  | >> | E ( | ) | 3 | f |
| Level 2: | B | > | F ( | ) | 3 | p |
|  | C | > | G ( | ) | 3 | p |
|  |  | > | E ( | ) | 3 | f |
|  | D | > | E ( | ) | 3 | f |
| Level 3: | G | > | G ( | ) | 3 | p |

\> : indicates a procedure on the next level
\>> : called by a lower level procedure
G : recursive
p : procedure
f : function

**Figure 13.2** Outline of output form for program shown in Figure 13.1.

procedures that it calls, either directly or by making use of other procedures. This output can then be used to construct a structure chart.

In its simplest form this program can simply show the calling hierarchy, but of course there is also scope to add information about the formal parameters for the procedure calls. For the purposes of the examples though, we shall include the parameters in the basic design. (Obviously this is one of the features that should be considered when assessing our design structures in terms of possible future extensions.)

Figure 13.1 shows a structure chart for a very simple Pascal program, while Figure 13.2 shows the type of trace listing that the dependency tracing program should produce when this simple program is provided as its input.

As is typical of such situations, the outline requirement given above is not a very full or rigorous specification for a program, and it will need some further elaboration as questions arise during the design and implementation of our solution. The next two sections of this chapter are concerned with producing top-level designs for the program using two quite different design methods. These two methods have been chosen both because they are quite different models for the design process, and because they are also quite widely used. In the section that follows we expand one of these into a more detailed design and then examine it in terms of the criteria that were described in Chapter 12. This section also illustrates some of the issues involved in the construction of a program using separate compilation.

230    CONSTRUCTING A MODULA-2 PROGRAM

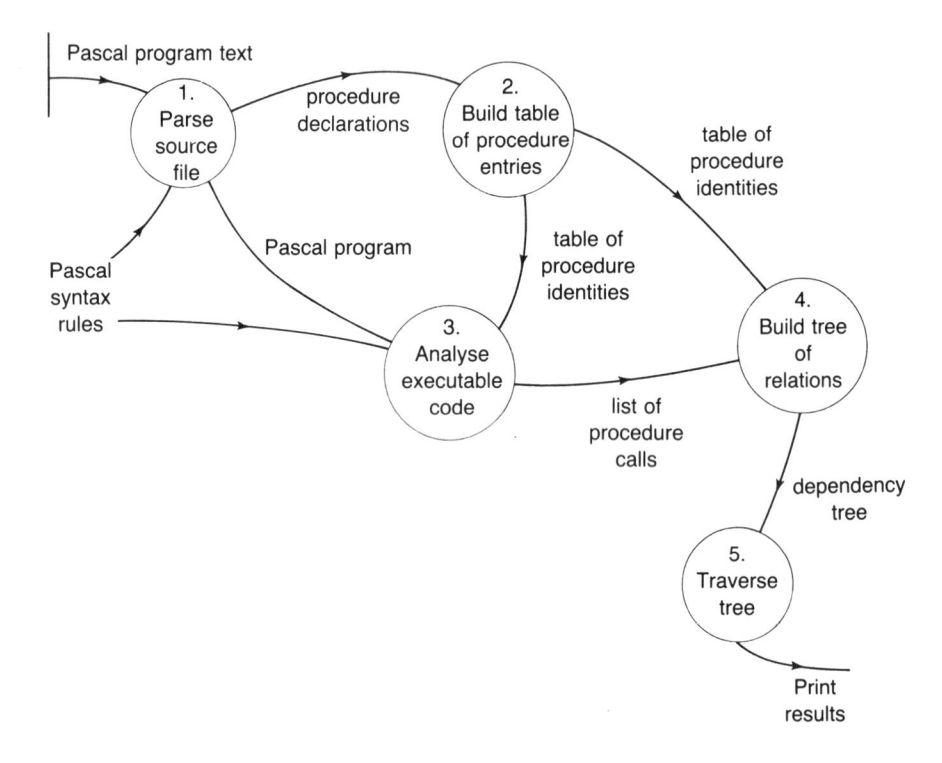

**Figure 13.3**   A first DFD for the problem of Figure 13.1.

## 13.2  A solution based upon Structured Analysis and Structured Design

As was explained in Chapter 12, the Structured Analysis and Structured Design method places considerable emphasis upon the *functional* aspects of a program when choices need to be made; but in its initial analysis, it also models the data *flow* that is involved in the problem. This section uses the method in a fairly simple manner, but it should provide sufficient detail for the reader to be able to understand how the method can be applied.

The design process begins with an analysis of the problem. It may well be that a number of questions will arise during this, and that some may concern details of the problem that were not made clear, or even identified at all, in the requirements specification. This can be regarded as a desirable feature of the method, since these questions should indeed be identified at an early stage, rather than being discovered (and subsequently resolved) during system implementation.

Figure 13.3 describes a first attempt at producing a data flow diagram (DFD) to describe the task involved. Examining this, we can see that

# A SOLUTION BASED UPON STRUCTURED ANALYSIS AND DESIGN 231

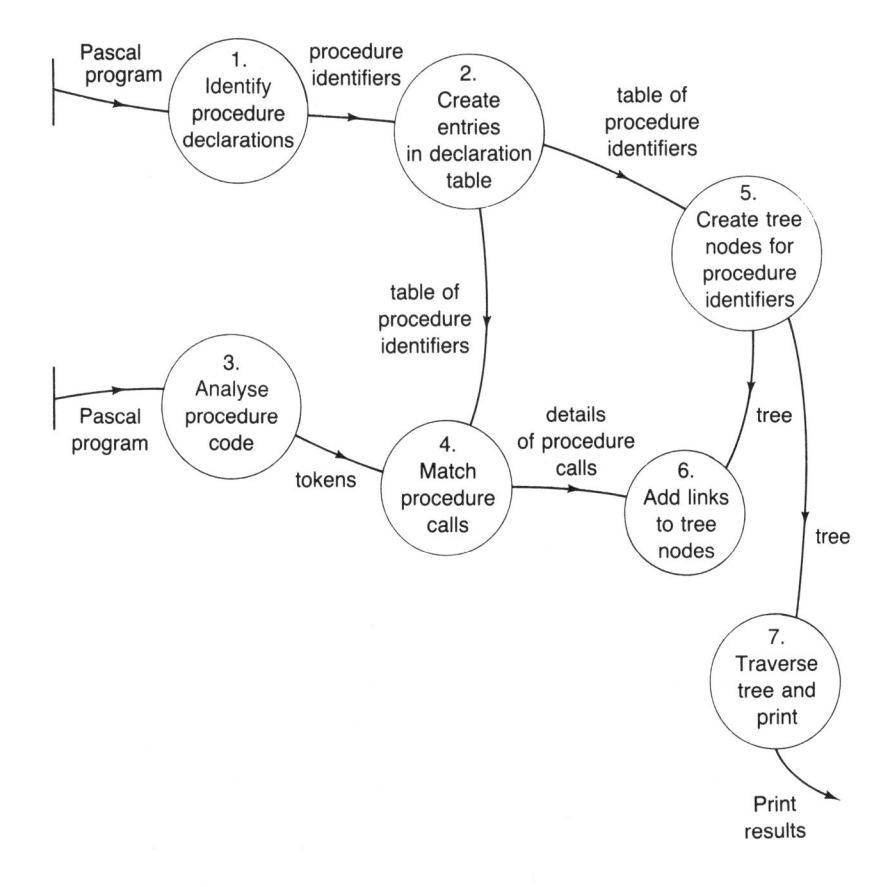

**Figure 13.4** A second DFD for the problem of Figure 13.1.

it immediately raises one question about the strategy that might be used in the solution, namely as to whether we should read the input Pascal source file once or twice. If it is read in only once, then it will be necessary to record both procedure declarations and procedure calls within a single pass – which is possible (since Pascal is designed for single-pass compilation), but which may involve additional complications for internal structures. However, at this point it is not necessary to resolve this question, since it really forms an issue of *implementation*. Instead of being diverted from the correct level of abstraction, we must concentrate upon analysing the *operations* that the program needs to perform to derive the necessary information about the Pascal source.

A it happens it turns out that this description is not the best one that can be produced, as will be discovered by attempting to expand it further: doing so soon results in a number of rather awkward structures.

```
ProcedureDeclaration = ProcedureIdentifier
                       ProcedureType      (* function or procedure *)
                       ParameterList      (* used for annotation *)

                       (* do we really need ProcedureType? *)

           TreeNode =  ProcedureIdentifier
                       ProcedureType
                       list of parent nodes
                       list of child nodes
                       ParameterList      (* formal parameters only *)
                       level              (* start high, migrate down *)

      ProcedureCall =  ProcedureIdentifier
                       [caller]
                       ProcedureIdentifier
                       [called]

                       (* what about recursive procedures? *)
```

**Figure 13.5** A 'data dictionary' for the data flow diagram.

(These then complicate the structured design step.) So a second attempt is required, and produces the DFD shown in Figure 13.4.

Besides considering data flow between the different components, the task of structured analysis requires that the designer should also consider the forms of data that should be used. Figure 13.5 shows an example of a data dictionary that is created for this purpose, and which is intended to support the DFD shown in Figure 13.4. These initial descriptions are still fairly abstract, and are really only concerned with establishing the general forms that are required. The first rough workings will usually include some notes made by the designer as reminders for some of the various points that will need to be considered when expanding the design description. (For the purposes of this exercise, such notes are enclosed in 'starred parentheses', rather like the comments in a Modula-2 program.) Making such notes during the design process is a useful practice to adopt, and avoids the need to descend too far from the current 'level of abstraction' (Adelson and Soloway, 1985).

The next stage is to further analyse each of the operations that were identified as bubbles in the DFD and, where appropriate, to expand the details of these in further DFDs. To maintain control over the information involved in the different levels of the analysis, we use a simple numbering scheme to index the different levels of the diagram. Figure 13.6 provides a (simple) expansion of the task that is summarised in the first bubble of

A SOLUTION BASED UPON STRUCTURED ANALYSIS AND DESIGN 233

Pascal program → ( 1.1 Extract tokens ) →tokens→ ( 1.2 Select procedure declarations ) → procedure identifiers and parameter lists

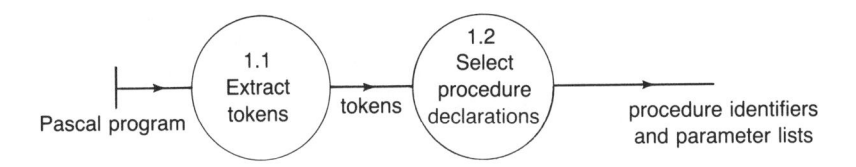

**Figure 13.6** A first expansion of the DFD of Figure 13.3.

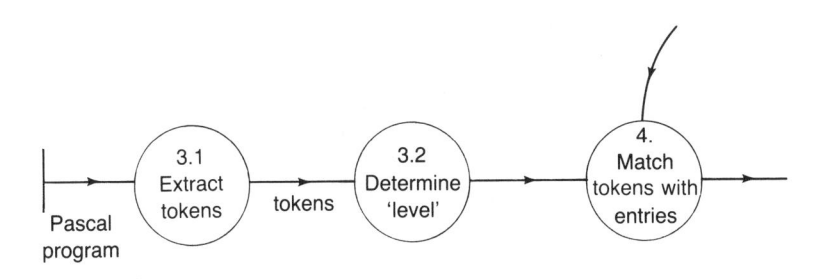

Pascal program → ( 3.1 Extract tokens ) →tokens→ ( 3.2 Determine 'level' ) → ( 4. Match tokens with entries ) →

(\*involves some global knowledge about 'level'\*)

**Figure 13.7** Further expansions of the DFD of Figure 13.3.

Figure 13.4, and the new bubbles are numbered in turn as 1.1 and 1.2. For the moment, there is no obvious expansion for the second bubble of Figure 13.4, and so Figure 13.7 shows an expanded version of the third and fourth bubbles (one of these is really more of a refinement of the original thinking). Finally, in Figure 13.8 these are reassembled to produce an expanded view of the complete system that was initially described in Figure 13.4. We have now established the main flow of information in the system, and so the data dictionary can be further refined too, resulting in the form that is shown in Figure 13.9. (Where necessary, this scheme of expansion and extended numbering can be continued to further levels, so allowing the designer to produce more detailed levels of description.)

The foregoing description is rather simplified in many ways, but it may make it obvious why comprehensive tomes have been dedicated to explaining structured analysis. However, we now have a fairly complete outline of the system required, and can proceed to consider how it can be transformed into a corresponding program structure via structured design. This task is achieved largely by performing a **transform analysis**, during which the non-hierarchical and potentially concurrent DFD that describes the structure of the *problem* is transformed into one or more hierarchical and sequential structure charts that describe the structure of the *system*. (In this case there need be only one structure chart and one process, but where a system needs to be realized as several processes, the method can be used to create more than one structure chart.)

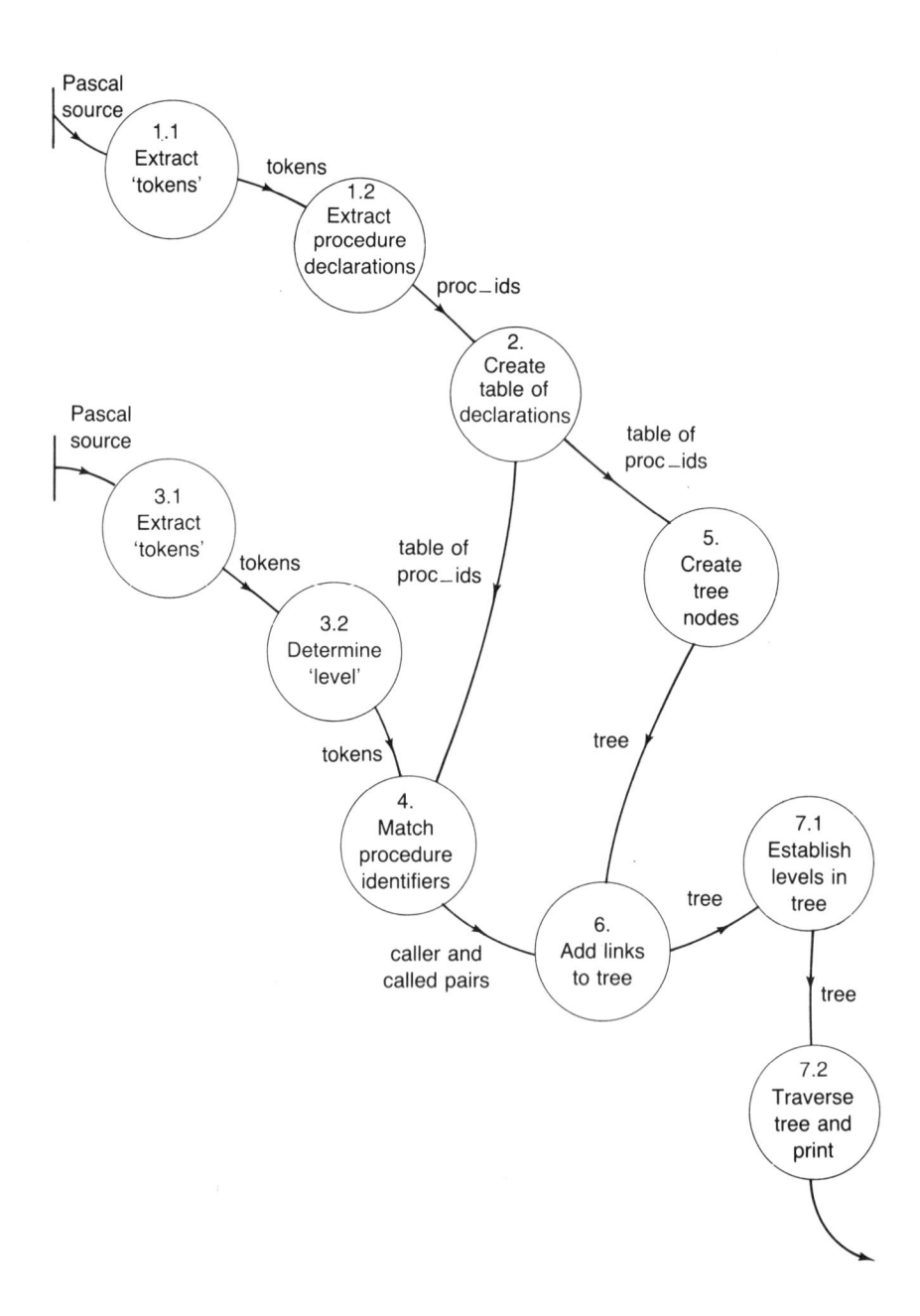

**Figure 13.8** A more detailed DFD for the system.

```
ProcedureDeclaration = ProcedureIdentifier
                       ProcedureType          (* function or procedure *)
                       ParameterList          (* formal parameters *)

       ParameterList = NoOfParameters         (* count of parameters *)
                       {FormalParameter}
      FormalParameter = ParameterIdentifier
                        ParameterForm         (* VAR or VAL *)
                        ParameterType
```

(* do we really need procedure type ? *)
(* procedure type is needed if we want to annotate with data flow information, as a function procedure is another parameter for this purpose *)

```
            TreeNode = ProcedureDeclaration
                       linked list of parent nodes
                       linked list of child nodes
                       level in tree          (* established by traversal *)
       ProcedureCall = ProcedureIdentifier    (* caller *)
                       ProcedureIdentifier    (* called *)
```

(* what about recursive procedures? *)
(* recognized by identical fields in a ProcedureCall record *)

Note: While this has not been carried into great detail, some of the questions have been answered. Both questions and answers should be kept on record.

**Figure 13.9** A revised data dictionary.

The first task in structured design is to identify the 'central transform' of the program. This is the point at which the input and output data flows of the DFD reach their most abstract level. The central transform is not necessarily easily identified, and it may require some experimentation to locate it with any certainty. Experienced designers suggest that if selecting one of the 'process' bubbles of the DFD for this task proves unsuitable, it may be necessary to create a new one that will take on a co-ordinating role.

In this particular problem, the input and output data flows are not particularly significant or distinguished features, since much of the content of the problem is centred around the handling of information held in a central data structure – or more correctly, in two such structures. (This emphasis on data flow is a reminder of the strong data processing orientation of this method!) One of these is the table of procedure declarations,

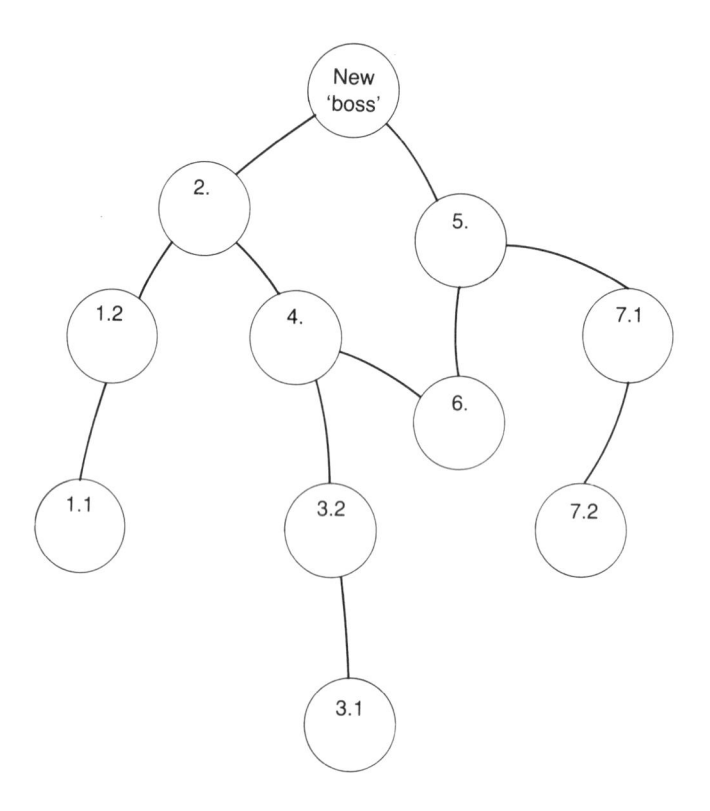

**Figure 13.10** First step in reorganizing the components of the DFD.

which is used to help in identifying procedure calls: while the other is the 'tree-like' linked data structure that will represent the control flow in the final structure chart. These can be considered as two distinct entities (even though one is transformed in order to create the initial form of the other) and, since both are central to the problem, it seems reasonable to try creating a new 'arbitrating' bubble at a point between these. It will occupy a place between bubbles 2.0 and 5.0 in Figure 13.8. (This task of finding and using a central transform is much harder when using the original DFD of Figure 13.3, and is one reason why that was abandoned.)

Having chosen this 'central transform', the next step is to imagine 'lifting' this bubble, trailing the others below it, and so creating the form shown in Figure 13.10. With some reorganization of links and squaring of circles, it is possible to produce the first rough structure chart for this program, as is shown in Figure 13.11. On this structure chart we have also shown the relationship between each component procedure and the main data structures of the program, purely for the purpose of explaining it in the context of Modula-2, and for future use in coding it in Modula-2. Adding this information emphasizes that the hierarchical structure of the

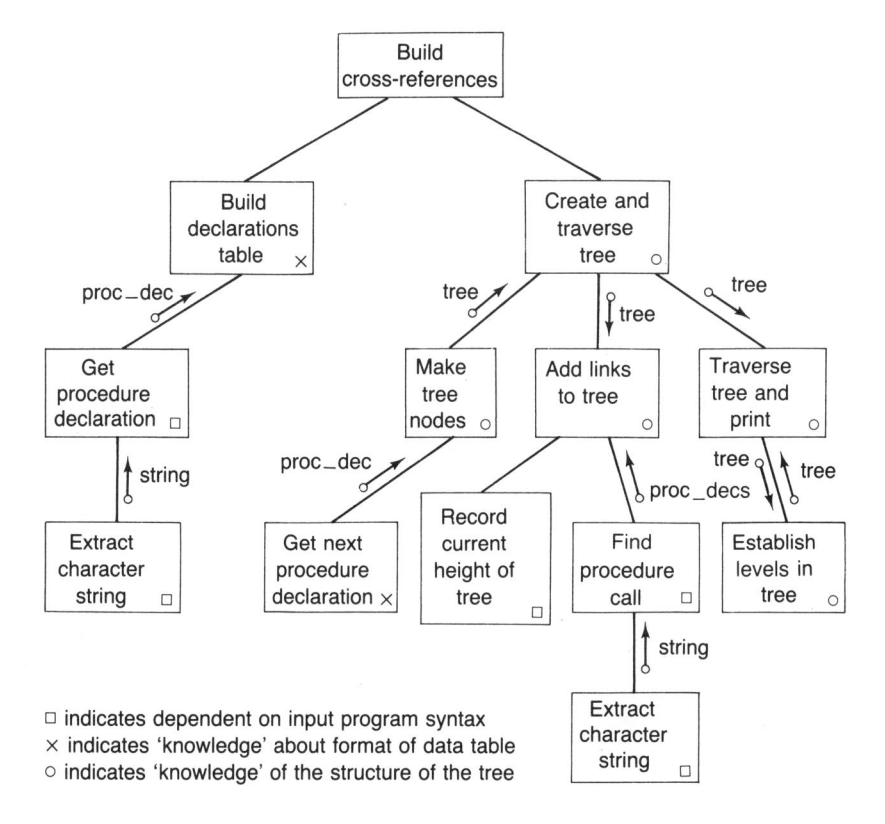

A SOLUTION BASED UPON STRUCTURED ANALYSIS AND DESIGN 237

**Figure 13.11** First rough structure chart.

program, and its packaging into modules, are usually quite distinct aspects of its structure.

The next step is to expand this first rough structure chart, making use of some of the design assessment criteria that were discussed in Chapter 12. It will also be necessary to expand more upon the detail of some of the operations to be performed by the program, including parsing the input text file. This latter task has so far received relatively little attention, but its appearance as a component on two major branches of the tree shown in Figure 13.11 suggests that decisions about how to perform this operation most effectively should not be deferred for much longer.

Figure 13.12 provides a more refined version of the structure chart of Figure 13.11. In the rest of this section we consider how well this design meets the various design criteria that have been proposed, and how it might be implemented in such as way as to make best use of the features of Modula-2.

In his excellent guide to the structured design method, Meilir Page-Jones (1980) lists a number of activities that should be performed as part of

238   CONSTRUCTING A MODULA-2 PROGRAM

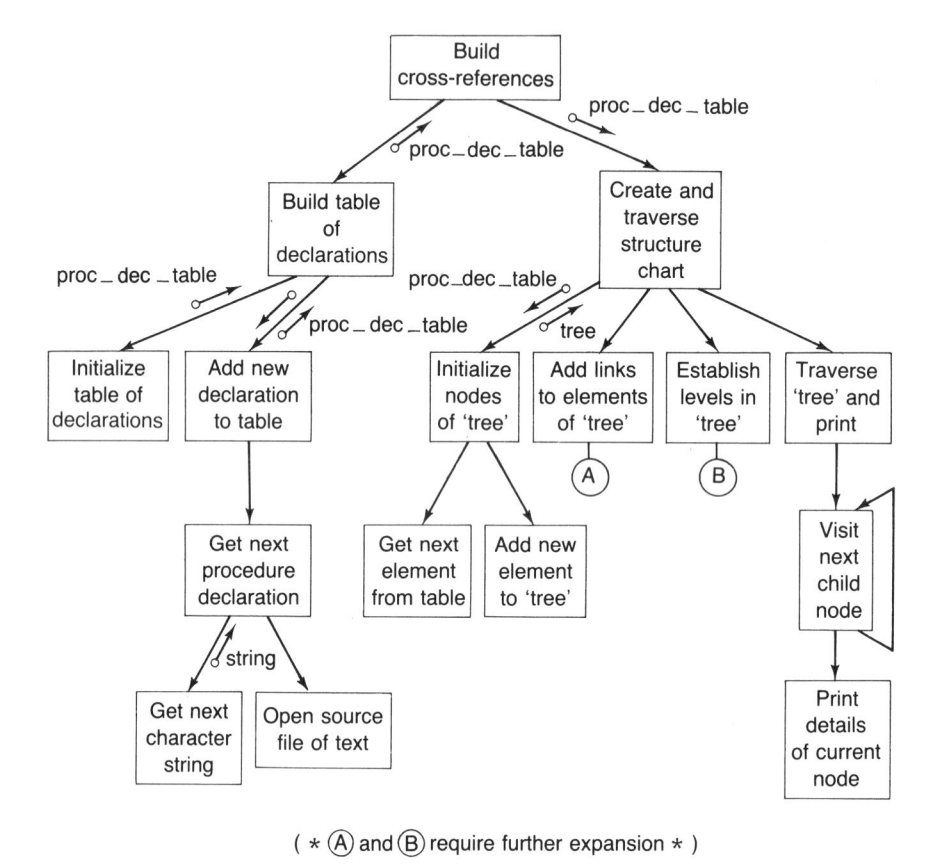

**Figure 13.12** A more refined structure chart.

the process of refining a first rough structure chart into something that might form the basis of a well structured program. Five of these activities that seem particularly worth considering here are:

- adding read and write modules;
- factoring out some of the functions (this involves creating new modules to take over sub-functions of larger ones);
- adding error-handling functions;
- adding details of initialization and termination;
- checking design criteria, and being prepared to change the design as a result of doing so.

Obviously some of these tasks are especially important in the design of data processing systems, but they are also issues that will need to be considered here – even though the emphasis may differ slightly. In particular, the organization of input and output, as well as the initialization of any data structures, need to be clarified at this stage of design. It therefore seems appropriate to consider how these tasks might be performed for the design described by Figure 13.12, and especially the last of them, which may of course require that we repeat parts of this design process. It is not appropriate to attempt to resolve all the issues that are involved in performing these tasks, but we will attempt to identify them in the context of this particular problem and of the solution that has been proposed.

**Adding read and write modules**

This is a relatively simple operation in this case, since the input and output streams both consist of a single file of characters. Associated operations, such as selecting the input file, may be dependent upon the facilities of the particular operating system used.

**Factoring out some of the functions**

This task requires a little more thought, and each box of Figure 13.12 needs to be examined with some care. From the short description given to each of these in the diagram, there seems to be relatively little scope for any further subdivision, but it is likely to appear more appropriate once the detailed design of each box is begun. Some of the routines concerned, especially those concerned with the analysis of the input program source, are likely to have quite complex algorithms: in this particular case, however, this will be aided by the facts that parsing and lexical analysis are relatively well understood problems, and that only limited amounts of information will be required.

In considering the factoring out, it is necessary to give some added thought to the way that each operation will be performed. One problem that might be encountered is how to handle recursive procedures in the input program. If too simple a tracing mechanism is used, an encounter with a recursive procedure will simply set the dependency tracing routines into a continuous loop! This problem does not necessarily need to be resolved at this point, but the very act of making notes about such aspects of a design is a useful practice to adopt. In their study of how experienced designers work, Adelson and Soloway (1985) observed that they tried to avoid descending too far from their current level of abstraction, but often made notes about points that could have led them into such a detour. These notes could then be used later to ensure that the relevant points were covered in the expanded design, so assisting with the verification process. So for the moment we shall defer any further attempts to factor out the design, and limit ourselves to making the one note about the need to consider how a recursive procedure is to be handled.

### Adding error-handling functions

For this particular problem, the error-handling aspect is not a major issue. It is reasonable to assume that an input file will contain the source of a program that already compiles successfully, and so should be syntactically correct and complete. This minimizes the complexity involved in handling the input (another reason for delaying consideration of the factoring). For convenience we will also make two further assumptions about an input file:

- the input program makes no use of forward references;
- all procedure names are unique within the first 12 characters.

Neither of these restrictions should prove unduly limiting. Provided that we keep them in mind during the rest of the design process, we can later add a facility for handling forward references if required. Similarly, the second requirement can easily be modified at a later stage, provided that we ensure the relevant declarations and expressions make use of an appropriate size constant.

Although in this program the error-handling features can be kept fairly simple, it may be useful to construct a list of the types of errors that the program might encounter, and the actions that it will need to take in each case. Again, this is one of the 'note-making' tasks of design.

### Add details of initialization and termination

The next task is rather harder to evade or defer at this point. The operation of initializing the program's own data structures, such as the table of procedure identifiers, is not likely to form a particular issue (as long we remember the need to include it), but organizing the actions needed for file handling may need more care. If a 'two-pass' approach is chosen, the program will need to open the source file twice and therefore will explicitly need to close it at least once. An associated question is to determine the level within the complete program structure to which we should assign the file-handling tasks.

Any knowledge about the file that is currently acting as the input Pascal source is likely to be known to the top-level module 'build cross-references', and so it seems appropriate that the operations involved in opening and closing files should be kept at this level. However, details such as recognizing the 'end of file' condition probably belong right down at the lowest levels – and so the knowledge of such system-dependent details should perhaps be confined to these levels. Since these are logically distinct aspects of file handling, this seems a reasonable separation to adopt.

**Table 13.1** Suggested forms of coupling/cohesion for the program outlined in Figure 13.12.

| 'Procedure' | Coupling | Cohesion |
| --- | --- | --- |
| (1) Build table of declarations | Data coupling (table) | Communicational |
| (2) Create and traverse structure chart | Data coupling (table and 'tree') | Sequential |
| (3) Initialize table of declarations | | Temporal (?) |
| (4) Add new declaration to table | Data coupling | |
| (5) Initialize nodes of tree | | Temporal (?) |
| (6) Add links to elements of 'tree' | | Sequential, communicational |
| (7) Establish levels in 'tree' | | |
| (8) Traverse 'tree' and print | | Sequential, logical |
| (9) Get next procedure declaration | | |
| (10) Get next element from table | | Communicational |
| (11) Add new element to tree | | Communicational |
| (12) Visit next child node | | Functional |

**Checking design criteria**

The final task involves assessing our design using such criteria as *cohesion* and *coupling*, and also checking that the program is complete. While we might also try to consider information-hiding, this feature is less easily assessed at this level, and so will not be attempted yet.

Table 13.1 provides a rough summary of the extent to which the different forms of cohesion and coupling appear to be present in the design of Figure 13.12. While *activating control coupling* has been omitted (since it is implicit in every procedure call represented in Figure 13.12), an attempt has been made to find which other forms can be considered as present in each element.

At this point it is worth standing back a little and attempting to assess how far the use of structured design has provided guidance on the best ways of making use of Modula-2.

- The method clearly helps with identifying function, so that we can determine which procedures will be required – but it does not help in assessing how well we can subsume any of these functions into the anonymous procedures that form the main bodies of the Modula-2 MODULEs.
- There is no specific guidance to determine how the components of the program can best be 'packaged' into MODULEs in the Modula-2 sense. It may be possible to back-track towards this goal by considering the use made of shared information, but there is no direct guidance.
- Because the initialization of internal and external structures is considered at a relatively late stage in the design process, the method gives little guidance about how to structure the main bodies of the MODULEs. Opening files, closing files and similar tasks could be handled within the main body of a subordinate module. More generally, there is also little guidance about which operations could be performed by the main module at the top of the program tree.
- Data types required and information about shared data structures are not clearly identified by the method.

So while it is certainly possible to develop this design into a Modula-2 program, there is little doubt that it will be necessary to extract explicitly and separately much of the additional information that will be needed for determining how the program should be partitioned into modules. In order to make use of the distinctive features of Modula-2, and particularly of its packaging facilities, there is a need to find distinct criteria that do not emerge naturally from this particular design process.

Perhaps this is really not surprising, since the structured design method predates the design of Modula-2. However, it does suggest that structured design needs to be reconsidered somewhat in order to get the best out of Modula-2. It may well be possible to do this.

In the next section, therefore, we develop a new solution using a design method (object-oriented design) that more closely parallels the form of Modula-2, and is largely based upon the same philosophy. We can then contrast the type of final program structure that is produced, and see to what extent this lends itself more naturally to being implemented in Modula-2.

## 13.3 A solution based upon Object-Oriented Design (OOD)

The term 'object-oriented' has come to mean slightly different things when used by designers and by system developers, but the same essential concepts are present in both interpretations. The idea of basing the design and

A SOLUTION BASED UPON OBJECT-ORIENTED DESIGN    243

**PROBLEM SPACE**

```
         Data                              Results

   ┌──────────────┐                   ┌──────────────┐
   │ Real-world   │   Real-world      │ Real-world   │
   │ objects and  │────algorithm─────▶│   objects    │
   │ operations   │                   │              │
   └──────┬───────┘                   └──────▲───────┘
          │                                  │
   The programmer's                    Human
   representation                    interpretation
   of the problem                      of results
  ────────┼──────────────────────────────────┼────────
          │                                  │
          ▼                                  │
   ┌──────────────┐                   ┌──────────────┐
   │ Programming  │   Computer        │              │
   │language objects│──algorithm─────▶│ Output data  │
   │ and operations │                 │              │
   └──────────────┘                   └──────────────┘
```

**SOLUTION SPACE**

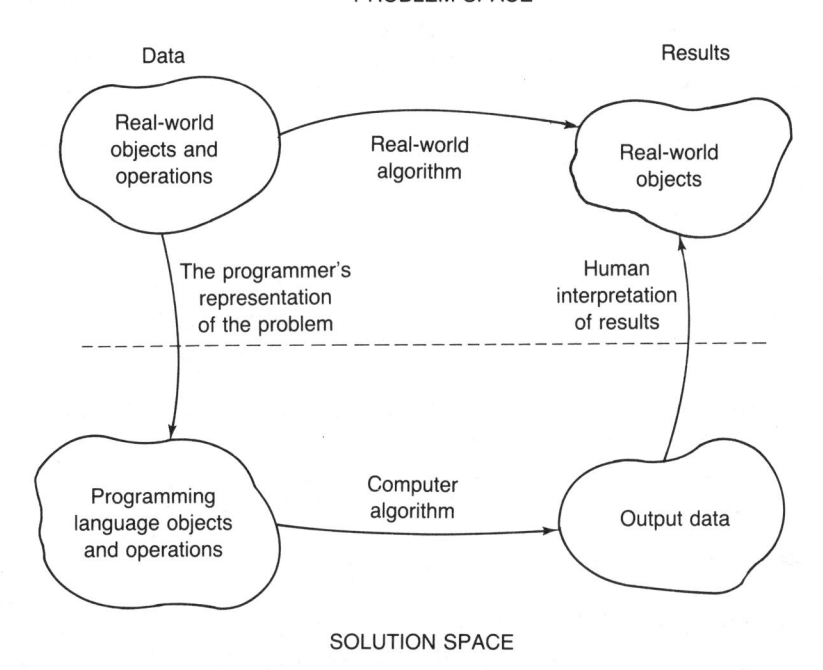

**Figure 13.13** Model for a typical programming task. Adapted with permission from *Programming Language Landscape: Syntax, Semantics, and Implementation*, Second Edition by Michael Marcotty and Henry F. Ledgard. Copyright © Science Research Associates, Inc., 1986. USA.

construction of a program around 'objects' really stems from the Smalltalk system (Goldberg and Robson, 1983); the idea of using it as a means of design in the form described here (often termed OOD) was first proposed by Russ Abbott (1983), and then further developed and refined by Grady Booch (1983, 1986). Both Abbott and Booch have been primarily concerned with exploring the rich set of Ada structures, but much of their thinking is also applicable to a language such as Modula-2, which contains the same packaging concepts.

The diagram shown in Figure 13.13 was originally proposed by Ledgard and Marcotty (1981), and it summarizes the concepts of this method. The upper half of the diagram represents the 'problem space', which contains real-world problems (such as providing an accounting system for a bank), and also the real-world solution, complete with appropriate algorithms. The tasks of the programmer and the designer are represented by the lower half of the diagram: these consist of finding models of the problem and its solutions that will mirror the real-world system, and hence mirror its solution too. This makes it possible to maintain the resulting system in a methodical and systematic way, by ensuring that any changes in the real-world system (perhaps a change in the tax laws that affect banking practices) can be mirrored in the solution space by modifying the corresponding objects.

The object-oriented philosophy is therefore based upon designing a program to manipulate various 'objects'. These will correspond in some way with the real-world objects, and will be subject to corresponding operations (such as withdrawal, depositing, opening accounts, etc. in the example of a bank). This idea can be developed further, in that it should also be possible to package the objects of the model in some manner that reflects the 'packaging' of the real-world objects. In this way, the scope 'walls' that are built around our information will be constructed around the representations of the objects, and may be used to conceal the details of their representation.

While Modula-2 is not so well endowed as Ada in its capability for representing objects, it is nevertheless considerably better provided than most other imperative programming languages. It is also close to Ada in style and form, so that the OOD method has the potential to provide a designer with more complete guidance on the final form of the design than is possible from a simple application of the structured design approach.

In his original paper, Abbott (1983) observed that the functioning of real systems can be described in English language statements by using a mix of verbs and nouns. Imperative programming languages are usually provided with ample means of representing operations (verbs), but comparatively inferior means for describing objects (nouns), and for describing the relationships between objects by using verbs and adverbs. Modula-2, like Ada, is rather more evenly equipped in this respect, and so would seem to be well suited to implementing a design produced by using the OOD method. This method has been described quite extensively in the literature on Ada design, but in this section the solution will be expressed in terms of Modula-2 and its structures.

When using OOD with Ada, Booch (1983) advocates that the method should proceed by means of the following steps:

- define the problem;
- develop an informal strategy;
- formalize the strategy by
  - identifying objects and their attributes;
  - identifying operations upon objects;
  - establishing the interfaces between objects;
  - implementing the operations.

Only in the last two sub-steps of this design process do we identify the language-specific aspects, when it becomes necessary to determine the details of such features as procedural interfaces and packaging, and to devise the algorithms that are to be used. So the basic sequence above seems equally suited for use with Modula-2, and will provide the basic structure for the rest of this chapter. (It is interesting to note that this approach changes the emphasis of the detailed design process too. Traditionally this task has been regarded as concerned largely with the derivation of algorithms, and the role of designing the data structures has been given far less emphasis.)

The first step above (define the problem) has already been performed in Section 13.1, in which we provided an informal English language requirement for the problem. So the two remaining steps are concerned with first roughing out a design (developing the strategy), and then expanding its details (formalizing it). Only at the end of the latter task is the design process concerned with the details of Modula-2 structures.

### 13.3.1 Develop an informal strategy

This step can be regarded as performing the top-level design task, and it is essential that the informal design produced by this process should be as complete and correct as possible. The informal English language description that is generated during this step will also contain a number of significant design decisions (such as the number of times the system will read through the source text of the program being analysed). As usually happens during the design process, it is also unlikely that we will get the strategy completely correct on the first attempt, and so the description produced will probably need to be further analysed and refined. (A useful means of checking this informal design description is to try to explain it to another person: in the process of doing this, they or you will probably spot many of the inconsistencies or significant omissions.)

So a first attempt at describing a solution for the example problem might read something like the following:

> 'The program first reads through the input Pascal source file, and makes a list of the procedures that are declared in that program. It then reads the input file again and this time it makes a note of each call that is made to any of the procedures that were previously identified, and also records the identity of the calling component. From these records it then constructs a tree that shows the interdependencies of the different procedures, and finally prints out a table that represents the tree by listing the called procedures and calling procedures in a suitable manner.'

The strategy outlined in this statement is very similar to that described by the DFD of Figures 13.4 and 13.8, although it is expressed in a rather different form. Indeed, Booch suggests that sketching out a DFD can be of assistance in producing a statement like the one above, since it helps the designer to identify the flow of information within the system. (It is always important to avoid having too 'partitioned' a view of design forms and techniques, since a technique from one method can sometimes be of assistance when using another design method.) Since the object-oriented approach rather lacks any graphical forms that might help with this initial step, the DFD is probably one of the most suitable forms to use.

The process of refining the above statement is informal too. Since the statement has so informal a style (lacking any rigid syntax that might assist with its analysis), it is difficult to find any way of performing a rigorous analysis, or even a check for completeness or consistency. Indeed, the limitations of this form provide yet another reason for trying to utilize diagrammatic representations, since a diagram may provide assistance by imposing some form of syntax and semantics upon the description.

A designer would normally expect to refine and check this statement. On this occasion, though, as it has already been considered at length in the previous section, it seems appropriate to accept it without further modification, and to proceed to the next stage in the design process. However, we should recognize that there are a number of design decisions that are already implicit in this statement, and which we might later wish to revise. One such is the sequencing described in the solution, in which a two-pass operation upon the Pascal source file is assumed. As we refine our thoughts, we might well choose to identify both procedure headings and procedure calls in a single pass through the file.

### 13.3.2 Formalize the strategy

This step in the OOD process incorporates both module design and detailed design, and is the point where this method begins to diverge significantly from the practices used in structured design. (The rest of this section concentrates on the first two sub-tasks, which essentially comprise the module design phase, and leaves the language-specific task of detailed design to be covered in the next section.) During the module design phase, the informal strategy is subjected to an analysis in order to identify both the 'noun phrases' and the 'verb phrases' contained in it. The former are then used to create an initial list of objects, and these are the first items that we seek to identify. The 'verb phrases' are then used to help identify the operations that are performed upon each of the objects, refining the list of objects in the process.

The process begins by extracting all of the nouns from the earlier description of the intended solution, and considering each in turn as a candidate for being an object. Each noun is also examined to determine whether it is a

- common noun: that is, a 'class' name such as 'book', 'account', 'file';
- mass noun: describing a unit of measure;
- proper noun: used to identify a specific entity.

The identification of common or mass nouns can help indicate where abstract data types will be needed, and so where the program might use specific instances or entities. Proper nouns will usually map onto particular real-world objects. Any adjectives that are associated with a noun can also be used to help in identifying the properties or 'attributes' of the associated object, and (where appropriate) the adjectives and adverbs may provide information about any specific timing constraints that may apply to a system.

To show this process more clearly, the informal description of our solution is repeated below, placing emphasis upon the nouns and the adjectives (these are also numbered as an aid to the later analysis).

> 'The *program* [1] first reads through the *input Pascal source file* [2], and makes a *list* [3] of the *procedures* [4] that are declared in that *program* [5]. It then reads the *input file* [6] again and this time it makes a *note* [7] of *each call* [8] that is made to any of the *procedures* [9] that were previously identified, and also records the *identity* [10] of the calling *component* [11]. From these *records* [12] it then constructs a *tree* [13] that shows the *interdependencies* [14] of the different *procedures* [15], and finally prints out a *table* [16] that represents the *tree* [17] by listing the *called procedures* [18] and *calling procedures* [19] in a suitable manner.'

(The process of analysis cannot be conducted in a particularly formal or codified manner, since an informal solution such as this will usually contain a number of synonyms and circumlocutions. The presence of these needs to be taken into account during the analysis.)

We are able to identify several objects that appear to play a significant role in our solution. (One possible way to verify our conclusions about the objects is to outline the top-level algorithm again in terms of these objects alone: any difficulties that are encountered indicate where we may have failed to identify necessary objects, and any ambiguities found may suggest where there might still be some redundancy.) Looking one by one at the terms that are italicized in the above description, we can draw the following conclusions:

(1) *program* This can be discarded, since it is simply a reference to the mechanism of the complete solution, and is not itself a part of the solution.

248   CONSTRUCTING A MODULA-2 PROGRAM

(2) *input Pascal source file*   From this we can identify *source file* as an object that the program will operate upon (open, close, read), and which will possess attributes of some form.

(3,4) *list* of *procedures*   This also seems a good candidate for being treated as an object, since the program will perform operations upon it (AddEntry, SearchForEntry, etc).

(5) *program*   This is simply a synonym for *source file*.

(6) *input file*   This is again a synonym for *source file*.

(7,8) *note* (of *each call*)   This could be an object, but as it seems to refer to performing an operation in this particular context, we can discard it. (Perhaps we should have expressed this as 'notes each call' in the informal strategy, which would be less colloquial!)

(9) *procedures*   The object that this reference is concerned with is a *procedure identifier*, and so this seems to be a good candidate for inclusion as an object.

(10, 11) *identity* (of calling *component*)   This seems to be a further synonym for *procedure identifier*. Considered in the light of the reference to 'note of each call' above, it might seem that 'caller' and 'calling' could be attributes of some form.

(12) *record*   Again, this is seen to be a synonym for *list* (entry) when we examine the context.

(13) *tree*   This seems to be a new object, or at least a new data structure constructed from existing objects. It seems appropriate to include it for now, and to reconsider it later if necessary.

(14, 15) *interdependencies*   This is really another reference to the attributes of *procedure identifier* (the preposition 'of' makes this particularly clear).

(16) *table*   This could be an object, although it seems to refer to some structure that is constructed from existing objects and that has some association with *tree*.

(17) *tree*   This is a repeat of (13) above.

(18) *called* (*procedure*)   This is simply an attribute of *procedure identifier*.

(19) *calling* (*procedure*)   This is also an attribute of *procedure identifier*. (With both (18) and (19) we need to consider how a recursive call will be represented.)

By taking the surviving nouns, and examining these in the light of the previously described classifications of common, mass and proper nouns, we find that we have the following candidates:

(a)  the common (class) noun *procedure identifier*;
(b)  no evident candidates for mass nouns;
(c)  a number of specific objects (proper nouns), namely
 – *source file*
 – *list of procedures*
 – *tree of relations*

The claims of *table* are rejected (and we can reserve the right to reject the *tree* if further analysis requires it).

One of the more obvious issues that arises from this process is the difficulty of systematically parsing statements that are made in a natural language such as English. In the above analysis of the informal solution we were able to identify several synonyms, and so the way that the statement describing a solution is phrased can considerably complicate or assist the process of identifying the objects. This could in turn have implications for the actual process of design using the OOD method.

The next step (which will also help in refining the questions left unanswered by the previous step) is to consider the actions – represented by the *verbs* – that are contained in the statement describing the informal solution. These are extracted and analysed in much the same manner that was used for the nouns. (The adverbs are included in this process too.)

> 'The program *first reads*[1] through the input Pascal source file, and *makes*[2] a list of the procedures that *are declared*[3] in that program. It then *reads*[4] the input file again and this time it *makes a note*[5] of each call that *is made*[6] to any of the procedures that *were previously identified*,[7] and also *records*[8] the identity of the calling component. From these records it then *constructs*[9] a tree that *shows*[10] the interdependencies of the different procedures, and *finally prints out*[11] a table that *represents*[12] the tree by *listing*[13] the called procedures and calling procedures in a suitable manner.'

(The previous point about the role of adverbs and adjectives in providing information about timing constraints is illustrated by the use of *then*, *again* and *this time*, in emphasizing the previously mentioned design decision about reading the source file twice.)

Obviously the problem of synonyms is just as relevant for verbs as for nouns, and so some of the terms used may again need to be further refined or clarified. Proceeding in a similar manner as before, we can now go through this list and examine the credentials of each of the actions that have been identified, seeking where possible to link each action to one of the objects that was identified in the previous step.

250  CONSTRUCTING A MODULA-2 PROGRAM

(1) *reads*  This is clearly an operation that can be applied to the *source file* (ReadItem).

(2) *makes* (a list)  This becomes the operation of adding entries to the *list of procedures* (AddEntry).

(3) *are declared*  This verb is simply concerned with the existence of objects (*procedure identifiers*), and so (following a general rule of OOD), it is ignored – unless we want to consider 'declared' as an attribute.

(4) *reads* (*again*)  This has already been covered in (1).

(5) *makes* (*a note*)  We can really express this more rigorously by regarding it as a synonym for the action of adding an attribute to a *procedure identifier* (or at least, modifying an existing attribute).

(6) *is made*  This simply identifies the attribute which is to be modified by the preceding operation.

(7) *were previously identified*  This can be considered as an existence reference and ignored (again, it might also qualify as an attribute).

(8) *records*  This identifies which attribute of *list of procedures* is to be modified.

(9) *constructs*  This is really an operation on the *tree of relations*, or, more correctly, it may involve a set of operations when it is more fully expanded.

(10) *shows*  This is another form of existence reference, and so it is ignored.

(11) *prints out*  This is an operation (or series of operations) that is applied to the *tree of relations* (and which could involve a further stage of object-oriented analysis of this form).

(12) *represents*  This can be considered as an existence verb and ignored.

(13) *listing*  This is really an operation upon an object that has not previously been considered, namely the *output file*. While this undoubtedly has attributes, they are largely organized by the supporting run-time libraries (such as FileSystem and InOut). Since this seems a relatively minor object in terms of the solution, it is included as a fairly unstructured design object at this stage, but will need to be considered more fully during the refinement of the design.

So, combining the results of these two analyses, we can now list the objects and the operations associated with each object (Table 13.2).

**Table 13.2** Objects and associated operations identified in an informal description of a program.

| Object | Operation |
| --- | --- |
| *procedure identifier* | AddCallerIdentity |
|  | AddCallingIdentity |
| *source file* | ReadItem |
| *output file* | PrintItem |
| *list of procedures* | AddEntry |
| *tree of relations* | AddRelation |
|  | ReadNode |

At this point it is necessary to resolve the question as to whether the last two objects should be considered as one object or two. From the previous experience with using the structured design method, we would expect that one of these objects will be transformed in some way to create the other, and so we can conclude that it should be possible to find some composite form that can be used to represent both of them. In this way, the final list of objects is reduced to four. (This should not be considered as unreasonably small: the process of reduction largely reflects the English language's generous provision of synonyms, and the tendency that most of us have to make use of these very widely.)

To complete this part of the design task, we now need to produce a fuller list of the operations that will be applied to this final list of objects. (In part, this suggests that the informal solution is inadequate, or at least inadequately expressed. However, some of the operations can be determined only by considering aspects of the solution in greater detail, and it is perhaps not surprising that it is not possible to determine a complete list of objects and operations from what is essentially only a top-level description.) For the present, the best way to generate a fuller list of operations is by working through the list of objects and considering the operations which will need to be applied to each of them. (It may help to identify the attributes first, and then to use these as an aid to selecting the operations.) Table 13.3 summarizes the attributes and operations associated with the four objects. (The step from 'character' to 'tokens' will need a further design cycle.)

The final composite structure has been termed a 'table', simply to ensure that it is recognized as being a composite representation, rather than because the term holds any structural significance. The last two operations performed on this object may also need further refinement.

At this point it becomes possible to see how the solution might be packaged using MODULEs. We can see that one module may be needed for handling the input to the program (and performing a lexical analysis upon it), a second may be needed to hold the information describing the 'tree',

**Table 13.3** Attributes and operations associated with four objects identified from an informal description of a program.

*Procedure identity*

| Attributes: | *procedure identifier*<br>*link to list of callers*<br>*link to list of called procedures* | Operations: | CreateProcedureIdentity<br>AddCallerLink<br>AddCalledLink |
|---|---|---|---|

*Source file*

| Attributes: | *file identifier*<br>*open/closed*<br>*end of file* | Operations: | ReadToken<br>OpenFile<br>CloseFile |
|---|---|---|---|

*Output file*

| Attributes: | *file identifier*<br>*open/closed* | Operations: | PrintString<br>OpenFile<br>CloseFile |
|---|---|---|---|

*Table of procedures*

| Attributes: | *entries*<br>*entry relations* | Operations: | AddNewEntry<br>AddLinkToEntry<br>DetermineLevelInTree<br>TraverseTree |
|---|---|---|---|

and a third (program?) module will be needed to control the sequence of operations, as well as to provide any print-out that is needed. (Actually, this latter task could also be separated off, in order to provide a better means of anticipating the subsequent development of new forms for presenting the information about the source program.)

When considered from the viewpoint of information-hiding, this decomposition also seems quite sound. A convenient and practical way to assess this is to consider the possible changes to the requirements that might arise. The two most likely reasons for making a change would appear to be:

- to restructure this program so that it can be used for analysing programs written in some other source language;
- to change the format that is used to present the output.

The first of these will affect only the MODULE that handles the input tasks, while the second affects only the program MODULE (or a subordinate module if we prefer to create one). If preferred, the information-hiding content can be further refined by using a local module within the input module, in order to hide any details of the interface with the operating system itself.

Figure 13.14 shows a structure graph that represents this design as developed so far. The next task identified in the OOD method is to

# A SOLUTION BASED UPON OBJECT-ORIENTED DESIGN 253

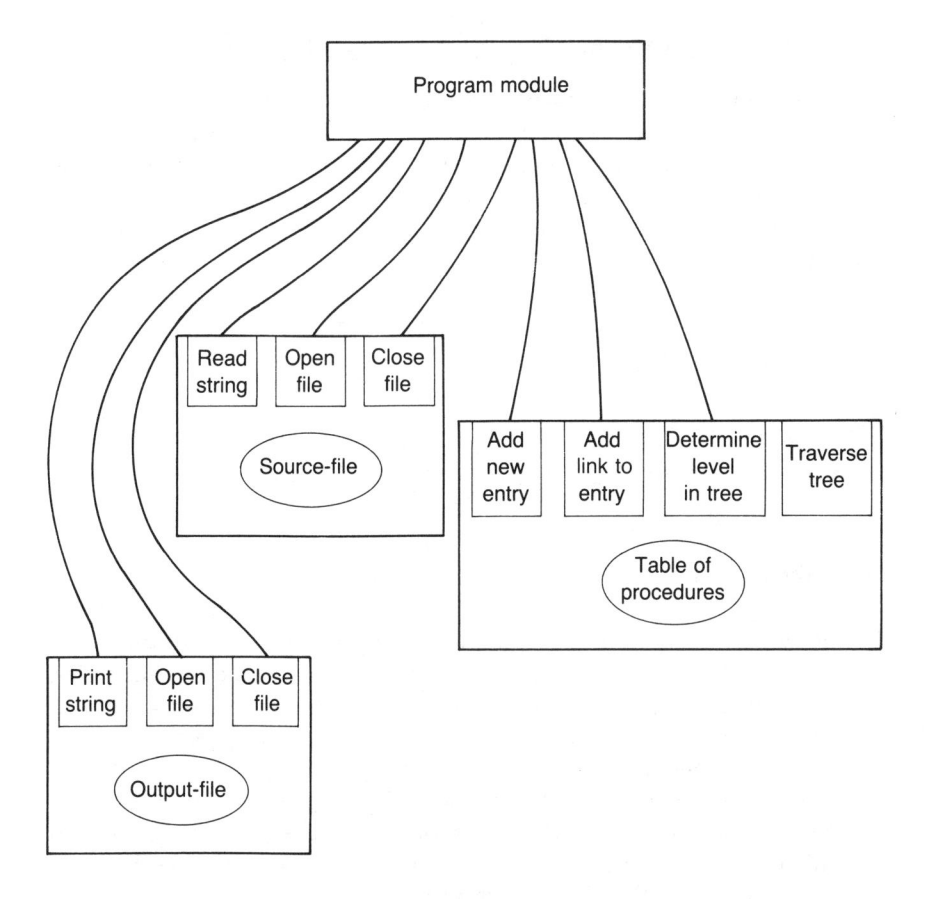

**Figure 13.14** Structure graph for initial design using OOD techniques.

'establish the interfaces', which involves us in determining the form of the procedures that will be used to provide these operations. In terms of Modula-2, this will essentially consist of specifying the definition parts that will be used for each MODULE. Since this is really the last task before the actual implementation, it can be considered as part of the task of detailed design, and so the design of the system has now been developed to essentially the same level of detail that was achieved using the structured design method in the previous section.

This is also the limit to which we can consider the design process as 'abstract', and in the next section we examine the task of detailed design as applied to Modula-2. We shall also try to compare the form of the design produced with the OOD approach to that which was produced with the structured design method.

## 13.4 Completing the Object-Oriented Design

In the previous section we examined those steps of the OOD process that are basically concerned with the abstract steps in the process of design (logical design). The last two sub-steps in the process of 'formalizing the strategy' are less abstract in nature and more implementation-specific (physical design), and these provide the topic of the present section. The two sub-steps are:

- establishing the interfaces between objects;
- implementing the operations.

When these tasks are considered in terms of the Modula-2 programming language, we can interpret them quite directly as comprising:

- the specification of the definition parts
- the construction of the implementation parts

for the MODULEs that were identified from the previous steps in the OOD process. In performing the former of these two tasks, it is quite likely that we will reveal inadequacies in the results from the preceding steps, and so a degree of iteration may still be required in the complete design process before the implementation parts can be constructed.

It is also possible that the previous design process may need to be repeated in order to *expand* the details for some areas of the design. In this example problem, as may already be evident, the task of parsing the input source file and extracting the 'tokens' provides us with just such a situation. Although for this case the module interface is relatively well defined and is not particularly complex, the task of implementing the operations rapidly reveals the need for a further complete cycle of the OOD process.

For the moment, though, our aim is to establish the interfaces between the objects identified for the example, and thus to produce a definition part for each of the MODULEs in our design.

The first MODULE that was identified in the previous section was that used to handle the input source file. A definition part for this (using fairly abstract, and as yet undefined, types where necessary) is as follows:

```
(* Module that extracts strings of characters or 'tokens' from a file of text making up a Pascal
program. *)

DEFINITION MODULE TextAnalyser;
EXPORT QUALIFIED token, GetNextToken, OpenFile, CloseFile, OpenedOk;
TYPE
    token = (EOF, procedureidentifier, parameteridentifier, endprocedure, other);
        (* the forms of interest *)
```

```
    PROCEDURE GetNextToken( VAR t : token; VAR name ARRAY OF CHAR);
       (* reads next token from the input file *)
    PROCEDURE OpenFile( fileidentifier : ARRAY OF CHAR) ;
       (* opens the file containing the Pascal program *)
    PROCEDURE OpenedOk() : BOOLEAN;
       (* TRUE if file found and opened by OpenFile *)
    PROCEDURE CloseFile() : BOOLEAN;
       (* closes file containing Pascal source program *)
    END TextAnalyser.
```

The list of token values defined above may need revising when we go on to consider the algorithms that will be used in the other modules. So the algorithms for this module, which provides relatively low-level services, should probably be designed as late as possible, since the requirements that will be made of it have still not been fully defined.

The second major module is concerned with storing the descriptions of the relationships between the procedures, and a first draft of its interface is given below:

```
    (* MODULE containing the data structure that describes the relations between the
       components in a program's calling hierarchy. The procedures exported allow elements to
       be added to the data structure, and provide information about elements already stored. *)
    DEFINITION MODULE RelationsTree;
    EXPORT QUALIFIED AddNewEntry, AddNewLink, DetermineLevel,TraverseTree;
       (* AddNewEntry stores a new procedure declaration *)
    PROCEDURE AddNewEntry(procedureidentifier : ARRAY OF CHAR;
                          noofparameters : CARDINAL);
       (* AddNewLink creates a new link between two existing elements *)
    PROCEDURE AddNewLink(callingprocedure, calledprocedure : ARRAY OF CHAR);
       (* DetermineLevel describes the level in the hierarchy for the element *)
    PROCEDURE DetermineLevel(procedurename : ARRAY OF CHAR;
                             VAR depth : CARDINAL);
    (* TraverseTree reorganizes the elements of the tree *)
    PROCEDURE TraverseTree();
    END RelationsTree.
```

Both of these definition parts should be considered as first drafts, since further consideration of the algorithms required may reveal the need to change the details of the interfaces, as well as possibly requiring new functions to be provided. (One issue that can be identified already is how the module will respond to an error in AddNewLink, if one of the two procedure identifiers has not been included in RelationsTree.) However, a benefit of developing a design in this manner is that we will need to change only the detailed form of the interfaces. As these will principally be concerned with the type values and the procedure parameters, any such changes are likely to have relatively few side-effects, since each module handles a well defined set of tasks.

The second task, which is concerned with implementing the operations, is basically one of producing a detailed design describing the algorithms and data structures of each module. If the design has been expanded sufficiently, then this task should be relatively straightforward (as for the MODULE RelationsTree and the main program module). Where there is clearly a further degree of complexity to be resolved (as in the MODULE TextAnalyser), a further OOD decomposition may be required.

One of the benefits of this design method is the strong separation of concerns that it encourages. This means that individual modules can be developed and tested in the knowledge that relatively little change (if any) will be required later in the development of the complete system. For this example, a suggested order for module development would be:

(1) RelationsTree;
(2) the program module;
(3) TextAnalyser;
(4) OutputFormatter.

There are good reasons for this ordering, since the algorithms of the RelationsTree operations and of the main program may help with the task of refining the definition part of TextAnalyser. (At the least, it should assist with the task of defining an informal strategy to be used for the TextAnalyser module.) Although RelationsTree is dependent upon TextAnalyser as a 'server' module, the appropriate operations can quite easily be dummied by producing a sequence of tokens from TextAnalyser that is intended to represent a simple tree of procedure dependency. The next chapter will have more to say about this technique. As an exercise, the reader might like to consider the OOD expansion that will be needed for the development of TextAnalyser.

Clearly this solution is incomplete in several ways, and there is some further design work that will be needed in order to:

- clarify how TextAnalyser will perform its task of extracting 'tokens';
- determine how exceptions might be handled (these might include errors in the Pascal syntax, running out of workspace, etc.).

However, the basic form of the design has now emerged, and may be expanded and developed to include such issues. (Of course, for a full design process these need to be considered before proceeding any further, since they may influence the fundamental design structures and require these to be redesigned.) So we will stop at this point, since the basic approach for applying such methods to Modula-2 should now be fairly evident. In the next chapter we shall consider the form of the development process more fully, and in particular, we shall examine how we use testing methods to verify our design choices.

# EXERCISES

**13.1** Take the structure diagram shown in Figure 13.12, and consider how this structure might be partitioned into modules if the program were to be implmented in Modula-2. What conclusions can you draw from this about constructional versus execution-time structuring of a program?

**13.2** Taking as a basis the method of design described in Section 13.3, expand the design for the module TextAnalyser using this approach.

**13.3** Using the OOD method of design described in this chapter, outline a design for a program which has to meet the following requirements:

> The program is to provide a 'browsing' facility that will allow a user to read through a file of text. Under normal use the program should copy the contents of the file to the user's screen, one 'page' at a time (with each 'page' filling the user's screen), with the next page being output when a response is typed in at the keyboard. (This is rather like the UNIX programs **more** and **pg**.) The default action will be to output the next page in sequence. Command options should allow the user to:
>
> - exit from the program;
> - re-read the previous page;
> - go back to the first page of the file;
> - go to the last page in the file;
> - search forward for the next section of the file containing a given string of characters, and output the page centred about these;
> - as the previous option, but searching backwards in the file, rather than forwards.

# Chapter 14
# Program Development, Testing and Documentation

14.1 A model of the software development process
14.2 Testing strategies
14.3 Module testing
14.4 Integration testing
14.5 Documentation
Exercises

This chapter is largely concerned with gathering up some of the threads of the two preceding chapters of Part II, and with interpreting these within the framework provided by the practices of software engineering. A major objective of this book is to describe how software-based systems of all sizes can be engineered using Modula-2, and this chapter deals with an important part of this engineering process.

## 14.1 A model of the software development process

One of the objectives of a software engineering discipline is to provide a framework within which the development of software-based systems can proceed in a well structured and organized manner. One useful and widely used model of this development process is the software life cycle, already discussed in Section 12.1.1. (However, it is important to remember that this is a *model* and not a rigid framework; see Gladden (1982) and Jackson (1982).) Most forms used to describe it include in some way the phases that we have previously mentioned:

- Requirements analysis
- Specification
- Design
- Implementation
- Testing
- Maintenance

Of course, these can be further subdivided, and part of this chapter is devoted to examining the main subdivisions of the testing phase. (For our purposes testing can be considered as marking the end of the activity of system production. The maintenance phase is really a separate activity altogether.) Testing is the one major phase of development that has so far received little attention in this book. Chapters 12 and 13 have examined some of the issues involved in requirements analysis and specification, as well as describing some of the methods that are widely used in system design, and we can probably consider the whole of Part I of this book as being concerned with the technical issues involved in implementation. (Note that *documentation* is not regarded as a separate task but rather is considered to be an essential component of every part of the life cycle.) So this seems an appropriate point to consider how the activities described so far can be validated and assessed.

Testing is not isolated from the other phases involved in software development. This particularly involves such issues as the order of module development, as well as the influence of testing strategy upon module choice and structure. We need to consider the different forms of testing that will normally be part of the development process and the purposes of each form of testing, as well as the way that it relates to the rest of the life cycle.

The major aim of software testing is to ensure that an item of software will perform all its tasks in accordance with the original requirements of the user or the intentions of the designer. (These should be consistent, of course, but at the detailed level they may not always be so, unless the design is tested against the requirements definition for verification purposes.) We should note that there are limitations upon what can be achieved through testing, and particularly that no form of testing is able to prove that software is 'correct' in any sense. That is, it cannot demonstrate the complete absence of errors, only that the subset of possible errors that are checked by our tests do not occur. Also, testing can never (or very rarely) be in any sense complete. Even simple programs have very complex structures in an analytical sense. Simply exercising every possible run-time path through a program may require impossibly large amounts of processing time, while still being a far from exhaustive test of all the conditions and states that can occur within the structures of the program.

A more desirable way of establishing that a program is 'complete' and 'correct' would be to use more formal mathematical techniques. Unfortunately the science of 'program proving' is still limited to use with very modest sized programs, and it would seem that conventional testing will be needed for a long time to come.

These reasons alone make it essential that such testing as can be performed during system development must be made as effective as possible. For large systems, the task of testing can absorb at least 40% of the total development effort (Sommerville, 1989). Unfortunately, the individual programmer who has only been involved with *programming in the small*, and who has not yet acquired any experience of working with larger systems, rarely regards testing as a significant or important task!

When considering the reasons for testing software, we can identify some fairly distinct sub-phases of testing, based upon different needs. A suggested set of headings for these is:

- *Module testing.* This is concerned with the testing of the individual components of a system. This usually takes place at the procedure/MODULE level. This process will also include the testing of all constraints and restrictions, as well as of any error-handling features.
- *Integration testing.* This is concerned with testing each structural unit as it is first assembled and then added to the complete system. At each step of integration we need to test the full effects of the added functionality and ensure that any previously tested features do not fail because of side-effects.
- *Acceptance testing.* This is a demonstration of the complete system to the customer or users to ensure that it meets their requirements.

Obviously these sub-phases may merge in practice, especially where fairly informal testing practices are in use. Since our purpose is to consider how systems are constructed using Modula-2, we will disregard acceptance testing and concentrate solely upon describing the aims of the other two sub-phases. We shall also confine ourselves to considering technical issues alone, omitting any discussion of how testing should be organized, and who should have the responsibility for each of the sub-phases involved. So the next section examines the nature of testing itself in a fairly abstract form, and then the following sections apply this thinking to the problems of module and integration testing.

## 14.2 Testing strategies

The basic process of testing program components may be considered as a fairly simple operation, which usually proceeds along the lines shown schematically in Figure 14.1. A 'module' is tested by applying a set of stimuli to it (namely the input data), and then observing the reactions that these produce, which are measured by observing the generated output. This output can then be compared with the predicted behaviour. (Herein lies one of the pitfalls of testing: someone needs to examine the results!) To make the testing process as thorough as possible, we need to select a set of inputs that will exercise all the operations of the system, and we must also predict the behaviour expected from the system in each case. While these

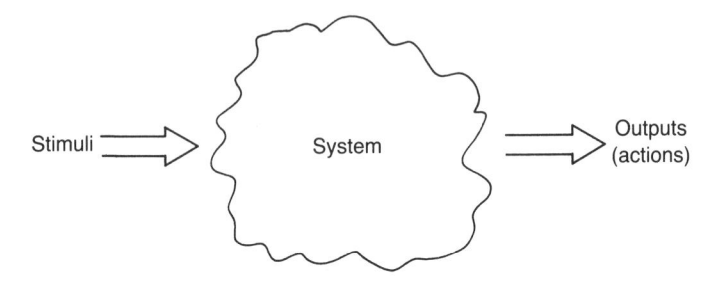

**Figure 14.1** Schematic description of the testing process.

objectives are easily stated in this way, they are not necessarily so easily achieved in any systematic manner.

We begin by considering the selection of a suitable set of inputs. We can again consider a general case, such as the one shown in Figure 14.2. A particular solution to a problem (as embodied in a program, module or procedure) can be considered to exist in a 'solution space', which may have many dimensions (although the diagram is restricted to representing only two). We normally expect that our solution can be regarded as valid for only a part of this solution space, represented by the inside of the irregular shape in the figure. Outside this area, although our solution may produce an answer, it is not regarded as being meaningful in terms of the problem. So one objective of our testing is to ensure that the solution produced has the correct 'shape': to do this we can try to establish that the following conditions are true:

- our solution should be valid at every point within the designated part of the solution space;
- our solution should be 'invalid' in the rest of the solution space.

Obviously we cannot test every possible element in this space, and so we try to test for the general conditions and also for the boundary conditions (usually just within and outside of the boundary). In terms of Figure 14.2 this means that we should test a set of representative points inside and outside the solution space, and a set of key points around the boundary.

Described in this way, the problem of selecting a set of test inputs may not appear to be particularly difficult. Unfortunately, for all except the simplest procedures, the solution space usually has many dimensions, and the 'valid' part may be very irregular. So testing the validity of even a modest set of boundary conditions can soon become a very large task indeed.

If we continue with the symbolic model of Figure 14.2 just a little further, and imagine it extended to several dimensions, we can see that each of the various boundaries provides us with different 'classes' of test. (That is, for a given boundary in a particular dimension, there will be a complete class of possible and equivalent test values that can be used.)

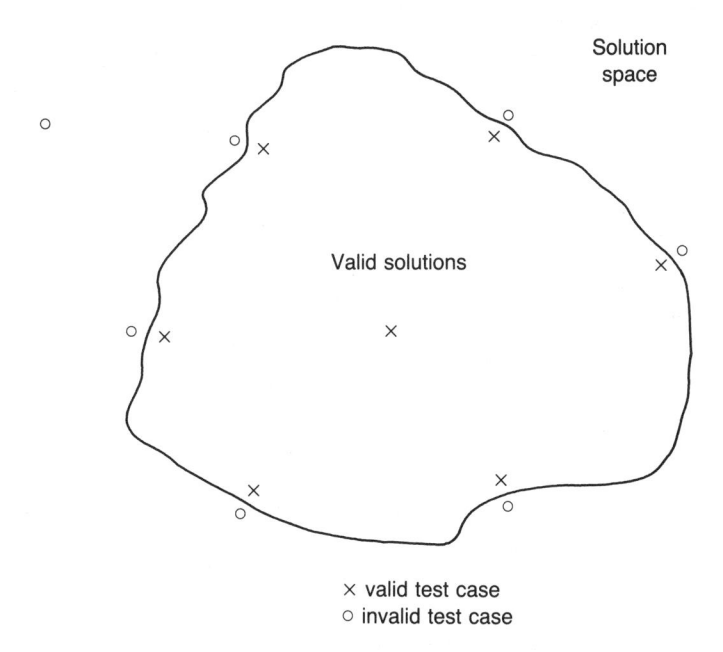

**Figure 14.2** Role of the test cases in the solution space.

Within each such class we can therefore select a set of representative values to use as our test cases.

At this point, a simple example may be helpful. An example introduced earlier was the BOOLEAN function procedure IsUpperCase. The purpose of IsUpperCase is to return a BOOLEAN status value that indicates whether or not the argument (a single character) is an upper case alphabetical character. We can easily identify two classes of input values:

- the 'valid' characters, 'A'...'Z';
- all other characters, including the lower case characters 'a'...'z', numerals and punctuation characters.

(It may already be apparent that it is easier to identify and classify a full set of valid cases than invalid ones, even for so simple a problem as this!)

Since we should test 'typical' values and boundary conditions, a set of suitable test cases from the above list might be:

- the valid characters 'A', 'M', 'Z' (selecting one from the middle of the range and the others from the two boundaries);
- the characters immediately before 'A' ('@') and after 'Z' ('[') in the ASCII character set;

|  |  |  |  |
|---|---|---|---|
| \multicolumn{4}{l}{Module tested: IsUpperCase} |
| \multicolumn{4}{l}{By:} |
| \multicolumn{4}{l}{On:} |
| \multicolumn{4}{l}{Outcome: Successful for all cases} |
| \multicolumn{4}{l}{Further actions: None} |

| *Valid/invalid* | *Inputs* | *Predicted output* | *Actual output* |
|---|---|---|---|
| V | A | T | T |
| V | Z | T | T |
| V | M | T | T |
| I | a | F | F |
| I | z | F | F |
| I | m | F | F |
| I | 0C (null) | F | F |
| I | 6 | F | F |
| I | ; | F | F |
| I | 177C (delete) | F | F |

**Figure 14.3**  Example of a test record sheet.

- the lower case characters 'a', 'n', 'z', and some other non-case-sensitive characters, such as the null character (0C), the 'delete' character (177C), a numeral, and a punctuation character.

(For this particular situation, we have assumed the use of the ASCII character set. It might be better if the characters were specified in a way that made the reason for their choice more explicit and less related to the particular character set in use.)

So even for such a relatively simple procedure as this, we soon end up with quite a large set of test cases. To tackle the task thoroughly we should also predict the expected result for each test case, and so will need to monitor the testing process via some form of 'score sheet'. (Figure 14.3 shows a very simple example of such a sheet, which could be used for testing the above procedure.)

While we can fairly easily identify a set of test classes and test cases for this very simple procedure, the task rapidly becomes very much more difficult as we consider more complex procedures and packages. (In this case, complexity probably begins with any procedure that has more than one input parameter and returns more than one value!) The difficulty is further compounded once we begin to integrate a complete system, since the test cases become much harder to select and the predicted results much harder to determine.

We can also see that it is likely to be much easier to test the components of a system 'from the bottom up', than 'from the top down'. This is because we can begin by testing small, simple components such as IsUpperCase, and then use our experience with these to assist in testing the larger components that are assembled during the integration phase. If we construct our software from the top down using 'stubs' and 'drivers', we may well face the problem of having to create highly complex test cases and solutions from the start, with no opportunity to build these up from simpler situations that might provide us with a 'feel' for the problems. The bottom-up testing strategy is also quite well suited to a Modula-2 program, since the MODULE structure provides a suitable system of layering.

So finding a practical testing strategy does require some means of selecting the test classes and representative test cases in a systematic manner. Unfortunately this problem is rather application-dependent, and is certainly not amenable to any form of analytical approach that can be described at the level of this text. However, from the above discussion we do now have some form of a model that can be applied to help with describing the main sub-phases of testing.

## 14.3 Module testing

In this context, a 'module' can still be considered as almost any separately identifiable component of a program, including procedures, local modules and separate modules. The principal need is to identify a component of the system that can be isolated in some way, so that its operation can be tested. Procedures are obviously already in a convenient form that can be used for this purpose. Separately compilable modules are also suitable, but the form of testing required for these differs significantly from that used for procedures. Procedures are 'active' elements that can be categorized fairly simply in terms of their 'function', so the testing process is concerned with actions and results. MODULEs, on the other hand, also incorporate 'passive' components, such as data structures, with which the active elements interact, so selecting the test cases is complicated by the need to test the interactions between these elements as well.

Since procedures are not separately compilable objects in Modula-2, we generally have to construct all, or at least part, of a MODULE, and then test the component procedures, along the lines previously described for IsUpperCase. Once the procedures have been tested in terms of their basic operations, we can proceed to consider their interactions with any data structures that may be present. To see this more clearly it may help to consider another example.

Suppose that a MODULE (NameQueue) is required to maintain a queue of records, each of which has a 'name' component, which in turn is stored as a string of up to 14 characters. The module provides two procedures for accessing the queue, AddQueueElement and RemoveQueueElement, which respectively add a new element to the back of the queue and remove the front element from the queue. So the definition part of NameQueue might look something like the following:

```
(* NameQueue provides support for a FIFO queue of character strings as defined by
   QueueElement. *)
DEFINITION MODULE NameQueue;
EXPORT QUALIFIED AddQueueElement, RemoveQueueElement, QueueElement, Done;
TYPE
   QueueElement = ARRAY [0..13] OF CHAR;
   (* AddQueueElement adds a new entry at the back of the queue *)
PROCEDURE AddQueueElement( newelement : QueueElement);
   (* RemoveQueueElement extracts the first element in the queue *)
PROCEDURE RemoveQueueElement(VAR first: QueueElement);
   (* Done is used to indicate success/failure of above operations *)
PROCEDURE Done() : BOOLEAN;
END NameQueue.
```

(The procedure Done has been declared as a BOOLEAN function procedure to allow for the possibility of failure in performing the main two operations, as when reading an element from an empty queue or if it becomes impossible to add another element to the queue.)

We can fairly easily construct a set of test cases for the two procedures, but testing the data structure involves a little more difficulty. The Modula-2 scope rules are such that the queue can be accessed and tested only by using the two procedures, and so any tests upon it will need to extend or complement the test cases used for the procedures. (Of course, there may be some overlap with the tests used for the procedures.)

Some possible tests of the queue storage mechanism might involve: names with a length of zero characters or one character; names with a length of 14 or 15 characters; mixtures of upper and lower cases in the names; and using sequences of procedures to build a queue of more than one string. Examples of such sequences might be: add three elements, and then remove them; add three elements, remove two, add one, finally remove all; and so on, with each sequence being a test case from a test class of sequences (test classes do not apply to the data values alone).

Again, the simplicity of the example may be deceptive (not least because the form of the queue elements will also need testing in some way), but it should suffice to show how we need to consider different aspects of a module in order to generate the necessary set of test cases.

A useful concept that can be used when testing both the 'active' and 'passive' components of a module in this way, is that of the **test harness**. In its simplest form this is a program module that applies the chosen test cases to the components of a module, and may also output a summary of the results. (To be effective the results will need to indicate very clearly the presence of any discrepancies from the predicted values, otherwise testing can easily degenerate into a rote task and significant results will be overlooked in the volume of output generated. This is a particularly significant point – sheer volume of output is not enough, someone needs to look at it too!)

More complex forms of test harness also exist, in which symbolic debugging may also take place, allowing for more thorough error tracing. Constructing even simple test harnesses and checking (testing!) them can involve considerable expenditure of effort concerning design, implementation (and even) testing of the harness itself. So the relatively large proportion of development effort that is often reported for the testing phase is easily explained! (Any test harnesses developed should of course be documented and saved for possible re-use during maintenance.)

## 14.4 Integration testing

We can view integration testing as essentially repeating the process of module testing for increasingly complex functions and combinations of modules. It is likely to become steadily more difficult to identify each set of test cases, and to predict what the results from a particular test should be. (This latter point is very significant, since testing is only of practical value where we can predict the result; unfortunately this point can easily get overlooked!)

One way in which we can seek to minimize this complexity is through our choice of the order in which integration should take place. However, for a large Modula-2 program, it is rarely practical to follow a completely 'bottom-up' strategy for construction: there may be interactions between the components that require the top-level sequencing to be included in some way, and the component modules do not form any sort of hierarchy other than through the IMPORT facility.

The use of 'stubs' and 'drivers' (dummy procedures that act as 'sinks' and 'sources' of data, respectively) may be convenient in those cases where the effect of the top-level algorithm is required at an early stage of testing. Large sections of a program may be simulated by providing implementation parts consisting of stubs and drivers, so providing the necessary degree of interaction while avoiding the complexity of the complete system. Since the interface of a module is specified fully by the DEFINITION MODULE, the stubs and drivers can later be replaced by their proper forms with minimum overhead and with no hidden side-effects.

Planning for 'bottom-up' integration encourages the construction of modules that are fairly general-purpose and can be re-used in other programs. (The NameQueue module is a possible example, although we need to consider carefully how to make it as general as possible. The form of QueueElement and the operations performed upon it might need to be modified for this purpose.) Re-using a tested MODULE helps reduce the overall volume of testing required, and the lack of true 'generics' in Modula-2 makes this a harder exercise. The Modula-2 MODULE structure lends itself very well to the construction of libraries of tested modules.

The choice of testing strategy, the design of tests, and the organization of the testing process are complex subjects, and this chapter has given only a very brief sketch of some of the issues involved. For Modula-2 the strategies may not be fundamentally different from those that would be used with any other programming language. However, one of the benefits of a modular structure and separate compilation is that we can isolate many aspects of testing, which in turn assists with the selection of the test cases and helps to structure the whole process.

## 14.5 Documentation

It is something of an uncongenial fact of life that most programmers regard writing any form of documentation for their software as a worthy but dull task. It is equally true that they would like others to provide useful, extensive documentation, but are rarely eager to produce anything to a comparable standard.

It is essential to appreciate that documentation *is* an important part of the program development process – so important that it is not usually regarded as a separate phase of the software life cycle. Documentation of one form or another is an essential component of every phase of software production and maintenance, and the burden of producing it should be spread across these too.

The documentation forms adopted for systems requirements analysis and for system design are usually method-specific rather than programming language-specific. Similarly, the task of documenting tests is more concerned with itemizing the test cases than with the programming language itself. So this section concentrates upon the one phase that is significantly dependent upon the nature of the programming language, namely the documentation of Modula-2 statements.

The form of Modula-2 does not have a direct effect on the main issues of documentation, such as its purpose (the intended readership and use), layout and style. However, the MODULE provides a form of structuring that needs to be explicitly incorporated into the documentation scheme, and it can complicate the use of diagrams for program representation.

This section is therefore concerned with only two aspects of documentation: internal documentation by the use of comments; and how the module may be represented diagrammatically.

DOCUMENTATION 269

We can identify the following places where comments are needed:

- an initial comment block, with entries identifying the MODULE, its purpose, date of creation, author(s), details of testing needs, etc., as well as the details of any updates.
- comments on declarations, amplifying the information embodied in the identifiers by explaining how a particular type, constant or variable will be used in the MODULE/procedure, and by any elements of a MODULE that might be exported;
- short comment blocks, used to describe the function of each procedure, and any other relevant information about it;
- in-line comments, placed so as to assist in identifying the points where the key decisions of an algorithm are effected.

The first category needs to be in a standard format (to ensure consistency and completeness), and is largely a matter of 'house style'. It can even be generated by making use of a 'pro forma' when a text-editor is used to create a module. A common student error is to omit this block when creating the definition part of a module – yet since this part is more likely to be read by a potential user than any other, the need for it to contain the relevant information is even more critical than for the implementation part and its presence is an important part of software engineering practice.

For modules with both definition and implementation parts it is also necessary to ensure that the comment blocks in each part remain consistent with one another. (A solution favoured by some programmers is to provide the full header block in the definition part of the module, and only a cross-reference to this in the implementation part.) Figure 14.4 shows an example of a header block.

Comments on declaration statements may not seem to be so important (after all, we all use meaningful identifiers, don't we?). However, the identifier that is meaningful to one programmer (who has a particular model of the solution in mind) may not be so clear to the person who inherits the program for maintenance without necessarily inheriting the model. In addition, most of us have only a limited imagination in making our choice of identifiers, and so an additional comment that defines the main purpose of a variable, type or constant can be immensely valuable. Don't forget the declarations within procedures too: the identifiers used there may be very overworked, and so may have even greater need for an explanation. Some examples of this style of comment are shown in Figure 14.5.

Each procedure declaration should ideally be accompanied by a *short* comment block that summarizes the purpose of the procedure and of each of its parameters. (If this cannot be summarized easily in a short statement, then the design must surely be suspect.) Preferences may vary as to the exact style to adopt: some prefer to have such comment blocks

```
(*
    1. Project Title:
         Software Development with Modula-2

    2. Module Title:
         An example comment block

    3. Description of Module:
         A module that will parse UNIX directory entries and list them on the user's screen.

    4. Stored in: /usr/fsa/db/figure14.4

    5. Version: 0.0

    6. Created on: Mon Aug 17 10:24:08 BST 1987

    7. Updates – date and nature:

    8. Definition modules required:
         InOut
         NameQueue

    9. Test routines or modules used with this module:
         directorytest.1
           up to
         directorytest.12

   10. Comments:
         Will need revision if the directory structure is modified to allow for longer names.

   11. Author: D Budgen
         *)
```

**Figure 14.4** Example of module header block.

placed before the procedure declaration, while others prefer to place it between the declaration and the procedure body. The only really key requirement is consistency of form. A further refinement to the form of the block is to provide pre- and post-conditions – see the examples in Sale (1986).

Making effective use of the in-line comment requires the largest element of independent decision making on the part of the programmer. (The other forms can be more easily codified as part of a house style.) Exactly where such comments should be placed is difficult to prescribe in any rigorous fashion. If used too frequently, the effect is rapidly destroyed, and the code and comments can become interwoven in a very confusing way. As a rule of thumb, only lines containing IF, ELSIF, ELSE, WHILE and UNTIL should be considered as the main candidates for an in-line comment, and not every one of these should qualify. Some assignment statements may

```
TYPE
    directory = RECORD              (* used to store info about a directory *)
            name : QueueElement;    (* directory identifier *)
            owner : CARDINAL;       (* owner identifier code *)
            parent : directoryptr;  (* identity of parent directory *)
    END;
    (* NOTE: If the parent directory is the rootdirectory, then the parent pointer will have a value of NIL. *)

    directoryptr = POINTER TO directory;

CONST
    rootdirectory = 'root';         (* base directory for system *)

VAR
    homedirectory : directory;      (* user's login directory *)
    currentdirectory : directory;   (* current at execution time *)
    depth : CARDINAL;               (* nesting depth from login *)
```

**Figure 14.5** Examples of comments on declarations.

also qualify for comments, but this should certainly not be considered as a general rule. In particular, such comments should *never* be placed other than at the end of a line, and certainly should never be positioned *within* an executable statement. (The effect of this practice is to make it astoundingly difficult to read the code of even a fairly well structured program.)

The *content* of a comment is also relevant to its use. A comment of the form

```
VAR
    mycode : CARDINAL;    (* my code *)
```

hardly enhances the information already purveyed by the identifier itself! It shows, though, how easily a practice can become debased if the spirit is ignored and only the form is pursued. For that reason, the practice of 'reading through' code with another programmer, with the author explaining its purpose in the process, should include the comments as well as the statements.

Comments are a double-edged weapon. Used too frequently or too sparingly they lose their effect and may obscure the very features they are intended to highlight. Used well, they can enhance even the clearest programming style by drawing the reader's attention to key issues. In that sense, the code and the comments should be considered as a complementary pair of forms used to describe the programmer's intentions about what is being achieved, represented, or stored.

When words fail us we often turn to pictures. Again, the importance of clarity and simplicity can hardly be overstated. The highly detailed diagram usually requires an immense degree of concentration from the reader: we should note that the most 'successful' forms, such as the data flow diagram, use a very simple syntax and only a small set of symbols to represent the user's ideas. As with the case of comments an attempt to include too much information will almost surely result in a failure to convey some of our information to the reader.

The designer (or programmer) needs to convey two principal items of information about a program to a reader. The first is the *hierarchical structure* of the program, which in turn reflects the transfers of control and data that occur within its component procedures. Such information is essentially language-independent, and is probably best conveyed through the use of a structure chart. This describes the *logical* structure of a program when it is viewed as a solution to some problem, and is concerned largely with the operations of the program as a whole. The second item of information to be conveyed is the organization of the packaging of the components and their mutual dependencies. This requires some form of diagram that shows module interconnections and dependencies. One elegant form available for this purpose is a structure graph, as described in Chapter 12 (Buhr, 1984).

It is important to appreciate that these two forms of information are essentially orthogonal, and are concerned with quite different aspects of the structuring of a program. The first is concerned with the *run-time call hierarchy* of the program, while the second is concerned with the *dependency relations* in its partitioning at compilation time. Attempts to combine the two forms are likely to bring confusion in their wake – the reader becomes overloaded with information and must perform extra work to extract the required information.

One last aspect which is concerned with purpose rather than form relates to the documentation of the *changes* that inevitably occur to a program during development and over its operational lifetime. It is only too common to find that changes have been made that render some of the original descriptions incorrect, yet these changes have not been recorded. For that reason, the header comment block should include a section for this purpose. Notes of changes should not only be clearly marked and indexed, but should also state the *reasons* for their inclusion. This is not least because the range of validity for some changes will be wider than that for others. A change made because of a weakness or error in logical structure is likely to have a universal validity, whatever happens to the program subsequently. A change made to provide optimization for a given machine or compiler has only a local or temporary relevance and, if it is not noted as such, can later cause great difficulties for the maintainer.

Ideally, our documentation should be such that it requires fairly natural (and effortless!) actions from the programmer. It should make key points in a concise and clear manner and should augment the information conveyed by the program itself. By establishing a set of guidelines such as those suggested in this section, it may be possible to ensure that we at least make progress towards these objectives. However, it should also be emphasized that they require the support of sound management practices to ensure that they are adhered to as fully as possible.

## EXERCISES

**14.1** Devise a set of test classes to be used with the modules TextAnalyser and RelationsTree that were described in Section 13.4.

**14.2** Devise a set of test classes that could be used with the program described in Exercise 13.3.

**14.3** Design a standard comment block that is suitable for use as the initial block in any of your own modules. In doing this, try to think about *future* needs, and the information that might be required by anyone who needs to change a module in any way. How might the details of a block need to vary for the different parts of a module?

**14.4** For the program design that was produced in Section 13.3, what order of integration would you adopt, and why?

# Part III
# SYSTEM PROGRAMMING IN MODULA-2

Chapter 15 **Breaking the Rules!**
Chapter 16 **Forms for Use with Concurrent Programming**
Chapter 17 **Low-level Input and Output**

# Chapter 15
# Breaking the Rules!

15.1 Why Modula-2 includes rule-breaking mechanisms
15.2 The module SYSTEM
15.3 The type WORD
15.4 The type ADDRESS
15.5 Some other non-standard facilities
Exercises

## 15.1 Why Modula-2 includes rule-breaking mechanisms

Having throughout this book extolled the virtues of strong typing and of using sound software engineering practices, we now need to deal briefly with some of the 'other' aspects of Modula-2.

The need to break the rules in a controlled manner arises because there are some problems for which the only possible solutions will require operations that conflict with the ideal of working with abstractions, and at a high level in an apparently machine-independent way. For example, system programming can involve handling the physical structures of the interfaces to input/output devices, and hence needing a way to specify that the data structures for these must occupy specific locations. In controlling the operation of devices, moreover, it may be desirable to refer to a programming object in different ways (by using different types). Embedded real-time systems typically abound with such requirements. Strong typing can also be too restrictive in less specialized situations – hence the need for the type transfer facilities, and a more generalized mechanism for creating these will be introduced in this chapter. The techniques currently used for writing generic modules also require the relaxing of some of the restrictions of the language.

So this chapter is concerned with some of what may be regarded as the 'shady' bits of system programming. It must be emphasized that once we use such features in a program, it will become much less easily transferable to another type of machine. This is because the form of these features will depend on both the physical machine architecture and the services provided by the operating system. So the facilities described in this chapter should be used with care and only when it is absolutely necessary to do so.

Even though the facilities described here can weaken the strict checking provided by Modula-2, it still remains a highly structured tool. While they allow it to perform the type of operations that we expect to undertake with a powerful system programming language such as C, it still retains a higher level of structuring than C. In Modula-2, even the rule-breaking is structured and has its own rules!

Many programmers may never find any need to use the facilities described in this chapter. Others may find it necessary to make limited use of some of them for such tasks as handling files of raw binary data, especially where these have not been generated by the standard Modula-2 library routines, or have been generated on another operating system. Some understanding of them is necessary in order to be able to use other facilities of Modula-2, such as co-routines (described in Chapter 16). So the material of this chapter also provides some necessary background for that of the next two.

## 15.2 The module SYSTEM

The data types and procedures that are used to provide a structured form of 'rule-breaking' in Modula-2 are supplied from the module SYSTEM. This is really a pseudo-module, in that it provides information that is already known to the compiler by describing some of the major features of the underlying machine architecture. Because SYSTEM is machine-dependent, any use of its facilities will immediately make it harder to move the program to another operating system, or to a computer with a different architecture.

Although the contents of SYSTEM are known to the compiler, for consistency a program is still required explicitly to import those contents to make use of them. (The presence of the words FROM SYSTEM IMPORT can also be a useful indication to the reader that this module is likely to be system-dependent and might do 'odd' things.) So SYSTEM has to be treated in the same way as any other library module, in order to preserve the logical structure of the program. (Because it is a pseudo-module, there will not be a SYSTEM.sym file in the libraries used with a compiler. Similarly, when compiling in 'verbose' mode, so that a compiler reports each module referenced, SYSTEM is not usually listed as being accessed.)

Wirth (1980) defines a number of types and procedures that should be provided from SYSTEM. These include the types

    WORD    ADDRESS

which will be described in the next two sections, and the procedures

    TSIZE    SIZE    ADR    TRANSFER    NEWPROCESS

The procedures TSIZE, SIZE and ADR are described in this chapter, while NEWPROCESS and TRANSFER are concerned with the creation and use of co-routines, and so their use is described in Chapter 16.

Implementations of Modula-2 may and do provide other data types and procedures in addition to those listed above. The procedure IOTRANSFER (described in Chapter 17) is commonly included in SYSTEM too, and other non-standard types such as BYTE, as well as procedures such as REGISTER, are frequently included in SYSTEM in order to provide a program with the means to access the architecture-dependent features of a particular computer system. Before making use of SYSTEM, a programmer is advised to consult the local documentation to find out what features are provided for a particular compiler.

## 15.3 The type WORD

We generally refer to the main subdivision of a computer's memory as a 'word'. It is not a well defined term in the context of computer architecture (which in turn is an area not renowned for the use of well defined terms) but, as a general guide, the size of a word is often equivalent to the amount of memory occupied by one machine-level instruction. This in turn is generally related to the amount of information that can be copied from memory in a single read access cycle. Some commonly used word sizes are 16, 24 and 32 bits, although many others have been used.

Machine-level operations usually include variants to manipulate a number of different forms and amounts of data, but the word is the most commonly handled quantity. However, some operations may involve using multiples of a word (often termed 'longwords'), while others may involve subdivisions (usually in the form of 8-bit 'bytes').

In Modula-2, WORD is a data type that can be used in much the same manner as others: we can declare variables of the type WORD and then assign values to them, and may also pass parameters of type WORD. However, there are no other operations that may be applied directly to such a variable, which is logical enough since the type is provided to facilitate type breaking rather than for the direct manipulation of information.

One of the main roles for WORD is to provide a means of specifying 'generic' parameters in procedure declarations. Wherever the *formal* parameter of a procedure is specified as being of type WORD, then the *actual* parameter that is substituted for this when the procedure is called can be of any data type that occupies one word of memory storage. These types normally include BITSET, INTEGER and CARDINAL, and may include REAL as well. As an example of this, a procedure that is declared as:

> PROCEDURE ReadObject(filenumber : CARDINAL; VAR data : WORD);

can be used to read any item of data from the selected file into a variable that is of one of the compatible types. This facility can be particularly useful where a file contains a mixture of data types, or where one field is used to determine the way in which the rest of the record should be interpreted.

This use of WORD as a 'place-holder' can be extended further to include any data type that requires a larger quantity of storage. If the *formal* parameter of a procedure is specified as being an open array of form

> ARRAY OF WORD

then the *actual* parameter that is supplied may be of almost any data type.

WORD can be useful in a number of ways. One of these is for supporting the use of generic data types, as discussed in Chapter 12 (Beidler and Jackowitz, 1986; Wiener and Sincovec, 1985). Another use is to perform operations upon files that have been written by other programs that may include forms not standard to Modula-2, or to the particular implementation. The following example considers the DEFINITION and IMPLEMENTATION parts for such a module (WtmpLogRecords), which is used to extract wtmp records from a file used on UNIX (Edition 7). (wtmp is a rather typical UNIX abbreviation, the origins and meaning of which seem lost.)

On the UNIX system, provided the appropriate accounting routine is enabled, a new wtmp record will be created in a central file on each occasion that any user logs on to the system, and another wtmp record (with slightly different contents) will be added whenever the user logs off. The contents of this file can then be used to provide information about the use of the system. For this example, the file is assumed to have been written on a machine with a 16-bit word size, and each record has the structure:

> ⟨terminal_name⟩ : 8 characters
> ⟨user_identifier⟩ : 8 characters
> ⟨time_of_day⟩ : 32-bit long integer

The module WtmpLogRecords contains procedures that read the blocks of a file (each block is 512 bytes long) into a buffer, using some very low-level file-handling routines in the process, and extract the wtmp records from the buffer. The latter procedure returns the data for each entry in the file as fields of a Modula-2 RECORD. (Where the information was originally written as 32-bit integers, this is returned as an array of two 16-bit integers.) This module provides a good example of information-hiding, in that the details of file handling and buffer manipulation are kept concealed within the module WtmpLogRecords, and are invisible to any routine that calls on the facilities provided by the module.

The definition part of the module WtmpLogRecords is as follows:

```
(* module to provide access to wtmp records on a UNIX system *)

DEFINITION MODULE WtmpLogRecords;

EXPORT QUALIFIED ReadLogRecord, Logrecord;

TYPE
  (* the type Logrecord maps on to a wtmp record *)
  Logrecord = RECORD
    terminal : ARRAY [0..7] OF CHAR;
    userid : ARRAY [0..7] OF CHAR;
    time : ARRAY [0..1] OF INTEGER
  END;

(* the procedure ReadLogRecord returns a record and a status value indicating whether or not
   the end of file has been found. Status 0 is normal, −1 indicates the end of file or error *)
PROCEDURE ReadLogRecord(VAR r : Logrecord; VAR status : INTEGER);
END WtmpLogRecords.
```

Note that the *formal* parameter r that is used in the declaration of the procedure ReadLogRecord is declared to be of type Logrecord. This is because this procedure will normally have an *actual* parameter of type Logrecord, and by declaring it in this manner, the use of the module SYSTEM is kept hidden within the implementation part of the module.

An implementation part for this module is shown in Figure 15.1. Note that, in order to conceal the use of the type WORD, it is necessary for the procedure ReadLogRecord to act as a 'buffer' between a user module and the inner procedure GetLogRecord which actually manipulates the data buffer. Such a structure makes it possible for the strong typing mechanism to protect the use made of the WtmpLogRecords module, and it hides the type-breaking process within the implementation module.

The type WORD can also be used on other occasions, as when creating a workspace in memory for system purposes (an example of this will be discussed in the next chapter). For such a purpose, the form ARRAY {size} OF WORD is generally a convenient form to adopt.

Two aspects of such uses of the type WORD ought to be emphasized here. One is that, while it does provide a form of type breaking, it should be used only when it is necessary to create our own *type transfer* procedures (such as ReadLogRecord above). The second point, once again, is to remember that the use of WORD is both machine- and implementation-dependent, and its presence will of necessity render it that much harder to port a program to run under another operating system or on another computer architecture.

282   BREAKING THE RULES!

**Figure 15.1** Implementation part of the module WtmpLogRecords.

(* module to handle the wtmp file. It reads in the blocks of the wtmp file and passes out the 20 byte
   records via the procedure ReadLogRecord. *)
(* status return values are:
     0 : normal
    −1 : end of file or error *)

IMPLEMENTATION MODULE WtmpLogRecords;

FROM Files IMPORT Lookup, ReadF;
FROM SYSTEM IMPORT WORD;

CONST
  buffersize = 256;                                 (* size of one block in words *)
  recordlength = 10;                                (* size of one record in words *)

VAR
  buffer : ARRAY [0..buffersize−1] OF WORD;         (* block buffer *)
  fileno : CARDINAL;                                (* file identifier *)
  block : CARDINAL;                                 (* block number within file *)
  i : INTEGER;                                      (* index of buffer position *)
  reply : INTEGER;                                  (* used to hold i/o status return *)

  (* Procedure ReadLogRecord obtains the next Logrecord from the file by calling GetLogRecord. It
     hides the details of file organization from the user. *)

PROCEDURE ReadLogRecord(VAR r : Logrecord; VAR status : INTEGER);
BEGIN
  GetLogRecord(r,status);
END ReadLogRecord;


  (* Procedure GetLogRecord fetches the next record from the buffer and updates the buffer when a
     block is exhausted. *)

PROCEDURE GetLogRecord(VAR r : ARRAY OF WORD; VAR status : INTEGER);
VAR
  j,temp : INTEGER;                                 (* temporary counters *)
BEGIN
  status := 0;
  IF i=buffersize THEN                              (* at end of block *)
       ReadF(fileno,buffer,block,2*buffersize,reply);  (* so fill buffer *)
    i := 0 ; INC(block)
     END;
  IF i < (buffersize − recordlength + 1) THEN       (* record fully in buffer *)
    FOR j := 0 TO (recordlength −1) DO              (* so copy from buffer *)
      r[j] := buffer[i+j]
    END; (* for *)
    INC(i,recordlength);

```
    ELSE                                         (* record partly in buffer *)
      temp := (buffersize−1) − i;                (* read available part *)
      FOR j := 0 TO temp DO
        r[j] := buffer[i+j]
      END; (* for *)
      ReadF(fileno,buffer,block,2*buffersize,reply);   (* refill buffer *)
      i := 0 ;
      INC(block);
      INC(temp);
      FOR j := temp TO (recordlength −1) DO     (* read remainder *)
        r[j] := buffer[i];
        INC(i);
      END; (* for *)
    END; (* if *)
    status := reply;
  END GetLogRecord;

BEGIN
  block := 0;                                    (* initialize file *)
  Lookup(fileno,'/usr/adm/wtmp',reply);
    (* get first block *)
  ReadF(fileno,buffer,block,2*buffersize,reply);
  block := 1;
  i := 0;
END WtmpLogRecords.
```

**Figure 15.1** *cont.*

Following from this latter point, there are two procedures provided from SYSTEM that can help to improve the portability of any programs that need to make use of WORD. These are

   SIZE    TSIZE

The function SIZE(v) returns the amount of storage allocation that is used for variable v, while TSIZE(t) returns the amount of storage used for an element of type t. (In the 1983 revision, SIZE became a standard procedure that could also take a type identifier as its argument, so rendering TSIZE redundant.)

SIZE and TSIZE provide the programmer with some scope for reducing the degree of system dependence implicit in the use of the type WORD, and so it is a useful practice to make use of them wherever possible.

## 15.4 The type ADDRESS

In the same way that WORD provides a system-dependent generic form that can be used as a 'place-holder' for most scalar types, so the type ADDRESS provides one that can be used with any pointer type. This is defined as:

```
TYPE
    ADDRESS = POINTER TO WORD;
```

and a pointer value of type ADDRESS is compatible with *any* pointer type.

Just as WORD can be used as a formal parameter of a procedure, if ADDRESS is used for the type assigned to a formal parameter in a procedure declaration, then a variable of any pointer type can be substituted as the actual parameter. So this provides a further mechanism for bypassing the type-checking operations.

One way in which ADDRESS differs from other pointer types, however, is that in addition to the normal assignment operation that can be used with any pointer type, it is permissible to perform arithmetic operations on a variable of type ADDRESS. However, the extent to which this facility can be used is dependent upon the particular machine and implementation of Modula-2. This is because, in order for these operations to be practical, it is necessary for an element of type ADDRESS to occupy the same storage space as the other variables that are combined with it in an arithmetic expression – for example, as is needed for a type such as CARDINAL.

This facility makes it possible to perform such operations as constructing an indexed address directly (this is sometimes termed a base + offset address). A very simple example is given in the program shown in Figure 15.2. (It is assumed that ADDRESS is essentially equivalent to CARDINAL for this example.)

In this example, the variable base contains the address of the start of the data buffer. The data held at a given offset within this buffer is extracted directly by using indexed addressing. (At the machine-code level this form of addressing is very common, and the architectures of many popular machines such as the DEC VAX-11 and the Motorola MC68000 include several variants on this form.) For the example in Figure 15.2, the value returned by the program will depend upon the form of memory addressing that is used by the computer. For example, on a byte-addressing machine, using four bytes for a CARDINAL variable, the value printed out should be '25'.

This example also makes use of the function procedure ADR, which needs to be imported from the module SYSTEM. The function procedure ADR(v) returns the location in memory that has been assigned to store the variable v (which may be of any type), as a value of type ADDRESS. Note that this provides a 'back-door' mechanism by which pointers can be linked to statically declared data. (Of course back in Chapter 11 it was stated that pointer variables could be used to provide access only to anonymous variables that had been created dynamically!)

```
MODULE Indexed;

FROM SYSTEM IMPORT ADR, ADDRESS;
FROM InOut IMPORT WriteCard, WriteLn;

VAR
    base : ADDRESS;                        (* will be used to point to base of buffer *)
    offset : CARDINAL;                     (* contains offset from base of buffer *)
    data : CARDINAL;                       (* holds result of read operation *)
    location : ADDRESS;                    (* temporary holder for indexed address *)
    buffer : ARRAY [0..299] OF CARDINAL;
    i : CARDINAL

BEGIN
    FOR i := 0 TO 299 DO buffer[i] := i END;   (* load a test pattern *)
    offset := 100;
    base := ADR(buffer);
    location := base + offset;
    data := CARDINAL(location↑);
    WriteCard(data,6); WriteLn;
END Indexed.
```

**Figure 15.2**   Program module containing an example of indexed addressing.

## 15.5 Some other non-standard facilities

Modula-2 implementations may also provide a number of other types and functions in SYSTEM. Two of the more common ones are BYTE and REGISTER, both of which provide further degrees of access to the computer's storage facilities at the machine level. Two further facilities that may be included in an implementation are a 'code insert' mechanism and the specification of absolute addresses.

### 15.5.1 Code inserts

The Modula-2 Report (Wirth, 1980) omits to include any form that can be used to insert special machine-level instructions into a Modula-2 program. While for high-level programming the practice of inserting machine-level instructions is both unnecessary and highly undesirable, there are a few special problems that may only be handled by means of some such facility. One example involves the operations performed by some of the parts of an operating system, such as context switching between processes. Such operations may require special instructions to modify the status of the computer itself, and to perform operations such as accessing the stack area of a user task.

Since such instructions are not normally generated by a compiler, some implementations of Modula-2 include a procedure in SYSTEM, with a name such as CODE, through which the programmer is able to insert special instructions when necessary. (These may be in the form of assembler mnemonics or numerical op-code values.) Another, rather more controlled, form allows the implementation part of a Modula-2 library module to be written in another programming language, such as assembler code. The definition part for such a module then needs to provide some information to inform the link-editor that this is the case, and that the normal version checking cannot be applied. The second form seems much more in the spirit of Modula-2, while the former seeks to minimize the extent of the 'non Modula-2' components.

### 15.5.2 Absolute addressing

The examples of this non-standard facility that are provided in this book are based upon the architecture used in the PDP-11. This is because absolute addressing is generally used to perform operations closely connected with a feature of the hardware architecture termed 'memory mapped input/output', which was popularized on the PDP-11 and has subsequently been included in the architecture of many other machines. (Anyone familiar with the architecture of machines such as the Motorola MC68000 should find no difficulty here.)

The term 'absolute addressing' implies that a computer program is able to make references to the data held in a specific location within a computer's memory (and hence is able to perform operations upon the contents of this location). While a programmer certainly does not need to be concerned with such information for almost all programming purposes, there are certain tasks – especially those that are involved in low-level input/output – that may require this. Examples of these operations will be discussed in Chapter 17.

The form that is normally used to specify an absolute address in Modula-2 is not strictly standard, largely because it needs to reflect the way in which memory may be segmented on a particular computer architecture. It consists of a small extension to the syntax of the standard form used for declaring variables: to allocate a variable to a specific location in memory, the designated address is placed in square brackets following its identifier in the declaration statement. Such a variable can usually be of almost any type, and its type will normally be selected so as to permit the appropriate operations to be performed using the clearest form of expression.

As an example, two such declarations are:

```
VAR
  printerstatus[177564B] : BITSET;
  printerbuffer[177566B] : CHAR;
```

(The reasons for choosing these values will be explained in Chapter 17.) The address of each memory location has been given in base eight (this is the normal PDP-11 convention). The 'control and status' register, in which specific bits are used to select specific operations and indicate particular status information, is declared to be of type BITSET, while the data buffer is declared to be of type CHAR, since this is the form of data that will be copied to it.

Variables that are declared using this form can be accessed and used in an identical manner to those variables that have been declared in the normal way. So a statement such as:

```
printerbuffer := 'A';
```

is quite valid, as is the statement:

```
printerstatus := printerstatus + {6};
```

This concludes the immediate survey of non-standard and system-dependent forms in Modula-2. This chapter has been essentially preparatory for the next two chapters, which require some knowledge of the forms described. It should again be emphasized that all the forms described in this chapter should be used only when it is absolutely necessary, and that their purpose is to assist in programming rather specialized and machine-specific tasks in a structured manner.

## EXERCISES

**15.1** Obtain a listing of the module SYSTEM as provided with your local implementation of Modula-2. Find out:

(a) the size of a WORD in bits;

(b) what additional types are provided (if any);

(c) which types can be mapped on to a single WORD.

**15.2** Write a simple stack module that provides a 'WORD stack' which is implemented using an array of type WORD, together with procedures Push and Pop. Then write a short program module which pushes the contents of both INTEGER and CARDINAL variables on to the stack and then retrieves them. What happens if values are retrieved into a variable which is of the 'other' type to that of the source?

[Hint: try this for large INTEGER and for negative INTEGER values.]

**15.3** Modify the workings of the stack module described in Exercise 15.2 so that the stack pointer is a pointer of type ADDRESS rather than a simple array index (you may need to use the standard function procedure ADR too).

# Chapter 16
# Forms for Use with Concurrent Programming

16.1 Principles of concurrent programming
16.2 The co-routine concept
16.3 Co-routines in Modula-2
16.4 Some examples of co-routines
16.5 Co-routines as concurrent processes
Exercises

## 16.1 Principles of concurrent programming

The programs that have been considered up to this point have all been *sequential* in form. A sequential program is one in which the program is executed on a single central processor; it begins execution at some point in time, and each statement of the program is then executed in turn as a sequence of operations. Only one operation is performed at a time, and the next operation will not be started until the previous one has been completed.

However, that is not the way in which we perform tasks ourselves, nor is it analogous to many of the situations that we may wish to model by using a computer. Many everyday situations require that we perform a number of operations simultaneously that are not necessarily independent of one another. The act of riding a bicycle is a good example of this: the cyclist must pedal, balance, steer, and also observe the actions of the rest of the traffic. All these actions are individually sequential, but they must also take place at the same time – that is, they must be performed in parallel – and they must be synchronized with each other, so that the cyclist neither falls off, nor gets run over by a car, and safely reaches the intended destination.

Employing concurrent operations within computer programs has long been recognised as a very important topic, and it may be realized in a number of ways. Even where we have a single central processor that can perform only sequential operations, a multi-tasking operating system can produce the illusion that the single processor is executing several programs at once. Of course, the programs are not actually executed at the same time – rather, the operating system provides short bursts of processor time for each in turn. (This is sometimes termed 'round-robin' scheduling.)

In more powerful computer architectures, the arithmetic and logic unit (ALU) of the central processor may be capable of performing a number of different arithmetic operations at the same time, such as addition, division and multiplication. In order to exploit this facility, the compiler must optimize the code of a program so that the computer's scratchpad memory (its registers) are allocated to different types of operation in such a way that no conflicts occur over their use, and so that the different operations can be performed in parallel.

Increasingly, microprocessor systems have architectures that involve a number of relatively small processors, with each one executing its own programs but also sharing access to a central block of memory, through which it can exchange information with the other processors. Collectively, these forms are all examples of what is often termed 'parallel processing'.

In all these systems, each of the components is basically sequential, being directly concerned only with its own actions, and so it requires the use of some co-ordinating mechanism in order to synchronize these with the actions of the other components. By whatever means this effect is produced, it can be a very valuable tool for modelling the many real-world processes that are non-sequential in form.

In recent years, the topic of **concurrency** has received quite a lot of attention, and it is now fairly well understood, in the sense that we possess a number of models that describe how it can be handled and used. There are a number of good texts that explain the issues involved (Ben-Ari, 1982; Holt *et al.*, 1978; Peterson and Silberschatz, 1983), so this section will provide only a brief introduction to these in so far as they apply to Modula-2.

Writing the programs for a concurrent system involves selecting a form of communication between the concurrent elements, and then resolving two major issues, namely **mutual exclusion** and **synchronization**. Mutual exclusion may need to be provided at any point where a program requires to access a shared information area, and it is concerned with ensuring that any changes to the information are made in a controlled manner by only one component at a time. In order to prevent possible corruption of the shared information, any part of the program that changes an item within the shared area must include extra code whose purpose is to temporarily *exclude* other parts of the program from access to the shared area while the change is being made. It may also need to wait until no other part of the program is accessing the information before it can begin the exclusion process.

The need for *synchronization* likewise arises from the relative independence of the component parts. It is concerned with *events*. A section of the program that 'produces' information needs to notify some independent 'consuming' part that information has now become available for it – that is, that an event has occurred. (The information may be the event itself, as in the case of a clock interrupt, or some data that is quite separate, such as a character from a terminal keyboard.) Events are often concerned with the flow of data through a system, and may also be concerned with activating another part of the program to perform some task.

Most imperative programming languages are sequential in form, so that the language constructs available enable us only to specify sequences of operations, rather than segments of a program that can be executed concurrently. Relatively few programming languages can specify which segments of a program can be executed independently (in parallel). Because of this, a system with concurrent features usually requires the means of providing synchronization and mutual exclusion to be provided externally, via such a mechanism as the 'system call' of an operating system.

To illustrate this latter idea, the segment of code below uses the two keywords COBEGIN and COEND (or PARBEGIN and PAREND) to identify segments that may be executed independently of one another. (Any code between a COBEGIN and a COEND is a sequential segment, and where such segments appear at the same level of nesting within a program, they identify parallel threads within the program.)

```
BEGIN
  i := 0; j := 7; x := 10;
  COBEGIN
    REPEAT i := i + 1 UNTIL i > x + 10            } Segment A
    IF j < x THEN j := x + 20 END                 } Segment B
  COEND
  x := x + j + i;
END
```

The operations involved are deliberately trivial, so that the independence of the two segments can be seen clearly. In the code segment A, the variable i is modified, and the value of variable x is tested. In segment B, the variable j is modified, and again this utilizes the value of variable x for comparison purposes. So the result of executing the program as a whole is independent of whether segment A is executed before segment B, or vice versa, as long as the operations of both of these segments have been completed before the next statement following the end of the block is executed.

If we were now to make a small alteration, so that segment A now contains

```
REPEAT i := i + 1 UNTIL i > x + j
```

then the result of executing segment A depends upon the values of both x and j. Since the value of j is modified by the operations of the code of segment B, the two segments are no longer independent of one another, and the result of executing the complete block will now be dependent upon the order in which statements of the two segments are interleaved during execution. The variable j is now an example of shared information, and this demonstrates in a simple way why we need to control access to such shared data.

We can often find fairly trivial examples of sequences of operations that are essentially independent of one another in our own programs, so that the order of the operations performed by the statements within a block of code is immaterial. The optimizing compilers used with powerful computers seek to identify such sequences, and then utilize this knowledge to organize the machine-level code so as to keep the components of the ALU working in parallel. However, dividing up a program on a larger scale is a much more difficult task, both conceptually, since it requires a different view of programming, and physically, in that the programmer needs to take considerable care to keep the components of a program separate. So writing *multi-thread* (parallel) programs is very much more difficult than writing *single-thread* (sequential) programs. In addition, since the operations that support mutual exclusion and synchronization will usually require calls to the operating system, they may represent a significant overhead in the program's overall use of computer time.

A number of programming languages incorporate some form of concurrent programming features in the structure of the language. Concurrent Pascal (Brinch-Hanson, 1977), Ada (ANSI, 1983; Burns, 1986) and occam (occam, 1984) are examples of three quite different approaches. (Modula-2 provides yet another!) One good reason for providing such features *within* the programming language, rather than by using multiple processes with an operating system, is that it allows the programmer to combine a number of concurrent segments within the address space of a single process. This enables these segments to share access to code and data as necessary, and gives scope for making effective use of such ideas as information-hiding. Such a language can, of course, also be used for constructing the operating system itself. On the other hand, constructing a system from separate processes running under the control of an operating system requires that the concurrent features must be provided by the operating system. Also, since each process occupies its own address space, it will have no means of accessing the address space of another process, and hence of sharing information via shared variables. So the exchange of information will require such facilities as shared data segments and/or a message-passing mechanism. While this is a valid model for constructing large concurrent systems and has some strengths, in that it is easier to construct such a system with a team of programmers (Simpson and Jackson, 1979; Budgen, 1985), it is apt to involve larger run-time overheads.

Modula-2 provides some relatively simple structures that can be used for writing concurrent programs. While these are not as comprehensive and powerful as those of occam or Ada, they are nevertheless useful in their own right. (Of course, Modula-2 can also be used to construct sequential programs that are then combined into a concurrent system via some operating system support (Budgen, 1985), and it provides some nice features for doing this, but the standard features are worth exploring a little in their own right.)

The Modula-2 model of concurrent programming is quite a simple one, and is primarily oriented towards the use of multiple programs within a single processor. However, this is not a specific requirement and there is no reason why a Modula-2 implementation should not provide support for the use of multiple processors.

Before proceeding to examine the Modula-2 model of concurrency more fully, the next section provides a little more background by explaining a little about the notion of a *co-routine*.

## 16.2 The co-routine concept

Virtually every programming language contains some facility for declaring and calling subprograms. Modula-2 has the procedure and the function procedure, Pascal has functions and procedures, FORTRAN has functions and subroutines, and so on. (In assembler coding, the term that is commonly used to describe a subprogram is 'subroutine', and for consistency of style we will use this term throughout the discussion of this section.)

Despite the wide use of subroutines for structuring programs, the co-routine mechanism, which is really quite closely related, is encountered only rarely. The nature of a co-routine is perhaps best explained by comparing its form with that of the subroutine.

Whenever a subroutine is called during the execution of a program, control is passed to the first executable statement of its main body, which is sometimes termed the **entry point** of the subroutine. So while execution might be terminated at a number of optional points within its body (perhaps via several different RETURN statements), execution will *always* begin from the one entry point.

Figure 16.1 shows this flow of control in diagrammatic form for a set of three subroutines, A, B and C. The unbroken line represents the flow of control that occurs when a set of nested calls are made to these three subroutines. (Subroutine C is called twice from subroutine B.) When using subroutines, the transfer of control has a strictly hierarchical basis, as is reflected in the form of the diagram.

The idea of the co-routine is rather similar, in that on the *initial* transfer of control to a co-routine, execution will begin at its entry point.

294    FORMS FOR USE WITH CONCURRENT PROGRAMMING

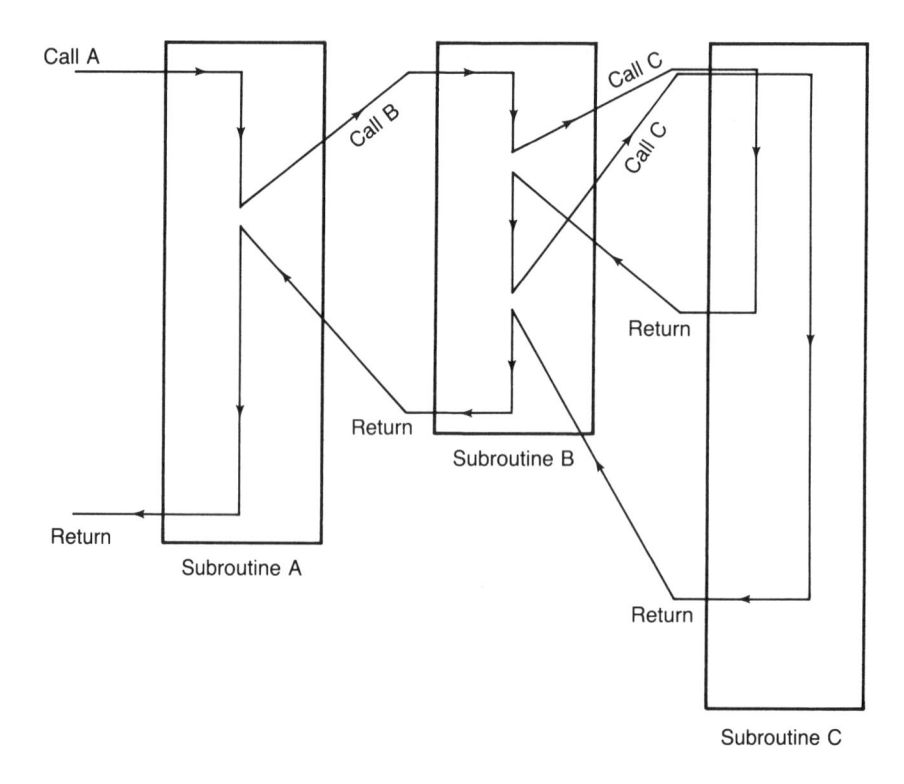

**Figure 16.1**   A typical flow of control for three subroutines.

If, however, it suspends execution and passes control to another co-routine, then if and when control is returned to the first co-routine, it will continue executing from the point where it was suspended. Figure 16.2 shows the flow of control that might occur between three co-routines, A, B and C. We refer to a 'call' to another co-routine as a **transfer**, a term that indicates that control is being transferred to an equal, rather than to a subordinate.

There are some practical issues arising in implementing a scheme of co-routines that can restrict the benefit of using them in many situations. One limitation is that it is not very practical to pass parameters on a transfer operation. Another (which is more related to the implementation issues that can arise in a simple machine architecture) is concerned with how the local variables of each co-routine can be preserved between transfers. We will be returning to this particular problem in the next section. However, despite these limitations co-routines can provide a very useful and powerful structuring tool, although there are relatively few examples around that show how this can be done (Allison (1983) provides

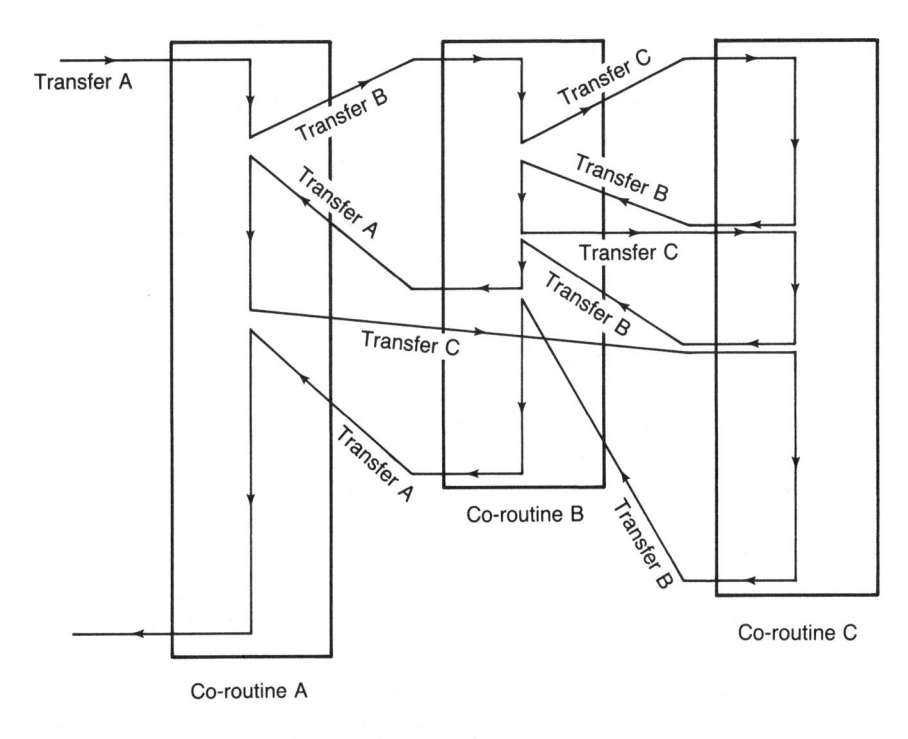

**Figure 16.2** A typical flow of control for three co-routines.

an elegant example). To some extent the lack of examples is caused by the nature of the design methods that were discussed in Chapter 12. These are almost always hierarchical in form, and any design produced by such methods will be more easily implemented using subroutines than co-routines.

The control flow shown in Figure 16.2 may suggest an analogy with the way in which a multi-tasking operating system is organized. In such operating systems, the execution of each process will be suspended and resumed – possibly many times each second – under the control of the scheduler. Each time a process is suspended, either because it needs to wait for a resource or because it has been 'pre-empted' by the scheduler to let another process be executed, the current 'state vector', which describes its state of execution, must be preserved so that the process may be correctly resumed when the scheduler next selects it for execution. Co-routines are suspended and resumed in much the same way as processes, and the underlying run-time system similarly needs to preserve the necessary information. However, there need not be any pre-emption for co-routines, and control is transferred only through their own actions. (This is sometimes termed **co-operative scheduling**.)

## 16.3 Co-routines in Modula-2

Modula-2 has no 'static' language constructs used for declaring a co-routine (COROUTINE is not a reserved word, nor is it a predefined type). Instead, co-routines are created *dynamically* during the execution of a program using the procedure NEWPROCESS. In order to construct a co-routine, we write the code for it in the form of a parameterless procedure. This is then used as the 'template' from which a co-routine is created when the program is executed.

Creating a co-routine dynamically in this way requires that a number of items of information should be associated with it, namely:

- the identity of the parameterless procedure that acts as the 'template' for the co-routine;
- the identifier of a pointer to a 'control block' (which must be different from the identifier of the procedure) which will be used to hold information about the status of the co-routine. (Because the allocation of information to the 'control block' is dynamic, it is possible to later re-allocate this identifier for use with another co-routine, though this should only be done with great care);
- a workspace area that will be used to hold the local stack space of the co-routine, and also the state vector of the co-routine whenever it suspends execution.

When a co-routine is created using the procedure NEWPROCESS, imported from the module SYSTEM, this information must be supplied through its parameters. The procedure heading for NEWPROCESS is

```
PROCEDURE NEWPROCESS(source : PROC; buffer : ADDRESS;
    buffersize : CARDINAL; VAR coidentity : ADDRESS);
```

So a call of NEWPROCESS requires that values be provided for the following four parameters:

- the identifier of the procedure to be used for the 'template' of the co-routine;
- the address of the workspace to be associated with this co-routine;
- the size of the workspace;
- the identifier to be used for the pointer to the 'control block' associated with this co-routine.

An example of a call to NEWPROCESS might be

```
NEWPROCESS(ProcName, ADR(workspace), SIZE(workspace), CoStateBlock);
```

where: ProcName is the identifier of the parameterless procedure used as a template; workspace will usually have been declared as an ARRAY OF WORD; CoStateBlock is the identifier for the 'control block' used for this co-routine.

(The type PROCESS was originally included in the language, and was used to provide a control block pointer. In later definitions of Modula-2, and in later compilers, this has been dropped, and the fourth parameter of NEWPROCESS is of type ADDRESS rather than PROCESS.)

Two quite important observations can be drawn from the form of the procedure NEWPROCESS. The first is that, since co-routines are declared dynamically, there is no reason why we should not generate several instances of co-routines, using one procedure as a template. This is precisely the form that is used for modelling a quite complex set of interactions with many co-routines, using only two procedures as templates, in the paper by Lloyd Allison (1983). One of the examples of the next section also shows this technique, although for a rather simpler problem.

The second (less desirable) observation is that a call to NEWPROCESS requires the amount of workspace that is to be allocated to a co-routine to be declared explicitly as a constant. For most systems there will be a suggested minimum size for this. Since this workspace is used to hold system-dependent information about the state vector of the co-routine when it is suspended, as well as information about any procedures that are called from within the co-routine (usually by providing a local 'stack space'), the amount required for a co-routine at any time may vary according to the algorithm contained within it. A co-routine that makes many procedure calls – some of which can generate further (nested) calls – will need more workspace than one that makes none. Since the amount of workspace needed will also depend upon the implementation of the underlying run-time system, it is very hard to give any general guidelines to help to determine the size of the workspace. So when programs using co-routines are transferred to another machine, or another operating system, the amount of workspace required may change too. This need to provide system-related data structures makes the use of co-routines in Modula-2 much less abstract than the **task** mechanism that is used in Ada.

The **transfer** operation used to exchange control between co-routines is performed by calling the procedure TRANSFER (which is also imported from the module SYSTEM). This is declared as :

PROCEDURE TRANSFER( VAR coroutine1, coroutine2 : ADDRESS );

where coroutine1 and coroutine2 are pointers to co-routine control blocks. (Again, on older systems, these parameters will be of the type PROCESS.) The first identifier, coroutine1, should be the identifier of the control block used for the co-routine that is currently executing, and informs the run-time support system which associated workspace should be used to save the co-routine's state vector information. The second identifier, coroutine2, is the identifier of the control block for the co-routine that is to resume execution on the transfer of control, and again, because of the links set up by the previous calls to NEWPROCESS, this informs the system which workspace contains the information needed to resume co-routine execution. Since the transfer of control will alter the information stored in the workspace of the second co-routine as well as that held for the first, both parameters need to be variable.

While the operation of TRANSFER is fairly clear once the co-routines are executing, one point that is not evident from the above description is how the first co-routine is to be activated on the initial transfer. If TRANSFER is to be used for this first call, then the programmer needs to provide some form of specification for the first parameter – yet it would appear that no co-routine is executing at this point. To get around this, the executing program (generally the main body of one of its modules) must be regarded as a co-routine too, and an additional identifier MAIN of type ADDRESS (or PROCESS) is usually declared for this purpose. Since the program already has a workspace, there is no need to associate one with it via a call of NEWPROCESS: when the first call of TRANSFER is made, the status of the program itself is saved in the main workspace, and a link to this is stored in the control block associated with MAIN. (In the first example of the next section, this is also used when the co-routines have finished their task, and it becomes necessary to transfer control back to the main thread of the program.)

## 16.4 Some examples of co-routines

This section provides three example programs to show how co-routines may be used in Modula-2. The first two examples are primarily concerned with showing how the co-routine mechanism works, and have therefore been kept as simple as possible. The third example is larger and is intended to demonstrate the use of co-routines in solving a rather more realistic problem, namely the construction of a text formatting program. Although this solution has some quite attractive features, it must be admitted that it is somewhat contrived, since there is no particular reason to use co-routines for the solution in preference to more conventional programming techniques.

To begin with the basic mechanisms. The example program CoExample1 shown in Figure 16.3 contains three co-routines, each formed from a different procedure. The joint operation of the co-routines prints out a line of text, and the first co-routine also keeps a count of these, returning control to the main program once the task is complete.

When this program is executed, it prints a line containing the start-up message Start playing:, followed by 21 lines each consisting of the string Ping – Pong and then a final message, Game finished. This sequence of messages

**Figure 16.3** Example of the use of co-routines.

---

(* Simple example of the use of co-routines to print a line of text: each co-routine prints a separate part of the line. *)

MODULE CoExample1:

FROM SYSTEM IMPORT WORD, ADR, ADDRESS, NEWPROCESS, TRANSFER;

FROM InOut IMPORT WriteString, WriteLn;

CONST
  workspacesize = 400;                         (*select default workspace size*)

TYPE
  Workspaces = ARRAY [1..workspacesize] OF WORD;

VAR
  MAIN, FIRST, SECOND, THIRD : ADDRESS;    (*co-routine identifiers*)
  firstwspace, secondwspace, thirdwspace : Workspaces;

(* now the code for the co-routines *)

```
PROCEDURE First;
VAR
  i : CARDINAL;
BEGIN
  FOR i := 0 TO 20 DO
    WriteString('Ping ');
    TRANSFER(FIRST,SECOND);
  END; (* for *)
  TRANSFER(FIRST,MAIN);
END First;

PROCEDURE Second;
BEGIN
  LOOP
    WriteString('- Pong');
    TRANSFER(SECOND,THIRD);
  END (* loop *)
END Second;

PROCEDURE Third;
BEGIN
  LOOP
    WriteLn;
    TRANSFER(THIRD,FIRST);
  END; (* loop *)
END Third;
```

```
BEGIN                                        (* main body of program *)
  WriteString('Start playing:');
  WriteLn;
  NEWPROCESS(First, ADR(firstwspace), workspacesize, FIRST);
  NEWPROCESS(Second, ADR(secondwspace), workspacesize, SECOND);
  NEWPROCESS(Third, ADR(thirdwspace), workspacesize, THIRD);

  (* now start the system running *)
  TRANSFER(MAIN,FIRST);
  WriteString('Game finished');
  WriteLn;
END CoExample1.
```

**Figure 16.3**  *cont.*

demonstrates a complete sequence of transfers, including the original one from the main body of the program to the first co-routine and a final one back to the main body for a clean exit.

Because the task of this program is so simple, the mechanisms are fairly prominent in the code. There are some points to note . First, the co-routine control block accessed through MAIN, which is used for the co-routine corresponding to the main body of the program, requires no call to NEWPROCESS and no workspace needs to be allocated for it.

Second, the size of the workspace is system-dependent (to get this program to work on your own system may require a different value, although a value of 400, as used here, is fairly generous). Generally, if the program crashes at some point, it may well be worth increasing the workspace. Unfortunately the information needed to estimate the size of the workspace is rarely available to the programmer.

Finally, and arising from the last point, debugging such programs needs a little care, as we need to distinguish between program failures that are caused by programming errors and those that are caused by not having allocated sufficient workspace for a co-routine.

The second example program is shown in Figure 16.4, and is an extension of the first. The program now contains just one procedure that can be used as the template from which to create three message-printing co-routines.

There are several points that can be usefully noted from this second example. First, in order for each process to 'know' its own identity, the program needs to provide a shared variable currentprocess. This could lead to problems of mutual exclusion if the program were to be shared among a number of processors, and so needs to be handled with care. (This is also an example of the type of structure that can be used to overcome the lack of any form of parameters for a transfer.)

**Figure 16.4** Further example of the use of co-routines.

---

(* Example of co-routine use, with multiple co-routines created from a single process template. *)

MODULE CoExample2;

FROM SYSTEM IMPORT WORD, ADR, ADDRESS, NEWPROCESS, TRANSFER;

FROM InOut IMPORT WriteString, Write, EOL;

```
CONST
  processcount = 3;         (* no of instances of co-routine *)
  workspacesize = 400;      (* co-routine workspace size *)
  maxmessage = 30;          (* maximum message length per co-routine *)

TYPE
  buffer = ARRAY [1..workspacesize] OF WORD;              (* workspace form *)
  messagebuffer = ARRAY [0..maxmessage] OF CHAR;

VAR
  MAIN : ADDRESS;
  PRINTER : ARRAY [1..processcount] OF ADDRESS;           (* co-routine instances *)
  workspace : ARRAY [1..processcount] OF buffer;          (* workspace instances *)
  message : ARRAY [1..processcount] OF messagebuffer;
  messageterminator : ARRAY [1..processcount] OF CHAR;    (* ends each message *)
  currentprocess : CARDINAL;                              (* index for current instance *)
```

(* co-routine template – prints the message in its buffer, followed by its particular terminator, then passes control to next instance *)

```
PROCEDURE Printer;
VAR
  thisprocess : CARDINAL;                                 (* local copy of instance *)
BEGIN
  LOOP
    thisprocess := currentprocess;
    WriteString(message[currentprocess]);                 (* print message *)
    Write(messageterminator[currentprocess]);
    IF ( currentprocess < processcount ) THEN INC(currentprocess)   (* determine next *)
    ELSE currentprocess := 1;
    END; (* if *)
    TRANSFER(PRINTER[thisprocess],PRINTER[currentprocess]);
  END; (* loop *)
END Printer;
```

BEGIN (* module main body *)

(* initialize the messages *)

messageterminator[1] := ' ';
messageterminator[2] := ' ';
messageterminator[3] := EOL;
message[1] := 'Ping';
message[2] := ' — ';
message[3] := 'Pong';

(* create the co-routine instances *)

FOR currentprocess := 1 TO processcount DO
   NEWPROCESS(Printer, ADR(workspace[currentprocess]), workspacesize,
              PRINTER[currentprocess]);
END; (* for *)

(* set the system running *)

currentprocess := 1;
TRANSFER( MAIN, PRINTER[currentprocess]);
END CoExample2.

**Figure 16.4** *cont.*

Second, while this example is a little longer than the previous one, its form is far more flexible, and to extend it to include further co-routines would require little more than some additional assignment statements to initialize variables.

Third, unlike the previous example this program does not stop. (A useful point to note is that the system should stop if any co-routine reaches its final END. However, some implementations may not handle this situation gracefully if the terminating co-routine is other than the one formed from the main body of the program.)

Finally, as a side-issue, this program also shows examples of the declaration of two-dimensional arrays, for the variables workspace and message, and the facility for treating these as one-dimensional arrays when assigning a string (in the case of message) or when referencing a complete array (as in the calls to NEWPROCESS).

The third example program is rather larger, although it makes use of only two co-routines. While not necessarily the best or most obvious solution for this problem, it serves to show a little more of the way in which co-routines might be usefully employed.

The program, TextFormat, is a rather simple text formatter that takes as its input text files that contain embedded formatting commands, in the

**Table 16.1** Format options for TextFormat.

| Command | Interpretation |
| --- | --- |
| .br | Line break. Causes the current line to be output at that point, and starts a new output line. |
| .in off | Left margin indent. Adjusts the left margin by the number of spaces given in the signed offset off. Positive offsets move the margin to the right, negative offsets move it to the left. Causes a line break. |
| .ll off | Right margin adjust. Adjusts the right margin by the number of spaces given in the signed offset. Does not cause a line break. |
| .cc c | Change control character. Modifies the current command identifying character to the value of the character c. |
| .nf | Stop filling. The program will normally fill out lines with words to the best of its ability. When this output is in effect, each line is output in exactly the form in which it was input. Causes a line break. |
| .fi | Fill lines. Reverses the effect of .nf and resumes filling of output lines. |
| .ls val | Line spacing. Lines are normally single-spaced – with no interval between lines. This corresponds to a default interval of 1 (i.e. val = 1). This command changes the interval, and outputs (val−1) empty lines between each line of text. Causes a line break. |

form used for the **roff** family of text formatters that will be familiar to UNIX users. Such an input file will consist of raw text together with formatting commands, each of which appears on a separate line and normally begins with a period character. The output from the program consists of the text component of the input file, formatted according to the specification formed by the embedded commands.

For simplicity, the formatter described here possesses only a small set of commands, listed in Table 16.1. Note that one of these allows the user to modify the command character that appears at the start of a line containing a command (which is the full stop by default), so that by using a sequence such as

```
.cc #
... this line represents continuation of the sequence
#cc .
```

the user's text can contain a line that is output as

> ... this line represents continuation of the sequence

(Note that it is usually wise to return to using the default command character in the way shown here, to avoid errors when we forget that we have changed it!) The source text of the example program is shown in Figure 16.5.

The program TextFormat is constructed around two co-routines. One of these performs the main task of text formatting, transferring text from the input buffer to the output buffer and organizing its layout in the process, according to a table of conditions. The second co-routine processes the formatting commands themselves. These cause the second co-routine to modify the shared table that contains the current formatting conditions and may also require it to perform certain operations on the output buffer. While neither co-routine is performing a particularly simple task, their structures have been simplified by making use of subordinate procedures.

Several points are illustrated by this example. First, the use of co-routines does not make the flow of control within a program easy to follow. This is often found in concurrent programming exercises, where the flow of control and manipulation of shared data are fragmented between different sections of a program.

Second, input and output buffering has been separated off into local modules (these could equally well have been separate modules), in order that the code in the main part of the program should not have any means of accessing the input and output buffers directly, but only via the procedures provided. This is another example of information-hiding.

Third, to further illustrate the use of information-hiding as a design principle, the structure of the program has been chosen so that each of the items of information about formatting status (the current control character, the width of a line, etc.) is *used* by the statements in only one of the three modules. For example, the value of the variable controlchar is used only in the code of the main module and those of the variables leftmargin and linewidth are used only by the procedures in the Outputs module. The one exception to this is the value of filling, which is used by routines in all three of the modules. This really represents an example of an incorrect design choice: if NextString passed back each textual 'token' complete with any leading spaces, the Inputs module would not need to import the value of filling. This is in turn an example of processing the input information at too early a point – the leading spaces before each input word should not be stripped off within the module Inputs.

Fourth, the parsing of the commands would seem to be ideally suited to the CASE construct. Unfortunately, the syntax of CASE requires that the labels of the branches should be scalar values, and not arrays of CHAR. So the next best choice is to use ELSIF. No ELSE clause is needed on this

**Figure 16.5** TextFormat program.

---

(* demonstration program to show the use of co-routines in Modula-2 *)
(* this is a simple 'roff' type text formatter program with the following subset of commands:
.br — line break
.in — left margin offset
.ll — right margin adjust
.cc — change control character
.nf — stop filling (leaves lines 'raw')
.fi — fill lines out
.ls — line spacing
for the .ll and .in commands, the argument is in characters, for the .ls command, the argument is in lines *)
(* written by : D. Budgen *)

MODULE TextFormat;

FROM SYSTEM IMPORT WORD, ADR, ADDRESS, SIZE, NEWPROCESS, TRANSFER;

FROM InOut IMPORT WriteString, Write, WriteLn, Read, OpenInput, EOL, Done;

CONST
  period = '.';                                      (* default command character *)
  wspacesize = 1000;                           (* default workspace for co-routines *)
  maxsymbol = 80;                                (* maximum input word size *)
  defaultfilling = TRUE;                          (* normally providing filling of lines *)
  initiallinewidth = 72;                            (* default characters/line *)
  initialpagelength = 66;                        (* default line/page *)

VAR
  (* first the status table that defines the current formatting mode *)
  leftmargin : CARDINAL;                         (* size of the left indent *)
  linewidth : CARDINAL;                           (* position of right margin *)
  pagelength : CARDINAL;                        (* number of lines per output page *)
  lineinterval : CARDINAL;                         (* line spacing *)
  controlchar : CHAR;                              (* current control character *)
  filling : BOOLEAN;                                  (* control of output line filling *)

  (* buffer space to hold the current 'token' *)
  token : ARRAY [0..maxsymbol] OF CHAR;
  length : CARDINAL;                                (* token size *)

  (* the co-routine (process) workspaces and co-routine declarations *)
  formatwspace : ARRAY [1..wspacesize] OF WORD;
  commandwspace : ARRAY [1..wspacesize] OF WORD;
  MAIN, FORMAT, COMMAND : ADDRESS;

  (* the two co-routines which form the core *)

  (* Command — decodes the current formatting command and any arguments that it has, and then updates the formatting mode, flushing the output buffer if necessary *)

## 306  FORMS FOR USE WITH CONCURRENT PROGRAMMING

PROCEDURE Command;

(* GetOffset — is a procedure that is used to calculate the argument value for those commands that need an argument. *)

PROCEDURE GetOffset(VAR offset : INTEGER);

VAR
   negative : BOOLEAN;                             (* used to indicate sign of argument *)
   index : CARDINAL;                                (* provides a general counter *)

BEGIN
   index := 0; negative := FALSE; offset := 0;
   NextString(token,length);
   WHILE ( token[index] = ' ' ) AND (length > index ) DO
     INC(index);                                      (* strip any spaces (if not filling) *)
   END; (* while *)
   IF ((length-index) > 0) THEN
     IF ( token[INDEX] = '+' ) THEN INC(index)
     ELSIF (token[index] = '−' ) THEN INC(index); negative := TRUE;
     END; (* if *)
     FOR index := index TO (length−1) DO
       IF (token[index] >= '0') AND (token[index] <= '9') THEN
         offset := (offset*10) + INTEGER(ORD(token[index]) − ORD('0'));
       END; (* if *)
     END; (* for *)
     IF negative THEN offset := offset*(−1); END;
   END; (* if *)
END GetOffset;

VAR
   first, second : CHAR;                          (* holds the command characters *)
   change : INTEGER;                             (* holds offsets from arguments *)

BEGIN
  LOOP
    first := token[1];
    second := token[2];

  (* the .br break command *)

    IF (first='b') AND (second='r') THEN FlushBuffer;

  (* the .in command − indent and break *)

    ELSIF (first='i') AND (second='n') THEN
      GetOffset(change);
      IF ( INTEGER(leftmargin) + change ) >= 0 THEN
        leftmargin := CARDINAL( INTEGER(leftmargin) + change);
      END; (* if *)
      FlushBuffer;

## SOME EXAMPLES OF CO-ROUTINES    307

```
(* the .ll change line length command – no break *)

  ELSIF (first='l') AND (second='l') THEN
    GetOffset(change);
    IF (( INTEGER(linewidth) + change) > 0 ) THEN
      linewidth := CARDINAL( INTEGER(linewidth) + change);
    END; (* if *)

(* the .cc change control character command *)

  ELSIF (first='c') AND (second='c') THEN
    NextString(token,length);
    IF (length = 1) THEN controlchar := token[0] END;

(* the .nf stop filling command for raw text *)

  ELSIF (first='n') AND (second='f') THEN
    FlushBuffer;
    filling := FALSE;

(* the .fi resume filling command *)

  ELSIF (first='f') AND (second='i') THEN filling := TRUE;

(* the .ls change line spacing command *)

  ELSIF (first='l') AND (second='s') THEN
    GetOffset(change);
    IF (change > 0) THEN
      FlushBuffer;
      lineinterval := CARDINAL(change);           (* take new absolute value *)
    END; (* if *)
  END; (* if *)
  TRANSFER(COMMAND,FORMAT);                       (* return control *)
  END (* loop *)
END Command;

(* Format – handles the basic text processing sequence *)

PROCEDURE Format;

BEGIN
  WHILE ReadLine() DO
    NextString(token,length);                     (* get first token on line *)
    IF length <> 0 THEN
      IF token[0] = controlchar THEN TRANSFER(FORMAT,COMMAND)
      ELSE
        REPEAT
          PutString(token,length);
          NextString(token,length);
        UNTIL length = 0;
```

```
      END; (* if *)
      IF NOT filling THEN FlushBuffer END;
    ELSE
      PutNewLine;                            (* add empty line *)
    END (* if *)
  END; (* while *)
  FlushBuffer;                               (* empty last line from buffer *)
  TRANSFER(FORMAT,MAIN);
(* return control at end of input *)
END Format;
```

(* InitialConditions – is a routine that sets up the default formatting conditions when the program starts up *)

```
PROCEDURE InitialConditions;
BEGIN
  leftmargin := 0;
  linewidth := initiallinewidth;
  pagelength := initialpagelength;
  lineinterval := 1;
  controlchar := period;
  filling := defaultfilling;
END InitialConditions;
```

  (* the two local modules that handle input and output buffering *)

  (* Inputs – contains the routines to read in the lines of source text, and returns the words of the line as a set of 'tokens' or strings of characters *)

```
MODULE Inputs;

  IMPORT filling, EOL, Read, OpenInput, WriteString, WriteLn, Done;
  EXPORT ReadLine, NextString;

CONST
  Null = 0C;
  bufferlength = 120;
  Tab = 11C;

VAR
  textbuffer : ARRAY [0..bufferlength−1] OF CHAR;   (* input line buffer *)
  lineindex : CARDINAL;                             (* line position index *)
```

  (* ReadLine – procedure to fetch next line of characters from the input file *)

```
PROCEDURE ReadLine() : BOOLEAN;
VAR
  i : CARDINAL;
BEGIN
  i := 0;
```

```
      REPEAT
         Read(textbuffer[i]); INC(i);
      UNTIL (textbuffer[i−1] = EOL) OR (i = bufferlength) OR NOT Done;
      lineindex := 0;
      RETURN Done
   END ReadLine;


   (* NextString – procedure which obtains the next character 'token' from the input buffer *)

   PROCEDURE NextString(VAR token : ARRAY OF CHAR; VAR length : CARDINAL);
   VAR
      i : CARDINAL;
   BEGIN
      i := 0;

      (* if mode is for formatted text, strip leading spaces *)

      IF filling THEN
         WHILE ( (textbuffer[lineindex] = ' ')
            OR (textbuffer[lineindex] = Tab) ) DO
            INC(lineindex);
         END (* while *)
      END; (* if *)
      IF ( textbuffer[lineindex] = EOL ) THEN length := 0;   (* no more *)
      ELSE

      (* if mode is for 'raw' text, include leading spaces *)

         IF NOT filling THEN                         (* copy leading blanks *)
            WHILE ( textbuffer[lineindex] = ' '
               OR (textbuffer[lineindex] = Tab ) DO
               token[i] := textbuffer[lineindex];
               INC(i); INC(lineindex);
            END (* while *)
         END; (* if *)

      (* now copy the token, ending with a space, tab or end of line *)

         WHILE ( textbuffer[lineindex] <> ' ' ) AND ( textbuffer[lineindex] <> Tab)
            AND ( textbuffer[lineindex] <> EOL ) DO
            token[i] := textbuffer[lineindex];
            INC(i); INC(lineindex);
         END; (* while *)
         length := i;
      END; (* if *)
      token[i] := Null;                              (* terminate string *)
   END NextString;
```

310  FORMS FOR USE WITH CONCURRENT PROGRAMMING

```
BEGIN (* main body of Inputs *)
  WriteString('Enter File name:');
  OpenInput('test.1');                    (* this bit is system dependent *)
END Inputs;

(* Outputs – is the module which provides the output buffering *)

MODULE Outputs;

IMPORT WriteString, Write, WriteLn, leftmargin, linewidth, maxsymbol, lineinterval, filling, pagelength;

EXPORT PutString, PutNewLine, FlushBuffer;

CONST
  fullstop = '.';                         (* sentence terminators *)
  shriek = '!';
  question = '?';

VAR
  linenumber : CARDINAL;                  (* position of line on page *)
  charposition : CARDINAL;                (* current character on this line *)
  started : BOOLEAN;                      (* whether buffer yet used or not *)
  outbuffer : ARRAY [0..maxsymbol] OF CHAR;  (* output buffer *)

(* PutString – procedure to output the next token *)

PROCEDURE PutString(token : ARRAY OF CHAR; length : CARDINAL);
VAR
  i : CARDINAL;
BEGIN                                     (* start new line if insufficient space left *)
  IF ( (linewidth – charposition) < length ) THEN FlushBuffer END;
  FOR i := 0 TO (length–1) DO
    outbuffer[charposition] := token[i];
    INC(charposition);
  END; (* for *)
  IF ( charposition < linewidth ) AND filling THEN
    outbuffer[charposition] := ' ';       (* add space between words *)
    INC(charposition);
    IF ( charposition < linewidth )       (* check for end of sentence *)
      AND ((outbuffer[charposition–2] = fullstop)
      OR (outbuffer[charposition–2] = shriek)
      OR (outbuffer[charposition–2] = question)) THEN
      outbuffer[charposition] := ' ';     (* second space for sentence *)
      INC(charposition);
    END; (* if *)
  END; (* if *)
  started := TRUE;                        (* mark outbuffer as being in use *)
END PutString;

(* PutNewLine – adds an empty line(s) to output *)

PROCEDURE PutNewLine;
VAR
  i : CARDINAL;
```

```
BEGIN
  FlushBuffer;                              (* clear buffer out first *)
  FOR i := 1 TO lineinterval DO
    WriteLn;                                (* add empty lines *)
  END; (* for *)
END PutNewLine;

(* FlushBuffer – to output current buffer contents *)

PROCEDURE FlushBuffer;
VAR
  i : CARDINAL;
BEGIN
  IF started THEN
    FOR i := 0 TO (charposition-1) DO
      Write(outbuffer[i]);
    END; (* for *)
    FOR i := 1 TO lineinterval DO
      WriteLn;
    END; (* for *)
  END; (* if *)
  InitLine;                                 (* get buffer ready for next line *)
END FlushBuffer;

(* InitLine – organizes output buffer for a new line and marks it as unused *)

PROCEDURE InitLine;
VAR
  i : CARDINAL;
BEGIN
  IF leftmargin > 0 THEN
    FOR i := 0 TO (leftmargin-1) DO
      outbuffer[i] := ' ';
    END; (* for *)
  END; (* if *)
  charposition := leftmargin;
  started := FALSE;
  INC(linenumber);
  IF (linenumber > pagelength) THEN
    linenumber := 1;
  END; (* if *)
END InitLine;

(* main body of Outputs *)

BEGIN
  linenumber := 0;
  InitLine;
END Outputs;
```

```
BEGIN (* main body of TextFormat *)

  InitialConditions;
  NEWPROCESS(Format, ADR(formatwspace),SIZE(formatwspace),FORMAT);
  NEWPROCESS(Command, ADR(commandwspace),SIZE(commandwspace),COMMAND);
  TRANSFER(MAIN,FORMAT);
END TextFormat.
```

**Figure 16.5** *cont.*

occasion, because the formatter is intended simply to ignore any commands that it does not recognize. Since formatting commands are likely to occur only infrequently in a text file, there is probably little point in trying to order the tests to improve efficiency.

One last point concerns the use of symbolic constants within modules. To avoid an undesirable coupling, the period character '.' is defined in the CONST blocks of both the main module and the module Outputs. It is declared twice because it is used in two very different ways. In one case it is a default control character (and hence potentially alterable), whereas in the second it is the terminator of a sentence of text, and hence very unlikely to be replaced. If the module Outputs simply imported period, then a later change in the design of the formatter, requiring a different default control character, might have curious side-effects!

Designing a program for implementation using co-routines has received very little attention (partly owing to the lack of co-routine structures in most programming languages). However, the basic forms are very similar to those of multiple processes, and hence those design methods that are based upon building concurrent models of a system, such as JSD, seem to have some potential for being used in this role.

A program based on the use of co-routines can be implemented and tested in much the same way as a program with a more conventional sequential form. We can create subprogram 'stubs' in just the same way as we do with other large programs. In the third example, the obvious order of development is to first get the routines of module Inputs to work so that we can input test data; then to expand that part of the module Format needed to recognize commands; then to do the same for the routines of module Outputs; and finally to expand the routines that handle the changes caused by each command.

One other question that arises is how best to represent the structure of such a program. The conventional structure chart requires that subprograms are represented in such a way as to show their hierarchy – yet with co-routines we have no hierarchy! Figure 16.6 suggests a possible form, illustrated for the structure of TextFormat, which uses the standard structure chart representations and links the co-routines via arcs. (We cannot simply

SOME EXAMPLES OF CO-ROUTINES 313

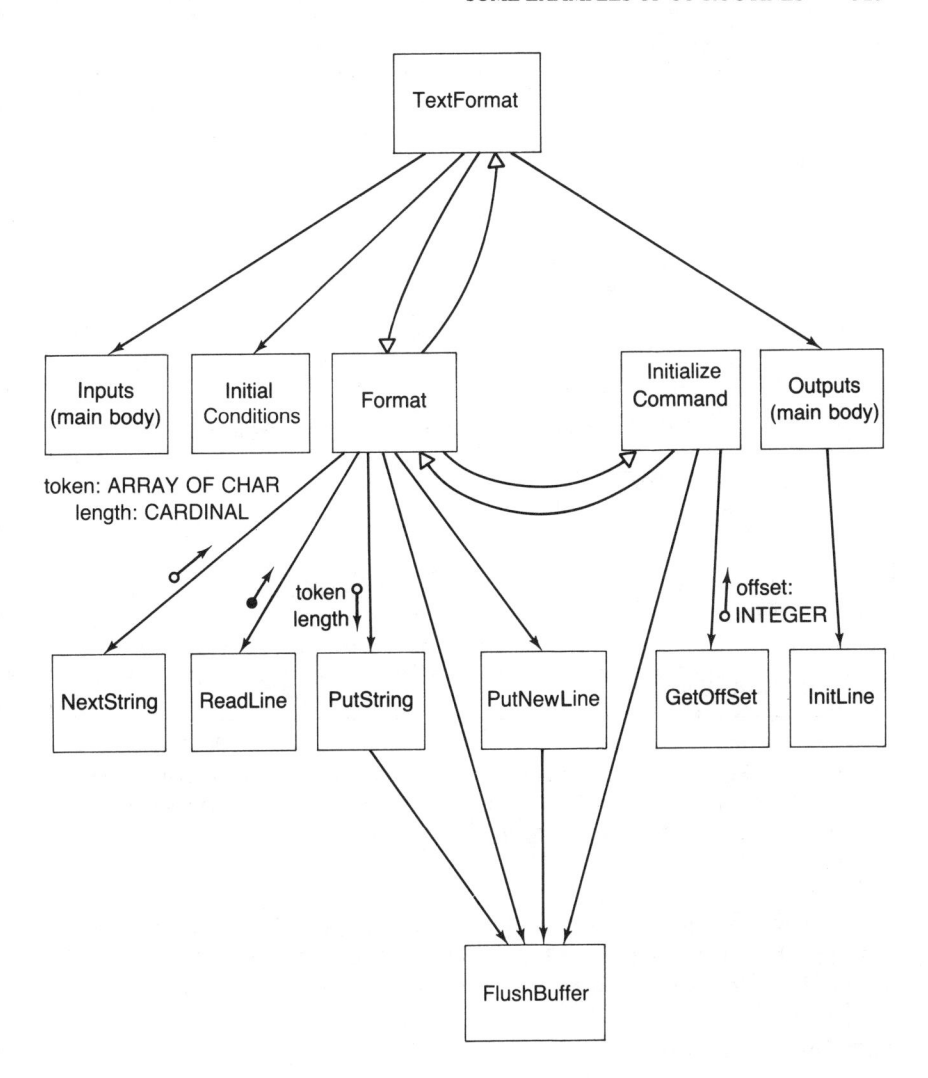

**Figure 16.6** Modified structure chart for TextFormat. Note that (i) no library procedures are shown; (ii) control flow arrows with filled heads ( ⟶ ) indicate transfer of control by procedure call; arrows with empty heads ( ⟶▷ ) by co-routine transfer.

use horizontal lines to represent 'transfer', since we may have a lot of co-routines with a fairly complex flow of control between them.)

Returning to the representations that were discussed in Chapter 12, Figure 16.7 shows how the program TextFormat can be represented using structure graphs (Buhr, 1984). This representation can be considered as complementing that of Figure 16.6.

MODULE TextFormat

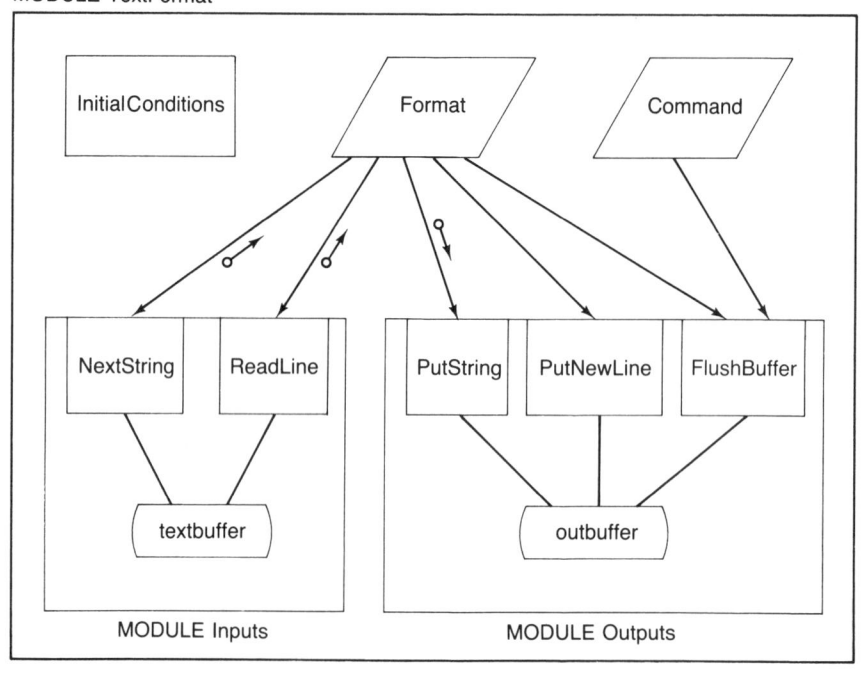

**Figure 16.7** Modified structure graph representing TextFormat. (The parallelogram used by Buhr to represent an Ada **task** is used here to represent a *co-routine*. Some details have been omitted, including library procedures.)

This section has shown some simple examples of co-routines used as a straightforward programming tool. The next shows how they can be used to provide a form of concurrent programming system, by means of making decisions about transfers of control through an external executive rather than within the co-routines themselves.

## 16.5 Co-routines as concurrent processes

When discussing concurrent programming, the term 'program' is generally reserved for the source form of a program (namely, the textual description of its algorithm and data structures). The term 'process' describes the execution of the binary image that is generated by copying the compiled binary form of a program into the computer's memory, and then setting it running. So processes are dynamic entities and we can create many instances of processes from one program. An example is the use of the text-editor on a typical multi-user operating system. There is usually only one copy of the compiled form of the editor stored on disk, but at any given time there may be many instances of the editor process resident in the computer's memory, each being used by a different user. Each time a user invokes the editor, a new process will be formed by copying the binary image of the editor program into the computer's memory.

As mentioned previously, the executive component of an operating system will often *interrupt* the currently executing process in order to *resume* execution of another process. The status of the pre-empted process is preserved by the operating system so that it can in turn be resumed at a later point.

The analogy with the way that co-routines operate in Modula-2 should be fairly evident: in the latter the TRANSFER routine preserves the status of the suspending co-routine for later re-use, and causes the other co-routine to resume execution at the point where it was suspended. Similarly, both co-routines and processes are *dynamic* entities created from static templates – in the one case this is a parameterless procedure, in the other it is a binary image on disk. However, in an operating system, the acts of pre-emption and resumption are largely *transparent* to the processes, and may be caused by the actions of an external agency, which is the operating system, as well as from requests issued from a process. This means that each process does not need to contain any special provision for organizing suspension and resumption and does not need to know anything about the other processes that are currently active (except where there is a need to synchronize with these, or to access shared data). So by moving the decision about which co-routine is to be resumed out of the co-routines, and providing some form of external 'executive', it is possible to make a set of co-routines behave very like a set of concurrent processes in an operating system (Budgen, 1985). (It should therefore be fairly evident why the type PROCESS was originally provided in Modula-2, and why the procedure used to create co-routines is termed NEWPROCESS!)

Strictly speaking, this is an example of what is sometimes termed **quasi-concurrency**, in which the co-routines behave as processes within the 'true' process that is formed from the complete Modula-2 program. Of course, when this outer process is executing under the control of an operating system within a single processor, its internal system will possess no means of pre-emption – although there are circumstances in which this can be implemented, which will be examined in the next chapter. For the moment, we will limit ourselves to considering those cases where the internal 'executive' can gain control of the situation only when a 'process' yields control to it, usually by making some request for a service such as access to shared data. (As we have seen, this form of non-pre-emptive scheduling is often termed 'co-operative' scheduling.)

So Modula-2 provides the programmer with the means of constructing a set of parallel processes, together with the necessary scheduling, synchronization and mutual exclusion operations. These latter features are necessary because of the need for the processes to share information in

316   FORMS FOR USE WITH CONCURRENT PROGRAMMING

**Figure 16.8**  A simple two-process system.

```
(* A simple two-process system with both producer and consumer processes acting as co-routines
   and performing their own scheduling. *)

MODULE sharing;

FROM InOut IMPORT ReadInt,WriteInt,WriteString,WriteLn;
FROM SYSTEM IMPORT ADDRESS,WORD,ADR,NEWPROCESS,TRANSFER;

CONST
   wspsize = 100;                       (* workspace allocation *)
   intformat = 10;                      (* size of integer printout *)

VAR
   p1,p2,main : ADDRESS;                (* co-routine identifiers *)
   wsp1,wsp2 : ARRAY [1..wspsize] OF WORD;   (* workspaces *)
   buffer : INTEGER;                    (* shared data buffer *)


(* producer – obtains an integer value from the user and stores it *)

PROCEDURE producer;
VAR
   x:INTEGER;                           (* local data buffer *)
BEGIN
   LOOP WriteString('(PRODUCER) Type a number :');
      ReadInt(x);
      buffer:=x;
      TRANSFER(p1,p2);                  (* Give consumer a turn *)
   END; (* loop *)
END producer;


(* consumer – obtains integer value from buffer and prints it out *)

PROCEDURE consumer;
VAR
   x:INTEGER;                           (* local data buffer *)
BEGIN
   LOOP
      x:=buffer;
      WriteString('(CONSUMER) Your number is : ');
      WriteInt(x,intformat); WriteLn; WriteLn;
      TRANSFER(p2,p1);                  (* Give producer a turn *)
   END; (* loop *)
END consumer;
```

CO-ROUTINES AS CONCURRENT PROCESSES    317

```
BEGIN (* Main program *)

    NEWPROCESS(producer,ADR(wsp1),SIZE(wsp1),p1);
    NEWPROCESS(consumer,ADR(wsp2),SIZE(wsp2),p2);

    TRANSFER(main,p1);                    (* Start the producer *)

END sharing.
```

**Figure 16.8**  *cont.*

(* this module provides a very simple executive that will support two co-routines acting as quasi-processes *)

DEFINITION MODULE twoprocesses;

EXPORT QUALIFIED split,suspend,stop;

  (* split – this starts the two co-routines running *)

PROCEDURE split(p1,p2:PROC);

  (* suspend – called from a co-routine and allows the executive to select the other for execution *)

PROCEDURE suspend;

  (* stop – called by a co-routine to stop the system running by transferring control back to the main program *)

PROCEDURE stop;

END twoprocesses.

**Figure 16.9**  Definition part for the simple two-process executive.

order to perform any sort of joint task. However, the analogy should not be taken too far, for an important difference is that the processes which are controlled by an operating system will usually have their own unique address spaces, while the pseudo-processes created from co-routines share a single address space.

Figure 16.8 shows an example of a simple system of two co-routines, although for consistency they will now be termed 'processes'. One process acts as the 'producer' of data (which it obtains from the user's terminal), while the other acts as a 'consumer', taking the data that the producer places in the shared buffer, and printing out its value.

In this system, the two processes explicitly transfer control to one another in turn, and so there is no need to provide any synchronization between them or use mutual exclusion to protect their use of the shared data buffer. The producer is able to inform the consumer that data is available in the buffer by the act of transferring control to the consumer, while the consumer likewise informs the producer that the buffer is now available for re-use by transferring control back to the producer.

To turn these co-routines into more realistic processes we need a more realistic executive, and Figures 16.9 and 16.10 provide the definition and implementation parts of just such an executive. This is still very simple in form, in that it can handle only two processes, but the procedure suspend already contains a very primitive scheduling algorithm for selecting the next process to be executed.

Figure 16.11 provides an example of a two-process module that makes use of this executive in order to perform the same producer–consumer activity that was shown in Figure 16.8. Transfers of control to another process now take place via calls to the executive and, as an important side-effect, the knowledge of the details of the module SYSTEM and its system-dependent contents is entirely concealed in the executive module. (This is another example of information-hiding.)

The resultant system is still a very simple one. Because the two processes co-operate, there is no need to protect access to the shared data buffer by any form of mutual exclusion and no need for inter-process synchronization. However, this simple example demonstrates how different the same system can appear when reconstructed in this form, and also shows something of the benefits that arise from separating the concerns of the different parts of the program in this way. This becomes even more significant if the system is extended to handle more processes and to include some form of pre-emption mechanism.

An example, with a listing, for a much more powerful executive system can be found in Budgen (1985), and may be of interest to any reader who wishes to see how some of the more technical issues of concurrent programming can be managed in Modula-2. In particular, this paper demonstrates some of the power of Modula-2 when applied to writing a real-time executive in a high-level language.

**Figure 16.10** Implementation part for the simple two-process executive.

```
IMPLEMENTATION MODULE twoprocesses;

FROM SYSTEM IMPORT ADDRESS,NEWPROCESS,TRANSFER,WORD,ADR;
FROM InOut IMPORT WriteLn,WriteString;

CONST
  wspsize = 100;                        (* workspace allocation *)
VAR
  mainprocess,process1,process2 : ADDRESS;   (* process identifiers *)
  wsp1,wsp2 : ARRAY [1..wspsize] OF WORD;    (* workspaces *)
  state : (main,proc1,proc2);                (* current process status *)

  (* split – starts up the two processes *)

PROCEDURE split(p1,p2:PROC);
BEGIN
  IF state <> main
  THEN WriteString('Illegal split – two processes already active');
    WriteLn;
  ELSE NEWPROCESS(p1,ADR(wsp1),SIZE(wsp1),process1);
       NEWPROCESS(p2,ADR(wsp2),SIZE(wsp2),process2);
       state := proc1;
       TRANSFER(mainprocess,process1);
  END;
END split;

  (* suspend – suspends the active process and selects another *)

PROCEDURE suspend;
BEGIN
  CASE state OF
  main: WriteString('Main process cannot suspend'); WriteLn |
  proc1: WriteString('SWAP 1→2'); WriteLn;
        state:=proc2; TRANSFER(process1,process2) |
  proc2: WriteString('SWAP 2→1'); WriteLn;
        state:=proc1; TRANSFER(process2,process1)
  END
END suspend;

  (* stop – transfers control back to the main program *)

PROCEDURE stop;
BEGIN
  CASE state OF
  main: WriteString('Main process cannot stop'); WriteLn |
  proc1: state:=main; TRANSFER(process1,mainprocess) |
  proc2: state:=main; TRANSFER(process2,mainprocess)
  END;
END stop;
```

```
BEGIN
  state:=main;                    (* initialize current process *)
END twoprocesses.
```

**Figure 16.10** *cont.*

**Figure 16.11** The simple two-process system, using the external executive.

```
MODULE parallel;

FROM twoprocesses IMPORT split,suspend,stop;
FROM InOut IMPORT ReadInt,WriteInt,WriteLn,WriteString;

CONST
  intformat = 10;     (* size of integer printout *)

VAR
  buffer:INTEGER;     (* shared data buffer *)

  (* producer - obtains an integer value from the user and stores it *)

PROCEDURE producer;
VAR
  x:INTEGER;
BEGIN
  LOOP
    WriteString('(PRODUCER) Type a number ( <0 to stop ): ');
    ReadInt(x);
    IF x<0 THEN stop END;
    buffer:=x;
    suspend;          (* Give consumer a turn *)
  END; (* loop *)
END producer;

  (* consumer - obtains integer value from buffer and prints it out *)

PROCEDURE consumer;
VAR
  x:INTEGER;
BEGIN
  LOOP
    x:=buffer;
    WriteString('(CONSUMER) Your number is : ');
    WriteInt(x,intformat); WriteLn; WriteLn;
    suspend;          (* Give producer a turn *)
  END; (* loop *)
END consumer;
```

```
(* main body of module *)
BEGIN
    WriteString('Main starts'); WriteLn; WriteLn;
    split(producer,consumer);
    WriteString('Main continues'); WriteLn; WriteLn;
END parallel.
```

**Figure 16.11** *cont.*

This ends the initial discussion of concurrent programming in Modula-2. With its system-dependent features, and the need for relatively low-level programming considerations, this is not one of the most elegant aspects of Modula-2. However, it can be a very useful and powerful programming tool, as demonstrated by the system described in Allison (1983). Indeed, its relative simplicity makes it a means of constructing a wide variety of application forms. In the next chapter we will see some further examples of the use of co-routines, and will encounter a mechanism for using a form of pre-emption.

# EXERCISES

**16.1** Using as a basis the program listed in Figure 16.4, produce a program using four co-routine instances with each instance printing out one line of the following verse:

> Speak roughly to your little boy,
> And beat him when he sneezes:
> He only does it to annoy,
> Because he knows it teases.
>           (*Lewis Carroll*)

(For an additional feature, the fourth co-routine might ring the 'bell' by using the appropriate character (7C) at the end of the verse.)

[Hint: for this exercise you may need to experiment with the value to be given to workspacesize.]

**16.2** Make a list of the changes needed to the simple executive listed in Figure 16.10 for it to be executed to cope with:

  (a) large numbers of processes (consider a linked list of workspaces?);

  (b) a random selection mechanism for determining which process is to be run next.

**16.3** Try to think about how you might adapt any of your existing programs to make use of co-routines, as opposed to a hierarchical structure of procedures.

**16.4** Write a simple program that extracts and prints the comments contained in a Modula-2 module (you should be able to test this using your solutions to the exercises of course!). Do this by using two co-routines that are selected according to whether the text being parsed at any time is 'code' or 'comment'.

# Chapter 17
# Low-level Input and Output

17.1 Background issues and device input and output
17.2 Memory mapped input/output
17.3 Controlling input and output by device polling
17.4 Interrupts and concurrency
17.5 Handling multiple interrupts
Exercises

## 17.1 Background issues and device input and output

While previous chapters have been primarily concerned with software structures, the material of this chapter is heavily influenced by the details of the hardware organization of the computer. This is inevitable, since the topic is strongly machine-dependent and, while the descriptions and examples used in this chapter have been kept at as abstract a level as possible, they need to reflect real machine architectures to be of any real use. For consistency, all examples have been based upon a single computer architecture, that of DEC's PDP-11 range of minicomputers (Tanenbaum, 1984). This is partly because the PDP-11 was one of the earliest machines to have a Modula-2 compiler, but even more because its architecture has formed the basis for the design of many subsequent computers. (DEC's own VAX-11 and Motorola's MC68000 ranges are two of the most popular and prominent of these.)

The various peripheral devices that can be attached to a computer use a variety of internal signals to control their operations, and these are not necessarily compatible in any way with the signals used within the computer itself. In order that the computer can send data to devices and receive data from them, some form of **interface** is required that can transform between the signals used by the computer and those used by the

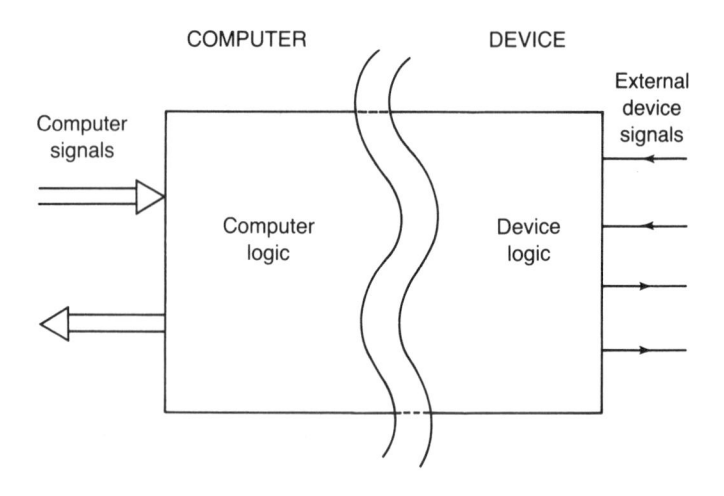

**Figure 17.1** Role of a device controller in a typical computer.

device. This interface is often termed the **device controller**. Figure 17.1 shows the role of a device controller in a diagrammatic form.

The side of the interface that is connected to the computer must present the computer with some set of primitive machine-level data structures that can be manipulated by the operations of the machine-level instructions. These usually take the form of word-sized **registers**, comprising arrays of bits organized in a manner similar to the memory of the computer. In almost all widely used computer architectures, there are two forms of operations that can be used for controlling data transfers between the computer and simple input/output devices. These in turn impose some requirements upon the way that the registers of the interface are used, both by the program and by the device controller.

The first of these two forms is termed **device polling** (or **test-ready**). The computer program that is handling the interface to the device controller repeatedly tests (or 'polls') the value of some data structure that forms part of the device interface, to determine whether the device is ready to receive data (output) or has data available (input).

While device polling has the attraction of being simple to organize, it is somewhat limiting in its scope. It is difficult to handle input from and output to more than one device at a time with this technique, and, more significantly, when implemented in a simple fashion it effectively constrains the computer to operate at the speed of the device. Since most devices are at least several orders of magnitude slower than the computer in transferring data, this can represent very poor utilization of the computer's power. In practice it is usually used only in situations such as those in which some 'dedicated' computer is given the task of handling the interface to some device.

In the second form the device interface generates **interrupts** when it has completed a data transfer and is ready to send or receive further data. When such an interrupt is received, the following sequence of actions will normally occur in the central processor:

- the processor suspends the currently executing process, saving any information that will be needed later to resume its execution;
- the processor resumes execution of the 'device driver' process that is used to handle the device interface;
- the device driver process organizes the copying of data to or from the device interface buffers, re-enabling the interrupt if more data is to be transferred, and then suspends itself to await the next interrupt;
- the processor resumes execution of the original process.

This scheme is an essential feature in most operating systems, and is virtually essential for the support of multiple users and multiple processes. However, its organization is considerably more complex than that of device polling, and it requires a more complicated device driver program.

The use of the terms 'suspend' and 'resume' in this context may already suggest that the co-routine mechanism of Modula-2 can be adapted to handle this type of operation. Since device polling is a simple sequential operation, this means that both forms of input/output can be programmed directly with Modula-2. The rest of this chapter will essentially be concerned with showing how each form is managed with Modula-2.

One last point of clarification may be necessary in this rather brief introduction to a quite complicated form of programming. The terms **program-controlled input/output** and **direct memory access** (or **DMA**) are often encountered in connection with input/output. They describe the ways in which data is transferred between the main memory of the computer and the buffers of the device controller.

Program-controlled transfers are used with the type of device controller for which the computer program itself needs to perform any transfers of data, using assignment operations. Typically, this form is suited to relatively slow and simple device interfaces.

For direct memory access transfers, the device controller needs to possess a degree of local 'intelligence', so that it can perform the data transfers without any program intervention. The device driver program simply needs to provide the controller with such information as the amount of data to be transferred, the location of the data buffer in the computer's memory, and any other device-related information that might be required. Once the DMA operation has been initiated by the computer, the device controller will perform the necessary transfers directly, and will signal to the computer only when the task is completed. A benefit of this form is that it allows the central processor to be used to run programs rather than to perform the relatively low-level task of input/output. DMA is also more suited to the needs of fast devices, such as disks, where data is transferred in 'blocks'.

Both forms of transfer can be controlled using either device polling or interrupts, in order to indicate that the device is ready to perform another transfer (program control) or that the direct transfer has been completed (DMA).

Since program-controlled input/output uses much simpler device interfaces than DMA does, most of the examples of this chapter will use this form, although DMA will be demonstrated for a fairly simple device.

## 17.2 Memory mapped input/output

One of the pioneering features of the architecture of the PDP-11 family, subsequently used in many other computer architectures, is the idea of the **external page**. The basic idea behind this is very simple.

Rather than using a special data highway (or 'bus') to provide access from the central processor to the device interface registers, the PDP-11 uses a single 'bus' to access both its main memory and the device controllers. In addition, a convention is adopted that a range of addresses that would otherwise be used for memory locations are used instead for the registers of the device interface controllers. When the computer accesses one of these addresses in any way, the data is read or supplied by the device controller, rather than by the main memory. (The device controller uses exactly the same signal conventions as are used by the main memory.) A particular benefit of this scheme is that the device controllers can be accessed by using the normal instructions of the computer. This approach also makes it much easier to develop controllers for new devices, since no 'knowledge' about their form is built into the architecture of the computer itself. (This is an example of the principle of information-hiding applied to hardware design rather than to software design!)

As we shall see, a further benefit of this scheme is that it makes it easier to handle these devices using a high-level programming language such as Modula-2, since the compiler does not need to generate any special input/output instructions for this task.

A program in a PDP-11 computer can access only a rather restricted range of memory locations (32K words, equivalent to 64 Kbytes), and by convention the top 4K words of this range are reserved for use by device registers. This leaves only 28K words in which to store programs and data, and the increased use of high-level languages, leading to larger programs, together with the rapidly falling cost of memory, has made this address space seem rather cramped. On later machines, such as the VAX-11 and MC68000 computers, the range of possible addresses that can be used by a

MEMORY MAPPED INPUT/OUTPUT 327

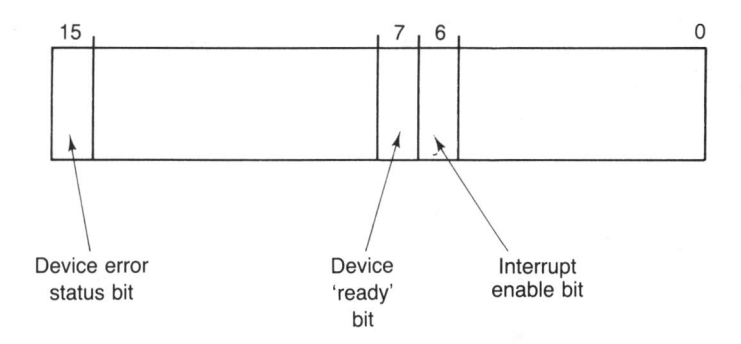

```
 15              7 6              0
┌──────────────┬─┬─┬──────────────┐
│              │ │ │              │
└──────────────┴─┴─┴──────────────┘
       │         │  │
       │         │  │
  Device error  Device  Interrupt
  status bit   'ready'  enable bit
                 bit
```

**Figure 17.2** Status/control register for console printer (PDP-11).

program has been greatly increased. So this form of device access (often referred to as **memory mapped input/output**) has become even more attractive, since the enlarged 'address space' also allows for a much larger range of device addresses within it.

On the original PDP-11 computers, a range of 4K memory addresses was referred to as a page (although in the context of virtual memory schemes, the term usually has a slightly different meaning). Because they were used for device registers, accessing interfaces that were external to the main memory, the highest 4K words became known as the external page. So on a PDP-11 with 16-bit words and byte addressing, this meant that any address with all three most significant bits set to 1 was located within the external page. A further convention was used to assign particular addresses in the external page for use by the registers of particular devices. A simple device such as a printer might need only two addresses, whereas some disk controllers might need as many as 20. A measure of the success of the PDP-11 as a machine, and of the limitations of this aspect of its design, is that the available 4K words of address space were soon fully allocated, and some multiple allocations became necessary. (Since most computers use only a small number of devices from the many that are available, this has rarely presented much of a problem.) On machines with quite different organization of memory segmentation, the term 'external page' may still be used, although the actual address space may be much larger.

To help with understanding the examples provided in the next sections, it is useful to look at the structure used by some of the device registers. Figure 17.2 shows the structure of the 16-bit word that is used as the status/control register for the computer's console printer. Bits are numbered from 0, and the most significant bit is bit 15. Such a relatively simple device has only one other register, which is used to buffer the transfers of data. and Figure 17.3 shows its structure. This form of device interface is typical of those used for many of the simpler devices. By convention, the status/control register is allocated an address of 177564B,

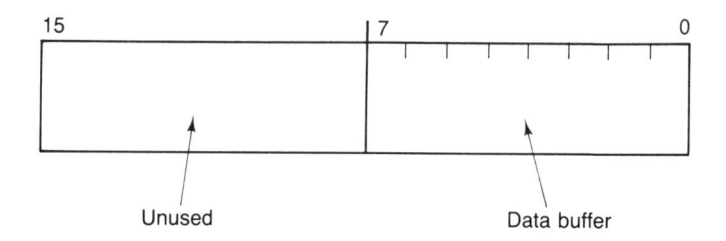

**Figure 17.3** Data buffer register for console printer (PDP-11).

while the data buffer is at 177566B. (The difference of 2 in the address arises because the PDP-11 is a byte-addressing machine. A word is accessed by specifying the address of its least significant byte, which is always even-numbered.)

Only a few of the bits available in the status/control register need to be used for such a simple device, and we will examine the roles of most of them here. The 'status' bits are generally set (to a value of 1) and cleared (to 0) by the device controller, and may be read by the program. In turn, the 'control' bits are set and cleared by the instructions of a program and are acted upon by the device controller. The three bits in which we are interested are:

- Bit 15. This is a status bit, set to 1 by the device controller whenever a fault occurs with the printer – such as running out of paper – and reset to 0 by the controller when the fault is cleared.
- Bit 7. This is a status bit, and is usually known as the 'ready' bit. It is set to 1 by the device controller when the printer is ready to receive another character, and to 0 whenever a computer operation copies data into the data buffer register.
- Bit 6. This is a control bit, known as the 'interrupt enable' bit: its role will be explained in section 17.4.

The data buffer register has even less structure, and only eight of its bits are used. When the printer is ready to receive another character, the controlling program simply copies the appropriate character code into the data buffer, in order for the device controller to print the corresponding character on the device. So only eight bits of this register are used, since an ASCII character may be represented by a 7-bit pattern, with a further bit usually included as an optional check bit.

This scheme is a very flexible and powerful one, in that a device controller can be designed with whatever control and status bits are necessary for a program to be able to organize the input or output for that device. This enables the computer to handle a wide range of devices, simply using its normal machine-level instructions to assign values and to test for the necessary responses. (The choice of bit 7 for the 'ready' bit is connected with this last point. As the PDP-11 is a byte-addressing machine, it possesses a set of instructions that can operate upon both bytes and words. Bit 7 is the 'sign' bit of the lower byte of a word, and hence of the word that is occupied by the status/control register, and so the value of this bit can easily be tested using arithmetic operations. This is really a machine-code issue and does not affect the way in which we handle these operations using Modula-2.)

Having now introduced the structures that a program needs to manipulate, and having explained what sort of operations are usually involved in transferring data, we make use of this information in the next section to introduce the handling of device interfaces from a Modula-2 program.

## 17.3 Controlling input and output by device polling

A device polling program is essentially a two-step operation:

(1) keep testing the value of the 'ready' bit in the device status register until it is set to 1 by the device;
(2) when the device is ready, copy the data to or from the data buffer (so clearing the 'ready' bit).

Since we can associate a variable of any type with the absolute locations (addresses) of the device registers, and the operation of testing the device status requires that the program should examine the value of an individual bit, the obvious data type to use for the device status/control register is BITSET. The choice of type for the data buffer is less obvious, and largely depends upon the type of data that is normally transferred to that device and the size of the buffer register (it could, of course, simply be WORD). For a character-oriented printing device, the most suitable type is CHAR, and, because the even-numbered byte of each word is the lower byte, this will be correctly mapped on to the lower half of the data buffer.

The implementation module shown in Figure 17.4 contains a set of routines that are used to handle the console of a PDP-11 by polling. (We have already seen the registers that are used for the output part of this in Figures 17.2 and 17.3.) Note that the keyboard is treated as a separate device. The registers used for the keyboard are very similar to those that have already been described for the printer.

Both the data buffers are declared as type CHAR. A variable of this type is usually allocated eight bits for storage (one byte), which is slightly larger than is actually needed, since the ASCII convention requires only seven bits to represent a character. Additional code is needed for the input routine as a result of this, because the eighth bit is used in different ways by different terminals: while many simply set it to 0, others may use it to

(1) The definition part

(* Base level module to poll the console device *)

DEFINITION MODULE Polling;

EXPORT QUALIFIED Put, Get;

PROCEDURE Put(ch:CHAR);    (* get a single character *)

PROCEDURE Get(VAR ch:CHAR);    (* print a single character *)
END Polling.

(2) The implementation part

(* Base level module to poll the console device *)

IMPLEMENTATION MODULE Polling;

CONST
  ready = 7;              (* the 'ready' bit *)
  bitmask = 200B;         (* identity of bit 7 *)
  sevenbits = 127;        (* largest seven bit number *)

VAR
  Instatus[177560B] : BITSET;    (* keyboard status *)
  Inbuffer[177562B] : CHAR;      (* keyboard input buffer *)
  Outstatus[177564B] : BITSET;   (* printer status *)
  Outbuffer[177566B] : CHAR;     (* printer output buffer *)

(* Put – used to copy a single character to the printer *)

PROCEDURE Put(ch : CHAR);
BEGIN
  REPEAT UNTIL ready IN Outstatus;
  Outbuffer := ch;
END Put;

(* Get – used to obtain a single character from the keyboard *)

PROCEDURE Get(VAR ch: CHAR);
BEGIN
  REPEAT UNTIL ready IN Instatus;
  ch := Inbuffer;
  IF ( ORD(ch) > sevenbits ) THEN    (* if bit 7 is set *)
  ch := CHR( ORD(ch) – bitmask ) END;
END Get;

END Polling.

**Figure 17.4** Example of device polling for a console device on a PDP-11.

provide parity checking. To ensure that these routines will work with different terminal devices, the device-handling routines will need to ensure that the eighth bit is cleared.

One useful point to note about the example is that the most appropriate way to express the operation of polling is to use a REPEAT–UNTIL loop, since we know that it will *always* be necessary to test the 'ready' bit at least once, and to keep testing it *until* the device is ready. (Even with a 'fast' printing device, the difference in speed between the central processor of the computer and the printer is such that there will usually be at least tens of thousands of loops executed between printing successive characters!)

A second point worth noting is the degree to which information has been kept concealed within this very low-level module. Such device-specific information as the absolute addresses of the registers and the identity of the 'ready' bit is completely confined within it. This makes it possible for a higher module that contains routines such as Write, WriteLn, WriteString and WriteOct to be constructed with no need for any knowledge of the way in which the output is handled physically, or even about the device being used. In this case the device is so simple that there is no need to initialize it in any way when the system starts up, but if this were to be required, the details of initialization could also be confined within the module by making use of its main body.

This latter point becomes much more relevant when controlling a more complex device, such as a disk drive, which has many more registers. For such a device it will be necessary, for example, to position its read/write head when initialized and to initialize various status bits in the interface.

The definition and implementation parts of a module that provides a rather more complex example of this technique are shown in Figures 17.5 and 17.6. This demonstrates how a DMA (direct memory access) transfer can be organized with a Cambridge ring network (Needham and Herbert, 1982). The Cambridge ring provides a means for very high-speed transfer of data along a continuous loop of cable, using the principle known as the 'slotted ring'. With this format, the data travels between the nodes of the ring in 40-bit 'packets'. Each such packet contains 16 bits of data, together with 24 bits of route and status information. (The apparently small payload of data in each packet is offset by the very high transmission rate, and by the ability of the ring to handle many interleaved transmissions at a time.) Each node on the network has an 8-bit address, and the address of a destination node must be explicitly included in the message, by placing it in one of the interface registers.

Because this is a more complex type of device, its interface requires the use of several registers for handling status and control information, and the module requires the procedure InitNode, which is used to initialize the state of the computer's own node. This latter routine also 'enables' the interface for that node, so that it will check each passing packet to see if it

```
(* Simple polling routines for handling a Cambridge ring node *)
(* provides a very low-level set of routines to handle 40-bit ring packets *)

DEFINITION MODULE RingPoll;

EXPORT QUALIFIED Packet, Nodeaddress, ReadPacket, WritePacket;

TYPE
    Packet = ARRAY [0..1] OF CHAR;    (* holds data component of ring packet *)
    Nodeaddress = [0..255];           (* 8-bit node address value *)

(* the two procedures used to send and receive packets by polling *)

(* reads a packet from the ring that has been sent from the node selected by 'source'. If 'source' has
   a value of 255 then packets will be accepted from any node on the ring. *)

PROCEDURE ReadPacket( VAR nextblock : Packet ; VAR source : Nodeaddress );

(* writes a packet to the ring, addressed to the node specified by 'destination'. No check is
   performed on the return status. *)

PROCEDURE WritePacket( block : Packet ; destination : Nodeaddress );

END RingPoll.
```

**Figure 17.5** Definition part of a DMA device driver using polling.

is intended for that node. It is also possible to define the range of sources from which packets are to be accepted, by setting up a 'window' in one of the registers to define the addresses of those nodes regarded as 'valid' sources. The routines contained in this module perform very primitive tasks, and for practical use it would be necessary to provide several higher levels of procedures to handle the necessary network protocols.

A couple of brief points should perhaps be made here about this example of the use of DMA transfers. One is that once the various registers of the controller have been loaded with the appropriate information, the device-handling process in the computer needs to signal to the DMA controller to direct it to begin the transfer. This usually involves setting a control bit, the 'go' bit, which will then be cleared by the device controller as it begins its task.

In the example, the size of each data transfer is always two bytes. (The example routines use an array of type CHAR for the data, which is really rather restrictive.) So the transfer count has been included here as a constant. By convention, the transfer count is always converted to a negative quantity, since this slightly simplifies the design of the device controller.

**Figure 17.6** Implementation part of a DMA device driver using polling.

```
(* Simple polling routines for handling a Cambridge ring node *)

IMPLEMENTATION MODULE RingPoll;
FROM SYSTEM IMPORT ADR, ADDRESS;

CONST
    ready = 7;                              (* identity of the 'ready' bit *)
    dmacount = -2;                          (* transfer count for dma *)
    GO = 1;                                 (* DMA enable bit *)

VAR
    sourcesr[174040B] : BITSET;             (* source window for new input *)
    txdest[174042B]   : Nodeaddress;        (* destination node for transmit *)
    rxsource[174042B] : Nodeaddress;        (* source node for next input *)
    txstatus[174046B] : BITSET;             (* transmit status information *)
    rxstatus[174050B] : BITSET;             (* receive status information *)
    rxcount[174054B]  : INTEGER;            (* input transfer count *)
    txcount[174054B]  : INTEGER;            (* transmit transfer count *)
    rxbuffer[174056B] : ADDRESS;            (* input buffer address *)
    txbuffer[174056B] : ADDRESS;            (* transmit buffer address *)

PROCEDURE ReadPacket( VAR next : Packet ; VAR source : Nodeaddress );
BEGIN
    rxcount := dmacount;
    rxbuffer := ADR(next);
    INCL(rxstatus,GO);                      (* start transfer *)
    REPEAT UNTIL ready IN rxstatus;         (* wait for data *)
    source := rxsource;
END ReadPacket;


PROCEDURE WritePacket( block : Packet ; destination : Nodeaddress );
BEGIN
    REPEAT UNTIL ready IN txstatus;         (* wait until device free *)
    txdest := destination;
    txcount := dmacount;
    txbuffer := ADR(block);
    INCL(txstatus,GO);                      (* start the transfer *)
    REPEAT UNTIL ready IN txstatus;         (* ensure transmission done *)
END Writepacket;


PROCEDURE InitNode;
BEGIN
    INCL(rxstatus,0);                       (* enable node *)
    sourcesr := BITSET{0..7};               (* set window to accept any source *)
END InitNode;
```

```
BEGIN
   InitNode;
END RingPoll.
```

**Figure 17.6** *cont.*

## 17.4 Interrupts and concurrency

When discussing the operation of an interrupt in Section 17.1, we observed that the flow of control involved closely resembles the transfer of control between co-routines in Modula-2. When an interrupt occurs, one process is suspended, another is executed to handle the transfer of data to or from the device, this then suspends itself and finally the first process resumes execution from the point at which it was pre-empted. The main difference between these transfers and those occurring between co-routines is that the former occur in a *pre-emptive* manner, being caused by the *external* event of the interrupt, rather than by an action of the currently executing process. (Interrupts are sometimes referred to as 'asynchronous events', since their occurrence is not synchronized with the operations of the computer in any way, whereas a call to TRANSFER from a co-routine is termed a 'synchronous event', as it will always occur at the same point within the executing program.)

An important issue that needs to be described at this point is the means by which an interrupt can cause the appropriate 'interrupt handler' routine to be activated. There needs to be some mechanism for identifying the routine programmed to perform data transfers to or from that particular device.

The link between the occurrence of the interrupt and the transfer of control to the device handler process is usually through the use of a **vector**. Each device has associated with it a fixed location, or vector, in the computer's main memory, usually positioned at one of the lowest addresses. This address is also programmed into the device controller, usually by means of switches or links in the hardware circuits. The vector in turn contains the address of the interrupt handling routine that should be used for this device.

So when the device becomes ready, and the device controller also recognizes that it has been configured to generate an interrupt (usually by enabling the interrupt bit in the control register), two things happen. The device controller sends an interrupt signal to the computer, using a dedicated signal line, and it also passes the value of the interrupt vector to the computer, using the data lines normally used for memory accesses. When the computer recognizes the interrupt signal, it suspends the currently executing process, and reads the address of the vector for the interrupting device from the data highway. It then obtains the address of the interrupt handler process from the appropriate vector, and finally transfers control to the handler process.

So a process that organizes the transfer of data using interrupts must copy the address of the routine that is to perform the actual transfers to the vector for the device, *before* beginning any transfers of data. To begin a data transfer, it must then *enable* the interrupt mechanism for that device. (Since many devices are sitting ready to do some work, an interrupt may occur immediately after the 'enable' bit is set, and so the correct sequencing of these two operations is vital.) Enabling the interrupt facility for a device usually involves setting the 'interrupt enable' bit to a value of 1. Whenever the device becomes ready, the device controller will check this 'enable' bit, and if both it and the 'ready' bit are set to 1 it will generate an interrupt. In order to terminate interrupt-driven transfers, the program in the computer must set the 'enable' bit back to 0 when the last transfer has taken place. By this means, processes within the computer can retain overall control of input/output transfers, without requiring the continuous monitoring of the device interfaces required by polling. Figure 17.7 shows the sequence of events involved in transferring data through a simple interface.

Writing programs that will perform input/output using interrupts is a rather complex task, and especially so when it must be integrated into the transactions of a large operating system. To show how such a transfer may be programmed, Figure 17.8 lists a program module that is a very simple example of this technique. It consists of a single Modula-2 program designed to be the only program running in the computer, and so to execute without the aid of an underlying operating system. (This is commonly the case when we need to write programs to handle interrupts, since most multi-user operating systems are designed so as to ensure that user's programs cannot directly access device interfaces – with good reason!)

This program again is intended for the PDP-11, and it utilizes what must be the simplest device available, the 'line clock'. This provides a simple timer for a computer system by setting its 'ready' bit at regular intervals. It requires only a status register (no data is transferred on an interrupt, since the occurrence of the interrupt *is* the data). When the interrupt is enabled, the line clock will interrupt the processor at the frequency of the electrical mains supply (in the UK this is 50 times per second, in the USA it is usually 60 times per second). If the device handler is designed to count these interrupts, then the computer's software can be provided with a simple timekeeping mechanism.

The program module shown in Figure 17.8 simply enables the clock and counts the interrupts. Every four seconds (200 interrupts) it prints a character on the console device in order to show that it is running correctly. (The library module Console makes use of the module Polling from Figure 17.4

336    LOW-LEVEL INPUT AND OUTPUT

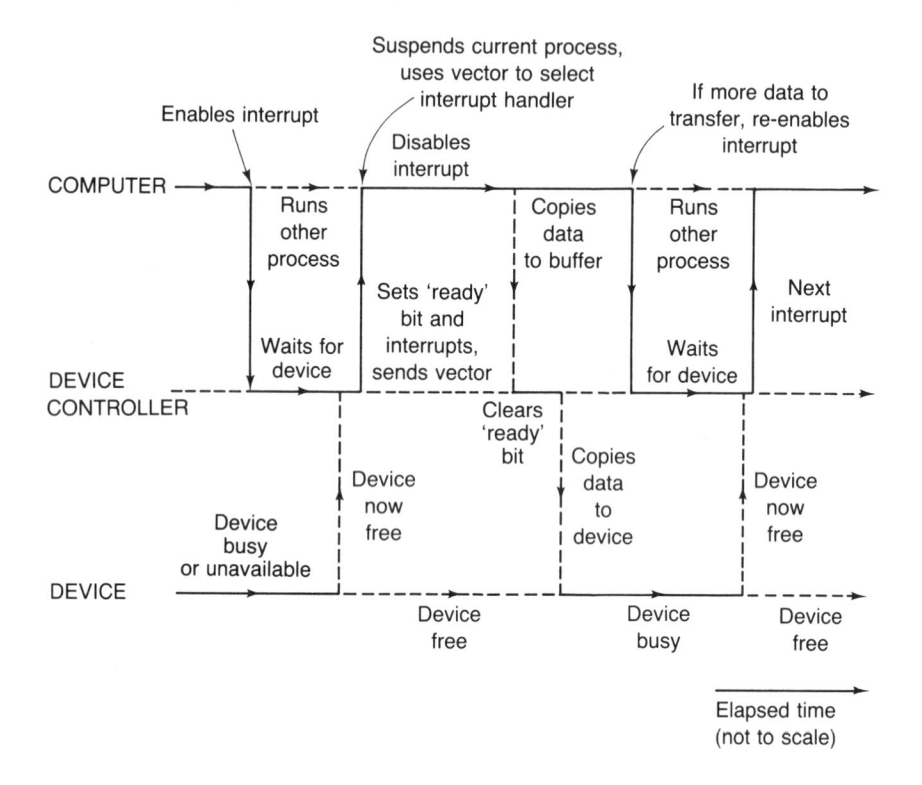

**Figure 17.7**  Data transfers for a simple output device using interrupts.

in order to print this character.) While the example is relatively trivial, it makes it possible to see the operation of the interrupt mechanism at its most elementary level. It also provides an example of the type of simple test program that can be used to isolate and check the operation of a particular feature. This type of test program can be very useful when programming with interrupts. It also introduces some new features that are explained below.

The first new feature is that of **module priority**. This is declared by the value in square brackets that follows the module identifier in the opening MODULE statement. The value (and form) of this is implementation-specific, and it complements the priority that is assigned to each interrupting device. The PDP-11 has five interrupt lines, each of which is assigned to a different priority level. Each device controller is also assigned to a priority level, and this determines which of the interrupt lines it uses to signal an interrupt to the computer. The central processor itself has a priority, which may be selected by the currently executing process: only those devices that have a priority greater than the current priority of the processor may interrupt it. Under normal conditions, a user's process will

**Figure 17.8** Simple example of interrupt handling with Modula-2.

```
(* interrupt handling test using the line clock *)

MODULE Clock[4];

FROM SYSTEM IMPORT ADDRESS,NEWPROCESS,TRANSFER,IOTRANSFER,ADR,SIZE,WORD;

FROM Console IMPORT Write, Writeln, Writestring;

CONST
   enablebit = 6;                         (* interrupt enable bit *)
   clockvector = 100B;                    (* vector address for clock *)
   fourseconds = 200;                     (* tick count for 50 Hz, 240 for USA *)
   wspacesize = 100;                      (* default workspace limit *)

VAR
   clockstatus[177546B] : BITSET;         (* status register for clock *)
   PRO, CON, MAIN : ADDRESS;
   wsp1,wsp2 : ARRAY[0...wspacesize-1] OF WORD;
   count1,count2 : INTEGER;               (* counters used in test *)

   (* Service – runs to handle an interrupt, incrementing count1 and then returning control to the
      interrupted process *)

PROCEDURE Service;
BEGIN
   Writestring('Begin service'); Writeln;
   LOOP
      INC(count1);
      IOTRANSFER(PRO,CON,clockvector);
   END;
END Service;

   (* Check – enables clock, and then keeps checking the counters to see if the 4-second period has
      elapsed, printing a '1' whenever it finds this has occurred and then resetting the counters for the
      next period *)

PROCEDURE Check;
BEGIN
   Writestring('Begin check'); Writeln;
   INCL(clockstatus,enablebit);           (* enable clock *)
   LOOP
      IF (count1 – count2) > fourseconds THEN
      Write('1'); count2 := count1 END;
   END;
END Check;
```

```
(* main body of program, starts everything running *)
BEGIN
    count1 := 0;                                              (* set up counters *)
    count2 := 0;
    NEWPROCESS(Service,ADR(wsp1),SIZE(wsp1),PRO);             (* create processes *)
    NEWPROCESS(Check,ADR(wsp2),SIZE(wsp2),CON);
    Writestring('Clock test starting'); Writeln;              (* write message and begin test *)
    TRANSFER(MAIN,PRO);
END Clock.
```

**Figure 17.8** *cont.*

execute with the processor's priority set to a low value (so allowing all interrupts to occur), but during the execution of key sections of a program, it may well be desirable to raise the priority of the processor so that it is not interrupted. Such key parts usually include much of the resident executive or operating system, and sometimes an interrupt handler routine too. Obviously these parts need to be designed so that the processor will be assigned a high priority only for short periods, in order that interrupts are not ignored.

The priority allocated in the declaration of the module is used to determine the priority of the central processor when any of the routines within the module is executed. The value chosen in this example is 4, which corresponds to one of the lowest levels (the five levels have values of 3, 4, 5, 6 and 7, with the values 0–2 being equivalent to 3). So to interrupt this program, the line clock will need to have been assigned a priority of at least 5.

The mechanism is very useful for constructing interrupt handling code, although it might be more convenient if priority could be assigned to individual procedures too, and not just collectively via the MODULE declaration.

The second new feature of this example is the use of the procedure IOTRANSFER, which is imported from SYSTEM and called from the device handler. While performing a similar task to that of TRANSFER, IOTRANSFER has three parameters, and is declared as:

    PROCEDURE IOTRANSFER ( VAR Handler, Savedprocess : ADDRESS;
                               vector : CARDINAL);

where:

- Handler specifies a pointer to the process 'control block', which stores the details of the current process so that it can be reactivated when the interrupt occurs.

- Savedprocess specifies the location of the 'control block' that stores the details of the interrupted process when the interrupt occurs. On the first call to IOTRANSFER this should be used to specify the process to which control should return after initialization of the handler.
- vector specifies the address of the vector that is to be linked to the interrupt handler procedure (Handler).

(Again, as with TRANSFER, for some compilers the variables Handler and Savedprocess will be of the type PROCESS.)

Like TRANSFER, IOTRANSFER causes the calling process to be suspended. The second parameter is used at two points in the sequence. When an interrupt occurs, it specifies a link to a 'control block' that stores the details of the interrupted process. So, on a call of IOTRANSFER, this can be used to identify the process that is to be resumed after the interrupt handler has completed its work. This means that IOTRANSFER differs from TRANSFER in that it specifies the route by which the calling process expects to be reactivated, by associating a particular vector with the calling process.

Except for initialization, a call of IOTRANSFER will usually occur at the end of an interrupt sequence, returning control to the interrupted process until the next interrupt occurs. Note that IOTRANSFER is concerned only with organizing the routing of interrupts, and that the operations involved in enabling and disabling the interrupts and performing the data transfers are quite separate.

Within the example program module Clock shown in Figure 17.8, the interrupt handling is performed in the procedure Service, and the call to IOTRANSFER is positioned within an infinite service loop. (Since the clock does not require any transfer of data from a buffer, this routine simply increments the variable count1.) Figure 17.9 shows the flow of control that will occur when this program begins execution.

Examining the module Clock again, we can also see several other features that are required for the task of handling clock interrupts. The first is that the main body will initially transfer control to the first co-routine via a call of TRANSFER, so that the first entry to the interrupt handler is from the main body. This means that the code at the entry point of an interrupt handling procedure must handle any initialization necessary before suspending itself. In this example, as there is nothing special for it to do, it just prints out a message and suspends itself, after setting up the interrupt vector as part of the activity associated with IOTRANSFER. (This sequence is important, as it is necessary to initialize the value of this vector *before* enabling the interrupts.)

The first call to IOTRANSFER transfers control to the process CON (created from Check), and the initialization part of this writes a short message and *then* enables the interrupt. From then on this process will execute almost continuously, polling the clock counter and printing a character every four seconds. (The use of a separate process for this task is

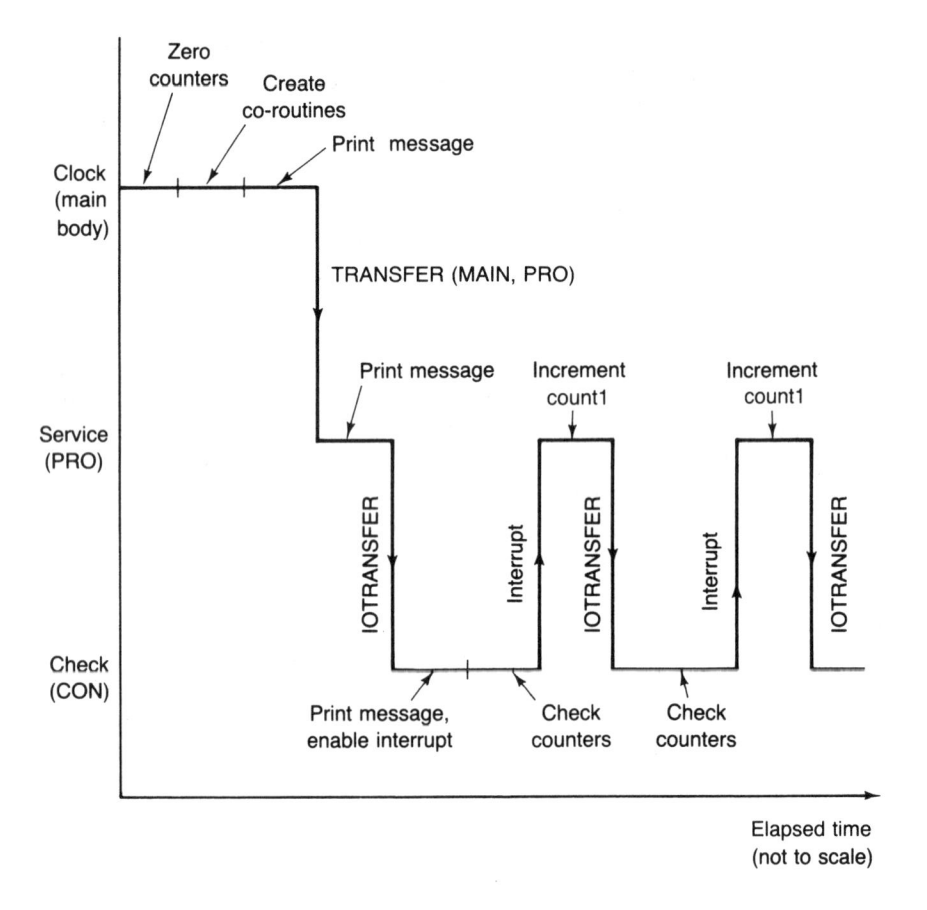

**Figure 17.9** Initial flow of control when Clock is executed.

not an essential feature of the design. Since the main body of the module is a co-routine, it could perform this polling task as well. However, partitioning the tasks in this way provides a cleaner structure, and leaves the main body to perform system initialization tasks.) After each interrupt, the procedure Service returns control to the interrupted procedure (Check) via the use of IOTRANSFER.

This example is oversimplified, since the variable count1 is unprotected. If an interrupt were to occur during the subtraction operation in

IF (count1 − count2)

then a corruption could occur. Because of the relatively slow rate of interrupts for this device, such a corruption should not occur in this example, but the point should be noted as an example of the type of situation that requires the use of some form of mutual exclusion.

Of course, in a 'real' program the interrupt handler would usually transfer control back via some executive routine, and this would select the next 'normal' process to be executed. So it should be emphasized that Check is really standing in for a number of processes that would be performing some useful task rather than just polling the results of interrupt handling!

Two minor programming points are also worth mentioning briefly in the discussion of this example. The first is the use of the LOOP form within the device handler process. Since the operations of the device handler are to be performed an unknown number of times (effectively for ever), this provides the ideal construct for the purpose. The second is the use of the procedure INCL in order to enable the interrupt bit – an elegant solution, which is made possible by the use of the type BITSET. (Equally, of course, the device can be disabled by using the procedure EXCL.)

Where the library modules provide the necessary support, it may also be possible to use IOTRANSFER in a process running under the control of an operating system. There are obviously likely to be some limitations upon this (for one thing, few multi-user operating systems are likely to permit user processes to access the vectors directly), but the facility does make it possible to run a program that handles asynchronous events.

Figure 17.10 shows a simple example of a program that runs on the UNIX operating system and 'catches' a UNIX signal via the IOTRANSFER mechanism. This allows the user to interrupt the program through the use of a device such as the keyboard, and then to restart it.

Unfortunately very few real systems have only one interrupting device to be handled in the manner shown in these examples. Equally, very few have only one process to allow us to specify explicitly the second parameter of IOTRANSFER in this way. The next section deals briefly with some of the issues that can arise when we need to handle multiple interrupts, and yet wish to keep the benefits of the modular structures offered in Modula-2.

**Figure 17.10** Program to handle asynchronous signals.

```
(* a simple example of a program that handles asynchronous signals generated from the keyboard
   and relayed through the operating system – in this case, UNIX *)

MODULE SignalHandler;

FROM InOut IMPORT WriteString, WriteLn, Read, EOL;
FROM CLibrary IMPORT SignalType;      (* enumerated type describing valid UNIX signals *)
FROM SYSTEM IMPORT NEWPROCESS, ADDRESS, IOTRANSFER, TRANSFER, WORD, ADR, SIZE,
    TSIZE;
```

```
CONST
  workspacesize = 300;


TYPE
  Workspace = ARRAY [0..workspacesize-1] OF WORD;


VAR
  wspace1 : Workspace;              (* workspace for interrupt handler *)
  Handler, Main : ADDRESS;          (* co-routine 'control block' pointers *)
  terminate : BOOLEAN;              (* used to end program gracefully *)



(* the interrupt handler process. Prints a continuous series of messages, until stopped by a signal. *)


PROCEDURE SignalHandler;
VAR
  ch : CHAR;                        (* buffer for keyboard input *)
BEGIN
  LOOP
    IOTRANSFER(Handler,Main,SigInt);  (* SigInt is specified signal *)
    WriteLn;
    WriteString("Interrupt handler: <return> to continue");
    WriteLn;
    WriteString(" enter any other character to end program : ");
    Read(ch);
    WriteLn;
    IF (ch <> EOL) THEN terminate := TRUE END;
  END; (* loop *)
END SignalHandler;



(* main body – prints a continuous sequence of messages until stopped *)


BEGIN
  terminate := FALSE;               (* ensure will run first time! *)
  NEWPROCESS(SignalHandler, ADR(wspace1), SIZE(wspace1), Handler);
  TRANSFER(Main,Handler);           (* connect Handler to signal *)
  REPEAT
    WriteString('Main process: ↑C to stop');
    WriteLn;
  UNTIL terminate;
END SignalHandler.
```

**Figure 17.10**  *cont.*

## 17.5 Handling multiple interrupts

Since there are many different ways of organizing a system that handles multiple interrupting devices, this last section is limited to making a few fairly general points about how the forms shown in the previous examples need to be modified and extended.

We begin by considering a system that is to be constructed as a single Modula-2 program, with no resident underlying executive. The first constraint is that of *priority*, which requires that key parts of the system, and most notably the interrupt handling routines, shall be executed with a sufficiently high priority to ensure that other external interrupts are locked out. (It is not strictly essential to prevent further interrupts from all other devices occurring while an interrupt handler is servicing an interrupt: computer hardware structures are generally able to nest interrupts, just as procedure calls are nested, so it may be appropriate to allow more important devices to interrupt. However, the analogy with nested procedure calls should not be taken too far, since multiple interrupts from a device that is locked out will not be queued in any way. Overall, the design complications that arise from allowing this to happen rarely make it worthwhile.) At the same time, in order for interrupts to be recognized, the main part of the program needs to be executed at a relatively low priority.

The fact that priority can be allocated only to complete MODULEs, suggests that the interrupt handlers should be contained within separate or local modules. Since the idea of confining device-related information to a module has additional attractions for the designer, this is generally a good strategy to adopt.

It is, however, necessary to consider the topic of *initialization* of such structures with some care. The previous section has already provided an example of a useful method of initializing the interrupt handler: using TRANSFER to make an initial call to the entry point of the process. This then performs any necessary initialization tasks, before suspending itself at the beginning of the main service loop.

Some changes are now necessary, though. Where such a structure is retained, it is important to ensure that after initialization the interrupt handler always returns control to the main body of its own module. Since the main bodies of subordinate modules are normally executed before that of the program module, each subordinate main body must be executed fully before the main program begins execution.

While the discussion of this section has been limited to considering only one form of program organization, the points are general enough to apply to a range of system structures. Programming by interrupts is always a complex task, since it combines hardware concepts such as priority with software concepts such as concurrency of processes.

Although this chapter has only skimmed the surface of this important, though specialized, topic, it should at least have demonstrated how interrupts may be managed using Modula-2. Traditionally such techniques have been the domain of assembler code programming, but there is now no reason for not writing interrupt handling code using a high-level language such as Modula-2 – at least where the computer architecture makes this possible. While it is true that an assembler version may be optimized more easily for faster execution, this is no longer so critical an issue as it once was. The benefits of using Modula-2 in terms of clarity and ease of modification should not be underestimated.

## EXERCISES

The nature of the material that is covered in this chapter renders it difficult to suggest any specific exercises. However, if the run-time support system for your Modula-2 implementation can pass asynchronous signals (in the manner shown in the example listed in Figure 17.10), then the following exercise should be worth trying.

17.1 Write a program that continuously reads the 'time of day' and writes this out on a terminal

(a) by polling the time of day;

(b) by catching clock signals and updating the time from these.

In the second case, the 'idle' time may be used for polling the clock in the form used in case (a) and keeping a count of the number of times it is polled. From this count it may be possible to compare the overheads of polling with those of interrupts.

## Postscript

To make the most effective use of a software tool such as a programming language, we need to have an understanding of the structures that it offers, as well as of the general principles of program design. For a system programming language such as Modula-2, we also need an understanding of machine architecture in order to make use of some of the facilities that it offers. In attempting to cover a wide range of ideas about Modula-2, this book has inevitably skimmed over many issues that should really be treated more fully; this has been necessary in order to keep the focus on the main objective of understanding how to use Modula-2. However, the works in the References list that follows can provide much fuller treatment of this background material. I hope that the reader of this book will gain as much pleasure from these, and from using Modula-2 itself, as I have done.

# References

Abbott R. J. (1983). Program design by informal English descriptions. *Comm. ACM*, **26**(11), 882–94

Adelson B. and Soloway E. (1985). The role of domain experience in software design. *IEEE Trans. on Software Engineering*, **SE-11**, 1351–9

Allison L. (1983). Stable marriages by co-routines. *Information Processing Letters*, **16**, 61–5

American National Standards Institute (1983). *Reference Manual for the Ada Programming Language*

Beidler J. and Jackowitz P. (1986). Consistent generics in Modula-2. *ACM SIGPLAN Notices*, **21**, April, 32–41

Ben-Ari M. (1982). *Principles of Concurrent Programming*. Prentice-Hall, ISBN 0–13–701078–8

Bergland G. D. (1981). A guided tour of program design methodologies. *IEEE Computer*, October, 13–37

Booch, G. (1983). *Software Engineering with Ada*. Benjamin/Cummings, ISBN 0–8053–0600–5

Booch G. (1986). Object-oriented development. *IEEE Trans. on Software Engineering*, **SE-12**, 211–21

Brinch-Hanson P. (1977). *Architecture of Concurrent Programs*. Prentice-Hall, ISBN 0–13–044628–9

Budgen D. (1985). Combining MASCOT with Modula-2 to aid the engineering of real-time systems. *Software–Practice and Experience*, **15**, 767–93. (See also the letter in Vol. **16**, June 1986, 603)

Buhr R. J. A. (1984). *System Design with Ada*. Prentice-Hall, ISBN 0–13–881623–9

Burns A. (1986). *Concurrent Programming in Ada*. Cambridge University Press, ISBN 0–521–30033–9

Cameron J. R. (1983). *JSP and JSD : The Jackson Approach to Software Development*. IEEE Computer Society Tutorial, ISBN 0–8186–8516–6

Cameron J. R. (1986). An overview of JSD. *IEEE Trans. on Software Engineering*, **SE-12**, 222–40

Cornelius B. J. (1988). Problems with the language Modula-2. *Software–Practice and Experience*, **18**, 529–43

De Marco T. (1978). *Structured Analysis and System Specification*. Yourdon Press, ISBN 0–917072–07–3

Dietel H. M. (1984). *An Introduction to Operating Systems*. Addison-Wesley, ISBN 0–201–14502–2

Fairley R. E. (1985). *Software Engineering Concepts*. McGraw-Hill, ISBN 0–07–019902–7

Gladden G. R. (1982). Stop the life cycle, I want to get off. *ACM Software Engineering Notes*, **7**(2), 35–9

Goldberg A. and Robson D. (1983). *Smalltalk–80: The Language and its Implementation*. Addison-Wesley, ISBN 0–201–11371–6

Goldsby M. E. (1986). Concurrent use of generic types in Modula-2. *ACM SIGPLAN Notices*, **21**(6)

Holt R. C., Graham G. S., Lazowska E. D. and Scott M. A. (1978). *Structured Concurrent Programming*. Addison-Wesley, ISBN 0–201–02937–5

Inmos Ltd (1984). *Occam Programming Manual*. Prentice-Hall, ISBN 0–13–629296–8

Jackson M. A. (1975). *Principles of Program Design*. Academic Press, ISBN 0–12–379050–6

Jackson M. A. (1983). *System Development*. Prentice-Hall, ISBN 0–13–822130–8

Jackson M. A. and McCracken D. D. (1982). Life cycle concept considered harmful. *ACM Software Engineering Notes*, **7**(2), 29–32

Jensen K. and Wirth N. (1974). *Pascal User Manual and Report*, 3rd (1985) Springer-Verlag ISBN 0–387–96048–1

Knuth D. E. (1986). *The TeXbook*. Addison-Wesley, ISBN 0–201–13447–0

Ledgard H. and Marcotty M. (1981). *The Programming Language Landscape*. Science Research Associates Ltd

McCabe T. J. (1976). A complexity measure. *IEEE Trans. on Software Engineering*, **SE-2**, 308–20

Myers G. J. (1977). An extension to the cyclomatic measure of program complexity. *ACM SIGPLAN Notices*, October, 61–4

Naur P. and Randell B. (1968). Software engineering. *Proc. NATO Conference*, Scientific Affairs Division, NATO, Brussels

Needham R. M. and Herbert A. J. (1982). *The Cambridge Distributed Computing System*. Addison-Wesley, ISBN 0–201–14092–6

Orr K. T. (1981). *Structured Requirements Definition*. Topeka: Ken Orr & Associates

Page-Jones M. (1980). *The Practical Guide to Structured Systems Design*. Yourdon Press, ISBN 0–917072–17–0

Parnas D. L. (1972a). A technique for software specification with modules. *Comm. ACM*, **15**, May

Parnas D. L. (1972b). On the criteria to be used in decomposing systems into modules. *Comm. ACM*, **15**, 1053–8

Peters L. J. (1981). *Software Design: Methods and Techniques*. Yourdon Press, ISBN 0–917072–19–7

Peterson J. L. and Silberschatz A. (1983). *Operating System Concepts*. Addison-Wesley, ISBN 0–201–06097–3

Sale A. (1986). *Modula-2: Discipline and Design*. Addison-Wesley, ISBN 0–201–12921–3

Shepperd, M. (1988). A critique of cyclomatic complexity as a software metric. *Software Engineering J.*, **3**, 30–36

Simpson H. R. and Jackson K. (1979). Process Synchronization in MASCOT. *Computer J.*, **22**, 332

Sommerville I. (1989). *Software Engineering* 3rd edn. Addison-Wesley, ISBN 0–201–17568–1

Stevens W. P., Myers G. J. and Constantine L. L. (1974). Structured design. *IBM System J.*, **13**, 115–39

Tanenbaum A. S. (1984). *Structured Computer Organization* 2nd edn. Prentice-Hall, ISBN 0–13–854605–3

Warnier J. D. (1974). *Logical Construction of Programs*. Van Nostrand Reinhold Co., ISBN 0–442–22556–3

Wiener R. S. (1986). Protecting against uninitialized abstract objects in Modula-2. *ACM SIGPLAN Notices*, **21**(6)

Wiener R. S. and Sincovec R. F. (1985). Two approaches to implementing generic data structures in Modula-2. *ACM SIGPLAN Notices*, **20**, June 56–64

Wirth N. (1971). Program development by stepwise refinement. *Comm. ACM*, **14**(4), 221–7

Wirth N. (1977). Modula: a language for modular multiprogramming. *Software–Practice and Experience*, **7**, 3–35

Wirth N. (1980). *Modula-2*. ETH Report No. 36

Wirth N. (1982). *Programming in Modula-2* 1st edn. Springer-Verlag, ISBN 0–387–11174–5

Wirth N. (1985). *Programming in Modula-2* 3rd edn. Springer-Verlag, ISBN 0–387–15078–1

Yourdon E. and Constantine L. L. (1979). *Structured Design: Fundamentals of a Discipline of Computer Program and Systems Design*. Prentice-Hall, ISBN 0–13–854471–9

# Selected Solutions to the Exercises

Needless to say, the solutions presented here are largely selected on the basis of supplying solutions to the easier questions and to those questions that are not too implementation-dependent.

**3.1** As might be expected, this should print out the two lines:

> 9 is a digit
> t is lower case

If it doesn't, then you have probably made an error in copying the example modules!

**3.2** The compiler should generate a

> type incompatibility

message (and so it should not be possible to execute this at all).

**4.1** (a) Pisquared, sevenUp and linecount are all valid identifiers;

(b) page_length may be accepted by some compilers, but the underscore character is not part of the Modula-2 character set, and so this is not strictly a valid identifier;

(c) 6by10 and $size are invalid identifiers as they begin with non-alphabetical characters.

**4.3** It is valid, but hardly recommended as a style to be adopted!

**5.1** This one is implementation-specific, but as an example, on a system where MaxInt had a value of 32767:

> WriteCard( CARDINAL(MaxInt+1),12) returned a value of 32768;
> WriteInt(MaxInt+1,12) returned a value of −4294934528;

so beware!

349

350 SELECTED SOLUTIONS TO THE EXERCISES

**6.1** As you might expect:

> Wednesday has an ordinal value of 2
> Saturday has an ordinal value of 5
> Modula2 has an ordinal value of 5
> COBOL has an ordinal value of 9
> Hearts has an ordinal value of 1

**6.4** My own suggestions are:

(a)  [1..31]    (CARDINAL)

(b)  ['0'..'9']   (CHAR)

(c)  [−10..30]  (INTEGER)

but of course, the last one depends on where you live!

**8.1** Obviously the question should really be answered in the knowledge of the fuller context of these operations, but in simple terms:

(a) could use REPEAT...UNTIL, since there will always be many iterations, and termination of the loop is determined by an external factor;

(b) could make use of FOR, as it has known bounds and is a regular sequence;

(c) appears suited to the use of WHILE, since termination is determined by external factors, and there is also the possibility of reading a line with no characters at all.

**9.2** The standard procedures MAX and MIN each return a value which is of the same type as that used for the parameter, and so the suggested program will also need to make use of ORD to obtain a numeric value for the ordinal.

**9.3** You sould certainly try this one, although it is unfortunately prone to reflect inadequecy of run-time checking in some implementations!

**11.1** A common error in designing RECORD types is to fail to consider the type of operations that will be applied to a particular field. For example, even if a field of a record contains a numeric value, if we are only going to print this, or otherwise handle it as a string of characters, there is little point in storing it as an integer value. In such a case, it would be more appropriate to store it as an array of characters. (An example of such a situation is the 'identification' number that we sometimes associate with staff, students, bank accounts etc. Such a number is very rarely used for any sort of calculation, and any checking or matching is likely to be on the basis of characters. This is particularly true if we use sub-fields within the number to identify particular sub-groups or branches etc.) For the suggested exercises, two outline solution forms are as follows (these make use of some fairly obvious enumerated types):

(a) a description of a ship:

```
shipform = RECORD
    name         : ARRAY [0..maxchars] OF CHAR;
    registration : ports;
    tonnage      : CARDINAL;    (* metric tonnes *)
    beam         : CARDINAL;    (* metres *)
    length       : CARDINAL;    (* metres *)
    propulsion   : enginetype;
    screws       : CARDINAL;
    purpose      : shiptype;
END; (* shipform *)
```

(There are some questions about units, of course, and these can only be resolved by determining a standard.)

(b) a description of a room:

```
roomdetail = RECORD
    purpose : roomtypes;
    level   : floors;
    length  : REAL;    (* metres *)
    width   : REAL;    (* metres *)
    windows : CARDINAL;
    sockets : CARDINAL;
    heating : heatforms;
    doors   : CARDINAL;
END; (* roomdetail *)
```

This one offers some scope for variant forms to cover such items as bathrooms (which may be en-suite). There is also the problem of handling multiple forms of heating, etc.

12.2 You need to make some assumptions, but a possible solution to problem(b) is shown in Figure Sol. 12.2b.

12.3 A structure diagram for this program is given in Figure Sol. 12.3.

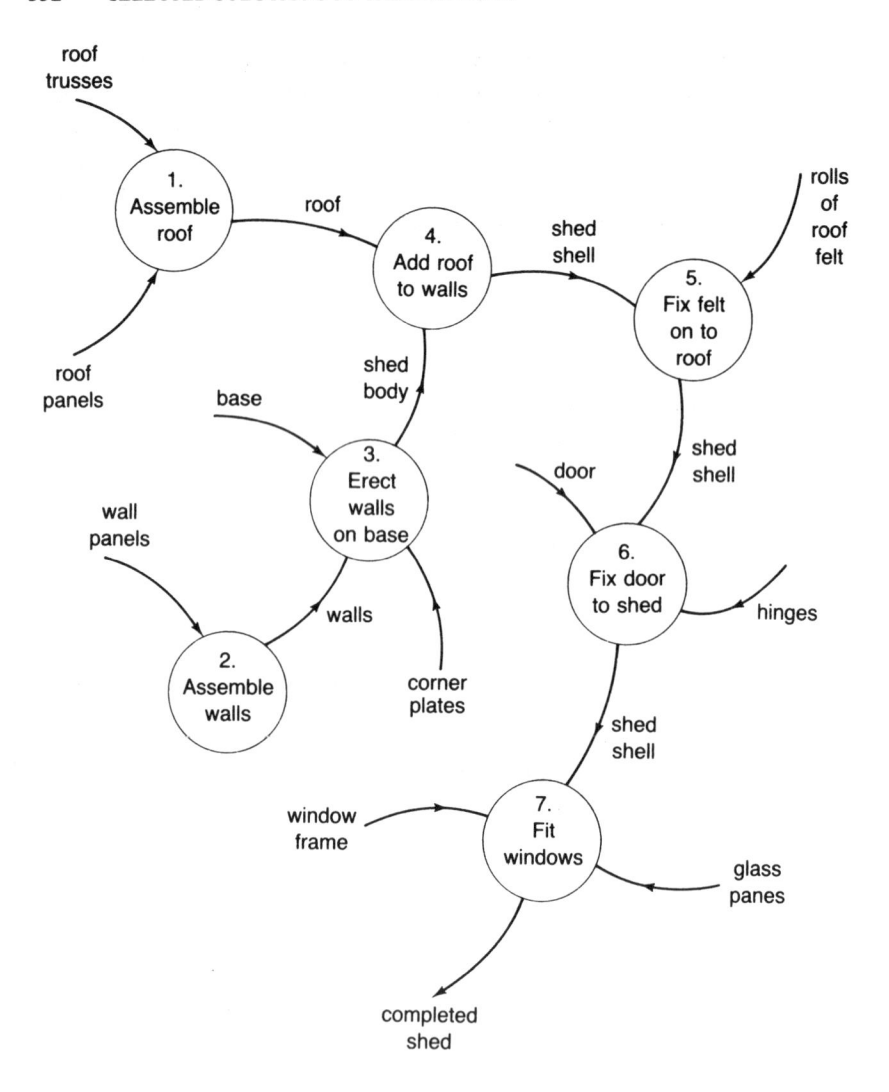

**Figure** Sol. 12.2b.

**14.2** A selection of possible test cases that might be used for this program are:

(a) some 'valid' situations:
- a file with length greater than two pages;
- a file containing a test search pattern in the middle of the file;
- a very long file;

SELECTED SOLUTIONS TO THE EXERCISES 353

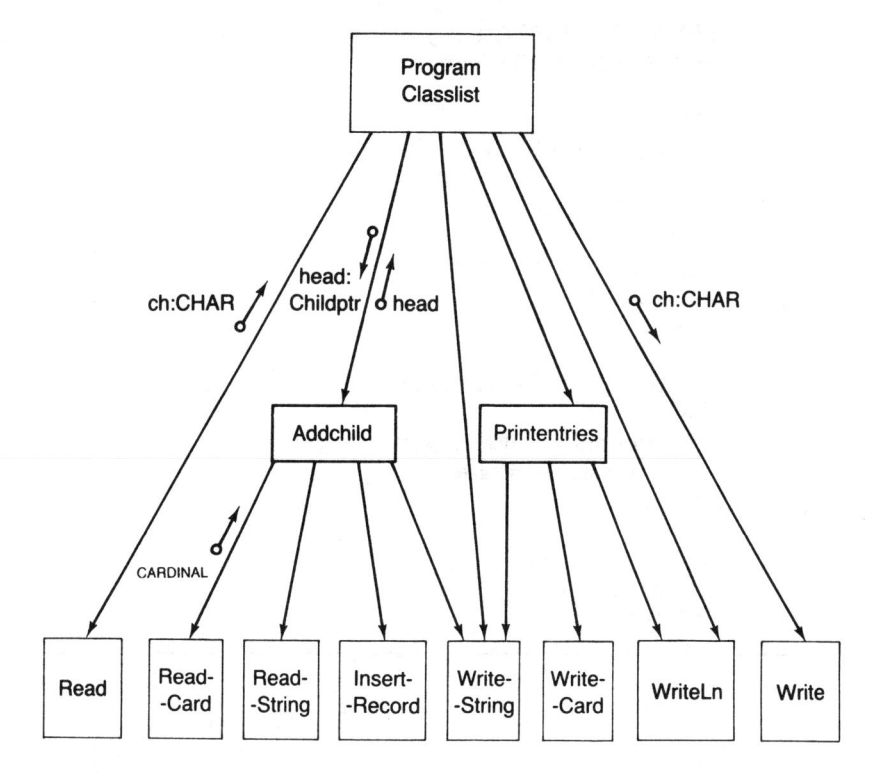

**Figure** Sol. 12.3.

(b) some boundary situations:
- a file of less than one page in length;
- a file of length slightly more than one page;
- a file with the test search pattern in the first page;
- a file with the test search pattern on the last line.

For this situation, invalid test classes are less obvious, but may include non-ASCII files, files with no test search pattern, etc.

**15.2** The very bare bones of a 'WORD stack' module are listed below (there is scope for you to refine this, and to add your personal comment block at the beginning!). It should be possible to write a program module that makes use of this stack and that makes no reference whatever to the type WORD. (Just use Push and Pop with CARDINAL and INTEGER parameters.)

```
IMPLEMENTATION MODULE Stack;
FROM SYSTEM IMPORT WORD;

VAR
   stackpointer : CARDINAL;
   stack : ARRAY[0..99] OF WORD;
PROCEDURE Push(element : WORD);
BEGIN
   stack[stackpointer] := element;
   INC(stackpointer)
END Push;

PROCEDURE Pop(VAR element : WORD);
BEGIN
   IF (stackpointer > 0) THEN DEC(stackpointer) END;
   element := stack[stackpointer];
END Pop;

BEGIN
   stackpointer := 0;
END Stack.
```

# Index

.  36, 46, 150, 167
,  36, 46, 160
:  36, 44, 46, 51, 95
;  36, 40, 41, 46, 52, 120, 166
|  36, 46, 95, 96
*  36, 44, 54, 69
+  36, 39, 44, 54, 67
−  36, 44, 54, 68
/  36, 44, 65, 69
=  36, 44, 52, 57, 74, 85
'  36, 58
"  36, 58
&  36, 44, 45, 63
~  36, 44, 45, 64
_  36
#  36, 44, 45, 57, 85
↑  36, 44, 173
^  36, 173
<  36, 44, 57, 85
>  36, 44, 57, 85
£  36, 45
:=  39, 44, 52
..  76, 89, 96, 97
<>  44, 45, 57, 85
>=  44, 57, 85
<=  44, 57, 85
[]  36, 46, 76, 286, 336
{}  36, 46, 47, 66, 79, 89
()  36, 46, 56, 87, 117
(**)  46, 47

Abbott, Russ  243
ABS  126
absolute addressing  286–7, 329

abstraction  188, 189, 201, 231, 232, 277
acceptance testing  261
actual parameter  *see* parameter
Ada  4, 6, 17, 24, 120, 121, 202, 223, 297
addition operator  54, 284
ADDRESS  278, 283–5, 297
address in memory  51
ADR  279, 284
ALGOL  4, 6, 10
algorithms  194, 204, 210–14
Allison, Lloyd  297
ALLOCATE  172, 177
ampersand character  45
AND  38, 45, 63, 86, 87
anonymous data objects  172
anonymous procedures  139
architectural design  *see* top-level design
arithmetic operators  *see* addition, subtraction, division, multiplication
ARRAY  38, 159, 280
array  103, 159–65
   assignment  161, 162
   boundaries  *see* array size
   declarations  159, 160
   dimensions  160
   index  159, 160, 163
   (as) parameters  122, 163–5
   (of) records  166, 167
   size  159, 163
   type  159
ASCII  45, 58, 59, 265, 328

355

assessment  *see* design assessment
assignment  (*see also* array assignment)
   compatibility  49, 76
   operation (statement)  39, 40, 52, 59, 63, 75, 161

B (suffix)  53, 58
base types  76, 77, 79, 88
base + offset addressing  284
BASIC  10
BEGIN  25, 38, 46, 139
bell character  60
binding (pointer types)  170
bit manipulation  *see* BITSET
BITSET  66–71, 78, 85, 329
   constant  66
   variable  66, 67
black box testing  15
block diagrams  209–10
blueprints  189, 203
Booch, Grady  202, 243
BOOLEAN  57, 62–5
   expressions  62, 84
   operators  63–4
   type  62
boundary values (arrays)  *see* array size
brace characters  46, 66, 78, 89
British Standards Institution (BSI)  5, 28
BSI  *see* British Standards Institution
Buhr, R J A  209
BY  38, 104
BYTE  279, 285
byte  279, 284


C
   character suffix  58, 60
   programming language  14, 15, 123, 278
Cambridge Ring  331
CARDINAL
   constant  52
   type  50, 51
   type transfer function  56, 126
CAP  126

carriage return character  60
CASE  38, 84, 95–8, 168, 304
   selector  168  (*see also* path selector)
case sensitive  20, 23, 36
central transform  235, 236
CHAR  58–60
character
   constants  58
   handling  58–60
   strings  161, 162
   type  *see* CHAR
CHR  59, 60, 123, 126
COBOL  4
code inserts  285–6
cohesion  215–17, 241
comment  38, 47, 268–72
common-environment coupling  *see* coupling
commutative operations  54, 67, 69
comparison operation  56, 59, 75
compiler
   checking  49, 119, 134, 139, 169, 172
   directive  *see* EXPORT, IMPORT
   version keys  22
compilation order  18, 21
composition in design  196
concurrent
   execution  205, 289–93
   objects in design  194
   operations  289
   processes  314–21
   programming forms  289–321
conditional expressions  70, 84, 85–9, 91, 107, 130
conditional loops  107–10
CONST  38, 49, 52
constant  40, 103
   declarations  *see* declarations
   expressions  40, 53, 103
   identifiers  37
Constantine, L L  115, 191, 194
control coupling  *see* coupling
control variable (FOR)  102–7
co-operative scheduling  295, 315
CORAL-66 programming language  15
co-routine  293–321, 325
counting  101, 102–7, 128

# INDEX

coupling   27, 145, 207, 215, 217–20, 241
cyclomatic complexity metric   220

data coupling   *see* coupling
data dictionary   213, 232, 235
data flow diagram (DFD)   194, 195, 205, 230–6, 246
data permanency   *see* permanency
data type   6, 17
DEALLOCATE   172, 177
DEC   75, 129
decimal number base   53
declaration (of)
   array   *see* array
   comments on   269
   constants   17, 51, 52, 116
   objects   6, 17, 38, 39, 49, 73, 138, 152
   procedures   117
   types   17, 116, 153, 165
   variables   17, 51, 58, 62, 67, 74, 78, 116, 166
DEFINITION   24, 25, 29, 38, 138
definition part (of a module)   17, 18, 25, 138, 152, 253, 254, 269
delay (in program)   110
delimiters   46, 55
dereferencing (of a pointer)   172, 173
design   183, 186–203
   assessment   213–20, 223
   decisions   245, 246, 304
   for change   193
   methods   *see* Structured Design, JSP, Object-Oriented Design
   metrics   214
   re-use   220–4
detailed design   188, 210–14, 245, 246, 253
device
   control   324, 326, 328
   driver process   325
   input/output forms   323–6
   interface   323, 324
   polling   324, 329–34
   registers   326, 327
direct memory access (DMA)   325, 326, 331

directive   *see* EXPORT, IMPORT
DISPOSE   172
DIV   38, 45, 55
division operator   55, 65
DO   38, 103, 167
documentation   213, 260, 268–72
Done   30, 63
dynamic storage allocation   169–77

E (scale factor)   65
ELSE   38, 90, 96
else clauses   89–91
ELSIF   38, 91
elsif clauses   91–5
empty (null) set   66, 79
END   25, 28, 38, 41, 46, 84, 85, 90, 94, 96, 103, 117, 165, 167, 302
entities   *see* objects
entry point   116, 293
enumerated types   74, 75, 88, 89, 102, 127, 153, 159
EOL (InOut)   30, 31
equality operator   57
error handling   94, 97, 112
EXCL   79, 80, 129
EXIT   38, 111, 112
exit from loops   *see* loop termination
exponent (for REAL numbers)   65
EXPORT directive   26, 27, 38, 80, 81, 145, 147, 153
expressions   38–40, 120
extensions to file names   *see* file naming conventions
external page   66, 326, 327

factorial   130
fields (of a RECORD)   165–9
   separators   165
   identifiers   165, 167
file naming conventions   17, 18, 20, 138
FLOAT   65, 126
floating point   65, 95
FOR   38, 102–7, 161
formal parameter   *see* parameter
FORTRAN   4, 6–7, 10, 11, 12, 13, 14, 29, 38, 84, 105, 121, 123, 219
fractional values   65, 102

FROM   26, 27, 38, 147, 151
function procedures   17, 116, 123–5

generic objects   221–3, 267, 277, 279, 280
global data structures   15
greater than operator   57
greater than or equal to operator   57

H (suffix)   53
HALT   125, 129
hello world/hello user programs   8, 28
hexadecimal numbers   53
hierarchical structuring   116, 137, 139, 141, 191, 207, 271, 295
HIGH   129, 163, 164

identifiers   6, 23, 35–9, 208, 269
IF   38, 84–95
imperative programming languages   3, 10, 11
IMPLEMENTATION   24, 25, 29, 38, 138
implementation constraints   50, 66, 77, 78, 163 (*see also* portability)
implementation part (of a module)   17, 19, 27, 138, 152–4, 254
IMPORT directive   19, 21, 26, 27, 38, 80, 81, 138, 147, 151
IN   38, 45, 70, 78, 88
INC   75, 129, 223
INCL   79, 80, 129, 341
increment (FOR loop)   104, 105
independent compilation   14–16
index value
 (of array)   *see* arrays
 (of FOR loop)   *see* control variable
inequality operator   57
information-hiding   9, 122, 143–6, 200–1, 218, 252, 292, 304, 326
initialization
 (of variables)   139, 142, 153, 208, 240, 331, 339, 343
 FOR loop   103
 WHILE loop   107, 108 (*see also* loop initialization)
InOut (MODULE)   29–31, 63

INTEGER
 constant   52
 type   50
 type transfer function   56, 126
integer
 operations   54–7
 types   50–7
integration testing   261, 267–8
interrupt   325, 334–44
 enable/disable mechanism   328, 335
 handling techniques   325, 334–44
 vector   334, 335, 339
IOTRANSFER   279, 338–42
iteration forms   101 (*see also* loop, FOR, LOOP, REPEAT, WHILE)

Jackson, Michael   196
Jackson structured programming   *see* JSP
JSD   202, 312
JSP   196–200, 212

key   (in .sym file)   22
Knuth, Donald   8

labels   95, 96, 97
Ledgard, Henry   243
less-than operator   57
less-than-or-equal operator   57
level of abstraction   *see* abstraction
library modules   29, 51, 75, 278
life-cycle   *see* software life-cycle
line clock device   335
line feed character   60
limit (FOR loop)   103–5
link-editor   14, 16, 21, 22, 29, 36, 138, 286
linked lists   107, 173, 174
LISP   3
local
 declarations   116, 121
 modules   146–51, 154
 objects   17, 138, 144, 145
 variables   116, 121, 130, 145
logical AND   45, 63, 86, 87
logical OR   64, 86, 87
logical design   186, 204, 254
logical structuring   8, 16, 115, 116, 137, 152, 189, 203, 271

longword   279
LOOP   38, 111–14, 341
loop
  body   101
  counting   101
  forms   101–14
  initialization   103, 107, 108, 110, 113
  termination   103, 105, 107, 109, 111, 112

main body (of MODULE)   24, 138, 139–42, 153, 208, 242, 298, 300, 339
maintenance   114, 136, 183, 185, 199, 202, 220, 244
MASCOT   205
MAX   128
memory mapped input/output   286, 326–9
metrics   *see* design metrics
MIN   128
MOD   38, 45, 55
model-building in program design   157, 170, 243
MODULE   23–5, 38, 46, 137–54, 201
module
  development   260
  identifiers   37
  priority   336, 338
  testing   261, 265–7
modulus operator   *see* MOD
monolithic compilation   16
Motorola MC68000 processor   66, 284, 286, 323, 326
multiple exits from
  loops   112
  procedures   124
multiplication operator   54
mutual exclusion   290, 292, 300, 315, 341

negation operator   54
nested procedures   116, 117
NEW   172
newline character   38, 60
NEWPROCESS   279, 296–8
NIL   171, 172
non-printing characters   58, 60

NOT   38, 45, 64, 87
note-making (by a designer)   232, 239, 240
nouns   37, 193, 244, 246, 247
null
  character   162
  set   *see* empty set
  statement   41, 42, 96

objects   73, 189, 193, 201, 244, 247, 249
Object-Oriented Design (OOD)   201–3, 242–57
octal numbers   53, 58
ODD   128
OF   38   *see also* ARRAY
opaque export   153–4, 219
open array   122, 129, 163–5, 280
operations upon objects   39, 43, 51, 54–71, 75, 116, 158, 170, 189, 193, 231
operators   38, 39, 43–5, 54–71, 85
OR   38, 45, 64, 86, 87
ORD   59, 60, 75, 123, 127
Orr, K   196
ordered data structures   *see* structured types
ordinal values   58, 59, 75, 78, 127

package (Ada)   24, 202, 209
packaging   137, 141, 189, 223, 237, 242, 244, 251, 272
Page-Jones, Meilir   237
parallel processing   *see* concurrent programming forms
parameter   12, 15, 19, 75, 294
  actual   13, 119–21, 163, 208, 279, 280
  arrays (as)   163–5
  formal   13, 119–21, 163, 205, 208, 279, 280
  lists   120, 121, 122
  separators   120
parentheses   56, 86, 87, 116, 135
Parnas, D L   143, 200
Pascal   4, 5, 6, 7, 10, 13, 15, 16, 17, 24, 29, 45, 77, 84, 89, 102, 117, 123, 144, 145, 201
path selector   84, 95–7

PDP-11 computers   50, 66, 97, 286, 287, 323, 326, 327
period character   150, 167
permanency (of data)   117, 118, 145, 147
POINTER (TO)   38, 170
pointer types   153, 169–77, 284
  operations on   170, 172, 173, 284
portability   59, 77, 144, 278, 281
precedence of operators   56, 87
PROC   135
PROCEDURE   38, 46, 116
procedure   115–36 (*see also* function procedure, standard procedure)
  as parameters   134, 135
  call   116
  comments (on declarations)   270
  declarations   116, 117, 119
  headings   120, 123, 134
  identifiers   37
  inner   116
  (as design) object   189
  parameters   75, 116, 118–22 (*see also* parameter)
  structure   116, 117
  types   134–6
procedural programming language *see* imperative programming language
PROCESS   297, 315
process   314
program controlled input/output   325, 326
program module   24, 28, 137–9
programming in the large   182
programming in the small   182
prototyping   183, 187
pseudo-code   189, 211–13

QUALIFIED   27, 38, 147, 150–1
qualify record fields   167
quality
  of designs   214, 215
  of software   185
quasi-concurrency   315
quote marks   58, 161

range (of values)   50, 96, 159
REAL type   65–6, 76, 95, 102

RECORD   38, 165–9
  fields *see* fields
  types   153, 165–9
  variant sections   168–9
recursion   130–4, 207, 239
REGISTER   279, 285
relational operators   56, 59, 63, 75, 85
REPEAT UNTIL   38, 109, 110, 331
requirements analysis   183
reserved words   23, 37, 38, 41, 45, 55, 123, 130
RETURN   38, 124, 165
re-use
  of design *see* design
  of sub-programs   14

scalar types   74, 157
scale factor   65
scope   46, 117, 118, 145, 146, 152, 201, 244, 266
selection forms   83 (*see also* IF, CASE)
selection *see* path selector, CASE
semicolon character   120, 166
  as statement separator *see* separators
  as statement terminator   52
separate compilation   20–2, 29, 80, 138, 139, 152
separation of concerns   220, 256
separators   38
  parameters   120
  paths (in CASE)   96
  record fields   165–6
  statements   38, 40, 41, 110
SET OF   38, 77
set
  constant   78, 79, 89
  difference operator   68
  intersection operator   69
  membership   70, 78, 88
  size limits   78
  subset/superset operations   85
  symmetric set difference operator   69, 70
  types   66–71, 77–80, 88, 157
  union operator   67, 106
  variables   78, 79, 80
signed numbers   50, 51
SIZE   128, 279, 283

## INDEX

Smalltalk 243
software design *see* design
software engineering 8, 185
software life-cycle 183–6, 187, 259, 268
space character 38, 39, 47, 54, 55
specification 183
stamp coupling *see* coupling
standard data types 50–66
standard procedures 125–9, 134
statement 38, 39
  separator *see* separators
  sequence 43, 83, 84, 115, 130
  termination 52
stepwise refinement *see* top-down
Storage (MODULE) 177
storage units (for data) 128
strings *see also* character strings
string
  constant 161, 162
  delimiter 161
strong typing 4, 49, 119, 169, 170, 189, 277, 281
structure (in programs) 136
structure chart *see* structure diagram
structure clash (JSP) 198
structure diagram 141, 142, 192, 197, 205–9, 210, 228, 233, 271, 312
structure graph 209–10, 252, 253, 272, 313
Structured Analysis 194, 230–42
structured data type 102, 157–77
Structured Design 194–6, 230–42
stubs and drivers 265, 267
sub-programs 11, 12, 14, 115
sub-range types 6, 51, 75–7
sub-routine 293, 294
subtraction operator 54
symbolic constants 52, 312
synchronization 290, 291, 292, 315
SYSTEM (MODULE) 278, 279, 296, 297, 338

tag field 168, 169
team of programmers 15, 16
template 134, 223, 296, 300, 315
termination (of statements) *see* statement
test cases 15, 263, 264, 266

test classes 262, 264, 266
test harness 15, 266, 267
testing 183, 184, 259–72 (*see also* acceptance, integration and module testing)
TeX 7
THEN (*see* IF) 38, 84
then clause 84–9
throw-away programs 182
tilde character 45
TO 38, 103, 170
top-down 11, 189–94
top-level design 188, 245
TRANSFER 279, 297, 298, 315, 334
transfer of control (between co-routines) 294, 297
transform analysis 233
trees 130, 134, 171, 196
TRUNC 65, 127
truncation of values 55
TSIZE 172, 279, 283
twos-complement 50
TYPE 38, 73, 134, 159
type
  checking 49, 50, 56, 73, 75
  compatibility 76
  conversion 59, 65, 125–8
  definitions 73 (*see also* declarations)
  identifiers 37
  transfer 56, 59, 125–7, 277, 281
typing (strong) 4, 49 (*see also* strong typing)

unary operators 54
underscore character 36
UNIX operating system 17, 341
UNTIL 38 (*see also* REPEAT)
user-defined data types 7, 15, 19, 27, 37, 73–81

VAL 127
value parameters 81, 120–1
VAR 38, 49, 51, 121, 160
variable
  declarations *see* declarations
  identifiers 37
  parameters 81, 120–1, 124
variant sections *see* RECORD

VAX-11 computers 50, 66, 284, 323, 326
VAX/VMS operating system 17, 36
vector
  interrupt *see* interrupt
  quantity 157, 159
verbs 37, 193, 194, 244, 246, 249
visibility 17, 19, 27, 28, 118, 130, 138, 147, 209

Warnier, J D 196
waterfall model 184 (*see also* software life cycle)
WHILE 38, 107–9
Wirth, Niklaus 6, 15
WITH 38, 167–8
WORD 278, 279–83
word size 279
workspace (co-routine) 296, 297